Moral Choices

Moral
Choices

Memory, Desire, and Imagination in
Nineteenth-Century American Abolition

Peter F. Walker

Louisiana State
University Press
Baton Rouge and London

Copyright © 1978 by Louisiana State University Press
All rights reserved
Manufactured in the United States of America

Design: Dwight Agner and Patricia D. Crowder
Type face: VIP Aldus
Composition: The Composing Room of Michigan, Inc.
Printing and binding: Thomson-Shore, Inc.

LIBRARY OF CONGRESS CATALOGING IN PUBLICATION DATA

Walker, Peter, 1931–
  Moral choices

  Bibliography: P.
  Includes index.
    1. Abolitionists—United States—Biography.
  2. Conway, Moncure Daniel, 1832–1907.
  3. Swisshelm, Jane Grey Cannon, 1815–1884.
  4. Douglas, Frederick, 1817 (?)–1895. 5. Slavery
  in the United States—Anti-slavery movements.
  I. Title.
  E449.W185   322.4'4'0922   [B] 78–5922
  ISBN 0-8071-0262-8

For Daryl
This is your book, too

In Minnesota there were silos
farther than we could see. Under
the setting sun they looked like
blazing observatories and we
seemed in a land where every one
was his own astronomer.

Contents

	Acknowledgments	xiii
	Introduction	xv
Part One	Moncure Conway: Apostate Slave Master	1
I	*Mission to England*	3
II	*Virginia*	21
III	*The "Moral Choice"*	43
IV	*North*	77
Part Two	Jane Swisshelm: Emancipated Woman	87
V	*The Wax Doll and the Covenanters' Daughter*	89
VI	*The* Visiter	136
VII	*St. Cloud*	171

Part Three   Frederick Douglass: Orphan Slave   207
    VIII   *Biography, Autobiography, and the Search for the
            Lost Past*   209
      IX   *Nantucket: Confirmation, Betrayal, and Rebirth* 229
       X   *The Highland Chief, the African Queen, and the
            Garden of Eden*   248

Part Four   "The Great Things"   263
      XI   *Self-Creation and Social Imagination*   265
     XII   *Henry Wright: Abolition, Sexuality, and "The
            Great Day Coming"*   278
    XIII   *Salmon Chase: Abolition, Union, and "The Great
            Moral Revolution"*   305
     XIV   *Thomas Cooley: Abolition, Law, and "The Day of
            Better Things"*   330

            Notes   351
            Selected Bibliography   373
            Index   383

Illustrations

following page 206
Moncure D. Conway
Jane Swisshelm
Frederick Douglass
Henry C. Wright
Salmon P. Chase
Thomas M. Cooley

Acknowledgments

For providing me access to much of the material on which this book is based, and in some instances making special arrangements for my using it, I am grateful to members of the staffs of the American Antiquarian Society; Boston Public Library; Butler Library, Columbia University; the Manuscripts and Photoduplication divisions of the Library of Congress; Spahr Memorial Library, Dickinson College; Perkins Library, Duke University; Houghton Library, Harvard University; the Massachusetts Historical Society; the Minnesota Historical Society; the New York Historical Society; New York Public Library; the Reference and Inter-Library Loan divisions of the Wilson Library, University of North Carolina; the Ohio Historical Society;

the Pennsylvania State Historical Society; the Western Reserve Historical Society.

Martha Slotten, Spahr Memorial Library, Dickinson College; Jon Pankake and Janet White, Minnesota Historical Society; Patti McIntyre, Reference Division, Wilson Library, University of North Carolina; Jack Barnwell, Lynchburg, Virginia; and Bud Walker, while he was at the Divinity School, Harvard University, went out of their way to find fugitive sources and information for me.

I am grateful to the late Dr. George Ham and members of the senior staff of the Department of Psychiatry, Medical School, University of North Carolina for permitting me to participate in the Seminar on Psychoanalytic Theory.

James L. Godfrey made it possible for me to have an unencumbered semester and gave me access to the resources of the Cooperative Program in the Humanities. I am indebted to him for this help and other kindnesses.

Ashbel Green, Frank Klingberg, Frank Ryan, Jack Semonche, Henry Lee Swint, George Tindall, and Joel Williamson read portions of early versions of the manuscript. I am glad to have had their help and encouragement.

Peter Filene, James McPherson, and Lewis Perry read the entire manuscript and were generous with their special talents. Excepting changes responsive to Perry's and McPherson's recommendations, and those suggested by Martha Hall, my splendid editor at the Louisiana State University Press, the book's content is substantially that of the original manuscript, which the Press received in 1974. The lines of argument are exactly the same.

For generosities of a most special, endearing kind I am grateful to Gwen Duffey, Peter Filene, and Jonathan Yardley.

With skill and good humor, Laurie Christesen, Secily Jones, Jane Lindley and Linda Stephenson typed the manuscript.

The most characteristically and
peculiarly moral judgments that a
man is ever called on to make are in
unprecedented cases and lonely
emergencies, where no popular
rhetorical maxims can avail, and the
hidden oracle alone can speak.
WILLIAM JAMES, *Principles of
Psychology*

Now it is true beyond possible
gainsaying that the operations which
we call creative leave us in the end
confronting mystery. But that is the
fated terminus of all our quests.
JOHN LIVINGSTON LOWES, *The Road
to Xanadu*

That each individuality is ultimately
conditioned by the forces of social
history will be demonstrated more
forcibly than in any other way by this
linking up of past, present and vista of
the future. It is precisely when a . . .
character . . . is allowed to grow
naturally out of the past he has lived
through that the ties between man
and society within his own
personality are brought to the surface
and rendered unmistakably clear. For
the past, which looked at historically
is the same for all, takes on a separate
shape in terms of each human life.
GEORG LUKÁCS, "Solzhenitsyn and
the New Realism"

Introduction

The essays in this book invade
private lives in order to better understand public lives. They are
accounts of several abolitionists active in the final phase of the antislavery enterprise in the United States. Furthermore, they are re-
strictive accounts. I have aimed at answering the question of *why*
these people became abolitionists. The following pages, therefore,
are about American abolition, but they make no claim to being a
history of abolition.

We know something about the cultural foundations of the attack on slavery in the United States, the social conditions that prevailed at the time the attack entered its final phases, the organizations that channeled the attack, and considerable about the rhetoric, strategies, and tactics employed by the abolitionists. But what we do not yet know much about is why certain people embraced abolition. Cultural history can lay out the great lines of force coming into focus on the abolitionists, sociological analyses can account for the measurable externals that describe them as a social group (and from the externals deduce a theory to explain individual behavior), but neither history nor historical sociology allows the individual to play his historical role. So we come at last to biography.

The difficulty with biography is not, as Sir Lewis Namier said, that so much of it is bad, but rather, as Claude Levi-Strauss has pointed out in *The Savage Mind*, that it is "low-powered history." Richest in point of information, biography is least explanatory in terms of historical processes. When we try to explain history through the lives of men, what we really do is illustrate history by personality. We turn an individual into a symbol, talk of representative men, and have them speak for history. For all of its attractiveness, turning a person into a symbol robs him of his concreteness and takes an individual experience, abstracts it, and raises it to engross an historical experience. But when we do this we are apt to forget that we are illustrating, not explaining, and inevitably we make a life bear too much.

Substituting illustrative personalities for historical explanations is common for the study of American abolition; and nowhere in American historical writing has the battle over the bodies of illustrating men and women raged more fiercely. An essay on the literature could be written in terms of the swings of fortune that the reputation of William Lloyd Garrison has taken. But the problem cannot be resolved by eliminating a biographical consideration of the people who led the attack on slavery; the problem is to make the best possible use of biographical material.

Abolition was conceived by the abolitionists themselves as a moral commitment and undertaking. Before their indictment of slavery had run its course, they had scouted every conceivable argument against slavery, but the bedrock of their position was that slavery was immoral. To become an abolitionist was at bottom a moral choice. What we need to know is why certain people made their moral choices.

Culture and society create the moral choices available to people who create their own moral slogans–"popular rhetorical maxims," William James called them—which are invoked to justify a moral choice. But the possibility of choice and the availability of slogans do not explain why the choice was made. The tendency has been either to accept the slogan as the reason for choosing abolition or to disregard the slogan and look for perversity and aberration behind the choice.

In these essays I have gone beyond the moral slogans, but I have not sought perversity or neurosis or even deviance. I have looked for particular human responses to particular human situations. I have listened for what James called the hidden oracle. It speaks to different people in different, often surprisingly unexpected ways, and studies in neither society nor history are sufficient in themselves to enable us to hear the oracle as it has spoken to other men and women.

I have written about these people for several reasons. All *seem* to have been on the periphery of abolition, and I believe we are apt to have as much access—maybe more—to a disputed social enterprise by way of its second- and third-echelon personnel as we can from its more celebrated spokesmen. So much is at hazard, both for the leaders and for those who would turn them into illustrative history, that the heart of the matter is difficult to come by. The leaders are, after all, the "founders," and they consequently have been pretty much preempted and invested with established historical personae. Coming to the lesser lights gives me a latitude of interpretative maneuver that I should not have had if I had stuck with some of the more celebrated abolitionists.

Another major purpose bearing on my writing about my principal subjects, Moncure Conway, Jane Swisshelm, and Frederick Douglass, has to do with the sources from which their lives must be reconstructed. Autobiography—that fusing of personal desire, memory, and imagination—is at the core of these essays. I have based my work on these people's self-writings. I have taken autobiography as a creative act, an imaginative response to internal necessities, whereby a self-writer has imposed his creative powers on the data of his life. I have attempted to answer the question of why Conway, Swisshelm, and Douglass were compelled to create themselves as they did, thinking that an answer to this question would illuminate the question of why they became abolitionists. In answering both questions I have not forgotten John Livingston Lowes's observation about the fated terminus of all quests for the origins of creative operations.

Apart from the autobiographies, the nature of the sources is substantively different. Each essay therefore proposes a different solution to the problem of the biographical reconstruction and interpretation of a life. Ordinarily biography hides the problems of method. Rightly so because if a biographer is simply writing a life story, there is no reason to inflict upon a reader what is really a wrestling match between a biographer and his subject. In the first three essays I have raised these internal problems as exercises in method. In these essays my method takes it for granted that the autobiographies are tendentious about abolition and the writers' relationships with it. I have therefore supposed that there is another, and richer, more complex, story of why each writer came to abolition. In providing alternative accounts of the writers' entries to abolition I have used variant strategies because of the different nature of the autobiographical material and the different nature of the other sources supporting the alternative accounts.

One of the great intellectual documents of the period, Moncure Conway's autobiography has been called; though because of its gigantic sprawl and the fact that Conway does not fit the received patterning for nineteenth-century history the book has gathered dust on library shelves. Blessed is he, Moncure Conway wrote, who can "enjoy the happiness of having no history." It is a strange and contradictory beatitude coming from a man who labored for nine hundred pages to produce a record of his own history. The autobiography tells a story contradicted by contemporary letters.

The letters tell enough about the situation in Conway House to permit the reconstruction of an alternate story. But the letters are from Conway's mother and father. It is their voices that speak. Absent from the contemporary materials is the son's voice, one he resolutely refused to allow to speak when later he told his version of the story. None of his contemporary letters survive. The problem is to hear him speak in response to his mother and father. In order to do this I have followed the theory that a creative writer does his "dreamwork" in his fiction. As I have followed the theory, I have been mindful of the dubiety of the general proposition itself as well as the hazards of a specific application. My doubts on both counts have been lessened to the extent that I am satisfied that in Conway's case the method is justifiable. It is apparent in his fiction that Conway's creative powers were limited. It was impossible for him to invent and sustain characters and situations. He simply could not do it. His fiction never transcended his experiences; his materials for his stories were not the bases for his stories, but were the stories themselves. But if the result was bad fiction, it is nevertheless unimpeachable biographical material. I have, therefore, read Conway's fiction—a few short stories and his novel, and several essays in which there are invented characters—as the answering voice in the conversation established by his father's and mother's letters. As his answering voice becomes audible we begin to understand why he delivered himself of that strange and paradoxical beatitude in his autobiography. He was not only chastened by his personal history. He was scathed and harrowed by it.

In the Swisshelm essay I have been obliged to deal with the problem of using an autobiography as the sole major source for recovering a person's life. Excepting a handful of fugitive notes and letters and her newspapers, Jane Swisshelm left no paper trail, and a Swisshelm biographer wanting to know about her personal life reaches a virtual deadend with *Half a Century*. Notwithstanding, the autobiographical form suggests a biographical method. As much as we might wish it otherwise, there is always an element of free association in any written history. Autobiography is the work of memory; at its best, the artistic winnowing of memory. Free association is, after all, nothing but the rushing, unfettered talk of memory. Jane Swisshelm's autobiography shows clear signs that her controls were fragile to begin with and that they broke down as she wrote her book. She was never given to rigorous analytical thought or disciplined exposition, and she began her book when she was aged and chronically ill. With nothing but her newspaper files to guide her she worked almost exclusively from memory. Only in the loosest sense did she stay within the subjects she announced at the beginning of the book, and only in a rambling, disconnected way did she develop the theses she set out to prove. Before she finished writing her book many memories had flashed through her mind, often causing her to leap back to earlier matters or rush ahead heedless of chronology, theme, or narrative development. My starting point with *Half a Century* has been Swisshelm's remembered reality. Having established that, I have then asked myself why she remembered as she did. To answer this question I have placed her remembered reality inside the contemporary circumstance insofar as it can be reconstructed from standard historical sources, and I have compared her recollection with her perception of the reality at the time. The major source that I have used to do the latter is her contemporary journalism. Because of her editorial control of her newspapers and her compulsive inclination to turn her editorials into personal statements, her columns take on the double characteristic of a publicly printed personal journal and a personal correspondence. I have therefore read her journalism as private papers. Most of the quoted material in the essay comes from either Swisshelm's autobiography or her newspapers. In Chapter I only sources other than the autobiography are cited. In Chapters II and III references to the leading autobiographical or newspaper source follow quotations in the following manner: *Pittsburgh Visiter* (PV [and date]). Uncited quotations come from either the autobiography or the newspapers.

For the Douglass essay my method is comparative. I have drawn heavily on the Douglass biographies by Philip Foner and Benjamin Quarles. Easily the most thorough and reliable of the several Douglass biographies, they provide a partial framework for my essay. Since I wanted to know why Douglass became an abolitionist, I was interested in how Foner and Quarles conceived, asked, and answered the question. In the essay their biographies are established

as counterpoints for my own inquiry. The three Douglass autobiographies have given me another set of counterpoints. The
essay proceeds from a comparison of the two biographies to a comparative reading of the three autobiographies in which I have
watched Douglass as he changed his mind about himself and about
his relationship with abolition. In making the comparisons I have
spared the reader tedious collations. If the reader wants to make
them for himself, my references to specific passages in the autobiographies will make this easier.

The second part of this book is frankly elliptical and provisional.
In it Conway, Swisshelm, and Douglass reappear and are joined by
Henry Wright, Salmon Chase, and Thomas Cooley. In these latter
essays I have dropped the consistent autobiographical base of my
method. My emphasis on *memory* is therefore reduced but not my
concern with *desire* and *imagination.* I also have kept my interest
in the *why* but in pursuing it I have diminished the depth and extended the range of my inquiry. I have looked for human responses
to human situations that carry beyond biography and make connection with history. In these sections I have, using Levi-Strauss's
words, "dove-tailed" a lower-powered history with a higher-
powered history. Particularly, I have been interested in imaginative human responses to undesirable human situations that resulted in the creation of ideas intended to promote moral social action
and morally justify social consequences. The essays on Wright,
Chase, and Cooley are more foreshortened than those on Conway,
Swisshelm, and Douglass because the perspective is changed. I
have traded off information for explanation. I have also traded on
the work of historians writing on these larger matters. My specific use of their work is acknowledged by citation. My general
use of some of these writings is unacknowledged because the informing sources are so much a part of the historical literature of
the nineteenth century that to cite them seemed pedantic. Because
these sections may seem to skirt the edges of what I have tried
to avoid—forcing biography to do history's work—the reader
might bear in mind that what Georg Lukács has called the "separate shapes" of individual lives "linking up past, present, and vista
of the future" remains at the heart of these latter essays.

I have avoided using the conventional phrase *abolition move-*

ment. I have contented myself with either *abolition* or *abolition enterprise,* which is what William Lloyd Garrison sometimes called it. Neil Smelser's closely reasoned strictures on *movement* partially explain my dropping the conventional usage. But of more force is my desire to convey what *enterprise* suggests, as opposed to the bland *movement:* a bold venture in a troubled, hazardous world. The essays in the first part of the book, I think, made that clear in individual terms. The essays in the second part of the book explore the point more generally.

I have not quarreled with myself over the definition of *abolitionist* because of the protean nature of abolition itself. During the antislavery crusade the word was not defined except as it was done restrictively to exclude, either pejoratively or protectively, as was the case for Salmon Chase who so thoroughly minced the word that he is a semanticist's delight but a historical categorizer's despair. I have taken the term to apply to someone who openly attacked slavery, denounced it for being immoral, and promoted schemes to destroy it as rapidly as possible. Applying the word with more discriminating precision is apt to cause one to take sides with a faction and make the word stand in place of a particular tactics, itself often murky and contradictory. I am gratified that of the six people discussed here, five conform with James McPherson's current attempt to define and categorize the abolitionists, and the sixth, Thomas Cooley, might without unseemly exegesis be brought under McPherson's rubric.[1] Probably the most useful defining distinction comes from Jane and William Pease who have suggested the existence of two abolitionisms, one for whites and one for blacks.[2] If the Peases are on the right track, as I think they are, then the abolitionists in this book are in the white tradition, as are their desires and imaginations and most of their memories.

Part One

Moncure Conway: Apostate Slave Master

I

Mission to England

Moncure Conway does not represent one single man on this side of the Atlantic.
WENDELL PHILLIPS

Moncure Conway is in England upon his own responsibility alone.
WILLIAM LLOYD GARRISON

A man sails the north Atlantic in early spring because he must. The passage in mid-April is hard, for once the Gulf Stream is left behind winter lies on the horizon. So it was on a voyage in 1863.

Aboard the *City of Washington,* bound out of Boston for England, Moncure Conway spent much of his time with his diary:

April 21 [he wrote]. I repair to the library a good deal, and for the first time make good acquaintance with Victor Hugo, to whom I am carrying a bust of John Brown. The Execution of John Brown was yet in suspense when Victor Hugo declared that it would be "Washington slaying Spartacus"; and when it occurred Victor Hugo drew with his pencil a sort of fog through which were barely visible a gallows with a dim human form hanging from it: beneath the picture was written simply the word Ecce![1]

Along with the bust of John Brown, Conway was carrying letters of introduction to open his way in England. Written by Ralph Waldo Emerson, William Lloyd Garrison, and George W. Curtis, the letters were addressed to their friends and opposite numbers, Thomas Carlyle, Robert Browning, Leslie Stephen, and John Bright. American literature and abolition were communicating with English literature and antislavery. Their emissary was Conway, recently coeditor of a Boston paper, the abolitionist *Commonwealth*. Underwriting the expense of Conway's mission were men in the forefront of American abolition, three of the Secret Six, the conspirators who had supported John Brown's Harpers Ferry raid, Frank Sanborn, the other editor of the *Commonwealth*, the wealthy philanthropists George Luther Stearns and Gerrit Smith, as well as Wendell Phillips, Elizur Wright, and the membership of the Theodore Parker Society. If one's credentials are established by association and by money from other men's pockets, Conway's provenance was impeccable. He was making the Atlantic passage as the accredited representative of the cream of American radical, moral dissent.

He was thirty-one years old, a slender man of medium height. His long nose, already showing the spatulateness that became more pronounced with age, swept upward to a high, broad forehead. His plain, almost raw-boned face was gentle, and was animated by a gay insouciance that unfailingly drew people to him. He had been in the pulpit since he was nineteen, but there was little of the parson's manner about him. He had cultivated felicity and he wore its habiliments easily. The opera, an after-dinner cigar taken with a good port, and the company of witty, learned men, where Conway's "rich wit was more refreshing than the champagne," were as much his style as the lucid sermons he had delivered in the First Unitarian Church in Washington, where he first turned his pulpit into an abolitionist platform.[2]

Conway had swiftly risen in abolitionist ranks as a polemical speaker and writer until, two months earlier, he was handpicked to make the mission to England. His accomplishments were solid and his achievements were undeniable. His *Rejected Stone: Or Insurrection vs. Resurrection in America* and *The Golden Hour* were the most popular books on abolition circulating in the United States in the spring of 1863. "These two little books stand sole and preeminent. . . . They have," wrote a reviewer in the *Atlantic Monthly*, "created the [public] opinion out of which the President [has drawn the Emancipation Proclamation]. . . . They are . . . the brightest and simplest which this exciting period has produced."[3] Discounting the reviewer's inspired notion of the way public opinion is created, his words nonetheless attest to Conway's standing in the radical wing of American abolition. He was very successful, he was famous, and he was well regarded by the top people in the leadership.

Small wonder it was that Conway relished the memory of Mrs. Jared Sparks's warning. Mrs. Sparks, the wife of the president of Harvard, had cautioned him, when he became an abolitionist to beware of martyrdom. Surely martyrdom was the last thought in Conway's mind as he waited for the shores of England to rise on the horizon. He regretted having left his wife and children at Concord, but they were among good friends, the Emersons and Frank Sanborn; and the Boston circle, Phillips, Garrison, and the others, could be counted on to help. His family would be well cared for in his absence, and he was eager to go.

I had said my say in America; I had borne my testimony . . . in all the towns of Ohio, in every important town of New England, and in the chief cities of New York, in Philadelphia and surrounding places, and in Washington. I had written innumerable articles and letters in papers and magazines, and my two books on the crisis were in wide circulation. It appeared, therefore, a fair time for me to go for a few months to represent the moral and political situation as viewed by American antislavery people.[4]

Conway's mission was to "persuade the English that the North is right" in the Civil War. By making personal contacts with influential Englishmen and by public speaking he was to convince the English that despite its ambiguities and apparent contradictions the Civil War was an abolition war. He was to help create a public opinion that would swing British policy in support of the Union government.

If British policy was already turning in that direction, it was not yet clear. There were many points of unresolved conflict between the two governments, difficulties so vexing that they would soon bring the famous threat from Charles Francis Adams, the American minister to Great Britain. "It would be superfluous," he wrote the British foreign secretary, "in me to point out to your lordship that this is war." In Parliament a movement to recognize the Confederacy as an independent nation loomed in the offing. And at home the Union field armies had so far failed at their two great tasks. They had neither split the Confederacy nor broken the Virginia front. Despite the Emancipation Proclamation, abolition of slavery in the United States seemed almost as distant in the early spring of 1863 as it had in 1860. As Conway and his friends assessed the situation, they were convinced that the "leaden hour had come." The success of the Union field armies was inextricably linked with British policy. Freedom for the American slaves seemed to hang in the balance when Conway was recruited to go to Britain to try to tilt the balance.

Several weeks later aboard the *City of Washington* Conway scarcely dreamed that his few months[5] in England would stretch into twelve years or that before the summer was past he would be repudiated by his sponsors with a vehemence that he never understood. His repudiation is one of the most illuminating incidents in American abolition, the significance of which vastly exceeds the brief flurry it caused in official governmental circles or the uproar it created among radical abolitionists. For what Conway did in his self-confessed inexperience in diplomatic and political affairs was provide a gauge whereby many of the values and priorities of American abolition might be measured with clarity and precision. Unwittingly he put the most radical of the abolitionists to the test of their own doctrines, and the result was their unequivocal disavowal. Wendell Phillips was more generous than most of them when he repudiated Conway. At least he gave Conway the benefit of good motive. "I think," Phillips said, "that his intentions were as honest as the midday sun is clear. [But] I know at the same time that he does not represent . . . one single man on this side of the Atlantic. I do not say I believe it. . . . I know it."

A cardinal tenet of American abolition, one that was invoked to separate the doctrinally pure from those of less finely tempered mettle, and one that has subsequently been used by such historians as Stanley Elkins to explain abolition was anti-institutionalism.

"Signing off" is Henry David Thoreau's splendid phrase for anti-institutionalism. It amounted to a sense of being at odds with the-way-things-are and a willingness to act on that sense. It was a deliberate dissociation, a physical and moral withdrawal from institutions that a person believed corrupting and immoral. Signing off was a common practice among the more radical antebellum reformers. Churches and political parties were the institutions they usually came out of, and Thoreau's default on his poll tax is simply a well-known illustration of the range of a dissident's refusal to lend his support to sinful practices and the institutions supporting them. Signing off was an escape from guilt by association, and it was a practice well suited to preserve a person's moral integrity, often at minimum price and inconvenience.

Signing off, as such historians as Aileen Kraditor have shown in rebuttal to the anti-institutional thesis, was the mode of only a radical minority of abolitionists, and "their attitude proves nothing about American abolition as a whole."[6] But if the anti-institutionalists staked out the limits for abolition's response to sin and immorality, then it remains profitable to pursue them as they reached their limits and see how far they were standing outside the American value system and outside abolition as a whole.

Underlying signing off was a belief in the autonomy of the individual, a determination to be headed by no other authority, and it expressed a desire to achieve a radical innocence, freedom from the guilty burdens of history and sin that were perpetuated and transmitted by institutions. Thoreau is signing off's most celebrated practitioner, and he himself confessed to the insuperable obstacles confronting a radical who desired to free himself of the trammels of sin. He could not, he said, find the whole list from which to sign off. Try as he might to jump the tracks and make a run for pure innocence, he could never break clear of authorities that his conscience told him were malign. Thoreau got the idea of signing off, which he improved with his sparkling phrase, from an obscure New Hampshire radical lawyer and editor, Nathaniel Peabody Rogers. Rogers' story itself is an object lesson in the hazards of rejecting any form of allegiance or control. It was over the question of

authority—the simple question of the legitimacy of one like-
minded man's authority over another—that Rogers broke with
William Lloyd Garrison, and was stripped by the Garrisonians of
his editorship of the *Herald of Freedom*, a radical abolitionist
newspaper in Concord, New Hampshire.

Rogers was one of the three men spared the critical bite of
Thoreau's pen when he took the measure of his friends and acquaintances. The other two were John Brown and Wendell Phillips.
They were a Thoreauvian trinity of radicals refusing to knuckle to
any authority save the dictates of conscience. They were, so to
speak, the only men Thoreau cared to have as his traveling com-
panions as he made his dissenting journey toward innocence. And
one wonders if Phillips would have been allowed to continue
had Thoreau lived to hear his repudiation of Moncure Conway.
For Conway, in his mission to England, was only proposing that
the radical abolitionists truly sanction and act on the anti-
institutionalism they had long espoused.

Signing off's characteristic political expression was disunion. For
the abolitionists who signed off, their slogan was "The Constitution is a covenant with Death and an agreement with Hell," and
their policy was "No Union with slaveholders." The history of the
Garrisonian attack on slavery is rich with instances in which the
policy of disunion was advanced, and it was the official position of
the American Anti-Slavery Society after 1844. Before the outbreak
of civil war the idea had become so pervasive that such orthodox
politicians as Horace Greeley supported disunion as the only way
out of the moral and political dilemma the nation found itself in.
Let the errant sisters, Greeley said of the seceding states, go in
peace. At the hands of a Greeley the destruction of the American
union was an expedient, but beneath the expediency lay the old
bedrock claim of innocence, the desire to be free of any partnership
with the slave states. The case was never put more clearly than by
Wendell Phillips. Writing in the *Liberator* in 1848, Phillips said,
"Dissolution of the Union is a course, by which a man or State may
immediately disconnect themselves from the sin of slavery. . . .
Disunion startles a man to thought. It takes a lazy abolitionist by
the throat, and thunders in his ear, 'Thou art the slaveholder.'"

It remains a fine point as to whether the abolition disunionists meant what they said as they turned signing off into a propaganda for disunion. It did indeed startle a man to thought. Disunion was an admirable tactic for forcing a hearing for the abolitionists and driving a wedge in complacent minds. To that extent disunion was a propaganda designed to shock one into listening and thinking; it did not necessarily compel one to act. But Phillips clearly implied that at the end of thought lay action. It was quite possible for disunion to be more than a propaganda of shock. It could be a tactic for action and an end in itself. If the disconnection were made, surely there would be no complicity in sin, and at last a true innocence would be attained.

Even the most skillful defender of Garrisonianism does not retreat from the contention that disunion was understood as a method whereby guilt would be relieved and slavery abolished.[7] Thus in the final analysis disunion provides a rigorous test for determining the depth of "guiltiness" and the strength of an unqualified devil-take-the-hindmost desire to destroy slavery. In short, disunion provides a gauge for measuring the two pillars upon which radical American abolition purportedly rested: guilt about slavery and the determination to destroy slavery at the expense of established institutions.

During the secession crisis of 1860–1861 disunionists were "thundering against compromise" because they "sincerely believed that disunion would destroy slavery," but when war came they abruptly changed course. James McPherson, the best student of abolitionists' activities during the Civil War, uses Wendell Phillips to illustrate how, when war came, "most abolitionists did an about face" on disunion. A wracking soul-searching followed the attack on Fort Sumter. Finally, Phillips completed his examination of conscience and stood before a packed audience in the Boston Music Hall to make his report. He admitted that he enjoyed the reputation of being the leading disunionist among abolitionists, but that now that war had come he found no inconsistency between his old disunionism and the "'hearty and hot'" welcome he gave "this war," which was admittedly a war for union, not abolition. Because, he told his audience, a war for union could be converted to an abolition war. "Seize the thunderbolt God has forged for you, and annihilate" slavery. "It was," reports McPherson, "the greatest speech of his life." Phillips had not recanted. He had simply combined his long-standing demand for abolition and justice for Negroes with a practical means for obtaining it. In his speech "Under the Flag," Phillips offered his listeners a vision of the future. "Years hence, when the smoke of this conflict clears away, the world will see under our banner all tongues, all creeds all races,— one brotherhood,—and on the banks of the Potomac, the Genius of Liberty, robed in light, four and thirty stars for her diadem, broken chains under her feet, and an olive-branch in her right hand." When the speech was over, "the high priest of disunion had taken up the cudgels for Union and liberty, and abolitionists everywhere enthusiastically closed ranks behind him."[8]

But there is the sentence with which Phillips, mustering himself for duty with the "men marshalled for war," introduced his vision of the future: "I believe in the *possibility* of justice, in the *certainty* of union."[9] Here is a critical distinction made by a man desperately trying to reconcile his proud self-proclaimed record of disunion with his new advocacy for union. One might expect Phillips, without any hint of contingency, to yoke justice with union, making one the necessary condition of the other, or, going further, making justice the necessary precondition to union. But his vision of the time "when the smoke . . . clears away" is prefaced with a qualified doubt. Even the double metaphor invoked in the vision suggests Phillips' emphasis. *Justice* for "all races" is handled almost perfunctorily. It is with *union* that the peroration soars and adorning figures are employed to embellish it. Unquestionably abolition and equalitarianism are firmly linked with the restored union, but it is obvious that Phillips' imagination and interest have been seized by the idea of union.

Furthermore, Phillips' set-piece speeches against the South and the Union delivered during the secession crisis, "Disunion" and "Progress," present difficulties to anyone wishing to make Phillips a root-and-branch disunionist who must do a turn-about when Fort Sumter is attacked. First is his claim for a singular destiny for America. Second is his proposition that "The people of the States between the Gulf and the Great Lakes . . . are essentially one [and] nothing can long divide us." These two contentions are linked with what Phillips called the "unchangeable basis of national life." "Our bones and blood are made of it," he said; "America belongs to Americans." When these statements are coupled with Phillips' striking profession, in the middle of the "Disunion" speech, of "a Union whose life survives the ages," one sees the outline of a bedrock belief in American nationality upon which, rather incongruously, a superstructure of disunionist polemics was erected.

For all of his pyrotechnic dissent Phillips was a child of his age and his country. Above everything he was a nationalist, a believer in an American nation endowed with a unique mission in the world. One searches his collected speeches in vain, especially those delivered before his "about-face," for any hint that Phillips' mind was ever freed of a national consciousness or that he ever doubted that America was the "great daughter of the west of the Atlantic," the imperial successor of the last great empire, Trajan's Rome.[10] The leimotiv of Phillips' dissent, the graveman of his sustained argument as an agitator, was always what is wrong with the United States. It was never the United States is wrong.

Phillips assigned the United States a world-historical mission. He believed that the United States—the political Union—was an arena in which a providential national moral drama was being enacted. Without union the morality play was impossible. It could not, as it were, be staged; therefore in the last analysis the Union had to be preserved. Political union was the first condition to anything else. It is difficult to avoid the conclusion that the supreme "sin" for the disunionist abolitionist was, as it was for the confirmed unionist, a real attack on the Union, the political expression of American nationality which was, Phillips claimed, "the last best growth of the thoughtful mind."

What makes this matter important is the guilt that supposedly energized disunion and which was supposedly so explosively strong that it compelled the guilty to seek nothing less than complete release from their sinful complicity. But the disunionists' about-face was scarcely consistent with a compulsive drive toward innocence that admits to no constraints or qualifications. The

Union was no less sinful when the disunionists swung to support it in April, 1861 than it was when they inveighed against it; nor was the Constitution in 1861 anything other than that which they had proclaimed it to be years earlier, a covenant with death and an agreement with hell.

The conditionals with which Phillips surrounds his own about-face are sufficient to illustrate the difficulty of reconciling a compulsion for innocence with allegiance to the state, and the disunionists' wholehearted embrace of a war for union simply records it. They could hope that a war for union might somehow be transformed into a war for abolition; indeed they pinned their faith precisely upon that hope, but abolition lay hidden in the path of war, and there were no guarantees that the transformation would occur. Phillips said as much when he pledged himself and his fellow disunionists "to try the experiment." And trying the experiment was precisely what had earlier separated the disunionists from political abolitionists. The latter claimed "that there are hidden in the armory of the Constitution weapons strong enough to secure [abolition]." "Grant us time," Phillips has them saying, "for the experiment." Until the attack on Fort Sumter, Phillips had derided the political abolitionists. But when the war came, Phillips embraced the "experiment," at the end of which, he said, lay only one certainty: union. Justice, he said, was only a possibility, and in saying so he gave abolition over as a hostage to the fortunes of war.

Disunion vanished at Fort Sumter and in the Music Hall in Boston. But did guilt, the energizing force behind disunion, also perish? To answer the question one has only to read Phillips' speeches delivered during the war. In them one might expect to find something on the order of Lincoln's idea of the war expressed in his Second Inaugural. The war, Lincoln said, was a national blood atonement for slavery; and the war could not end until God in His own good time had exacted the full measure of expiation for the national sin of slavery. But what one finds in Phillips' speeches is absolution granted to the old disunionists and all loyal citizens. They are not guilty, even of the sin of complicity; nor is there any hint that they ever were guilty of anything. For themselves the war is not a bloodly atonement; it is a terrible evil in that "it takes the lawyer, the merchant, the mechanic from his industrious, improving, inspiring occupation, and lets him down into the demoralization of a camp." But the war is an evil necessary to bring to the South, where all sin and guilt have now been shifted, "our . . . better, purer, nobler, higher civilization." Guilt is no longer the portion of the nation; nor is it summoned to strengthen the resolve of those who wanted to destroy slavery; and the Union field armies are not cast as regiments of militant penitents but as legions of a New Model Army armored with righteousness. Sin, like disunion, had vanished from the lexicon of the compulsively guilt-ridden. The old question of the disunionists, will you be innocent or sinful?, also vanished. It was replaced by another choice: "This war means one of two things,—Emancipation or Disunion." These were the alternatives Phillips presented at the Music Hall. He told his audience to choose freedom for the slaves or the political disintegration of the American nation. There were no other choices thenceforward for Wendell Phillips and the disunionists who followed him. In April, 1861, innocence had somehow been translated from its earlier meaning of political disconnection to a statement of political loyalty. The political integrity of the Federal Union became synonymous with emancipation, and both hinged upon the success of the Union field armies. Unless the Union armies defeated the Confederacy, everything was lost.

In early 1863 the war was going badly for the Union. It was a springtime of hope for the Confederacy. William Gladstone's comment that Jefferson Davis had made an army, was making a navy, and, more important, had made a nation seemed less a political epigram than a prophecy on the verge of fulfillment. The Army of the Potomac had been bled viciously at Fredericksburg and had barely escaped disaster at Chancellorsville. Grant was mired in the swamps of the Mississippi Delta outside the defenses of Vicksburg. The writ of the Emancipation Proclamation ran no farther than the picket lines of the stalled Union armies. "The experiment" had been underway for almost two years, and the only things it had so far yielded were a grinding war, disaster, heartbreak, and a political policy that freed some slaves, kept others in bondage, and in its announced form had, as has often been said, all of the moral grandeur of a bill of lading. Only the most sanguine northerners could see the war as better than at an impasse. Both union and abolition seemed as far, perhaps farther, away as they had in 1861. Surveying the scene, Phillips claimed, "I do not believe in Southern exhaustion. . . . No, the South has not yet felt the first symptom of exhaustion"; and he was also talking about doubt and despair, dark political mistakes, and treachery. It was during this dispiriting time when nothing was going right, when all the tides seemed to be flowing in favor of the Confederacy, the leaden time, as Moncure Conway called it, that he, at Phillips' invitation, agreed to go on the British mission.[11]

At the end of April, Conway was in London.[12] His initial contact was with Peter Alfred Taylor, a member of Parliament and leader of an abolitionist pro-Union society. Taylor gave Conway the hospitality of his home, Aubrey House; the society gave him a base from which to work. More contacts were made, and within a few days Conway had access to some of the cream of British intellectual and literary circles. James Hope Stanfield, Henry Fawcett, Leslie Stephen, Dr. James Martineau, and Robert Browning, all welcomed him, and Emerson's letter of introduction opened Thomas Carlyle's door. With the former group, Conway was among ideological friends, and their talk was spirited and uninhibited. With Carlyle, however, he was circumspect and guarded. There was, Conway thought, "nothing [to] be gained by raising before him any red rag of Radicalism." Carlyle's "relentless confrontation of optimistic visions and reforms was like having vitriol thrown upon you." Conway wanted to keep on the good side of the great man, and he therefore left "the initiative of talk entirely with Carlyle."

Conway's public work was mostly speaking at dissenting chapels. These were the popular strongholds of antislavery in England because, as Conway observed, "Our cause had largely fallen into the hands of dissenting preachers." After a month's labor in the chapels he began to think "that I [am] teaching only the already taught." He doubted that he was making much headway in his mission. Certainly he had failed to persuade the English intelligensia that the Civil War was not only a nationalizing war but was also a struggle to free the slaves. And this was the sticking point. As Robert Browning told him, "English writers were confused on the whole issue."

They talked in Browning's library, and Browning reviewed the situation for him. Even for one favorably disposed toward the American abolitionists, Browning said, there were difficulties in believing that the war for union was also a war for abolition. The Emancipation Proclamation itself was offered as evidence that the Lincoln government refused "to abolish slavery where [it was] within their reach." Some of his friends, Browning said, believed what the Confederate propagandists in England claimed, that the true purpose of the proclamation was to stir up slave insurrection behind Confederate lines. The effect might be the wholesale slaughter of white southerners, a disruption of the Confederate war effort, and military victory for the Union, but an inconclusive resolution of the slavery issue because there would still be slavery in the United States.

This was the question constantly nagging the minds of the "English writers of reputation." Where was the clear, unequivocal signal that the American Civil War was an abolition war? Where was the guarantee that the Union war aims went beyond "territorial integrity," the aim of nationalistic wars. Where was, Browning asked Conway, the undeniable proof "that the coercive measures of the North" were aimed at emancipating the slaves and reestablishing the Union on a basis of universal freedom? And was it not possible, Browning asked, that in the absence of such proof that the American abolitionists themselves had misjudged, that they had made a mistake in supporting the Lincoln government? Browning pressed on. Was it not possible that with the best of intentions the abolitionists had helped plunge the United States "into an abyss of blood" on the other side of which lay nothing much more than the antebellum status quo?

The best Conway could do was reply that it had to be assumed that slavery was the root issue and that the war would not be over until slavery had been destroyed everywhere in the United States. But assumptions were not assurances; and hopeful wishes were not guarantees. The two men came to friendly impasse. As Conway remembered it, Browning said that American abolitionists should declare before the world that they had no desire to subjugate the South except for the liberation of the slaves. Such a disclaimer would clear the abolitionists of the charge that they had helped drag the country into a war that "repelled discriminating thinkers" in England. It would put them unequivocally on record that they had embraced war solely as a means of eradicating slavery. The question was how to make that point. How could Conway find a way to clear up the "confusion" and regain the moral purity of the abolitionists that, in the eyes of his English friends, had been so damagingly compromised as the Garrisonians had swung in support of the Lincoln government?

Conway told Browning he would "challenge" the Confederacy. He would make a proposal that would simultaneously free the slaves, end the war, and restore the initiative of moral leadership to the abolitionists. In one stroke everything would be resolved.

Conway asked Browning for a pencil and paper and wrote out some notes. The challenge emerged as a letter to James M. Mason, the Confederate commissioner to Great Britain, and was worked into its final version in Aubrey House, the home of Conway's London host, Peter Alfred Taylor, from which it was sent on June 10, 1863:

Sir,—I have authority to make the following proposition on behalf of the leading antislavery men of America, who have sent me to this country:—

If the States calling themselves 'The Confederate States of America' will consent to emancipate the negro slaves in those States, such emancipation to be guaranteed by a liberal European commission, the emancipation to be inaugurated at once and such time to be allowed for its completion as the commission shall adjudge to be necessary and just, and such emancipation once made to be irrevocable,—then the abolitionists and antislavery leaders of the Northern States shall immediately oppose the further prosecution of the war on the part of the United States government, and, since they hold the balance of power, will certainly cause the war to cease by the immediate withdrawal of every kind of support from it [and with its cessation] a restoration of peace and the independence of the South. . . .

Any guarantee of my responsibility and my right to make this offer shall be forthcoming.

I am, sir, yours, etc.,
M. D. Conway

Here was everything, and more, for which radical abolitionists had ever contended: the rejection of violence as means of settling social questions; a separation of the slave states from the free states; the resolution of the free guilt the radicals claimed was their deepest motive for everything they undertook, the driving force behind their sustained indictment of sinful institutions. Furthermore, there was in Conway's challenge a program for the abolition of slavery. The old disunion thesis had never carried with it a program for abolition. It assumed that once separated from the United States the slave states would find themselves incapable of sustaining slavery, that somehow slavery would crumble from within, dissolve itself when confronted by a hostile world and its own inner contradictions. But Conway's challenge went beyond that. It guaranteed "immediate" abolition instead of assuming that a problematical future would somehow dispose of slavery, and at a price that was scarcely a price at all. It was only what the radical abolitionists had asked for before they embraced war as a problematical experiment in abolition. Conway also committed an enormous blunder. He proposed the political independence of the Confederacy.

Instantly the storm broke over Conway's head. James Mason rushed the letter into print in the London *Times*, hoping to divide the Lincoln government and the abolitionists Conway claimed to speak for. Conway was raked over the coals by Charles Francis Adams, the American minister to Great Britain. Conway lamely confessed his inexperience in diplomatic and political affairs and admitted that he had no authority to make the proposal on behalf of any abolitionsts. This admission satisfied Adams; he concluded the interview by saying in his dour manner that he hoped "no evil will result in America" and dismissed Conway.

Conway wrote Ellen, his wife, telling her to sell their Concord house and bring their children to England. He thought that there was no other way to protect them from "all the anger" that would be unleashed as soon as news of what he had done reached America. Notwithstanding his attempt to prepare himself to "suffer obloquy" he came down with a raging fever and a blistering skin infection. Consultation with a medical specialist brought no relief. Physicians, Conway said, "could not do much for a case of worry and for wounds of heart and mind."

Conway's deepest wounds came from his sponsors, Garrison, Phillips, and others of the Boston-Concord coterie. They attacked him with a "vehemence" he said he could never understand. Once they learned what he had proposed to James Mason they tumbled all over themselves trying to disassociate themselves from his "folly and presumption." But it was not sufficient to clear their skirts of somehow being involved in calling off the union war in favor of abolition. They did their best to clear themselves of any relationship with Conway himself. Wendell Phillips had the integrity to frame his denials in equivocal terms, but Stearns and Garrison were less careful with the facts of the matter, and Garrison himself deliberately misrepresented his connection with Conway. The radicals' repudiation was as thorough as they could make it because they, like Mason and Adams, saw the deadly trap Conway so innocently had laid for them.[13]

What Conway had done was commit them to cleave to emancipation at the expense of American nationality. He asked them to be true to their own words. Here lies the point to which we have been drawn: the sin-guilt and the consequent compulsive desire to be guiltless that supposedly informed radical abolitionists and drove them headlong in an explosive assault on institutions, the preeminent of which was the Federal Union, the American national state. But what of these compulsions? Long since they seem to have dissipated. And sin, according to Wendell Phillips, had been transferred to the Confederates who were foremost rebels, not slaveholders.

Conway plunged through union and the idea of American nationality in his flight toward innocence. But when he got to the other side he found himself alone. The most charitable thing his mentors in anti-institutionalism could say about him was that he had meant well. For themselves they stayed inside union and the idea of American nationality. Twice the test had come to the disunionists to break outside toward the innocence lying beyond. Both times they shied away.[14]

We catch intimations of the nature of classic American radicalism in the mid-nineteenth century. American radicals, for all their brave words, remained conditioned by an overwhelming nationalism. Their discontents and desires were trammeled by a national consciousness, a belief in the curative, restorative, and redemptive quality of America. For them, American nationality was indeed, as Wendell Phillips claimed, "the last best growth of the thoughtful mind." Neither their imaginations nor grievances were ever sufficient to permit them to break outside a nationalistic conception of the good and moral society.[15]

Important to understanding this homegrown radicalism are the institutions embedded in the idea of American nationality. Free speech, free toil, schoolhouses, and ballot boxes, Phillips listed them in April, 1861. When he restated them in 1863, they remained essentially the same: "Free speech, free types [i.e. newspapers and the mechanical means of the free trade in ideas], open Bibles [i.e. religious freedom] [and] the . . . rule of the majority." Phillips provides a list of the conventional institutions of an aspiring, socially mobile people operating in the free marketplace, all of which are guaranteed by the national state.

But Moncure Conway, what of him? With him we see the hazards of applying a general theory to the concrete realities of personal experience. Conway seems a splendid illustration of the proposition of the guilt-ridden reformer. Radical abolitionist, intellectual, abstract thinker, student of the doctrines of Concord, holder of no traditional institutional connections or allegiances, and easy prey to obsessive guilt over slavery, in explosive expiation he smashes through institutions. A "crisis thinker," his only measure of effectiveness is a satisfactory answer to the question of how many people are listening to me? And in his efforts to drum up an audience and enlarge it, his message became increasingly wild and erratic.

Two difficulties await us. When Conway got on the other side of institutions he found that he had no followers, not even his friends from Concord and Boston, who had taught him the doctrines. And

for Conway, slavery was not a sinister abstraction, always at a remove, the creation of the imaginative stirrings of guilt. He was a
child of the slave system. Heir to slaves and scion of a Virginia
dynasty of slaveholders, he grew up, quite literally, in the bosom
of slavery.

The one man who so excellently acts out the part of the compulsively guilty anti-institutional reformer described by the brilliant
interpretation poorly fits the model. We come again to William
James's observation about moral choice: popular rhetorical maxims
help us little; indeed they are apt to mislead when we try to understand why moral choices have been made.

II
Virginia

Falmouth, Virginia, was once
the head of navigation on the Rappahannock, but when the river
shifted, the little town was left as high and dry as the rocks in
the riverbed. Across the Rappahannock, Fredricksburg became the
entrepôt to this portion of the Virginia Tidewater, and Falmouth
became an eddy in the backwater. Bypassed but scarcely decrepit,
Falmouth remained the seat of Stafford County, and if its fortunes
did not grow, they did not decline. The hard times in Southside
Virginia that sent families and slaves wholesale into the Gulf states
were little felt in Falmouth. The old families did not move on,
and there was a "rough corner" in the town that gave sufficient
pleasures to the raffish countrymen on Saturdays to keep them

21

content on their depleted lands for the rest of the week. There was stasis, perhaps, in Falmouth, but also placid stability. It was into this little world that Moncure Daniel Conway was born on March 17, 1832, and for most of his life in Falmouth he lived in the largest house in the town to which Walker Peyton Conway moved his family in 1838.

When Conway told his life story in his *Autobiography*, he arranged these early materials to provide an answer to his question, "Who . . . made me? . . . Can I not pick my skeptical soul out of these old people?" He tells a splendid story of Tidewater consanguinity. Generations of Stones, Peytons, Daniels, and Moncures are sketched in to yield portraits of dissent—a signer of the Declaration of Independence, a member of the William and Mary chapter of the Illuminati, assorted freethinkers, nonjurors, and emancipationists—and a secure claim to membership in the Maryland and Virginia gentry that he passed off with the comment, "Virginia democracy forbade us to derive from out ancestors any dignity."

There are some distinguished names in Conway's list of forbears, but they are always at a remove, something on the order of "George Washington's great-grandfather was thus Mrs. Peyton's [Conway's own great-grandmother] great-grandfather." A more accurate measure of his place in the Tidewater pecking order is the professions of his father and grandfathers. One grandfather was a county clerk, the other a physician and surgeon. His father served one term in the Viriginia legislature and then retired to Falmouth to farm, practice law, and serve as presiding justice of Stafford County. There was a whiff of the declasse about Walker Peyton Conway. To the consternation of his own father he gave up his Episcopalianism, joined the Methodist Church, and fitted out the basement of his big house in Falmouth as a prayer meeting room, where twice a week the local Methodists came for services led by the town tailor. These meetings, Conway wrote, were "engraved in my memory,—this fine intellectual father of mine, accustomed to preside over courts, and the refined elegantly dressed lady beside him, surrounded by poor, dusty, patch people, of whom some could hardly write [and] some . . . he had picked out of the ditch."

Notwithstanding their descent into Methodism—"our family [was] the first of good social position in our region belonging to that sect"—Walker Peyton Conway's family was, as the saying goes, well-connected. He may have been, as his son said, "singularly free from ambition," but he had relatives who were not so free and who had gone much farther than the bar of Stafford courthouse. But the lines of connections ran in both directions and that fact gave some force to Moncure Conway's observation that "'poor white' was always a phrase forbidden in genteel families." The prohibition was less a genteel mannerism than it was a self-protective device, because in the course of a generation or two "many of the 'gentry' became 'poor white,'" and it was always possible to make an invidious comment about one's own family by using the term. Conway's cousins lay in either direction. One was a justice of the United States Supreme Court; another survives in the record only because Walker Peyton Conway and his brother-in-law made a place for her as a teacher of their children. Otherwise she would have slipped off the margin of social respectability with the other Gaskins, "originally Gascoigne." One did indeed resurrect his relatives with prudence, with a care for the demands of Virginia democracy, just as one interested in genealogy struck *poor white* from his vocabulary.

A discriminating selection of ancestors permitted Conway to begin his Virginia line in 1640 and to continue it through the generations, weaving in the Moncures, the Daniels, and, in those arabesques so necessary for the confirmation of identity through connection with the refracted glory of the ancients, practically every name of consequence in colonial and Revolutionary Virginia, finally to emerge at his own generation with an unbroken succession of Tidewater gentry stretching out behind him.

All were substantial people, and all were slaveholders. Walker Peyton Conway owned property valued at $100,000, part of it in slaves.[1] Some of his slaves were at Inglewood, his farm outside Falmouth; some were on another farm, unnamed; others were at the "cotton factory" in Falmouth; the rest were at Conway House, the big brick house in town.

It was a comfortable world into which Moncure was born. Inglewood, where his first memories came from, was a "little Avalon." Sherbourne and Glencairn, the homes of a cousin and an uncle were adjacent. Erleslie, Grandfather Conway's home, was close by, and they all ran together in the memory of an early seren-ity. "I dreamed of the distant beauties of Palestine, though the cedars of Lebanon were thick on our Falmouth hills, and no rose of Sharon ever equalled those of our garden. The wondrous Judas-tree at our door, and our fig-trees, myrtles, fireflies, meadows, crystal streams, all the materials of a paradise were around me."

Moncure, called "Monc" or "Monk," was the second child and second son. The first born was Peyton, the father's namesake, two years older. Mildred was five years younger, and she was followed by Catherine, who lived only a few days, and then by Richard and Peter. Peyton had the prerogatives of the firstborn. He was also "handsome and dashing... always ready to wrestle or fight." Moncure was born in an "applextic [sic] state" and was considered a delicate child. "Palpitations and fever," the symptoms of his pre-carious health, caused his mother to "spend an anxious life" about him even after he had left Conway House and Falmouth.[2] By his own account, Monc was not popular among his comrades. "I was," he said, "homely, was not spirited, and was a poor creature be-side . . . Peyton." He hated the wrestling and fighting that Peyton piled into. Monc preferred Mildred's company. And, he remem-bered, "I worshipped rather precociously the beautiful ladies of Falmouth, and numerous aunts and cousins from the country, [some] of whom were always visiting us. I did their errands and attended on them with eagerness, and they were so gracious to me that I cared little for the boys. Moreover, I was beginning to form friendships with people met in story-books. Much as I disliked playground squabbles, I found it pleasant to assist in the slaughter of dragons. . . . Fairy tales . . . dreams were built on the stuff of me [sic]; I was surrounded with a sleep—a source of dreams—and my little life was rounded out."

Inglewood, with fields like the Garden of Eden opening out to-ward the Rappahannock; Erleslie, where his grandmother seemed "the queen of the whole world"; Conway House, presided over by the "fine" man and his "refined" elegant lady; Peter Humstead, the black factotum who had come as part of Margaret Daniel Conway's dowry; Humstead's wife Maria, "nearly always laughing," all these were the web and the texture of the young boy's life. It was a social fabric and life experience interwoven with slavery. Pluck one strand loose and it inevitably raveled into the peculiar institution, all the way back to the first slaveholding Conway in Virginia. From this earliest progenitor the acquisition and management of slaves had underpinned the fortune and status of the family. Monc's experience of slavery was as concrete and as inescapable as the return of the seasons along the Rappahannock.

Before the memory of any playmates, came his recollection of "the comely coffee-coloured" Maria Humstead, who nursed him. He and Peyton roamed the fields with Peter and Maria Humstead's son Charles. "Handsome, brilliant, merry, with an inexhaustible store of stories and songs, this coloured genius was the most romantic figure" of Monc's childhood. But Charles's career was summarily ended. Fascinated by the Falmouth fire engine, he set fire to an abandoned outbuilding in order to watch the engine work, and Virginia law was relentless for the slave-as-arsonist. Walker Peyton Conway had the choice of having the boy arraigned for a capital crime or selling him out of the state. Charles's forced sale was the only time Walker Peyton Conway ever sold a slave; and the memory of Charles and the incident was so powerful that he and his incendiary prank appear intact in Conway's novel, *Pine and Palm,* written forty years after the event. At Falmouth there were flashes of the savagery in slavery. Monc watched as a master led his four female slaves from the Stafford County courthouse where he had charged them with conspiring to poison him, possibly (because the women were all old) in order to be reimbursed by the state should they be convicted and executed. But there was no evidence to support the charge and the women were acquitted. The master led them to his wagon, tied their hands to it, ripped their dresses down their backs, started the horses, picked up a rawhide, and the whole dismal procession disappeared down the road with the master whaling the women. The sight was a horror, but it was the only time Monc witnessed brutality. When the Conway slaves were whipped, it was "with no more severity and with less frequency" than the Conway children themselves were punished.

The one "horror" that Monc saw at Stafford courthouse remained in his mind all of his life, but it was mitigated in those early years in Falmouth by the knowledge that had been perpetrated by a renegade. No such scandal had ever attached itself to the tribes of Moncures, Daniels, Peytons, and Conways. The Conways cultivated the ways of paternalism. Their slaves were "servants." No slave was ever sold except Charles Humstead, and he was sold to save him from something worse. Their slaves were never hired to anyone but a neighbor whose character was vouchsafed by personal knowledge. The slaves were given the same religious instruction the Conway children received in the little Sunday school Margaret Conway conducted in her basement. Above all was the instruction the Conway children received about their slaves, and all slaves: "treat them with kindness."

But there were limits. Word seeped out into Falmouth that Margaret Conway was offering "equal" instruction in her Sunday school, and furthermore, she was teaching the Conway slaves to read, which was forbidden by Virginia law. The consequence was that she had to break up the Sunday school. Her husband, the presiding magistrate at Stafford courthouse, and his family, all had to be above suspicion on matters about slavery. There were fine variations of life in the Tidewater permitting eccentricity and those subtle deviations that gave the aberrant a certain singularity that allows a community to congratulate itself for its tolerance. But on slavery the margins of deviance were narrow, the best measure of their extent being the genteel euphemisms and the latitudes implied in the injunction of kindness. Beyond that the system was firm and unyielding. One acquiesced to it and made peace with himself as best he could.

Aberration. Jumping the tracks in spectacular derailments that carried him beyond two communities, Falmouth and Concord, leaving him the repudiated exile from both. It is always in one's mind when dealing with Moncure Conway. The knowledge of the end shapes the perceptions of the beginning.

There was Walker Peyton Conway's own aberrancy. The high-spirited young man, bearing the best of the cavalier tradition that blooded Virginians loved to impute to themselves, cutting a dashing figure at dances, card parties, and hunts, the beau geste flawlessly summoned when gallantry bid, suddenly kicking it all over, storming out of his father's house for the "vulgar fanaticism" of Methodism.

Walker Peyton Conway's conversion to Methodism was followed by his marriage to Margaret Eleanor Daniel. Margaret was twice orphaned. Her mother died, then her father, and she was left by her stepmother to be reared by an uncle. The uncle, John Lewis, was a teacher and sometime poet and minor novelist, who treated Margaret more as a daughter than a ward, and the evidence of the training that he gave her remains in her letters. There is an obvious intelligence informed by sharp analytical powers suffused by a remarkable flexibility that allowed her to see different sides of a question. Reading her letters, one is confronted by a woman whose intellect is quite possibly superior to that of her husband.

John Lewis' wife was a "tyrannous Calvinist." Margaret Conway told Monc that she was "kept in a sort of hothouse of Presbyterianism" until her marriage to Walker Peyton Conway. During the time she lived with the Lewises, she said she was in "covert rebellion" against the eternal decrees that damned the unborn. Her gentle spirit and desire for the best for others were offended by this Calvinist harshness. But she willingly accepted the doctrine of perseverance that was taught by the Lewises. Her entire life was, she told her son, a struggle to come as close as a mortal might to the "secret things which we are told belong [only] to God." Her struggle was a hard, enduring one. "I am," she confessed, "naturally indolent in body and mind and love to follow any inclination suggested by the weakness of the affections of my nature. I sometimes think surely my mission on this earth includes any sacrifice of natural inclination."[3] But this was a battle she fought within herself. Her exterior battles were always fought for the betterment of others. She took it, she said, as a solemn duty "to combat those things which I think involve what is [wrong] in the doings of those I love, or to whom nature has given me ties."

A high-strung woman—by her own admission "fear[ful] of [her] unfortunately excitable temperament and her nerves" which would not "stand any tention [tension] for any length of time"[4]— there were nevertheless some moments when her soul was at peace, when she believed she was close to the "secret things." Then she would sing the line from the slave song: "I never foun' no peace or res'/Till I jine the Methodess."

But more was needed for Margaret Conway's serenity than her quiet Wesleyan piety. Perhaps she told her husband, as she later warned her son, "Perverted female instincts, thro' a want of proper sympathy and cultivation from those they love had made more *bad women* than any other cause; and this is the reason why there have been sometimes such outlaws among women in married life, it usually begins in a [little] disappointment in some matter involving feeling, comparatively small in itself but becomes the lever that moves her whole after life."[5]

What dreams she carried with her when she left the Lewis' "hothouse" for Inglewood are unrecoverable. But clues to her dreams for herself appear in her warning to her son about a woman's need for sympathy and cultivation: "Always aim to preserve your own identity of character and style . . . even when it is painful"; her lament that her life "has brought on my premature decay of all my powers"; and her cryptic comment that the "necessity of my position includes every sacrifice of natural inclination [which is] often too painful for endurance."

There is never any specificity about these remarks. It is as though the actual facts of her grievance must be left unstated. A veil of abstractions is always drawn before the woman and her situation. The direct statement that would tell why she felt diminished, unsatisfied, wearied by some unnamed adversary that elicited her "love and duty" is always absent. Perhaps she knew that her son would understand, that there was no need to go beyond the allusions that puzzle a later reader.

The relationship between Walker Peyton Conway's conversion to Methodism and his wedding to Margaret Daniel is best explained by the single sentence their son wrote about it: "It may readily be understood that she would not be suffered to wed a gay and worldly youth, and also falling in love with a pious young lady would naturally sober such a youth."[6] The story has all of the elements of a trade-off. A young man deeply in love gives up his religion and his high-living ways in order to marry a pious girl of a different persuasion. There is less of a "conversion" than an accommodation, and if anything was abandoned, it was not religious belief (for the Episcopal Church in Stafford County was moribund, and Walker Peyton Conway's outraged father himself had never been confirmed in the Church) but the class claims of Episcopalianism. In the Tidewater, to be a Methodist was to demean oneself and one's family.

So there was the aberration. Two members of the Tidewater gentry had forsaken the religion of their fathers. It was permitted because the aberrancy concerned only individuals. The social fabric was neither broken nor threatened. No finely tuned and balanced social arrangements were deranged. The community remained intact, and even profited. Walker Peyton Conway's rebellion against his father was another proof of his integrity, his capacity for conscientious behavior. And the pious household that he and Margaret Daniel established became an ornament to Falmouth and a testament to the community's tolerance. No one thought the less of him until the rumor came out that Margaret Conway was teaching her slaves to read in the prayer meeting room in the basement of Conway House. Then the limits of permissible aberrancy were struck.

When Margaret Conway's Sunday school was disbanded the matter was not settled; nor was there peace of mind at Conway House on slavery. The Conways and the Daniels had for generations carried with them the "old Virginia anti-slavery" that certain Virginians prided themselves on. One of them, Travers Daniels, had gained some local notoriety by hanging his windows with curtains with scenes showing the English abolitionist Granville Sharp striking chains from Negroes, and several other members of the family had claims to antislavery positions.

When Walker Peyton Conway established his family in Falmouth, opposition to slavery was, as his son said, a traditional ritual, a device simultaneously employed to stroke uneasy consciences and to affirm status claims against the "new Proslavery Virginians" who were rising to power toward 1840. These men offended Walker Peyton Conway, causing him to leave active political life after serving one term in the Virginia legislature. But his

apparent hostility to slavery ran deeper than that. It was sufficiently strong to cause him to break with his brother Eustace when
the Methodist church split over slavery. Eustace Conway went the
way of the dissidents, supplying the money to build a proslavery
Methodist church at Fredericksburg. Walker Peyton Conway kept
his ties with the Baltimore Conference, the northern wing of the
split communion, and always cautioned his son against the proslavery Virginians. "Don't be the fool of those people! Slavery is a
doomed institution," he told Monc. But such comments "mys-
tified" the boy. To him, "Slavery seemed to be as permanent a fact
as the Rappahannock River." Moreover, it was obvious to the boy
that "neither my father nor any of the [old] Methodists were proposing to abolish slavery"; nor was there ever from his father a
complaint about either the burdens or the wrongs of slavery.

The father's words to his son suggest that Walker Peyton Conway was a circumspect man on slavery. He rose to troubled indignation only when his son set out to destroy the social system that
had supported the family for two hundred years. He was scarcely a
man who felt impinged or threatened by slavery, or even disturbed
by it. He prophesied its doom with equanimity, as though it would
fall at another time and in another place. Meanwhile he would
serve slavery well with the *oblige* that generations of training had
poured into him, all of which he could distill in one sentence. "A
single moments [*sic*] reflection would teach any common sense person the reason and propriety of our course." [7]

If there were no voices of disquiet or anxiety within Walker
Peyton Conway, there were those that spoke to his wife, the young
mistress of his household. We hear them later than those early
years at Inglewood and Conway House, but they come with such
clarity and explosive intensity that it is scarcely a presumption to
place them backwards in time and suggest that their quality was not
changed. Margaret Daniel Conway was a bitterly unhappy mistress of slaves. All that was lacking in these earlier times was the
opportunity for her to express herself in a way that might have
been recorded.

When she first went on record about slavery she professed her
"conservative spirit." Yet she called herself conservative only in

comparison with militant abolitionists. She despised their "noisy demogogism" [sic], and she feared the consequences of their "agitat[ing] continuously in the hope of reform without regard to its . . . effects on whole communities, white and black." But within six years she threw even this caution to the winds, pronouncing her daughter Mildred an "old fogy" for wanting abolition to come by constitutional amendment. For herself, she was willing for it to come through the presidential war power and be administered by the United States Army. She asked for abolition by arbitrary power and something close to martial law. Let the end come and let it be now, she said. The hammer blow was better than anything that risked delay. She had come to the end of her tether.[8]

Meanwhile she chafed under slavery. At Conway House she said she was the "greatest slave." "Oh! What a thralldom to me," she wrote Monc, "the white slave—mentally and bodily. I often think if some one would arouse me some morning from my sleep with the [news that the slaves were free] I should feel such a sense of freedom and relief from responsibility more oppressive as I grow older that I should be heard singing 'Te deum Laudamus' for my deliverance."[9]

The remarkable feature of these vivid outbursts against slavery is that there is no trace of them in her son's recollections. In his autobiography Conway was at pains to establish the antislavery lineage of the Conways, Moncures, and Daniels in order to lay a justifying base for his own abolitionism.[10] The impression Conway conveys of an antislavery feeling in his family is that his father could read the auguries of the future. But there is no sense of the dark currents of discontent swirling in Conway House. Nor is there any hint of what lay in the heart of Margaret Conway who found "peace" not in her home or her privileged society but in her de-classed church of poor whites and slaves.

If Conway were trying to provide a base for his abolition, what could be more useful than his mother's desire to be rid of slavery? He could have shown her attitude if not her explicit teaching. But in his autobiography he leaves no trace of that.[11] He gives us instead portraits of the "fine intellectual father" and the "refined . . . lady beside him," a conventionalized picture of the Tidewater gentry and their placid household. He blots out the matrix in which his career was formed, and his answer to his question "Who made me?" becomes an exercise in genealogy, a filiating evocation of the dead. It is as though he were fleeing from something he knew gave a better answer to his own question, the "refined lady" who once cried out to him, "Saving the black visage, I am the greatest slave here . . . the white slave—mentally and bodily."

If there were a trade-off with Walker Peyton Conway exchanging his easygoing Episcopalianism for his bride's Methodism, he made it his obligation to perfect the bargain to the last jot and tittle. One suspects that his austerity was less the regimen of the newly converted, who will out-orthodox the orthodox because of the fervor of his belief, than it was the determination to honor a bargain and provide the local Methodists an example that they might strive to emulate.

In Conway House even the "small affairs, actions, words, were ascribed everlasting importance and [the family] lived under the suspended sword of Judgment Day." Hymns in the prayer meeting room were raised with a tuning fork; there was neither choir nor musical instrument in these bare services. Walker Peyton Conway took exception with a visiting preacher about the sensuousness of the Song of Solomon. He said, "I do not think [it] ought to be in the Bible." At a revival he watched a pentitent sinner staggering forward to the mourner's bench. Calling to the preacher, Conway commanded, "Take that man away, he's drunk!" To which the preacher replied, "Indeed, brother Conway, if we don't get some of these people when they're drunk, we'll not get them at all!" Conway bowed to this wisdom, accepting the "grotesque side" of Stafford County Methodism as part of the larger labor that "mainly rested" on him and his wife. As for himself, he became a total abstainer, banishing playing cards as well as wines and liquor from his home, and on Sunday the only reading permitted at Conway House was the Scriptures and the *Christian Advocate*, the fourth page of which was proscribed "because it was literary and scientific." And so it was that the local Methodists looked up to Walker Peyton Conway with admiration.

There was a grim rectitude about the man, an inflexible determination to do right. He comes off the splendid patriarch, born and bred for the role, master of his house, and proprietor of his society, and perhaps driven deeper in his authoritarian role because of his own rebellion against his father. One looks in vain in his letters, and those of his wife as well as his son's reminiscences, for any ebullience of spirit in the man. He never rips off a phrase or indulges himself in any act that breaks the mold of circumspect rectitude. No one crossed him with impunity. His tactic was to try to bring an errant back into the fold with "rational efforts." If these failed and the errant was beyond the reach of his power, he was "hand[ed] . . . over to the mercy of God." But even then Walker Peyton Conway refused to quit. He promised to send up his "prayers, so long as his life lasts." Prayer was his last resort after appeals to "common sense . . . reason & propriety" had failed. [12]

This inflexible rectitude forced Margaret Conway to play the mediator between her husband and her children, especially the precocious Monc, who was soon "old enough to be troubled by the contrast between our Methodist and our social environment." Mediation also made her a confidante. The children confided in her, and it was she who softened the angularities of their father's austerity and tried to explain and reconcile the two worlds the family lived in.

There is no doubt that the son loved and respected his father and feared him, too. The question is what broke down Monc's love and respect, and what broke through his fear? Why did Monc rebel against his father and challenge him in his two most sensitive and vulnerable areas, religion and slavery?

Here we are dealing with a certified sacrificial rebel. None of the other people in this book made such an overwhelming repudiation of the authorities governing their lives. *Shipwreck* was the word Walker Peyton Conway gave to the whole business. And he meant that his son was losing both his immortal soul and the patrimony that had descended from the seventeenth century. Everything sacred and secular was being driven up on the breakers.

None of the conventional, historical wisdom about the abolitionists seems to apply to Moncure Conway. The fact that he

was a southerner does not merely add another dimension to the
problem of understanding him. It compounds it; because Conway
made his break a full generation after the genteel southern antislavery tradition had been snuffed out and the southern mind had
supposedly become closed on the subject. Little wonder he rarely
appears in our histories. One really does not known what to make
of him, or to do with him. He does not fit. "A kind of one-man lost
generation of the Civil War," he has been called.[13] And he raises
more questions than we are ever likely to answer.

The most illuminating things that Conway ever said about his
parents were said in his autobiographical novel, *Pine and Palm*.
This is a stereotypical story of the "reconciliation" genre common
after the Civil War, to which theme Conway gives a twist by having his reconciliation come before the war. Randolph, The Virginia
hotspur son of revered Judge Stirling goes to Harvard Law School.
At Harvard he meets his opposite number, an outspoken
abolitionist. There is the inevitable conflict, a slur on honor, a
quarrel, and a trumped-up duel which is arbitrated and resolved by
the young men exchanging places. They will travel in the other's
section for a year in order to explore and understand their opposite
(and misunderstood) societies. Before the story closes, with its inevitable understanding and reconciliation, sectional intermarriage,
and so forth, the reader has waded through a grotesquely wretched
novel, the subplotting of which defies description.[14]

In *Pine and Palm*, Conway's unconscious and repressions speak.
What they say is so unmistakable that we are given a major clue to
understanding this remarkable man and are provided with a basic
insight into the question *why*. But what we learn falls so far outside
the "popular rhetorical maxims" that Conway himself would have
blanched had he understood what he was really saying.[15]

The young hotspur converted to militant abolition is Conway
himself. His father, Judge Stirling, is everything a son could hope
for. One supposes that the judge is the presiding magistrate of Stafford County, Walker Peyton Conway. But he is not. Judge Stirling
was explicitly modeled after Conway's uncle, Richard Moncure,
"whose greatness of mind and character," Conway said, "raised
above me a standard to which I have always paid homage. No word

of unkindness, thoughtlessness, or of depreciation, ever came from him. Affectionate, simple, full of sympathy and humor [I] could always approach him." Judge Stirling-Richard Moncure is the father that Conway craved and never had, and that he created for himself. Above all he is a father who understands his son. As Randolph-Monc makes his lonely apostatizing journey from hair-trigger defender of slavery and southern honor to militant abolitionist and conductor on the Underground Railroad, the fantasized father supports him, never threatens to disown him, and always keeps his faith in his son. Gisela, Randolph's sister, reassures him when he returns to his Virginia home after a stint in Kansas with John Brown (Captain Gideon in the novel), "Don't lose courage. . . . Your suffering in trying to save others will make father feel prouder of you than ever." Thus after the supreme apostasy for a southerner—service with John Brown—the son is raised in his father's esteem.

What is at stake is not a matter of forgiveness, for it is not forgiveness that the son desires. Randolph wants his father's understanding. He wants his father to know that he has suffered only to save others, that instead of betraying his family and his section he has acted on what his family has taught him, "charity and humanitarian effort . . . nothing to do with dogmas, but a great deal to do with morality." Above all he wants his father's esteem, which can come only through sympathetic understanding. When Randolph's part in John Brown's Kansas operations is revealed to him he does indeed, as Gisela foretold, "feel prouder of you than ever."

"Affectionate, simple, full of sympathy, and humor" and always *approachable:* no such words were ever applied to Walker Peyton Conway, who, according to his lights, was a loving father and watched over his brood of children with all of the patience and compassion it was in him to give.

So Monc turned to his mother. She praised him, encouraged him, suspended judgment when she thought he was wrong, and tried to soften the austerities of his father. Even when he was a little boy, she "opened her heart with almost passionate fervour" to Monc. In *Pine and Palm* apparently there is no fantasy about Margaret Conway to compare with Judge Stirling, who reveals so much about Walker Peyton Conway. When the reader discovers that Judge Stirling is a long-time widower it seems that Margaret Conway is consigned to oblivion. But that is inconsistent with Conway's autobiography, and more especially with the manuscript record. The letters prove that mother and son were extremely close. Each plays confidant for the other; each is solicitous for the other's well-being and happiness; each craves the other's understanding, goodwill, and love. But in Judge Stirling's plantation home there is only "the picture of a youthful lady in gauzy white." It is a portrait of "indescribable charm." And the reader is left to infer that it is the portrait of the dead wife and mother.

Why is there no mother in a novel so patently autobiographical? All the materials were at hand for Conway to create a fictional version of Margaret Conway as mistress of The Palms. But to give Judge Stirling a wife and Randolph Stirling a mother would have deranged the truth Conway was telling about himself and his parents. For as Conway created the father he wanted, he also created the mother he desired. And he was able to handle his desire for his mother only by denying her existence. His desire had to be disguised and filtered through an equivocal story because it was too frighteningly overwhelming to be handled any other way.

Randolph Stirling's opposite is Walter Wentworth, an abolitionist. Wentworth, his closest friend at Harvard, accidentally becomes his mortal enemy and, like Randolph, makes his pilgrimage through an alien section out of which he emerges a partial convert—saved in a dramatic midnight meeting from being completely won over—to the enchanting life he finds there.

But Wentworth is more than Randolph's opposite. He is Conway's other half; his alter ego. The characters do more than illustrate sectional reconciliation. They reconcile Conway's own opposing selves. Wentworth's journey to the South permits Conway to affirm attachments and loyalties to the South, and more particularly to a social class in the South, a humane, admirable gentry. But more than that, Wentworth allows Conway to express and consummate his love for his mother.

Judge Stirling's etherealized dead wife is recapitulated by her daughter Gisela, with whom Wentworth falls in love and marries.

At first "Wentworth . . . felt certain that Gisela could never be his wife; she had built up her whole relation with him on a different basis. . . . [She was] always so free in his presence, so businesslike, so careless of the impression she might make that the possibility of any nearer relation between them had plainly never entered her mind." Even though she is older than Wentworth, he assures her that it makes no difference. Once that objection is removed it remains for Gisela to play her crucial part. It is she who shows Wentworth what previously has been masked by the simple, lordly gentility and happy slaves. Even at The Palms it is impossible to deny the horrors of slavery. Judge Stirling professes to despise the peculiar institution, but it is Gisela, mistress of The Palms, who bitterly denounces slavery, and it is she who prevents Wentworth from succumbing to it.

In the midnight meeting with Wentworth—was it a dream, Conway asks the reader—she reveals her love for him and her great unhappiness caused by slavery. Secretly she shows Wentworth a cowering slave whose family has been broken up by a forced sale. "'You said you had not witnessed the cruelties of slavery—look there,'" she commands, "through her tears, pity and anger." Then she tells Wentworth the truth about herself and slavery. "'Save me from slavery if you love me,'" Gisela begs him. He promptly takes her away from The Palms, marries her, and settles in Washington where he and Randolph merge their talents in a legal partnership, symbolically dissolving their separate identities.

In the Gisela-Wentworth story much that has lain hidden bursts into the open. A son's carnal love for his mother is scarcely exceptional, especially in the patriarchal antebellum South where Freud's protean theory about fathers and their sons was perhaps more closely acted out than anywhere else in American history. Moncure Conway could talk of his love for his mother only through the disguises of fiction. How he acted once he made his shattering discovery is foreshadowed by what we have learned from *Pine and Palm*, that "passable little tale" which confuses "actuality with reality," and splits an identity, sending half of it on a journey leading from a reflexive defense of slavery to militant abo-

lition and the other half on a mission to free the mistress of a
Virginia plantation from the social system that she begs her lover
to save her from: to destroy the father and steal the father's wife.

But an Oedipal relationship not only insists on the obvious, it
forces a caricature and drains a human life of its rich complexity. In
uncovering Moncure Conway's love for his mother we may have
found the core of the elusive *why* of his life, but we scarcely have
brought him to the point at which, with his mother's encouragement, he was ready to act the part of the primal son and make his
strike against his father.[16] As we remember that his rebellion was
singular in the form it took, we must all the more develop the
elements that gave his rebellion its singularity. Certainly no broad
psychosocial hypothesis helps us here. Only the life story can, the
details of his life that led him into his careening public career and
finally to his choice for his life's work. It is to these matters that we
now turn.

In our literature the Old South is usually evoked with a palpable
sense for the land. It is as though the South's physical quality has
informed the writers, beating in on them as it once impinged upon
its old inhabitants. Nowhere else in our historical writing (as well
as our creative literature) is the physical environment *felt* as much
as it is in the Old South. A result has been the facile corollary:
inasmuch as sensuousness, this overwhelming intrusion of the
physical, has been the predominating characteristic of southern life
it must follow that the alternative to sensuousness has been rudely
foreshortened. Intellect has been diminished, and cool rationality
is a casualty to the hotspur drive for gratifying the senses.

The fact remains that Moncure Conway was brought up and
lived out his life in the world of ideas. By the time his life was over
he had amassed a remarkable range of intellectual contacts and
interests. An ingratiating raconteur, he had talked with Emerson,
Carlyle, Huxley, Darwin, Browning, Mazzini, Garibaldi, Ruskin,
Cobden, Froude, John Stuart Mill, Herbert Spencer, Leigh Hunt,
Max Muller, and John Burroughs—the list in its entirety is
staggering—on their own terms. It would be easy enough to mark
him down as a facile dilettante, a packrat of ideas and personalities

whose own career was a tribute levied on the careers of other men. But such a judgment is reckless and harshly unfair. For if Conway was not an original thinker, he nevertheless had a quick, trained mind that delighted in ideas. And if he sometimes failed to grasp them, he nonetheless was willing to try to pursue their teachings wherever they led him. His ideas, his sympathetic biographer says of him, "covered such a wide variety that it was impossible to explore many of them thoroughly." [17]

It is difficult to think of another American of his time with such contacts and with such a range of interests. Henry Adams, almost precisely his contemporary, may have been equal; and James Russell Lowell. But Adams was grandson to presidents and son of the American minister to Great Britain, and Lowell was himself minister to the Court of St. James's. For all of his facile sociability, Conway's rites of passage into this world were underscored by pure ability, by a fine intellect, the shaping of which was begun in Falmouth, Virginia.

Monc's formal schooling in Falmouth is easy enough to trace. First there was the private school taught by his cousin, Betty Gaskins. Then he attended the Fredericksburg Classical and Mathematical Academy. The academy, descended from a school founded by James Marye a hundred years before, was in Monc's time the largest school in northern Virginia. Three masters presided over two hundred students, feeding them heavy doses of Greek, Latin, and mathematics. Monc, when he was entered in the academy, was the youngest student, a ten-year-old compelled to make his way among boys twelve to seventeen years old. He never could, he recalled, "mingle quite freely" with the other boys. The academy was a school for the gentry's sons, high-spirited and unburdened by the special claims of Methodism that so bedeviled Monc with his anxious, "precocious soul." The consequence was that he "shrank from the careless frolic of my playmates, who no doubt regarded me as a milksop." So he did the expected. He excelled in his studies, turning to his books and satisfying his masters. Notwithstanding, he found "no enjoyment" in his success. But the quality of his training was such that when he went to Dickinson College he was entered as a sophomore, and in less than a term he was advanced to the junior class. It was a notable accomplishment because he was only fifteen years old. But he remembered the achievement with a laconic comment, "I was sent to college too soon."

"My more lasting education," Conway called it, was at Conway House and Erleslie. It was in these homes that some of the finest minds in Virginia gathered. There was a galaxy of uncles and great-uncles. John Moncure Conway and Eustace Conway, brothers and lawyers, the latter a commonwealth judge; Richard Moncure, who became chief justice of Virginia; Travers Daniel, commonwealth attorney general; and two cousins, Peter Daniel, associate justice of the United States Supreme Court, and John Moncure Daniel, the brilliant young editor of the Richmond *Examiner*.

Monc, who was never on easy terms with his schoolmates, often sat with these men. Their conversations moved across theology, religion, jurisprudence, law, history, politics, and literature. The talk was ranging and deep, the gentle measured voice of Richard Moncure in counterpoint to the staccato of John Moncure Daniel. These two were particular heroes of the youth. Their sessions could be sharp and flashing, and Monc drank it all in, sometimes crouched for hours by an uncle's chair. The men were an academy themselves. Neither "condescending nor patronizing," they drew Monc into their conversations, letting him test his mettle against them. Here there were no "vague humiliations."

Another cousin, Elizabeth Daniel, daughter of Justice Daniel, drew him out even farther. After one of her visits to Conway House she asked Monc to write to her about the books he was reading, Dickens, Scott, Southey, and Moore. (Byron was proscribed because of his eccentric private life.) Their correspondence, which began when he was a lad of ten, lasted for several years. It was in these letters to Elizabeth Daniel that he learned "the exactness of statements and the extreme pains [it] took to express them."[18]

His father and mother encouraged him in his reading and thinking, too. But their encouragement always came with the admonition to "steer with the rudder of Faith . . . and never get beyond the way marks of revealed religon." Contrary to his parents, these uncles and cousins were teaching him to be "elastic" and to explore "thoughts unconnected with religion." He was growing rapidly.

His appetite for books and ideas was voracious; he was learning that the world of ideas was pleasant and that he was comfortable in that world. But there was still no direction, no informing purpose to his reading and for his developing intellect and abilities.

He had a love for words, and his life was already filled with them. Words would be the instruments of his vocation. But what vocation? What words? The words of the law, of the lawyer and the judge? The words of journalism, of the editor, and the literary critic? The words of the pulpit, of the preacher and pastor? Surrounding him were exemplars for each. There was the beloved uncle, Richard Moncure, bound for the commonwealth's supreme court and already famous for his refusal to take any cases except those that he believed to be incontestably right. There was cousin John Moncure Daniel, the young literary critic and editor of the Richmond *Examiner*, with all of his flashing worldly attractiveness. There were the itinerant Methodist preachers, some of them powerful in the pulpit and all of them laboring in the Lord's vineyard. But the law led away from writing and literature, and where in Virginia had a man ever made his living on literature alone? Journalism could lead to dissoluteness as the stories about "sinister" John Moncure Daniel's duels and mistresses suggested. And for all of their piety and good works the preachers were declassed, their fate bound by the social class to which they ministered; and if they sometimes spoke with brilliant phrases, their words rushed from inspiration and an untutored instinct for the cadence of King James's English, not from trained intellects.

Nothing was clear. The easy world of the Tidewater gentry was incompatible with Methodist morality. The bright world of words and ideas at Erleslie and Glencairn and the family rooms at Conway House clashed with the untutored evangelicalism in the Conways' basement prayer room and the church in Falmouth. His uncle John M. Daniel's encouragement to embrace "thoughts unconnected with religion" as he read and studied could not be reconciled with his parents' desire for him to always steer with the rudder of faith. There were too many contrarieties.

He later said, "I was not happy in this double life." Without direction or purpose, he floundered. His parents encouraged him to "take healthy recreations." Dutifully, Monc hunted and fished, but he thought that his mother and father failed to "realize . . . the way I was taking these things to heart nor the extent to which I was burdened." He "clung to the preachers, to [his] elders, and sang hymns about the vileness of a world [he] had not entered, and about death."

In the spring of 1847, when Monc turned fifteen, there were only vague signs of the stormy passage opening before him. He was waiting to "experience his vocation," resolve the contrarieties pulling at him, and find the channel into which his love for words could be poured.[19] Anguished self-pity, and several false starts laid him low. But his first step into these unhappy crisis years seemed to be a move toward a reconciliation of the two worlds he was caught between. His religion, which he knew only as the unlettered Methodism of Tidewater Virginia, was shown to be intellectually respectable. At Dickinson College he learned that Methodism was not hostile to intellectuality.

III
The "Moral Choice"

I was struggling at the center of an
invisible web.
MONCURE CONWAY

Dickinson College at Carlisle,
Pennsylvania, was owned and supported by the Methodist Church's
Philadelphia and Baltimore conferences. It was in the Baltimore
Conference that bitter battles were fought as the Methodist Church
divided on slavery in the 1840s. When the Virginia Methodists
split, Walker Peyton Conway refused to follow the schismatics.
One of the most prestigious and active Methodists in the Tidewater,
Conway was drawn deep into the struggle. There was, then, all the
more reason for him to send his sons to Dickinson. Not only would
he put them into a bastion of Methodism, he would also affirm his
loyalty to the Baltimore Conference.

Peyton, the eldest son, went to Dickinson first. At his request,

43

Walker Peyton Conway withdrew Monc from the Fredericksburg
Academy and packed him off to Dickinson at midterm in the spring
of 1847. Monc had no objections to joining Peyton. He had no
desire to finish at the academy. He had begun as an outsider and
he left that way. But his eight years of training there could not
be faulted. When he arrived at Dickinson he was entered as a sophomore; once again he was the youngest member of his class.

When Monc came to Dickinson the college was the showpiece
for the Baltimore and Philadelphia conferences. Nurtured out of
bankruptcy in 1833, it was, by 1847, strong, and its faculty could
claim genuine distinction.[1] Five men made up the faculty; one was
on the threshold of international eminence, and two others were
gaining national reputations. Spencer F. Baird taught the natural
and physical sciences. He left Dickinson to accept a position as assistant secretary at the Smithsonian Institution. Later he founded
the National Museum and the Marine Biological Laboratory at
Woods Hole. Before he died he had been honored by scientists
and governments around the world. Monc called Baird "the beloved
professor and the ideal student. He was beautiful and manly." William Allen taught chemistry and filled in with English composition
and rhetoric. He left Dickinson to become president of Girard College. Monc put "Bully" Allen down as "an abler man" than the
author of the textbook he taught. John M'Clintock, unlike the
masters at Fredericksburg, made Greek "interesting" to Monc.
M'Clintock also wrote on philosophy and theology for the *Methodist Quarterly*, which he edited. Monc came to love George R.
Crooks, who taught Latin, and took him as his patron. George
Sadler taught mathematics. He was, Conway said, "learned, but
had not the art of teaching." But even this dry mathematician held
Monc's respect. The Dickinson faculty seemed more like his cousins
and uncles gathered at Conway House and Erleslie. They encouraged him, brought him out, and caused him to want to do more.
Above all, the five of them were scholars in love with their subjects, and masters of them.

Here was a different Methodism than the one to which Monc was
accustomed in Virginia. Even the preachers showed a difference.
Their sermons were made to "bear on the listener's reason." For

the first time in his life, Monc saw a Methodism stripped of "rhetorical tricks." It seemed as if Methodism might be vindicated. At Dickinson there was no hostility between religion and the life of the mind. Baird was not a Methodist; and of the other four teachers, M'Clintock and Crooks were "broadchurch and original thinkers." But the Methodist Church supported them all. How far it was from Tidewater Virginia Methodism and its "thumping and loudness" and insistence on conformity.

Nor at Carlisle was there an invidious gap between social class and church. "It was indeed a revelation to find so many great men and refined ladies belonging to a sect that in Fredericksburg was in dismal contrast with the Episcopalian and Presbyterian churches." Unlike Fredericksburg, the "society" of Carlisle was accessible to the self-conscious, unsure boy who believed himself homely and shy, and carried with him some scars left by his Fredericksburg schoolmates' taunts about Methodism. For the first time in his life Monc's religion and his social class meshed.

At Falmouth Monc never heard the thunderclap of God's voice speaking to him, or experienced the onrush of God's mercy and grace, believing that he had been singled out for the revelatory experience that hurled a mortal into the arms of God. Monc had never known conversion. At Falmouth conversion seems to have been impossible for him because he would have been obliged to take his place in the ranks of "those dingy and illiterate peoples." But at Carlisle it was different. "To hear such learned and polite people talking about 'conversion' led me to think seriously about it."

In January, 1848, a Methodist revival swept the college. Before the revival was over, half of the student body had made their way to the mourners' bench where they and the congregation prayed for the conversion experience to come to them. Monc was the first student to take his place on the bench. Two days later he was converted, and he joined the Methodist church.[2]

Conversion was the first step toward vocation, toward finding the right words that waited to rush out of him. Joining the church was the second step. He was on his way to the Methodist ministry. The words of evangelical Christianity began to pour out of him in private student prayer meetings and in public class meetings. His way was opening for him. At last it seemed that the contrarieties tormenting him were being resolved. He "felt happy."

But we know that Moncure Conway's Methodist ministry lasted only a year and a half. Barely nineteen when he began preaching, before he quit his ministry the words of Methodism had soured in his mouth. "Brother," he was told, "you seem to be speaking to us from the moon." As he later said, he "gradually preached myself out of the creeds." What we wish to know is why he had to come to the creeds and how he had found the words of a Methodist preacher.

Monc's conversion, which he subsequently called "a boyish delusion," and which resulted in his physical and emotional collapse and his withdrawal from college, had several features to it. His conversion and joining the church was a calculated attempt to reconcile the needs that were tormenting him as he approached his sixteenth birthday. But most of all he needed to make himself acceptable to Catharine Emory, with whom he had fallen in love.

With only a few shreds of contemporary evidence surviving, Catharine Emory is elusive to biographical grasp. She is a wispy shadow falling across Monc's life. But it is certain she predominates an explanation of why Monc came to the "creeds" and why he preached them and, also, the circumstances of his repudiation of them.

She was Monc's first love and, other than his wife, the only woman he permitted himself to openly love.[3] The little evidence that survives suggests that Kate was a stolid, pious, circumspect girl. The late-born daughter of Bishop John Emory, she was, after her father's death, raised in the family of her brother, Robert Emory, Dickinson's president and polemicist for Methodist orthodoxy. She was Monc's age but "more mature in mind." The boy thought "a holy luster shown upon her countenance." She sang "plaintive melodies which had so often delighted his ear," and she prayed for him, sending up prayers "to the throne of grace on his behalf." She cut a lock of her hair and sent it to him with a prayer for God's blessing. Kate Emory also kept Monc at arm's length. Perhaps she sensed that this strange Virginian wanted her to relieve his "mournful truths, unexplained problems, unsatisfied desires." The "most daring propositions" sometimes burst from him, followed by "hours of fearful anguish and self-accusation on his part, [and] truthful forgiveness and gentle blessings on hers."[4] But their tepid reconciliations never settled anything.

What Monc wanted to tell her he wrote in some tempestuous short stories and an unfinished novel. The stories are about passionate unrequited love, ending in despair and unhappiness. One story closes with the young lovers embracing in a lurid double suicide. The novel was about incest, murder, and suicide, with a despairing hero who constantly thundered he was in hell.[5] "Wild, dreamy, pathetic," Monc described himself as he wrote his stories. No wonder he frightened Kate and she kept him at bay. The pious girl wanted Monc to be converted and saved. He was trying to save himself.

Abruptly Monc stopped writing the short stories about young lovers trapped in fatal love. "All at once," he wrote, "determined to be a Christian went to church—& to the altar."[6] The next day: "Went to the mourners bench again—too much self-righteousness." Then the following day: "Was strengthened in my determination to become a Christian—went to church in the morning . . . did me good—got ready to go to church [in the evening]—got to my knees to pray before I went—was converted—felt happy . . . .

Thy yoke is easy, Lord,
  But yet I need thy grace,
That I may reach the blest reward,
  And see thee face to face.

There remains a final piece of evidence connected with Monc's conversion experience. The night of his conversion, he said that he went to the mourners' bench without "feeling or conviction of anything. But I was *resolved* never to stop from that moment until I enjoyed religion in my heart, *if there was such enjoyment to be had.*"[7]

This cool, unvarnished qualifier is arresting. Monc had undertaken an experiment of the highest order involving the greatest risk. If he claimed conversion without actually experiencing it, he was guilty of blasphemy and dishonesty. For both his family and community, conversion was as far removed from an experiment as the Prince of Peace was from the devil.

There is, therefore, a triple character to Monc's "conversion" at Carlisle. It was the act of a "wild, dreamy pathetic" adolescent boy who wanted a straitlaced girl with a "holy luster" to love him. It was the act of a dutiful son attempting to remove his parents' anxiety about him and to reconcile their religion with the ambitions of his mind and his social class. It was also a calculated rebellion—the first signal that he was capable of setting himself against powerful authorities.

There were two weeks of euphoria; then Monc's journal records the downhill slide. He "Felt unwell." He cuts morning prayers and classes. He is given failing marks in some of his courses. He tries to compensate by giving "my experience" over and over again; but he judges his performances "not very flattering." All of his teachers are now giving him bad reports. "Here," he complains, "though a man be a Philosopher, he is forced to yield to power and recite the Elements of Chemistry." Even the pleasure of writing has soured. He increasingly complains of "not feeling very well in my mind." Monc was on the verge of collapse. Wracked by chills and fevers, he kept to his bed most of the time. He began to believe that he was going "crazy."

Alarmed, his father came from Virginia, and after talking with Monc and his teachers, decided to take him home. It was agreed that he might return in the fall without losing his class standing. The day he and his father left Carlisle, Monc awoke feeling "remarkable well." When they stopped at Baltimore for a consultation with a specialist in neurasthenia Monc's chills and fever had vanished; the doctor's diagnosis was inconclusive.

At Baltimore, Monc's medical consultation was combined with his father's church business. With Virginia Methodism already split, the Baltimore Conference was struggling to maintain itself in the state, and Walker Peyton Conway had emerged as the leader of the Tidewater loyalists. Monc accompanied his father at the long conversations on high-level church politics. This was his introduction to such matters, and for that alone he thought it was "worth my illness." But his greatest pleasure came as he heard his father praised. Only an adulating son could have written that it was clear that "everything . . . depended on my father." Never before had his father seemed so powerful, so awesome, his "efforts so herculean."

Once they returned to Conway House, Monc was apparently recovered. Uncle Richard Moncure arranged for him to serve as an election clerk. The two dollars paid him, the first money he had ever earned, pleased him tremendously. He wrote political satire for the Fredericksburg *Democratic Recorder*, some of which was copied by John Moncure Daniel's Richmond *Examiner*. He also wrote his historical fantasy, "Outaliski's Revenge," which was copied by the New York *Herald*. His father's business partner took him on a tour of the Valley of Virginia where Monc found Methodism genteel. At home, an "elegant" Methodist church was being built, the congregation was "larger and more intelligent," and the minister an "accomplished, cultured . . . thinker." Several old fashioned members of the congregation were frightened away by these changes. Looking about him each Sunday, Monc could not see a single "old Methodist bonnet."

The architect of these changes was Walker Peyton Conway whose work Monc had heard praised at Baltimore. Not only was he saving Tidewater Methodism from the proslavery schismatics, he was remolding the church. Now at last Monc could sit comfortably in his parents' church, and for the first time, he said, Virginia Methodism was able to "speak to my inmost soul." He was certain that his conversion was real.

Nevertheless, it was at this time that he wrote "Outaliski's Revenge," a tale recapitulating his relationship with his father that reveals the deepest kind of ambivalence.[8] Set in colonial Virginia, it is the story of the building of a magnificent church in Stafford County, the Conways' ancestral home. "Hughes," the architect, is a merciless masterbuilder, whose ambition is to build the church as a monument to himself. This "white tyrant" has as his workers the last surviving Indians in Stafford County, Outaliski and his son, who have been forced to bind themselves to Hughes as indentured servants. They are virtually his slaves but endure their brutalization because of their contract. The son, a delicate, sensitive youth, becomes sick. Hounded remorselessly by Hughes, he collapses on the unfinished tower. Hughes mercilessly beats the boy, who falls off the tower and is killed. Outaliski attempts to come to his son's relief, but Hughes commands him to keep working as their contract demands. Outaliski buries his murdered son and keeps working on the church. At last Outaliski and Hughes stand together atop the tower as the grieving father puts the last stone in place. He then throws Hughes off the tower, climbs down to his son's grave, and kills himself.

In September, 1848, Monc returned to Dickinson for his senior year, as usual, the youngest member of his class. Peyton remained at Falmouth, the victim of scarlet fever. Because of his peculiar entry in Dickinson half-way through the sophomore year and his foreshortened junior year, there was no hope of Monc taking academic honors, but he established himself as a prankster and something of a wit, and was invited to give the "comic" address at the college's Union Philosophical Society's annual meeting. At midyear he organized a student newspaper and as editor saw it through five issues. He continued writing occasional pieces of political satire and humor for the Fredericksburg *Democratic Recorder* and for John Moncure Daniel's Richmond *Examiner*. And during his senior year he had an article published in the *Southern Literary Messenger*.

Shortly before Monc graduated from college he asked Kate Emory to marry him. But she held him off and promised him nothing. She offered him, he complained, the "foam of champagne," but it was really "the juice of night-shade." The night following his graduation he stood in lonely vigil outside her house until dawn, his mind filled with thoughts of "self-destruction." With these bitter thoughts he returned to his room, packed his trunk and began the journey to Falmouth. He was seventeen years and three months old. He had finished Dickinson College in three full terms and two part terms. His graduation address was titled "Old Age."

When Monc returned from Carlisle he troubled his father. He read novels and poetry, and he wrote for the *Recorder*, the *Exam-*

iner, and the *Southern Literary Messenger.* His article in the latter appeared anonymously; and the first pieces for the *Recorder*
were published pseudonymously. But Walker Peyton Conway
penetrated the disguise, confronted Monc with the newspaper, and
ridiculed his son. Hiding behind such fanciful pen names as Cleofas
II and Alphonso III he continued to write for the *Recorder,* but he
always feared discovery and more of his father's disparagement.

There were some minor successes. Monc was appointed secretary of the Fredericksburg Southern Rights Association, an organization that "promulgated the philosophical, sociological, and
ethical excellence of slavery," as well as the political ideas of John
C. Calhoun. He also gave a lecture on Pantheism in the Fredericksburg town hall to which "the finest people in our region"
came. His lecture ended with "applause" and "congratulations."
He was being recognized and discussed about town and in Stafford
County. But these ventures brought his father's reproof. "Don't be
the fool of those people," he told Monc when he learned of his son's
involvement with the Southern Rights Association. And about his
subtle performance on Pantheism his father said dourly, "You will
make yourself unpopular by speaking above the vulgar com-
prehension."

Wherever he turned, the shadow of his father seemed to fall
across his path.[9] Walker Peyton Conway was closing him off,
pressing him harder toward the Methodist ministry. The central
metaphor of "Outaliski's Revenge" comes to mind. Higher and
higher the boy is driven, and death awaits him at the hands of the
tyrannical, master builder.

Monc fled to Richmond. He stayed with his uncle Eustace Conway, who persuaded him to return to Conway House. At home
Monc found his father angry, and talking about a "crisis." But he
had made his point. His future was open to negotiation. At his
father's suggestion Monc agreed to become a lawyer. Walker
Peyton Conway sent him to Warrenton to study law with a friend
of the family, Colonel William Phillips.

From March to December, 1850, Monc managed to convince
himself of his enthusiasm for the words of the law. Each word, he
thought, was "an instruction in precision; and how often, he asked

himself, might the change of a word decide a case. He read the law books rapidly, asking Colonel Phillips for more work. At last he seemed to be finding his way, if not with his father's blessing, at least with his permission and help.

But after nine months Monc wrote his father that his venture at becoming a lawyer was over. He was coming back to Conway House for Christmas; he had decided to become a preacher. He was applying for admission to the Baltimore Methodist Conference as a minister.

Monc returned to Conway House, studied Hebrew and read Methodist theologians. On his nineteenth birthday he received notice of his appointment to the Rockville circuit in Maryland, "one of the most important in the Baltimore Conference." Next morning he rode off on a handsome chestnut mare, a gift from his father, along with the saddle and fitted saddlebags. In the saddlebags Monc packed his Bible, Watson's *Theology*, Jeremy Taylor's *Holy Living and Dying*, Coleridge's *Aids to Reflections*, and the "Methodist Discipline." With them he packed Emerson's *Essays* and Carlyle's *Latter Day Pamphlets*. They "got on harmoniously," he later said, "for a time." He rode away with Walker Peyton Conway's farewell ringing in his ears, "Let the potsherds of the earth strive with the potsherds of the earth: seek higher things, my son."

Monc preached his first sermon three weeks later, taking as his text a passage from Genesis: "I have waited for thy salvation, O Lord." In the manner of Methodist preaching he had no written sermon. As he took his place in the pulpit a flash of panic seized him. What would he say? But the words came. It seemed as if Walker Peyton Conway's desire for his son had been consummated.

During the nine-month period of his law studies, which culminated in his second conversion, and as he called it, his "real" conversion, Monc suffered three illnesses. The first occurred shortly after he arrived at Warrenton, the second came midway through the studies, and the third coincided with his conversion, when he abandoned law and decided to preach. There is a consistency in these episodic illnesses that makes them one malaise. Each time he was laid low, listless, unhappy, besieged with "violent attacks of fever." Each was accompanied by a vision or revelation. Each occurred when he was under heavy stress, and was deeply engaged in an undertaking that bid to give a direction to his life's work that led away from the pulpit, the one place he knew his father wanted him to go. He was released from the attacks, which were more "mental and spiritual than physical," when he succumbed to his father's desire.

However, since Conway used the pulpit to deliver his abolition messages and assault his father's world, it is difficult to interpret his illness-dogged path to the pulpit as the acquiescent act of a dutiful son. The alternate possibility is that he made his way to the pulpit, not as a sacrificial act but as an aggressive one.

The euphoria of his start in law studies subsided after a few weeks. He began to feel "a repugnance to the idea of being a county lawyer." The first illness struck him, and he returned to Conway House to convalesce. It was here that the first vision, "a revelation," came to him: "Through a little rift I caught a glimpse of a vault beyond the familiar sky, from which flowed a spirit that was subtly inbreeding discontent in me, bereaving me of faith in myself, rendering me a mere source of anxiety in those around me." He thought he heard a skylark singing. He then imagined himself a skylark "set free . . . ascending toward the sky."

His revelation came after he had met two slave children, a boy and a girl, when he stopped at a spring to drink. "Both entirely naked," the children looked like "pretty statuettes of yellow bronze." After they had gone he "meditated more deeply than ever before on the conditon of their race in America." At Conway House he "thought again and again of those naked little [slaves] . . . whose minds were no doubt as pretty as their bodies, but without a stitch of clothing." He connected these with his mother's Sunday school. He remembered how she had been "warned" (by whom he does not say) never to teach slaves to read. He thought about the way slavery surrounded her with "debased faces of white people [with] their poverty of mind and body." He fantasized: "Above them all," the slave children, his mother, the poverty-stricken whites, "my inner skylark sang,—Glad tiding of great joy I bring to you and all mankind." But he asked himself, "Who [is] more powerless than I to bring glad tidings to anybody!" With his fantasy of the skylark the first episode ended.

When he told his father that he had heard a skylark on his walk, his father laughed at him and told him there were no skylarks in Virginia. In his fantasy Monc had turned himself into a creature that did not exist in Virginia. He soars over a tableau, the central figure of which is his mother. She is surrounded and trapped by ignorant, illiterate blacks and whites, the fantasy suggests. But he is powerless.[10]

Monc's second illness, about five months after the first, struck him as he was engaged in a single-handed campaign to promote a free public school system in Virginia. According to his autobiographical account, he wrote *Free Schools in Virginia: A Plea of Education, Virtue and Thrift vs. Ignorance, Vice, and Poverty* as a proud but worried young Virginian. He was disturbed by the attacks leveled against his state by critics who cited Virginia's deplorable schools as one of the reasons for the state's decline in power and prestige. His justification for a public school system recapitulated portions of the April skylark vision. "Everywhere swarmed the indigent white people, displaced, reduced to idleness by the slaves . . . their wretched cabins crowded with children growing up in ignorance, vice, hopelessness. Many of these children . . . were comely . . . . There was not even a Sunday-school within reach, and they could not read."

How pleasing, and how much easier, it would be for our analysis if the tableau in the skylark vision were duplicated with its original symmetry and clarity as Monc was moved to assume the role he had taken for himself in the vision, the rare bird, unknown to Virginia, bringing "glad tidings." But the tableau has now become lopsided. In its second form, only the poor whites are to receive the glad tidings. The slaves are there only as the implied causes of the poor whites' misery; and Margaret Conway has apparently vanished, remaining only, possibly, in the disguises of the out-of-reach Sunday school and the illiterate children. But we are dealing with a young man groping toward relief from his bedevilments. It asks too much of a youth that he suddenly resolve the ambivalences and contradictions lying within him and, for our convenience, admit to himself the goals he seeks, or even that he know himself what they are. We must patiently wait for him to extricate himself from his "fatal conditons."

As he was completing *Free Schools in Virginia*, Monc broke down. The familiar fever struck again. But he stayed in Warrenton to wind up the job. He intended to time the publication of his pamphlet with the opening of the Virginia Constitutional Convention, which he hoped would adopt a free public school system for the state. He paid to have hundreds of copies printed, and on the eve of the convention he mailed them to "every newspaper, public man, preacher in Virginia." [11] His efforts were ignored. He remembered only two men responding, both of whom were favorable. One was a professor at the University of Virginia Law School, John B. Minor; the other was Samuel Janney, a Quaker preacher and anti-slavery leader. [12]

Toward mid-October it was obvious that his scheme was stillborn. He had gotten no public hearing, and he had provoked no discussion. In the aftermath of his failure he was forced to confront his powerlessness, and the reason for it. He concluded that he had misjudged his audience and had chosen the wrong instrument to reach them. He must go directly to the "poor whites . . . the people [who] would be reached only by the living voice." He remembered a Methodist camp meeting that he had attended in August where he had seen the effect of sermons on large assemblies. The memory of that camp meeting came to him like a vision, the second of his three revelations. "I had a message for those masses of people. . . . how could it be delivered, unless from the pulpit?"

His rhetorical question exultantly answers the lament that concluded the skylark vision. "But who [is] more powerless than I to bring glad tidings to anybody!" It also opened the way out of the pamphlet debacle.

The three explicit elements in the vision are Margaret Conway, the slave children, and the poor whites. All are dependent on an implicit fourth element, Walker Peyton Conway. The vision is thus a metaphor for the little community in Conway House and the

larger community of a slave society. So tightly are all related that if
one element is touched the others must move; if the tableau is
upset, the social order becomes deranged. Glad tidings are bad news
for a man who is content with the way things are. It is his world
that the glad tidings bid to overturn, and him along with it. There is
much hostility and aggressiveness in Monc's skylark vision. There
is also a strategy for attack; and the object of attack is obviously the
master, patron, husband—and father.

All of this is easy enough to see (or logically derive from what we
know will happen), but what is lacking so far is Monc's *contemporary* perception of his father. We desire some corroboration for the
role the vision implicitly assigns to Walker Peyton Conway. We
need some indication that the free school program was an actual
working out of the vision, and that there was a hostile, deadly engagement between Monc and his father. We ask Monc to tell a
"truth" about which he himself was unaware (or tried to suppress),
of which there is no trace in the autobiographical recollections. In
these portions of the autobiography we are given Walker Peyton
Conway's response to the free school scheme (a brief enigmatic
"My father did not express agreement."); then there is nothing
until, in December following Monc's "real conversion," he is
"amazed" to learn of Monc's decision to abandon the law and enter
the ministry. But there is some of Monc's fictional writing that
presents Monc in his fantasized role of the skylark and Walker
Peyton Conway as an opponent of the "glad tidings." It is striking
proof of Conway's use of fiction to express his torments in an acceptable and permissible form.

Directly in the aftermath of his free-school fiasco Monc wrote a
short story, "A Webster Case in Europe." [13] Vairenne, the young
hero, is deeply troubled by the "poor peasants . . . of our land that
wander about in misery." A brilliant innovator and experimenter,
he undertakes some work in electricity, which, when it is made
public, will in some unspecific way revolutionize society. His uncle
and former teacher, Pentern, learns of Vairenne's discovery and
fears for his own reputation and position. Pentern kills Vairenne
with a diabolical secret poisoning device and publishes the brilliant
paper on electricity as his own. But the discovery is not applied to

improve the poor peasants' lives; it is used selfishly by Pentern to create an institute for himself and to further solidify his established position. The remainder of the story is denouement. The murder is discovered and solved, Pentern conveniently dies, and posthumous recognition comes to Vairenne.

The theme of the story is precisely the one that was developed in "Outaliski's Revenge": a youth is murderously sacrificed to the ambition of an older man. Now, however, the story line is adjusted to accord directly with Monc's own life. It is as though he made no attempt to disguise himself as he had in "Outaliski's Revenge." Monc also made another adjustment. In "Outaliski's Revenge" his ambivalence toward his father was so deep that he was obliged to split his father into two characters, Hughes the merciless master builder, and Outaliski the exemplary survivor of an earlier age. Hughes drove the youth to his death, and although Outaliski was obliged to permit the murderous sacrifice, he nevertheless avenged it once the demands of honor had been met. In "A Webster Case" this ambivalence is suggested, then swiftly resolved. As Vairenne graduates from the university, his father, an exemplary man, dies, as does, shortly, his mother, a woman who is "very intelligent and deeply devoted to her son." Vairenne is left a double orphan. This device serves two purposes. It projects Vairenne alone and unprotected to confront his antagonist (the father-as-Outaliski has literally died), and it allows Monc to tell his story without having to face what his story is all about: himself and his parents.[14]

Pentern recapitulates Hughes's characteristics: He is cold, able, and remorselessly ambitious. But unlike Hughes, in this new version of Monc's "truth," Pentern fears the youth because the youth himself has changed. Young and frail in "Outaliski's Revenge," he is no threat. But in "A Webster Case," he is in possession of extraordinary powers. Pentern acknowledges that Vairenne's innovative work makes his nephew a "redoubtable competitor for his chair" at the university, so he kills him.

As the story closes, the murderous family struggle has run its course, but outside Vairenne's family home, "a lovely country seat on one of the most graceful and picturesque bends of the river," life remains the same. No social arrangements have been deranged.

The peasants still wander about in misery, unaware of the great work that Vairenne had been on the verge of bringing to them. Pentern's world remains intact, just as Walker Peyton Conway's world remained unchanged by Monc's free public school proposal.

The truth content of "A Webster Case" is best attested by its subsequent fate in Conway's hands. In his autobiography he was at pains to mention his voluminous writings. Some of the most obscure and trivial pieces find their way into his book, duly noted, and commented on. But "A Webster Case," the story that established him as a writer of fiction in a prestigious literary quarterly, is not mentioned. One can only conclude that it raked too deep; it revealed too much about his "poor dead self," too much about the young man who envisioned himself bringing "glad tidings" to Virginia and whose attempt at prying apart the structure of Virginia society "was entirely ignored."

Six weeks after he wrote "A Webster Case" Monc was stricken again. The familiar symptoms of febrile illness and visionary revelation reappeared, and before the episode was over elements of the skylark vision also reappeared with much of their original symmetry. This episode concluded with his decision to come to the pulpit, and the resolution of what he later called the "moral crisis of my life."

Toward the first of December, Monc took for himself a startling new role. He erupted as a "wrangler" of the apologetics of slavery and racism. He wrote an elaborate essay, "The Diversity of [the] Origins of Races—Slavery," in which he advanced the theory of the multiple origins of mankind. He claimed that the Caucasian race was the highest of the several races, and he ended with the assertion "that this supreme race has the same right over the lower species of his genus that he was over quadrupeds."[15] The virtuosity of his synthesis was sufficient to win him a place in the leading study of "scientific" racism in antebellum America.[16] When Monc presented his essay before the little Franklin Lyceum in Warrenton he found himself "the centre of a . . . tempest."

Thoughtful southerners wrestled with the problem of reconciling slavery, religious orthodoxy, and current scientific findings and speculations on the origins of man.[17] The terms of the dilemma had been set several years before Monc created the furor in Warrenton. Instead of a single creation, as found in the Genesis account, many scientists claimed that there had been separate creations for the several races. From that contention it was but a step to arranging the races in a hierarchy and proving scientifically that the Caucasian was superior and that the African was inferior. Slavery became justified by the authority of science. But if one accepted the claim of the multiple origins of mankind, the orthodox version of creation found in Genesis collapsed. Monc put embarrassing questions to his Lyceum audience: If the Negro was not descended from Adam, he had not "like us whites inherited depravity." What were "our missions" to them? And if there had been a single creation, then all mankind had a common father and no amount of biblical exegetics could overwhelm the claim that the Negro was "a man and a brother."

Usually the dilemma was solved by avoiding it. Some sort of accommodation between science's claims and biblical authority was advised. Failing that, the "infidels" who were trying to twist the truth of biblical revelation to fit "some ridiculous little model in their own hearts" were reproached.[18]

In December, 1850, Monc joined the infidels. He rushed into the controversy, claiming that "the great Evil Spirit of the Earth is Conservatism" which blindly refuses to acknowledge the findings of science. He seized Louis Agassiz' cautious argument for the multiple origins of man and drove it to its farthest point: the Negro's relation to whites is precisely that of the quadrupeds; the Negro was an inferior animal, and the Caucasian has a "gift of Universal Empire over all that is beneath him."

Conway later explained his entry into the polemics of slavery and racism with the statement that predominates the entire Warrenton period. "It was not the vanity of a youth under nineteen, but *a spirit struggling for existence amid fatal conditions,* which led me to announce ... a theory that the negro was not a man within the meaning of the [word]."

Here Monc's state of mind is announced with unmistakable clarity. He was desperate. That desperation informs his essay. His argument in "The Diversity of [the] Origins of Races—Slavery" is composed of two complementary parts: an affirmation of Negro slavery and a repudiation of orthodox Christian doctrine. And when the complementary parts of his polemic are considered in another relationship, his explanation about struggling for existence begins to yield its deeper meaning.

Walker Peyton Conway was an orthodox Christian. Thus for his son to strike at orthodoxy was, as he said, "to subject myself . . . to . . . horrible uneasiness." [19] Walker Peyton Conway was also no outspoken advocate of slavery, and as southern politics began to rearrange itself with a hot defense of slavery at the core of the aggressive states' rights movement, Conway warned his son to steer clear of the Virginia states' rights party. "Don't be the fool of those people!" he told Monc.

The "Diversity of [the] Origins of Races—Slavery" fills fifteen pages with tedious, minutely written arguments and proofs. As its twin theses are developed, the essay becomes more than an expression of some "eccentric views" that meshed with the politics of the Fredericksburg Southern Rights Association. "Diversity" emerges as a carefully contrived attack on Walker Peyton Conway. It is a sequel to "A Webster Case," a tale of Vairenne's revenge on Pentern, whose world, despite Vairenne's brilliant plan to change it, remained intact. The writer of "Diversity" seemingly accepts the existing social order in slaveholding Virginia but strikes at the religion and politics that undergird it. For all its apparent incongruity, the intended effect of "Diversity" is precisely the same as Vairenne's work with electricity and Monc's public education proposal. It aims at the disruption of the world of Hughes-Pentern-Walker Peyton Conway. Furthermore, "Diversity" sharpens the personal conflict. It is the work of an "infidel" and a "fool." When he wrote the essay Monc adopted the two roles that he knew would be most abhorrent to his father.

Without suffering by comparison the essay might have joined the work of Beverly Wellford, George Fitzhugh, Thornton Stringfellow, William Smith, and others who were creating the proslavery polemic arising in Virginia at this time. But "Diversity" was never published. Immediately after it was written the essay was "thrown aside" to remain buried in Conway's papers until he exhumed it over fifty years later as one of the "wrappings of my dead self."

"Diversity" allowed Monc to strike a dramatic pose (and an unfelt blow against his father's verities), and it permitted him to explore one set of positions that established him as a fool and an infidel. But for all its satisfying impieties "Diversity" ran to a singularly unsatisfactory end. Slavery was maintained. Slavery's justifying foundations were radically, and for a man like Walker Peyton Conway, abhorrently, shifted; but if one were willing to forsake an old religion for a new science, they were secured. It is impossible to reconcile the essay's brutal claims with the "glad tidings" Monc had earlier hoped to bring to the slaves and the poor whites of Virginia. And surely in its dogmas there is no freedom for an unhappy slavemistress who protested that she was herself enslaved by slavery. Nor in them is there any relief for her son.

Monc's Warrenton journal concludes with this entry: "Had a violent fever last night." He was already disturbed when he went to bed. During the day, as he was completing "Diversity," he had become uneasy. He watched the "servants moving about the house, cheerfully yielding me unrequited services [never dreaming] of the ease with which I was able to consign [them] to degradation." He went to bed with this thought preying on his mind. The familiar illness struck, and his distress increased as the fever intensified. Then came another vision and with it the experience that Conway thereafter called his "real conversion."

Christ appeared in Monc's bedroom. He drew "near and said, 'What thou doest to the least of these my brothers, thou art doing to me.'" Monc received Christ's gentle words as a withering reproach. Immediately he understood that the dogmatic certainties of "Diversity" were undercut, that his work was a tissue of "superficiality, casuistry." An overwhelming sense of inferiority swept over him, and he trembled in the grip of the fever.

He describes the classic conversion experience. Pride and assurance have been shattered. He has been brought low before God, exhausted and wracked by his "real troubles." The quality that he prized most about himself, his intellect, has been exposed as a conceit and a fraud. He cried the ancient lament of the lost, "I'm afraid. . . . I go up on the hard bleak Rocks." "I am very wretched."

Then Monc heard "the Voice of God . . . saying 'I will set a mark on thee.'" As God *marked* Monc, He gave him a commission "to devote my life to the elevation and welfare of my fellow-beings, white and black." Once the voice of God spoke, the vision of Christ disappeared, the high fever passed, and Monc lay in his bed cool and calm. He understood that he was *called* to become a minister. Vocation and mission had at last been achieved. When morning came he wrote his father that he was giving up his law studies. He would seek ordination as a minister in the Baltimore Conference of the Methodist Church. He would "uplift fainting hearts and guide the groping."

With the achievement of vocation and mission, the basic symmetry of the skylark vision was restored. It had been skewed as Monc made his venture into the free school campaign, and it was deranged by his polemic in racism and slavery, but now it reassumed much of its original form. His ministry was to poor whites and slaves.

But a commission to accept slaves as "fellow-beings," given the proper exegesis, would place no particular strain upon a southern preacher; indeed southern ministerial careers of international renown such as that of Charles Colcock Jones had been forged of precisely such ideas and practices. Neither necessarily meant that Monc was prevented from becoming a conventional (but high-toned) purveyor of Virginia Methodism, nor that he must renounce Tidewater society and make war on its proprietors. He bore God's mark but what did the mark signify?

A "journeyman soul-saver," an uncle called him as Monc left Conway House to take his position as junior preacher on the Rockville circuit.[20] Mounted on the fine mare given him by his father he rode north. At Rockville he joined the senior preacher and began his itinerant ministry. He came to this circuit as spring was laying the first trace of green across the rolling countryside where, he later wrote, "slavery existed only in its mildest form, and there was no pauper population to excite my reformatory zeal. Nor was there even any sectarian prejudice to combat; the county was divided up between denominations friendly to each other and hospitable to me." Presbyterians, Methodists, Baptists, Catholics, a few Episcopalians, and an enclave of radical Hicksite Quakers lived amicably within Rockville circuit.

For a year and a half Monc lived among these people. The first year, from April, 1851, to March, 1852, he preached on the Rockville circuit. In March, 1852, he was appointed to the adjacent Frederick circuit, preaching there until December 4, 1852. He established himself on good terms with these people, and when he preached at Brookville he stayed with Episcopalians instead of Methodist families. He was often the guest of Roger Brooke, the bluff "chief" of the Hicksite Quakers at Sandy Spring. It was these non-Methodists that later in his life, he recalled with detail and tenderness. As for the Methodists, when he wrote of them he could not help but patronize "those dear people . . . in their humble homes."

Washington was nearby, and relatives and friends opened many doors there for him. Mrs. John Quincy Adams entertained him, as did Elizabeth Schyler Hamilton, Alexander Hamilton's widow, over ninety years old. On his own initiative he met "Grace Greenwood" (Sarah Clarke Lippencott), a journalist who introduced him to Dr. Gamaliel Bailey, editor of the *National Era*, the antislavery newspaper that was then publishing the original serial version of *Uncle Tom's Cabin*. But nothing came of the contact, Monc's first with a representative of organized abolition. He also wrote an article on international copyrights published in the *National Intelligencer*. The publication of this piece brought a response from Charles Sumner, an authority on international law and newly elected abolition senator from Massachusetts. But, as with Doctor Bailey, Monc made no attempt to pursue a connection that might have led to abolition work. In fact, when he was in Bailey's home, he said that on his circuit in Maryland and in his home county in Virginia, the two places where he had firsthand knowledge of slavery, the "negroes were not suffering." This remark characterized Monc's sermons. Not once during the entire time he preached from the Methodist pulpit did he utter a word against slavery.

As junior minister he was plunged in "flourishing and arduous" work. In his pastoral duties he was successful, and he was able to bridge the gap he opened between himself and his congregations with his preaching, for his preaching was not successful.

Monc refused to concede anything to the experience or expectations of his congregations. His sermons, on which he "took so much pains," carried his bewildered congregations in the direction of ideas and "the ideal life" which bore little relationship to received Methodist orthodoxies.[21] After "friendly hints" from some of his congregation, one of whom saying, "Brother, you seem to be speaking to us from the moon," Monc was told bluntly by his presiding elder that his sermons were "too profound." His father, after hearing him preach for the first time, told him, "One thing is certain, Monc, Should the devil ever aim at a Methodist preacher you'll be safe." Nor was Monc's pulpit style in the manner of Methodism. "My early training in law courts determined my method of preaching," he explained. "In preparing a sermon I fixed on some main point which I considered of vital importance, and dealt with it as if I were pleading before judge and jury."[22]

On his own in the itinerate pulpits, Monc could preach as he wished, but the camp meetings forced him to a style and a message that were impossible to avoid. In the revivals the preacher as hell-fire exhorter was unleashed; he was made obligatory by the institution itself. With pounding cadences he swept the faithful onward toward visions of eternal bliss and the unrepentant toward hell.[23]

Monc despised the camp meetings. He cultivated the habit of cross-examining the sermons of other preachers. In a camp meeting at which the presiding elder was to preach on the resurrection of the body, Monc, immediately before the man stepped into the pulpit, slipped a piece of paper into his hand. On it he had written a commonplace hypothetical: A soldier's body decays on a battlefield; grass springs up from it; a cow eats the grass; the cow is slaughtered and eaten by another man who in turn dies. If two men die with the same material substance in them, how can there be an exact resurrection of both of their bodies as they were at the moment of death? The preacher replied, "All things are possible with God," an answer that left Monc profoundly dissatisfied.

In this skirmishing Monc seems much like the village atheist dressed in the black Sunday clothes of a Methodist preacher. He came to the edge of demeaning himself badly by ambushing the unsuspecting elder with his question. More damaging, he laid himself open to the charges of bad faith and hypocrisy because he stayed in the Methodist ministry over a year after only a few "relics" of Methodism remained with him.

At the end of six months on the Rockville circuit Monc took "stock of what was left . . . that could honestly be preached in Methodist pulpits" and compared himself to a shipwrecked sailor: He jumps from a foundering ship to a jury-rigged raft. The raft is smashed to pieces; he grasps at a floating log until it is washed away; finally he clutches at "every stick, every straw." He tried to find comfort in Coleridge's assurance that doubts about difficult doctrines, the "bloody dogmas" of orthodox Christianity, came from misinterpreting them. He catechized himself with the classic question intended to shore up faith, "Could I . . . be certain that my doubts were not temptations?" He found himself sliding farther and farther from the doctrinal base upon which a Methodist preacher was supposed to stand. "The autumn of my first ministerial year," he later wrote, was a time of "rack and thumbscrew." He looked for help.

His two "rationalist" friends, Roger Brooke, a Quaker, and William H. Farquhar, the principal of the Quaker girls school, were, he thought, unable to understand his situation. They had never had any dogmas to unlearn. On the basis of what he had read in some fugitive issues of the *Dial*, Monc wrote to Ralph Waldo Emerson, hoping Emerson would understand what Brooke and Farquhar could not.

Monc's first "poor trembling letter" went to Emerson on November 4, 1851.[24] In it Monc said he was a nineteen-year-old Methodist minister who had "just commenced that office at the call of the Holy Ghost." He told Emerson that he believed that "the Christian Religion [was] the only way for the world to reenter Paradise." But since he had read Emerson's essays, he had found his beliefs upset. Emerson had taught him some "laws, when I see how they would act on the affairs of life, I have not the courage to practise." He wanted Emerson's advice and help.

Apparently Emerson answered him by return mail. He gently chided Monc for "not let[ting] me sufficiently into your own habit of thought to enable me to speak to it with much precision," and offered him some characteristically Orphic advice: "A true soul will disdain to be moved except by what natively commands it, though it should go sad and solitary in search of its master a thousand years. The few superior persons in each community are so by their steadiness to reality and their neglect of appearances. This is the euphrasy and rue that purge the intellect and ensure insight." And also characteristically, "I will not spin out these saws farther, but hasten to thank you for your frank and friendly letter, and to wish you the best deliverance in that contest to which every soul must go alone."

According to the *Autobiography* which quotes both letters, "This letter I acknowledged with a longer one (December 12, 1851) in which I say: 'I have very many correspondents, but I might say yours is the only letter that was ever written to me.'" With that Conway drops the subject of the Emersonian correspondence and returns the narrative to his life on the Rockville circuit and his struggle for "selftruthfulness." But the reader is given to understand that Emerson's reply was crucial for the young preacher during his "rack and thumbscrew" time. Emerson's words armed him with the courage to persist in his struggle. "Why then this sudden resolution?" he asks rhetorically. "Emerson was at the bottom of it."

In his autobiography as he writes of his tenure as a Methodist preacher, Conway makes his account turn on the "creeds," his struggle with doctrine, his attempt to save his old beliefs, while he was trying to achieve an intellectual honesty that had the unhappy effect of undermining the beliefs he was attempting to salvage. Fifty years later, still sensible to the old accusations of bad faith and hypocrisy, Conway makes it plain that he suffered great anguish as he found himself in that situation. "I gradually preached myself out of the creeds by trying to prove them by my lawyer-like method." After several months of such self-examination, he found himself trapped between his obligation for "self-truthfulness" and "the thought of turning my old home in Falmouth into a house of mourning, and grieving the hearts of . . . congregations that so trusted me." It was, Conway said, a thought terrible enough to keep him in the Methodist church for another year. Finally, no dogmas remained that he in good conscience could preach; he made his break with much pain. "My final month's round of appointments was a succession of heartbreaks." A journal entry is cited: "Farewell! [he bids the congregation at Jefferson, the last Methodist pulpit he occupied on his circuit] O how sad to go off." And he remains particularly sensible to the anguish his parents suffered as he repudiated their church and their expectations for him. "My old journal is a sort of herbarium of thorns that pierced father, mother, and myself." Nonetheless, he is obliged to accept "the truth" and whatever consequences that come with it. Encouraged by his Quaker and Unitarian friends, Conway entered Harvard Divinity School. He was once again launched. In place of creeds there was now a credo: "I must study it." Where he was headed he was not certain. Everything lay open.[25]

As he comes to this point in the story of his life, Conway has so insinuated himself in his reader's sympathy that it seems almost a breaching of friendship to suggest that the old warrior imposes too much on our credulity as he tells of his "rack and thumbscrew" time and explains his extrication from it as a triumph of right reason and humanitarianism. What we have already learned about Monc as he came to the Methodist ministry is simply not congruent with Conway's account of why he gave it up. Furthermore, it is in this portion of the life story that we have incontrovertible evidence that the autobiographical materials have been arranged to portray a man of rational goodwill. As we examine these materials we find in them sufficient clues to extend and conclude our inquiry in the question of why and by what means Monc found his way to his life's work.

In his third letter to Emerson Monc wrote with great distress about "the *circumstances . . . which God has placed me in.*" He said that he had to call everything that is wrong right. He chafed under a checkrein. Having been commissioned to speak the truth, he is compelled to be silent. The community into which he had been born and into which he has been called to preach is a "dead corpse."

He groans at the prospect of going through life dragging it along. He fears that he is in danger of losing his faith. "For God's sake," he cries, he needs " light."

This is not a plea for help on matters of doctrinal faith or the screed of a young preacher straining against the set ways of his congregations. It is Monc's confession that he has not yet executed the commission he has been given by God. When he is honest with himself he admits that he is delaying. "My Island is getting smaller each day. . . . I fear the time when the Eternal Things Above [will] drum me out . . . a Coward." His torment has become so great that he has thought about committing suicide.

He tells Emerson about the night of his "real conversion," the feverish night in Warrenton when he heard the voice of God. Now we are able to learn what the voice of God had said to Monc when he was called to the ministry and given his commission to "devote my life to the elevation and welfare of my fellow beings, white and black." In this second (and suppressed) letter to Emerson it comes exploding out of him what God's mark signified: "I heard the Voice of God saying *as It did to Cain for his sin*—'I will set a mark on thee.'" [26]

The mark of Cain, [27] God's safe conduct pass for the outcast second son in the land of his father, was delivered simultaneously with the call to the ministry and the commission to speak "the truth." Here at last we are in a position from which we may answer the earlier question about Monc's real conversion and his call to the ministry. His believing himself "marked" suggests that Monc did know from that night in Warrenton what he must do, what he believed himself compelled by God to do. He also knew that when he spoke "the truth" he would do so with safety but not impunity. Once his challenging, war-making words rolled off his tongue there could be no calling them back. Their meaning would be unmistakable. And the consequent recrimination and alienation were also known to him: "I shall walk alone [in] . . . Virginia . . . where I must live alone always." [28] "[It] is just my fate" to have to "speak the Truth . . . amongst talented Conservative Virginians *such as my father*."

In his confessional letter to Emerson it is not the "repulsive dogmas and atrocities" of the "creeds" that draw from Monc's pen his harsh words; it is the cultivated polished, talented conservative Virginians who are the "dead corpse" of the community he has been dragging along. It is about them, his father and his father's people, that God has commissioned him to speak the truth, and has promised him safety in the telling.

"The details," Monc said to Emerson, "would be worse." It is sufficient to say that "if I were to tell . . . what my real troubles were . . . I [would] have no sympathy on Earth."

Cain! "This is my grief . . . my fate . . . . for God's sake." [29]

A final question remains to be answered. Why did he hang on in the Methodist church for the better part of another year, preaching sermons that were equivocal on the creeds and silent on slavery? It was not until the late summer of 1852 that Monc accepted the commission which for over a year and a half he had believed that God thrust upon him.

On the Fourth of July, 1852, Monc preached at Dickinson College's commencement, the annual occasion at which the college celebrated itself as a bastion of Methodist education. Inviting a twenty-year-old junior preacher from a rural circuit to preach the commencement sermon was a resounding vote of confidence in his ability and prospects, as well as an acknowledgment of the standing of his father in the affairs of the college and the Baltimore Conference.

Monc had come to Carlisle as something of a princeling. The invitation was a sign that greater things than riding a circuit awaited him. Moving among the visitors, trustees, faculty, and old classmates (his class of 1848 was convening to receive their Master of Arts degrees), Monc relished the subtle signs of deference coming his way. He was introduced to the distinguished visitors and was invited to dine at the faculty's intimate dinners. After the tables were cleared, the conversations covered the spectrum of the church's interests, from doctrinal matters to "the increasing strength of the Church of Rome." Wherever the men ranged in their talk, they asked Monc to offer his views. At one of the dinners even his father leaned across the table to solicit his opinion about the "philosophical tendencies of the American mind." In private conversation with Professor M'Clintock and "some [other] highly intellectual Methodists," Monc confided his doubts about church doctrine. These preachers and theologians advised him that he could stay in his pulpit with a clear conscience. He was troubling himself needlessly. Many people, themselves included, these men told Monc, had "mental doubts," but they were of small importance. M'Clintock swept the conversation to an end by citing John Wesley, "'I am sick of opinions; give me the man's life!'" This private session with M'Clintock and his colleagues confirmed what Monc's invitation to Carlisle signified. He had been selected to rise high in the Methodist church, and he had the support of powerful men. On the eve of his commencement sermon there was much at Carlisle for Monc to relish. But most of all there was Catharine Emory.

When Monc came to Carlisle, the recipient of all the approbation and deference a twenty-year-old preacher could hope for, he came bearing them as trophies to lay at the feet of Catharine Emory. His invitation to preach the commencement sermon was his triumph and vindication; surely he was worthy of a bishop's daughter. Monc must have come to Carlisle prepared to claim Kate Emory for his wife.

Kate Emory greeted Monc with the news that she was to marry another Methodist preacher. Her engagement was being announced to coincide with the college's commencement, and it would be celebrated as part of the commencement festivities. Monc felt as if he had been *struck [by] lightning.*" It "*struck something in me deeper than the dogmas with which I had been concerned.... My ... faith and ... love crumpled together.*"[30] His Methodism was dependent on her. This is testimony from Conway's autobiography; even from that long retrospect he made clear the devastating effect of his final meeting with Kate. His imagery is explosive and reveals the crucial part the girl played in bringing Monc in open rebellion against the world in which he had been born. In his autobiography Conway declared that his love for Kate Emory was the "second of my births." He did not elaborate, as indeed he could not. But what we have already learned about Monc and Kate suggests that he meant that by being reborn of Kate Emory he had been given a new life, one that bid to free him from his "existence amid fatal conditions." It is difficult to avoid the conclusion that Kate Emory was a fusion of mother and lover, a surrogate Margaret Conway, in whom he had been able to deflect certain of his "dim, fantastic visions of happiness."

The *Autobiography* swiftly rounds out the account. He leaves Carlisle with "new hope and strength." He understands that he must minister "not by theologies and sectarian triumphs, but by feeding hearts that thirst and hunger for love and righteousness." Thenceforth he will "diffuse the spirit of peace and goodwill on earth." He eagerly writes a long article in which he says "the right of private judgment [in religion] must be insisted on, all intolerance of differences of opinion repudiated." The article, which is presented in the *Autobiography* as a plea for "free thought and free culture" throughout the world, is published in the Methodist *Christian Advocate and Journal*. He moves rapidly to disengage himself from the Methodist ministry. He decides to enter the Harvard Divinity School at midyear. He tells his parents of his decision, knowing "in every way it will be sad for them." With "unspeakable grief" he leaves his congregations, wishing that they would say, "'Come back and tell us freely all that is in your heart.'"

There is much prevarication here, more than anywhere else in the *Autobiography*.

What happened to Monc in the aftermath of Kate Emory's stunning blow has been anticipated. It remains to make his actions explicit and show how at last "the inner powerhouse of rage which must be submerged . . . as some of the fondest hopes and wildest phantasies are suppressed" was brought to the surface and (extending Erik Erikson's metaphor) closed its circuits and channeled its high tension energy in the conflict smouldering between a young man and the world into which he had been born.[31] When Kate Emory destroyed Monc's "fondest hopes," she freed the rage that he had for so long held within himself. It was now possible for him to make the rupture with his father. Before he left Carlisle he was poised on the verge of accepting his Cain-ness.

There are two articles, the only contemporary evidence surviving from this time, that Monc wrote shortly after he left Carlisle.

The first article, written in a blazing burst of energy, runs over twenty thousand words, and was published in seven installments. It was Monc's third venture into an extended polemic, and like the previous two, "Free Schools in Virginia" and "Diversity," was written under extreme stress when he was changing the direction of his life's work. If the writings are considered in this context, a rather clear pattern emerges. When Monc was at one of these stressful turning points that brought his anger as close to the surface as he dared allow, he relieved himself with equivocal words. He fired harmless barrages of words against an enemy who had no inkling that the salvos had been fired. This third polemic fits the pattern of these earlier "safe" attacks on Walker Peyton Conway and his world.

"Jesuitism," published in the *Christian Advocate and Journal*, seems to be a screed of the most savage Protestant bigotry.[32] Unexceptional as a specimen of the anti-Catholic propaganda of the time, "Jesuitism" rises above its own clichés only when Monc presents himself as an expert witness for the prosecution. He testifies *from positive personal knowledge* about the "baneful influence" of "the evil principle of Jesuitism," particularly instances of innocent children and young people who are "entrapped" by an indoctrinating "education" and a skillfully masked "hypocrisy." He has seen them trapped; he *knows*. His purpose is to sound the alarm: "Be warned and armed!" Before Monc is finished he has come close to calling for a jihad against the Catholics.

What saves "Jesuitism" from being only an example of the period-piece diatribes against American Catholicism is the polemic's full thesis. Monc argued that the evil principle of Jesuitism had survived in Protestantism. This "poisonous fruit" and "baneful influence" were "equally" in Protestant churches insofar as they trapped the young and crimped free thought for all people. To this extent certain Protestant churches are like the Catholic church insofar as they have laid waste to a land and "beggared, enslaved, [and] barbarised" its people. It is here that Monc's claim of being an expert witness becomes something more than apparent reckless perjury. Grotesque Catholic horrors are paraded across the pages of the *Christian Advocate and Journal*, but beneath them are matters about which he has personal knowledge. "Beggared, enslaved, barbarized," Monc is describing the society that Varienne was going to change and the skylark would undertake to destroy. "Jesuitism" is the most savage thing Monc ever wrote. It is pure naked rage, but it is a rage that has not been unequivocally focused on its real object.[33]

It was with the greatest effort that Monc now forced himself into his pulpits. Sometimes he could not complete his sermons and was left standing speechless in his pulpit with tears streaming down his face. He became reclusive, spending hours in long solitary walks during which he flagellated himself for saying "some bold things, but not boldly." The *Autobiography* says, "My mental troubles and the distress of my parents began to break down my health, and I arranged . . . to pass a week . . . in Baltimore." It was while he was at Baltimore that he decided to consummate his break with Methodism, become a Unitarian, and enter the Harvard Divinity School.

Monc wrote the companion piece to "Jesuitism" at this time. This second article is also a "safe" attack, but it goes beyond "Jesuitism" as Monc's rage was more focused and his animus more personified. He came to the verge of explicitness as he wrote what amounts to a descriptive self-diagnosis, in which there are three persons, unmistakably himself, his father, and his mother.

"Children and Their Literature" is an essay on child psychology, in which a brief review of some children's books is connected with a long, descriptive theory of childhood and its pathology.[34] A child, Monc wrote, begins his life living "in harmony with the universe." But a child is vulnerable to the teaching and precept of his father. His original harmony may be confirmed, or it may be damaged or destroyed, depending upon what his father teaches him. The young child is innocent and defenseless, and his father can force on him that which is "untrue," particularly "the fiends Puritanism and Jesuitism." Only as a child grows older can he understand that he has been maimed by his father. He comes to see *"the discrepancy between the outward and the inward of the household."*[35] He is able to understand that he has been deceived and duped and that his father's teaching was "his first lesson in hypocrisy" that he himself has unwittingly accepted and practiced. But even when "the fiends" have exerted their most crushing force there have been occasions when a child has not only survived but has turned to fight them. These have been the reforming saints, both religious and secular, who (in unspecified ways) have been "nurtured" by an "Apostate Mother" for their great work of destroying the fiends.

There is no wild savagery in "Children." Dispassion suffuses the entire essay. The hateful "fiends" are only stated, not defined or described. (One must read "Jesuitism" to understand what Monc meant by the word, and "Puritanism" is left for the reader to infer as the bleak zealotry of "Ironside discipline.") The hypocritical, maiming father—the personification as well as the teacher of "the fiends"—is presented with detachment, his son is a clinical specimen, and the Apostate Mother is nothing more than an allusive metaphor. "Children" retains its autobiographical character throughout, but as Monc's ideas develop the essay moves beyond being a statement on child psychology; it becomes an outline for an interpretation of history. There is a calm sweep through centuries during which there occasionally appears a young man whose task it is to break the monstrous power of "the fiends." He is a gentle intellectual reformer such as St. Francis, Pascal, and Emerson, whose "supreme end [is] to save hearts suffering not in eternity but in time, and in flesh and blood." As "Children" shifts from psychology to history it is as though some tormenting enraging matter has been resolved, a situation—a "fate"—accepted. The father, child, and apostate mother, each has played his part. The rest will be the unfolding of history.

Early in December, 1852, Monc preached his last sermon as a Methodist. Shortly before Christmas he arrived at Conway House where he waited until mid-February, 1853, when he left to enter Harvard Divinity School.

"'O my [God], do thou love me in this time of fire,'" Monc prayed after he had come to Conway House. For it was now that the conflict between him and his father broke into the open. At first there were long earnest sessions between them about Monc's "heresy." Father and son marched and countermarched over the familiar ground of religious and theological disputation like two ecclesiastical legists wringing proof and refutation from the same scripture. These arid inconclusive debates left Monc weary and impatient. He was marking time. "How little sympathy I have with the existing state of things. I am not,'" he said to himself "'in [this] world.'"

Walker Peyton Conway pointed to a book Monc was holding and said, "'These books that you read and now are about to multiply affect my feelings as if you were giving yourself up to excessive brandy.'" Here was the opening Monc had been waiting for. He told his father that his "doctrinal heresies"—the subjects of the books he was reading—were about "abstract and abstruse issues." They dealt with "fictitious hells." But he was concerned with "actual hells." He was, Monc said, "aiming at a new world." It "was of such a serious character" that he could enter it only by phases— "the abolition of slavery to begin with." He had, he told his father, "new ideas on slavery" which he no longer would try to "conceal." " 'I [have] found out how much hatred I had of the institution—and how much contempt for the persons engaged in it.'" *Hatred. Contempt.* 36

Much of what now happened in Conway House must be inferred: shock, recoil, hot exchanges between Walker Peyton Conway and Monc, each on the verge of bitter recrimination, desperately trying to save appearances and a semblance of civil discourse, with Margaret Daniel Conway "watch[ing] all the proceedings . . . with burning cheeks." By New Year's the struggle had spilled outside Conway House. Erleslie and Inglewood, once gay refuges from Conway House's austerities, were now places of acerbating reproach where Monc was "'persecuted about my radicalism.'" One of his uncles, Eustace Conway, became so "sore personally [and] so excited that for once he spoke to me in anger." Fifty years later the memory of these rancorous weeks lay in his mind like a "herbarium of . . . thorns." In the *Autobiography*, the contemporary hatred and contempt were glossed to the after-the-fact "distress" and "pain," but there is sufficient "emotion, embarrassment, and discord" in the palliated account to see Monc approaching the con-

summation of his Cain-ness. His father told him that when he left
Conway House he would be on his own. "'I have considered my
duty and reached this conclusion: I cannot . . . support you at Cambridge. . . . I cannot assist . . . grievous error.'" Monc's estrange-
ment was such that when he left Falmouth neither his father nor
any of his uncles or male cousins told him goodbye or wished him
well.

The morning Monc left for Cambridge, Walker Peyton Conway
was conspiciously absent from Conway House. Monc called for his
horse and took a short ride. The ride over, he tied the horse to a tree
in front of the house. He went inside and picked up the saddlebags
that had once held his copies of Watson's *Theology* and the
"Methodist Discipline." He carried the bags to his horse and laid
them empty across the saddle. He went back into Conway House,
told his mother goodbye, and walked alone to the railroad station.

IV
North

The personal events that strike
deepest in a man work out their
effects slowly.
MONCURE CONWAY

During the next ten years
Moncure Conway moved full circle. In 1853 he arrived in Cambridge, an exile from the slave society, as much repudiated by his Virginia kinsmen as repudiating them. In 1863 he fetched up in Venice in flight from the scathing renunciations heaped on him by his colleagues and friends of these past ten years, the leaders of American radical abolition. In Venice, suffering from a raging fever and skin infection diagnosed as the "morbid symptoms of the wounds of mind and heart," he ended the American phase of his career. He exiled himself from the United States permanently, returning thereafter only as a visitor. In the interval he established himself as one of the more celebrated abolition polemicists in the

United States and perfected those personal characteristics that fitted him as radical abolition's choice for the English mission.[1]

Conway's rise was spectacular in its swiftness and remarkable in its reconciliation of the antagonistic personalities and groups out of which the wartime abolition coalition was forged. In 1856, only two years after he graduated from Harvard Divinity School, he was nationally famous. His published sermons on slavery were circulating among Supreme Court justices and members of the Boston's Saturday Club, the nearest thing in America to an established literary-intellectual fellowship. From the Western Reserve in Ohio came unsolicited testimonials of support from anonymous men who linked him with his "exemplars Wesley, Luther, Socrates . . . Christ."[2] And in his rise to fame Conway did something no other radical abolitionist seems to have been able to do. He made himself acceptable to both the free spirits who believed that emancipation (and the whole matter of racial equalitarianism) was only the prelude to some dazzling new social order, and the hard-bitten men who reluctantly accepted emancipation as policy necessary to break the back of secession. The energy for the final assault on slavery had to be drawn from communard and from neo-Federalist, from such social enemies as Josiah Warren and Oliver Wendell Holmes, anarchist and autocrat yoked for emancipation. Despite his own storminess—and we shall come to that presently—Conway had the talent to mollify mutual antagonists. He was a bridge across which they could come in common purpose.

Arriving unannounced and unexpected at Modern Times, the radical experimental community on Long Island, Conway was given a chilly reception. But he charmed Josiah Warren, the community's leader, and was invited to stay and witness "an entirely original sociology" and "a vista of strange experiences" which he later idealized in some of his fiction.

To Holmes's exquisite disgust Conway came to a dinner given in his honor at the Parker House in Boston, trailing behind him "various unknown dingy-linened friends of progress." But Holmes, who had never met him, came away favorably impressed by Conway and reported him as "an out-and-out emancipationist," which Holmes was not. "He talked with a good deal of spirit," and

Holmes told his friend, the anglophilic elitist John Lothrop Motley, "I know you would have gone with him in his leading ideas."[3]

Conway's talent for bridging antagonisms was most clearly recognized (and used) midway in 1862 as it became apparent that willy-nilly the Civil War was becoming some sort of abolition war. The radical abolitionists' problem was to give the war the shape and the direction they desired. They wanted to create the broadest possible abolition base in the North, but at the same time they understood that their claims to leadership were suspect. For over twenty years they had marched along with the various unknown dingy-linened friends of progress that Holmes had reviled. The *Liberator* was indeed heard, but it was apt to be heeded only by those who were already convinced, and the Garrisonians wanted access to their erstwhile enemies.

In September, 1862, Conway was invited to Boston to edit the *Commonwealth*. This new abolition paper was to carry a Garrisonian message. The *Commonwealth*'s founders were confident of Conway's "vigor" and "recklessness" on that count. But they particularly wanted Conway to be the editor because they believed he would bring a "quality to the *Commonwealth* [that no] other journal could brag of." He could reach a different and a larger audience than that of the *Liberator*. Even Garrison who regarded encroachments on his domain as acts of lese majesty seems to have given the paper his unqualified blessing. As editor of the *Commonwealth*, Conway was "often in consultation with him and Wendell Phillips" and "there was no rivalry nor friction between [us]."[4] It was Garrison and Phillips and other members of the coterie of old radicals who, after he had edited the *Commonwealth* for six months, and when the Union army was mired in the swamps surrounding Vicksburg and stymied before the approaches to Richmond, chose Conway to make the voyage to England as their emissary to the English liberal intellectuals and literary lights.

Conway's path from Falmouth to London lay by way of Cambridge, Concord, Washington, and Cincinnati.

Entering Harvard Divinity School in the "middle" year at midterm, he graduated a year and a half later. When he arrived in

Cambridge he was something of an oddity trailing a whiff of notoriety after him. Self-advertised as a homeless southerner making his own way in the world, an apostate preacher not yet forgiven by his old church (*Zion's Herald* published an article written by a Boston Methodist minister attacking him), and with his talent for ingratiating himself, Conway was ripe for patronizing and was ready to use his patrons.

Mrs. Jared Sparks, the wife of Harvard's president, took him up as "a sort of protégé," as did Emerson who found him a home for the summer in Concord. Conway's journal says of these things: "O the ineffable delight!", and the *Autobiography* is a swirl of names and episodes in which he meets the celebrated and notorious. It is as though Conway set out to touch base with every intellectual and every reforming notable in New England. They are all there: Lowell took him swimming; Thoreau took him on a nature walk; Longfellow took him home for an evening; Theodore Parker took him on a search for a fugitive slave from Virginia; Wendell Phillips took him to Tremont Temple for an abolitionist rally after the Anthony Burns riot, and so forth.[5]

How much of the pleasure that suffuses these accounts is the sheer delight of a young man traveling exuberantly, unselfconsciously in circles that heretofore he had only dreamed of, and how much is the self-satisfaction of a calculated getting-on is a question that need not unduly detain us. But it would be a mistake to forget that Conway was enormously ambitious. He meant to get on, associate with the famous and the powerful, and use them as he pursued his own ambitions.

It also would be difficult to account for Conway's success without understanding that he had great vitality and a vast capacity for work. As he said in the *Autobiography*, "A disposition for hard work was characteristic of all our Conway race. Even in the cold northern climate I must rise early, and in that way I managed to read many excellent books." During his year and a half at the divinity school he was a supply preacher, played the chapel organ, organized a vegetarian mess, and served as a proctor in Divinity Hall (these things in order to support himself); arranged informal lectures at the divinity school, taught in a Cambridge night school for the poor, and audited Harvard College classes taught by Agassiz and Longfellow. These activities were in addition to his regular divinity school work, not to mention the concerts, operas, lectures, preachings, and his relentless quest of the New England notables.

During this year and a half in Massachusetts, Conway laid the base for his work for the next ten years. He made many of the acquaintances and friendships that would serve him well in the future. He learned the philosophical justifications for his war against "the fiends [of] Puritanism and Jesuitism," and insofar as antislavery was concerned, he quickly demonstrated that he was of the correct persuasion. The first Sunday he was in Boston he attended Theodore Parker's church. At Framingham Grove where the Garrisonians annually met to celebrate their work, and where Garrison ritually burned the Constitution of the United States, Conway delivered a brief speech advocating the peaceful separation of North and South. Shortly, he was writing for the *Liberator*.

Of the putative relationship between the teachings of the Concord philosophy and the doctrines of American radical abolition, there is no better example than Conway.[6] He embraced both with the zeal of the new, and true, believer. When he left Massachusetts in the fall of 1854 he was a certified probationer in the faiths of Emerson and Garrison.

From Cambridge, Conway went to Washington to be minister of the First Unitarian Church. When he arrived at Washington he was twenty-two years old. He grew a beard because, he said, he was "half a boy," and he thought the beard would give him a needed dignity among these people "unsurpassed for intelligence and influence" (characteristically, the *Autobiography* reels off the names of the "distinguished," "charming," and "brilliant" members of the Washington Unitarian society). He remained at the Unitarian church until the end of 1856, when he was turned out of his pulpit. It was the fight over his dismissal that earned him his spurs as a front-line radical abolitionist and catapulted him into national prominence.

Conway's three probative sermons were all on abolition, "Our special national sin—the greatest of all sins—human slavery." It was when Walker Peyton Conway heard of these sermons that he washed his hands of his son and wrote, "we hand you over to the mercy of God. . . . You are wad[ing] through . . . blood." He told him that he was not welcome at Conway House "until . . . your . . . reckless . . . horrible views . . . have undergone material changes." His mother wrote him, "You have brought down a tempest on y[our] head." Nevertheless, she said, "I think the style of your phillipic is very good." Throughout his tenure at Washington she praised Conway's sermons for being well composed and for demon-strating much "research," but she cautioned him to acknowledge his sources. "A trifle," she said, but "I should hate [for you] to be liable to the suspicion of plagiraism [sic] from any quarter." She also wondered whether he was "too ultra for even [the Washington Unitarians'] liberal notions." If, she told him, "I had prophecy . . . [I would predict] that you will not have the pleasure of officiating long in [the Washington church]." [7]

The Washington Unitarians were willing to abide Conway's abolition sermons. And they were able to swallow his disunion sermons as long as he cast them in Emersonian metaphors, such as, "The people of the United States are a firm. Wherever the firm deals with slavery, all deal with slavery. . . . Is not the only right thing for those who believe slavery to be sinful . . . to declare them-selves free from all share in [the firm]?" But when in this most political of all American cities Conway shifted to partisan politics and turned his pulpit into a Republican party stump he split his church wide open.

As a good Garrisonian he was a "no party" man until the Repub-lican mobilization in 1856, when he proposed political action to achieve the Garrisonian end. He preached John Charles Frémont's presidential candidacy with the thesis that a Republican victory "would be followed by secession of the slave states." Southern se-cession would simultaneously end the Kansas civil war and purify the nation of any complicity in slavery. This secession, prospec-tively peaceful, would carry the subsidiary result of the destruction of slavery itself, because with "The land of Freedom . . . extended [along] the Potomac and the Ohio. . . . Slavery could not last if the slaves had freedom within arms's length." Conway told his con-gregation that a Frémont vote was as "solemn as prayer." He taunted them to challenge him for preaching partisan sermons, "I feel the presence of [slavery's] great infernal power in this house today,—there lurking among you, whispering, 'Don't stand such preaching as this; if you do your friends will turn away from you, and you will be called an abolitionist.'"

After being warned to tone down his sermons, he was formally charged that "'He... persists in this desecration of his pulpit.'" The fight between Conway and his congregation went on for the better part of a year. Then they threw him out.

From Washington, Conway moved to Cincinnati. His mother wrote him as he headed West that he would have no communication from his father, but, she told him, his father's silence did not mean that "He can... kill native... love." As for herself, she said that his "trials and sorrows," so long as they were "endured for conscience [sic] sake" were her "most nourishing aliment."

"I am... pining to see you," she said, "and if I knew how to do it, would see you some where." But that was impossible. She cannot leave Conway House (and it is here that she launches into her most bitter recorded denunciation of slavery), "for you know that saving the black visage, I am the greatest slave here.... Oh! What a thralldom to me; the white slave—mentally and bodily."

"I shall see little of you henceforth, but I hope you will one day have a home where your sister and brothers can visit you." She herself would depend on his letters, and she begged him to write to her often. His silences were "enough for me to get the Hypo[chondria]... such an anxious life do I spend about you."[8]

In Cincinnati the Unitarian church gave Conway a home but it scarcely contained his energies. He cut a wide swath through the city. The *Autobiography* is sufficient to carry the story: "Cincinnati was the most cultivated of the western cities.... Into all the literary and artistic movements in Cincinnati I threw myself with ardor. I was adopted in the clubs, and wrote criticism of the classical concerts, the picture exhibitions, the operas, and plays.... In Cincinnati found myself for the first time able in indulge my passion for the drama....Society in Cincinnati was gay. There were picnics, dances, masquerade balls....A dancing and theatre-going preacher was previously unknown here." He became something of a dandy.

But some of Conway's most solid accomplishments lie in the

eight years he lived in Cincinnati. His first books, *Tracts for To-day*, *The Neglected Stone*, and *The Golden Hour*, come out of this time. His philosophical writing as a member of the Ohio Hegelians was sufficient to win him a place in the history of American philosophy, irrespective of his other work. He revived the *Dial* with an editorial hand that was praised even by Boston critics. He led the fight in the Conference of Western Unitarian Churches to force the churches to come out unequivocally against slavery, which caused the disruption of the Conference and the loss of the St. Louis and Louisville societies. Conway's part in the fight brought from his mother the strongest words of caution that she ever wrote to him: "It seems you are doomed to be in an excitement on the 'peculiar institution'—Well! I hope and pray that it is taken with an eye to your duty to God and Man, rather than to be a leader in a new cause. . . . I hope you do not venture upon this arena of strife without fervent prayers for enlightenment, that you may be 'as wise as a serpent and as harmless as a dove' in y[ou]r efforts to bias others." [9]

And he married. When she learned that he intended to marry, Margaret Conway predicted disaster, a "fatal blunder." "You," she said, "with your . . . abstract notions, and your resolute (not to say dogged) devotion to your own . . . will." "I do not think you are much gifted with insight into women's characters." "To see you married . . . w[oul]d be one of my greatest earthly trials, nothing so utterly separates a [mother from her son], nothing . . . not even his death, ever so fully snaps this tie." Her last letter laments the "sacrifice [of] the communion of my spirit with yours." [10]

Conway married Ellen Dana. Her father, Charles Dana, a down-on-his-luck Cincinnati businessman, had moved, with her mother, from Massachusetts. Ellen was an attractive woman, about Conway's own age. She danced with him and attended the theater and opera with him. But it was her "practical wisdom," "counsel," and "judgment" that seemed, as Kate Emory once seemed, to make her considerably older and wiser than he that he always praised. It was to Ellen that Wendell Phillips came to broach the Garrisonians' plan to send Conway to England, and it was she who managed the business and financial arrangements for the mission.

In the aftermath of the English debacle, Ellen sold the Concord house, disposed of the furniture, and took the children to join Conway in London.[11] She helped him establish himself as minister of the South Place Chapel where he began to remake his life.

For the remainder of his life, which carried him into the twentieth century, Conway found a place for himself in the advance echelon of the trans-Atlantic liberal intellectual community. He made his home in London, but traveled extensively about the world and occasionally visited the United States. In these years he promoted most of the libertarian impulses flowering in late Victorian society: rational free thought, woman's rights, birth control. He published a torrent of lectures, essays and books advocating these things.

Conway's later career duplicated his earlier American career. There was bumptious quarreling with the congregation of South Place Chapel that ended his association with any religious organization. There was his avid collection of the fashionable and celebrated men and women of ideas, literature, and reform. There was the ceaseless thrust toward new ideas he believed would liberate men from the old "fiends" that trammeled the full flowering of human individuality. The exception was his enlistment as a war correspondent in the Franco-Prussian War. His dispatches ascribe an excitement, satisfaction, and purpose to war that is altogether surprising. And one supposes that as he followed the Prussian army across the Rhine, Conway was unconsciously enlisting in a Civil War regiment, a notion he had in 1861 but rejected even though he feared some people would call him a coward. His catholic interests carried him in innumerable directions, but his tastes unerringly kept him in the company of the celebrated and powerful. Andrew Carnegie donated a building in his honor at Dickinson College.

In the decades of this multifarious activity Ellen seems to have supplied him with the strengths he had always sought from older women. Self-effacing, she never asked to share the limelight. Late in the century she stoically suffered from cancer.

When she died her last words to him were, "You will now have to take care of yourself." At Ellen's death Conway memorialized "her sense of duty, her unselfish nature, and instinct of helpfulness [that] had long become to her a religion too absorbing and satisfying to admit of much interest in problems beyond her powers." He undertook the *Autobiography* at her request and had barely begun it before she died. When he completed his account of *"Quorum magna pars fui,"* which runs toward nine hundred pages, Ellen had been mentioned on only six occasions. Of the last he wrote, "Here I say no more. 'That way madness lies.'"

Part Two

Jane Swisshelm: Emancipated Woman

V

The Wax Doll and the Covenanters' Daughter

Every human soul is . . . a company of two armies, and wherever there is one, there is strife.
JANE SWISSHELM

Other than three short notes and her newspaper pieces, only one contemporary item that she wrote survived the fire Jane Grey Swisshelm fed with her own writings. She claimed she destroyed her letters and other papers to keep them from her estranged husband. But her explanation scarcely rings true, for when she burned her papers James Swisshelm had been left far behind her. He would never again intrude in her life except in a legal battle carried to the Pennsylvania Supreme Court, and in her own imaginative desires.

This surviving letter was written to her old friend and ally, George W. Julian. Julian, an abolitionist, vice-presidential candidate on the forlorn Free Soil ticket of 1852, Republican congressman, and Radical par excellence, had fought the same battles as she in the days of sectional strife, Civil War, and Reconstruction. In 1872 Julian and Swisshelm went the way of many of the old-line reformers, abandoning Grant and the Regular Republicans for Horace Greeley and the will-o'-the-wisp dreams of reconstituting the party with the old ideology and moral force of the fifties. When the Liberal Republican movement failed to survive, Julian moved on to the Democratic party. But Jane Swisshelm returned to the Regular faith in 1876 and defended Rutherford B. Hayes's claims for the contested electoral votes of South Carolina, Florida, and Louisiana. She turned on Julian. Old and, by her own admission, tired and worn, she still had strength to fling her abuse in a scathing, half-legible scrawl across the paper. If, as she was ending her life, she could write with such fury to a friend, it was no wonder that in her better, stronger days her enemies had truly feared her attacks.

My Friend of the Olden Time,

Your letter reached me yesterday & made our parting more painful than before; but my duty is none the less plain & that is to do all in my power to lessen the influence you carry into the camp of the foes of Freedom.

Your present position is inexplicable to me on any ground but weakness or wickedness. I cannot belive you wicked & look backward for evidence of weakness. . . .

You are deceived by vulgar hooligans acting in the name of disembodied spirits, & by Mrs. Woodhull, the boldest, most disgraceful humbug of the age; & I must recall these facts to account for your [position] that Louisiana held as peaceful & orderly an election as Indiana!!!

I do not know what kind of an election Indiana held but I do know, from personal observation & a long & careful study of the habits & character of the Southern people, that they never had a peaceable or orderly election in any Southern State!

I lived among Southern people too long not to know that they do not know what peace & order means. Moreover, your testimony is contradicted by that of the Scallawags with whom you have associated yourself for they were [threatened] and intimidated. No doubt they made you believe everything had been lovely just as they did Horace Greely.

The best class of the Northern people are incapable of comprehending the duplicity & trickery & fraud & chicanery & [deceit] of those Southern scoundrels. Bah. It makes me sick to think of it. George W. Julian, the ally & champion of the old women-whippers of the South! I cannot talk about it & wish you had died a year ago, died before you sunk into this double damnation.

As for physical courage . . . I . . . never thought you had any. Neither had Sumner. . . . I also know that your temperament unfits you to judge, fairly . . . the character & merits of men whose only redeeming trait is brute courage. You are so far out of sympathy with the brutal affairs of the South that you cannot comprehend their plans, purposes & means for accomplishing them. You are their dupe, that is all! Blind Sampson grinding in the mill of the Philistines, & alas, grinding willingly. . . .I feel that I never want to see your face again. [1]

No stranger to screed himself, Julian gave as good as he got. He reminded her that she had also bolted in 1872, but was now "keeping step to the music of the political reprobates and thieves who owned and perfectly controlled the 'party of great moral ideas.' In allowing your partizan narrowness and dogmatism to run away with your reason would it not have been well to remember that the great majority of the people with whom you and I used to do battle against slavery were for Tilden & Hendricks." As a parting shot he offered her his "unreserved commiseration instead of ill will." [2] But the measure of Julian's wrath was not revealed until seven years later when he published his *Political Recollections*. There is no mention in his account of his public life of the woman who bore the title Mother of the Republican party in Minnesota, with whom Julian had worked to make the great political coalition against slavery.

It is difficult to imagine such an exchange between any of the other women enlisted in abolition and the men with whom they had fallen out—such women publicists as the Grimké sisters, Lydia Maria Child, Maria Weston Chapman, Lucy Stone, and Harriet Beecher Stowe. For all the passion her words may have contained, Maria Chapman set them down with the measured austerity that befitted a Brahmin; Lucy Stone's style was a reflection of her reasonable Unitarianism; and for the rest of them, *Godey's Lady's Book* might have served as a primer for style and sensibility. But Jane Swisshelm spoke with a voice distinctly her own. Furthermore, there was in her words a high-pitched insistence upon the self as an active participant in the struggle that denotes something other than self-celebration. Of all the abolition writers, her *I* most resembles that of Frederick Douglass. Touch these two and you find abolitionists whose personal grievance against slavery was so great that it gave a special quality to everything they wrote about the peculiar institution. For Douglass the animus came naturally and understandably enough, but Jane Swisshelm offers an altogether different problem.

Jane Grey Cannon was born into the comfortable but austere world presided over by her father, Thomas Cannon. When she was born in 1815, Thomas Cannon had been in America more than twenty years, and he had done well for an immigrant lad. He owned a store, warehouse, and city lots in Pittsburgh, and was engaged in various entrepreneurial activities. His greatest speculative venture came shortly after Jane's birth when he bought an interest in Wilkinsburg, a village laid out squarely astride the new Philadelphia turnpike east of Pittsburgh. He moved his family to Wilkinsburg, built a big house, opened a store, and waited for the village to grow and for the stream of travelers headed west after the War of 1812 to make him rich.

But however much business enterprise pervaded the Cannon household it was not the core around which the family was organized. Jane's grandmother Scott proudly instructed her on the genealogical intricacies that led back to Scotland and to her Presbyterian forefathers who had signed the Solemn League and Covenant and who, the grandmother claimed, had remained unflinchingly true to it. When she was three years old Jane could recite the bloodlines that carried her past a farmer grandfather who was nonetheless glossed into a gentleman who "rode a high horse, wore spurs, and had Hamilton blood in his veins" (Jane Swisshelm, *Half a Century*).[3] Beyond this grandfather the trail led to Irish heiresses and finally to Lady Jane Grey and royalty. Austere pride was the lesson the grandmother taught the little girl. It is difficult to say whether the pride was for fierce men who had fought for their deepest religious convictions or for a putative connection with the great-granddaughter of Henry VII who was brought to the block after being nine days on the English throne.

An austere piety shaped the Cannon household. The Covenanter traditions brought from Scotland and jealously guarded in the new land permitted no compromise or equivocation. Numerically small, the Covenanters were one of the two distinguishable secessionist sects from Scots Presbyterianism. Their authorized history is the record of contentious men's protests against deviation from the National and the Solemn League and Covenant, and from the Westminister Confession, which above all else demanded that righteous men rule the state. Long after the Cromwellian period the Covenanters were paying a heavy price for their zealous doctrinal purity. They were imprisoned and banished and their congregations withered. Quarreling among themselves as much as they fought unrighteous outsiders, the Covenanters led a rickety existence in America. They were never at peace over doctrinal matters. Schism was so prevalent that once they had no minister in North America. Their purges and counterpurges took such a heavy toll that the only way they could fill their pulpits was to appeal to Scotland and Ireland for new ministers who were pure in the old doctrine. Fitful attempts were made to merge with the other seceding church, the Associate Church, but these were half-consummated unions, for there was always a minority of Covenanters who pulled back at the first smell of compromise. While points of difference were as numerous as intractable, litigious men could devise, the central position the Covenanters never abandoned was the claim that "all power and ability civil rulers have are from Christ the Prophet of the Covenant." Unless the state unequivocally declared itself for God, its powers remained suspect, its laws were open to corruption, and a valid license was given the Covenanters to kick over the traces. Attempted unions between the Covenanter and the Associate churches had failed in 1782 and again in 1789 on this precise point. Both times the Associates were willing to give up the doctrine of the covenanted state. Some of the Covenanters accepted the compromise and slipped off into the amalgamated church. But a minority refused, even at the cost of losing all their ministers. Clinging tenaciously to the doctrine of the covenanted state, they remained outside the union. Pennsylvania was the Covenanters' stronghold. They were weakest in the South where they had always shied away from slavery. In 1800 the Covenanters took an unequivocal stand against slavery, denying communion to any slaveholder. The Northern and Western synods tried to succor the languishing Southern Synod by sending ministers to the southern congregations, but most of them did not stay. "The prevalence of slavery" is the recurring explanation for the Covenanters' failure in the South, and by 1820 the Southern Synod had all but collapsed.

The Covenanters' chosen home was the frontier where they were safe from new, unsound ideas that might corrupt their plain-spoken orthodoxy. Clinging to an outmoded theology and suffering from invidious social distinctions applied to the late-arriving Scots-Irish by the more English Americans, they were defensive, suspicious, and inclined to see devilish conspiracy on the part of their doctrinal opponents. Their congregations were tightly knit clusters of people who tried to keep an old system intact in the face of constant threats of compromise and contamination. If no Covenanter church were nearby for services, it was far better to worship in one's own home than hear heretical ideas coming from another denomination's pulpit.[4]

The Cannons learned this lesson at their own expense. They were *sessioned* for stopping on their way home from their Covenanter congregation to attend a service at an Associate Synod Church. After being disciplined by public rebuke the Cannons were all the more careful with their doctrine and their actions. Work in their home stopped on the Sabbath. Sunday was God's day. Nothing was permitted to distract the family from God's worship and from reflecting upon His wisdom, mercy, justice, and vengeance. The Sunday regimen allowed no coffee-grinding for breakfast, and it was a conscience-troubling event when once the baking had not been done beforehand. Only after much soul-searching did the Cannons light a fire in order to warm some leftover buckwheat cakes. They laid themselves unflinchingly on the Covenanters' "iron bedstead piety."

A volatile combination of sin and pride pervaded the Cannon household. There was the pride of relentlessly pursuing God's commandments and the pride of claiming blood relationships with royalty. The Cannon's Covenanter God sent them careening down a path in which they must despise the world prized by less exalted men, but the family tradition taught them that their rightful heritage included money and power. The unresolvable tension in the Cannon home may be seen in two pictures of Jane Swisshelm. One is a self-portrait; the other is a daguerreotype. Both pictures show a young matron in her twenties, dressed in proper black. Her hair is parted at the middle and pulled down to the back of her neck. But beyond that one would scarcely believe the pictures were of the same person. The difference, of course, is between what the camera saw and what Jane saw as she painted from her mirror's reflection.

The daguerreotype shows a woman quarter-turned from the camera. Her face is triangular; her cheeks slope sharply toward her chin. Her deep-set eyes are slanted and are heavily lidded almost to the pupils. Instantly the most striking feature of her face, her cool gray eyes pierce the distance as though scalpels lay behind them. Her nose is sharp. Her wide mouth goes straight across the face. Her left elbow rests, significantly, on two books, and she holds a sheaf of foolscap in her right hand. Her face is pleasing enough, more angular than round, and there is little doubt that intelligence and force lie behind it. All angles and sharpness, the daguerreotype is the face of a proper daughter of the Covenanters.

The self-portrait also shows a woman with her face quarter-turned, but the head is level. The eyes are wide and round. The face itself is more rectangular than triangular, with the line of the jaw and chin gently rounded. The wide eyes give the impression of openness, even receptivity, and the brows are distinct soft arches. Both lips are full and red. The face is serene and soft and, perhaps, regal. A white scarf falls in gentle curves between the breasts.

The God of Jane's fathers could not regard her as anything other than "a worm in the dust . . . a subject of punishment." The Covenanters were, Jane said, humble and self-distrustful. "I was almost fifteen when I overheard a young lady say I was growing pretty. I went to my mirror and spent some moments in unalloyed happiness and triumph. Then I thought, Pretty face, the worms will eat you. All the prettiest girls I know are silly, but you shall not make a fool of me. Helen's beauty ruined Troy. Cleopatra was a wretch. So if you are pretty *I* will be master, remember that."

Yet when she painted her picture she portrayed a woman who is soft, sensuous, attractive and by no stretch of the imagination self-destructfully humble. The level and confident eyes befit the daughter of Scots-Irish heiresses and men riding prancing horses, who (though they were invented from the whole cloth) laid claim on the world and its delights. Try as she might Jane could never escape the tension of desiring both the world and heaven. "My soul," she said, "is a Shunamite, a company of two armies, and wherever there is one, there is strife."[5]

In the Cannon home the antithetical desires for the world and for heaven were brought together, and the lessons derived from them were continually on display for the children. But there was never any doubt which lesson was primary. Even as the grandmother told her tales of the Scots nobility, she also told the story of the total depravity of man. When the children's questions took her outside the realm of the family's history her answers invariably came from the Bible. She simply looked up an appropriate passage and read it to them. Scripture as interpreted by Covenanter doctrine was the arbiter of all things.

Sinfulness was man's condition, and the imperfect world was his estate. Man's fate was his predetermined failure to bring his life into accord with God's perfection, and however relentlessly the Cannons pursued the Divine Law they were always confronted by the evidence of their shortcomings. For all of their attempts to keep the Sabbath holy there came times when, as a result of their own negligence, the cooking fire had to be lighted.

In the Covenanter Church there was a ceremony called "fencing the table." The minister led the congregation in an examination of conscience in order to determine their fitness to come to the communion table. He repeated the Ten Commandments, stopping at each to prohibit any who had broken it from coming forward. When he came to the eighth commandment he paused, then proceeded with this formula, "I debar from this holy table of the Lord all slave-holders and horse-thieves, and other dishonest people."

As a young child Jane watched the table being "fenced" and heard the uncompromising ban laid on slaveholders.

When she wrote *Half a Century*, the first reason Swisshelm gave for undertaking her autobiography was to show that abolition had not "originated in Infidelity," nor was it a "triumph of skepticism over Christianity." Abolition was, she claimed, Christian to its core, a divinely appointed war against sin in which no quarter was given. She then produced her life's work as proof of her proposition and grounded that work in the Covenanter church.

As a child she had read Revelations. But John preached the apocalypse, not the gospel. In the Revelations, God's predetermined judgment rides the wings of avenging angels, and in His own good time it comes crashing down upon the world in a holocaust. The picture John paints of the postmillennial new Jerusalem provides no place for gentle pietism and humanitarian compassion. They are as far removed from his eschatology as Death's pale horse is from the Lamb. Sinfulness perishes before the cut and thrust of righteousness' sword, and woe to him whose deeds have placed him in front of the sweeping blade.

What the young girl made of John's revelations remains obscure. We must content ourselves with her comment that John's account of the millennial apocalypse was her favorite literature when she was a child, and with the knowledge that it was easy for the Covenanters to identify with John's martyred remnant. But as we search for the roots of Jane's career as a brilliant polemicist we cannot neglect the message that John proclaims. In the wars of the righteous the tongue is a powerful weapon. Words slay men.

The end of the Napoleonic wars brought economic depression to America. Men investing in a war prosperity and allowing themselves to be drawn in deeper by the prospects of a peacetime exploitation of the New West, found themselves overextended. Thomas Cannon was one of these suffering investors.[6] His holding in the speculative village of Wilkinsburg disappeared in a tangle of contested land mortgages. All he had to show for his five-year effort was a house built on land to which he had no valid title. When the Wilkinsburg bubble burst he moved his family back to Pittsburgh. After he died in 1823 creditors tied up his estate in legal proceedings. To help support the family, Jane and her brother William were put to work. The recurring theme in Jane's memories of these years is that the law existed to make life more difficult for the widow and her children. Their hard circumstances were consequences of a state that had refused to make the contract with God, as Covenanter doctrine demanded. In the aftermath of her father's death the meaning of living in an uncovenanted state was difficult for the little girl to escape.

In time the family regained possession of the Wilkinsburg house and property; Mary Cannon reopened the store; and a way was found to send Jane to boarding school. Her schoolmates named her Wax Doll and, according to her account, she quickly made a spectacular success for herself. She easily out-performed her classmates. She sketched better than the drawing master, recited poetry for the benefit of the older girls, and was offered board and tuition if she would teach the younger ones. But after only six weeks Jane was called home to Wilkinsburg. Frail and undersized, she suffered from a persistent cough that the doctors diagnosed as the symptom of incipient tuberculosis. Thomas Cannon and four Cannon children had died from the disease, and Elizabeth, Jane's surviving sister, was suspected of having it. Mary Cannon was determined to save those who were left. She prescribed fresh air, a convalescent diet of dairy foods and vegetables, and a carefully supervised exercise program for her two daughters. The girls exercised with dumbells and were taught dancing though it was forbidden by the Covenanters.

As the battle against tuberculosis was being fought, the family was plunged into the courts again. This time Mary Cannon's father's estate was at issue. His executors proposed to sell off the property and bring affairs to an end. Mary Cannon intervened, had the executors dismissed, and had an arrangement made whereby she administered the estate. In her attempts to rehabilitate her family's health and fortunes, she faltered only once. Her "conscience was worked upon [by] the holy men of the church who furnished . . . advice." She succumbed to their demand that William, the son, be apprenticed to a cabinetmaker. William subsequently ran away, headed west, where he died, a victim, Jane said, of "authority."

Jane's recollections of William run like a bright thread through her autobiography. He is never overwhelming enough to crowd her off the center of the stage, but he is one of the two men she remembered most affectionately and vividly from her childhood. The other man was her long-time minister, the Reverend John Black. Between the two men Jane established an unspoken dialogue in which she suggested another dimension to the polarities within her.

Her minister John Black, a man of many parts and accomplishments, was exiled from Ireland for being implicated in the insurrection of 1797. A graduate of the University of Glasgow, sometime professor at the University of Pennsylvania, and minister of the Covenanter church in Pittsburgh, Black was master of the Covenanter congregations west of the Alleghenies. He was the hope of the Covenanters as they made their thrust toward the Ohio Valley in the early years of the nineteenth century. For over thirty years he was peerless in his leadership from Philadelphia to the western reaches of the "Ohio congregation." After outlining Black's life and listing his achievements, the covenanters' official historian, exhausting his superlatives, rested his case with, "He was a great man." [7]

When the Cannons made their first move to Wilkinsburg they went reluctantly because it meant giving up regular attendance at his church. When they returned to Pittsburgh after the Wilkinsburg failure they came heartened because they were returning to the great man's fold. To the young girl studying him Sunday after Sunday, year after year, he represented the finest flowering of the Covenanter tradition. Martyr to conscience and liberty, learned, a brilliant speaker, Black was the embodiment of force and grace. He never, unlike every other man she met, gave her reason to believe there was a flaw in him. "He seemed always to talk to *me*." It was John Black who "fenced the table" and denied the sacrament to any slaveholder. Jane said that whatever ability she had for distinguishing between truth and error was largely attributable to him. And if Black's message of pristine Calvanism was harsh and uncompromising, his authority was also uncompromised and eagerly accepted.

While William was confirming his rebelliousness, repudiating not only his mother's reluctant decision to force him in an apprenticeship, but also what underlay it, the advice of the church elders, Jane joined the Covenanter church. Now, at fifteen years of age, the signs of womanhood were on her. Having reached the age of accountability her mother matter-of-factly put the question to her: Was she not ready to join the church and take communion? "Not another word was said and the subject was never again broached between us, but here," Jane said, "a great conflict began."

Jane believed according to the Covenanter faith, but she was nevertheless troubled. Did she have, she asked herself, a "saving faith," or did she, "like the devils, believe and tremble?" But if she was saved it was at the cost of accepting the terrors of the world as being altogether righteous. They were part of God's inexplicable will and plan for mankind. She would be obliged to accept the "justice" of her father's death and, more excruciating, William's damnation. But "I could not be willing that William should be lost. . . . I was not willing that any should be lost. I could not stay in heaven and know that anyone was enduring endless torments in some other place! I must leave and go to their relief. . . . My whole soul flew in open revolt." She could not submit to the doctrine of damnation. "How should I find this acceptance with my heart full of rebellion?" she asked.

Jane went sleepless as she read Covenanter theology for the signs of a saving faith as distinguished from the evidences of self-deception. She read Ralph Erskine, the eighteenth-century Scottish theologian, preacher, and controversialist, whose *Belief Not Fancy* had been reprinted in Philadelphia in 1805 with money raised by Covenanter subscribers. Jane read *Belief Not Fancy* until she became "unable to think." She thought that "even the devils of hell were drinking cool water" while she was being forced through this torment. Then in the manner of federal theology she

worked her way around the proposition of an irrational God imposing His inexplicable will on the world. She proposed a bargain to
God. For His part God would bring her into the saintly fold. He
would likewise bring William into the fold. Then God could do with
her what he pleased. For her part of the bargain Jane said, "I would
be content to spend my whole life in any labor he [sic] should ap-
point without a sign of the approval of God or man, if in the end, I
and mine should be found among [the elect]." After proposing her
bargain to God she fell asleep in "perfect peace." When she awoke
she knew that the bargain had been struck, her vow had been
ratified. Several days thereafter she played the saint. She said that
she read a biography of Jonathan Edwards, kept a rigorous schedule
of prayer and meditation, and let all of her housework go by the
boards until her mother reprimanded her. Then, "I dropped my
roll [sic] of saintship, and went and washed the dishes."

Her comic descent from sainthood is a device by which Jane in-
tends to show her rejection of the Covenanters' "iron bedstead piety," but as much as she railed at some of the Covenanters' practices, she never denied their God. She stayed in the church all her
life (PV, April 13, 1850).

Jane had worked her way through Erskine's careful distinctions
between misleading "imagination" and supraworldly perceptions
of Christ. She believed she possessed the latter, and nothing would
ever shake that belief. All her life she claimed that she was secure in
the arms of her Covenanter God. But her security was purchased
by her admission that unqualified temporal love was God's enemy.
The imagination that Erskine warned his readers about was "the
seat of [temporal] love" as well as the cause of man's misapprehen-
sion of God. Unless all love were subordinated to one's love for
God, disaster was in the offing. Jane and her mother agreed that
James Cannon had died because they loved him too much. They
believed that William's rebellion against the Eternal Decrees and
his subsequent death was God's punishment for their loving him
too much. But when love drove one to excess it was possible to
retrieve the situation. One might pledge oneself anew to God's
work, promising to toil at the labor for which the faithful were
appointed, the creation of the covenanted nation.

Jane's autobiographical account races through the next several years. Time and life seem frozen for her. She is scarcely in motion, either physically or psychologically. She gives the impression that she never set foot outside Wilkinsburg. She taught school, a subscription school that she organized. She found the work congenial, and she abolished corporal punishment, the feature of her teaching experience that gave her the most satisfaction. She found hypocrisy in her church. Staunchly opposed to dancing, the Covenanters condoned quilting bees at which, without the forbidden music, partners stepped through quadrilles and ended with "promiscuous kissing." Jane was derisive of the church that allowed no dancing but permitted "plenty of kissing and rude wrestling to overcome the delicacy of women who objected to such desecration."

Except for the recollection of a few such episodes, these years all but vanish from her account of her life.

Jane came to maturity from a history and a social experience fairly typical of her time, but which, paradoxically, placed her out of the mainstream of American life. She was born in a contentious dissenting tradition; the family and the sect believed themselves God's beleaguered remnant. There is much self-righteous alienation running through Covenanters' accounts of themselves. With aggressive defensiveness they tried to conserve a seventeenth-century tradition in a society that was constantly demanding change and accommodations from them.

This summary of Jane at eighteen is accurate enough (given the surviving evidence) except for two particulars, her situation in the Covenanter church and her maturing sexuality. Both were important in preparing her for her subsequent career and in turning her toward abolition and woman's rights. And they are critical to an explanation of why her operations took the forms they did.

In 1833, the year Jane was eighteen, the Covenanter communion split in two wings, the Old Lights and the New Lights. Jane and her family followed their pastor, John Black, into the new school. The New Lights refused to reaffirm the traditional position that the Covenanters had formally affirmed with their 1806 "Testimony." The Testimony held that the Constitution of the United States was "immoral" on two counts, because of its "willful omission" of God and Christ and the Word of God as the "Supreme Law of nations and civil government," and because it sanctioned human slavery.[8]

As a child Jane had been catechized on the Testimony of 1806, and John Black had preached it without reservation. But after the War of 1812 the Covenanters' doctrinal cohesiveness became increasingly difficult to preserve, especially in the Upper Ohio Valley, the Covenanter stronghold. In an expanding society sectarians had to be exceedingly doctrinaire to remain insensitive to the worldly possibilities that political activity opened up for them. As early as 1821 the question of Covenanters' political participation was roundly debated in the synod, and Jane's recollection of the 1824 election makes it plain that the Cannons were partisans in Pittsburgh politics in the early twenties.

The Covenanters' Old Light historian was careful to keep the question of the schism squarely on the issue of doctrinal purity, but it was no accident that the centers of schism were the towns and cities, and that Pittsburgh, a booming entrepôt for the Midwest and the home of rising commercial and manufacturing interests, was the city in which the schismatic leadership was concentrated. In the election of 1824 the Cannons supported John Quincy Adams who was leading the wing of the old Republican party that was friendly to the claims of status, deference, and the systematic economic development of the nation. An aggressive Jacksonianism, though committed to helping the Pennsylvania metals industry, was opposed by the Cannons' circle, and that hostility was transmitted to the youngsters in the family. Jane's memory of the children's shrill partisanship—their belief that the Devil himself lived in the Jacksonian newspaper office—provides ample proof that the Covenanter communion was splitting on something other than doctrine alone.

When the question of participation in politics finally broke church polity in 1833, the schismatics took the position that the Constitution was a proper covenant between man and God.[9] They meant to use political power to obtain the ends they sought; whatever they did would be accomplished through the instruments of the law and the Constitution. Both were now binding on the New Lights.

One of the anomalies of Jane Swisshelm's life is that she moved to militant dissent and reform along a path markedly different from that followed by the typical antebellum militant, the "come-outer." For the come-outers, the characteristic pattern was to perceive sin and immorality in the traditions and institutions into which they had been born, then having been awakened to immorality, they came out of the traditions they believed held them in complicity with the sinful practice of an evil institution. Like Thoreau, they signed off. The Covenanters' Calvinism never allowed them to move in the direction of perfectionism on the model of such people as Henry Wright, William Lloyd Garrison, and Nathaniel Rogers, but their 1806 stand on immoral government anticipates the Garrisonian formula, "The Constitution is a covenant with death and an agreement with hell." In effect, Jane was a believer in a Garrisonian doctrine before there was such a thing; by the time it began to develop she was moving in the opposite direction. Following John Black's authority and the lead of the elder Cannons and Scotts Jane reversed the typical movement to militant reform and wound up fighting "sin" with the weapon ostensibly repudiated by the anti-institutionalists; party politics. In order for her to do this she and the New Light Covenanters had to invest politics with the most compelling moral content, and they had to give their allegiance to the Constitution, accepting it as a legitimate, binding covenant. The uprooting of allegiance was something that could not be done easily or without profound consequences. The most forceful lesson of her childhood had been in her stiff-necked forebears' refusal to compromise on the moral state. In order to remain faithful to the idea of the covenanted nation they were willing to become a leaderless remnant struggling for their survival as an identifiable sect. But now she was asked to follow her conscience in the direction that previously only self-serving and misguided brethren had taken: toward compromise and acquiescence in sin and immorality.

No doubt John Black's lead and the position of her family satisfied her and made for an easy accommodation, but there was another aspect to the matter. Jane gives the first clue to it with her recollection of the 1824 election. The Jacksonian newspaper office was given a wide berth because it was literally the abode of the devil. The Cannons had diabolized a particular political faction. They had not, as they should if they were clinging to pure Covenanter doctrine, diabolized all political factions. The difference cleared the way for the young woman to reject the distinctive claim her church made in behalf of its members—that they must abjure all politics—and enabled her to follow her beloved pastor, John Black, in 1833.

Diabolizing only one political party permitted the New Light conscience to reconcile compromise. Locating the devil in the party of the opponents cleared the conscience. Purity was maintained at the same time political activity was undertaken. The consequence was to pour a self-justifying moral imperative into one's own partisanship. The result was to make politics an apocalyptic struggle. It was war to the knife and the knife to the hilt. No quarter was asked and none would be given. The end comes only with annihilation of the satanic.

Of the other particularity about Jane at eighteen—her sexuality—little can be done with the subject but assume it, not assert it with any detail. Reticent in the manner of the nineteenth century about such matters, she provides in her autobiography only the most fleeting glimpses of herself as a sexually maturing woman. What may be safely asserted is the direction her sexuality was taking her, for here her record is more helpful.

She fantasied with romantic stories and struck attitudes of sexually sumptuous Helens and Cleopatras in front of her bedroom mirror. But she was driven away from the quilting parties by the amorous swains who wanted to make her a partner in those weekly wrestling and kissing matches. Her imagination told her there were better prizes: somewhere there was a "handsomely dressed ... grave ... seignor. A Russian count in a New York drawing room. ... The man of giant strength in full suit of black, riding a large spirited black horse. ... My black knight." So she must wait.

Whatever demands her libido was making lie in the realm of speculation. The only help Jane provides comes through inference. She liked to dance, the church rule notwithstanding. She objected to the wrestling and kissing at the quilting parties, but she was put off by the rough promiscuity more than the kissing itself. The only direct comment she ever made about her sexuality was simple but illuminating. When in middle age she abandoned her husband and opened the way for his divorce action, she accepted "the legal penalty—a life of celibacy."

We may assume that Jane grew into womanhood anticipating marriage with pleasure. But her husband must appear as romantic lover. There is little in the meagre sources to support the image of a militant feminist in the making, but there is ample substance in her fantasy to explain Jane's acrid recollection of the Wilkinsburg quadrilles: "Male and female partners keeping time to the music of their own voices, and making a denouement every few moments by some man kissing some woman, perhaps in a dark hall, or some woman kissing some man, or some man kissing all the women, or *vice versa.*" It is her sensibility that is offended. Her sensuousness and her eagerness to play a conventional female role remain intact awaiting the Black Knight.

Jane's inability to disencumber herself from fantasy is best seen by reading the account of her relationship with James Swisshelm in her autobiography. She could not, even in the closing years of her life, give a consistent picture of her former husband.

She begins their story as splendid romance. James rescues her and a wagonload of girls who are on an outing. A stormy night comes on, and the girls are trapped by a flooding river. Appearing out of the dark, James takes over the fractious team from the ineffectual driver, saving horses, wagon, and passengers. Once they escape from the river, James brings them to his home to dry out before his blazing living-room fire while he himself lurks in the shadows. Then, anonymous and black as the night out of which he so suddenly appeared, he sends them on their way with a "low, contemptuous but good-humored laugh." The episode is surrounded by "an air of enchanted castles, brigands, ghosts, [and] witches." With that, James vanishes from her story. Seven years later the anonymous young savior suddenly reappears at one of the raffish quadrilles where he "came and took possession of his prospective property [herself] with the air of a man who understood his business." It is here that Jane places a heavy demand on her reader's credulity. Everything that has gone before in the autobiography, although strained through the double filters of memory and selective arrangement, is at least plausible. But when she comes to James much of what she wrote does not make sense.

For two generations the Swisshelms had lived in the neighborhood. The family owned over six hundred acres of rich meadow and bottomland and a prerevolutionary gristmill and sawmill that, because of their connection with Braddock's campaign against Fort Dusquene, were local historical monuments. Ardent and well-to-do Methodists, the Swisshelms had built the local Methodist church out of their own pockets, and their home was the headquarters for Methodist preachers riding the circuit. Yet Jane would have us believe that in the tiny community of Wilkinsburg she remained blissfully ignorant of the identity of her knightly rescuer. The eldest son of the one of the leading families in the township, he went about for years identifying her as the woman he would bring to the altar and someday make mistress of Swissvale, the family home. She claims that he was so strange and foreign to her, she whose tongue delighted in the difficult sound of Old Testament names, that his name was not only unknown, it was unpronounceable.

She brings James into her autobiography as sheer fiction. Character is swiftly sketched in. The bases for conflict are laid, and it takes Jane less than a paragraph to get fully in her story: "My sister hated him, and my mother doubted him. . . . His family were the leading Methodists of the township [and] the income and energy of the family were expended in propagating a faith which we believed false. A marriage with him would be incongruous and bring misery to both." Two years later, November 18, 1836—she bridges the interval in one sentence—they were married and living at Swissvale. The day after the wedding they had a wrangling dispute that left Jane in tears.

In this short passage we are confronted by a writer who knows what she is about. With the greatest economy and simplicity Jane leads us to the central fact of her life, her relationship with James. A skillful writer working from a creative impulse seems to be shaping the materials of character and conflict into dramatic form. Furthermore, she apparently understands that the most satisfying conflict is ambiguous conflict; therefore James is never altogether in the wrong. In many ways he is admirable, and there is never a time when his case is prima facie bad. This handling of James is doubly intriguing because of Jane's unequivocal assignment of moral values and moral roles to all the people who appear in *Half a Century*, and because of a disinterested court record.

One of the leading nineteenth-century cases dealing with married women's property rights is *Swisshelm* v. *Swisshelm*. It was an incredibly tangled affair for which the court report does not attempt more than an outline. The report shows that James Swisshelm was quite probably a liar, cheat, and perjurer who attempted to swindle Jane out of property worth thousands of dollars. Only a portion of the Pennsylvania Supreme Court's opinion is necessary to make the point: "Taking the evidence in the most favorable point of view for the defendant [James], it would appear that he originally intended to strip his brother [of the land], but on discovering his wife's title, it became necessary to strip her." [10]

Yet Jane abruptly ended *Half a Century* when she came to the suit. On the last page she says that her old friend Edwin Stanton, the secretary of war, advised her to open the suit. Then she stops. She is unable to go the next step and lead the perfidious James out into the open. All she had to do was to quote the court record. Enough of the tawdry story was there in bald legal prose to satisfy anyone that the laws relating to married women's property rights were atrocious, and that James was a husband that only a wife determined upon immolation should be obliged to suffer. "No court of law or equity," the opinion says, "could ever permit so gross an abuse of the marriage relation." It was a splendid opportunity for her to bring out her talents for railing at hypocrisy and plain wrong-doing, and she was provided with a dramatic and telling culmination for one of the theses of her book, that woman's rights was founded on nothing other than a demand for simple justice. But she lay down her weapons and turned away.

Jane's difficulty with James in *Half a Century*, her inability to sort out her feelings toward him, to rage convincingly at him, and finally, to destroy him with the testimony in *Swisshelm* v. *Swisshelm*, raises perplexing questions about their relationship and their marriage. In the autobiography she was able to make the curt, summary judgment, "Our marriage had been a mistake, productive of mutual injury." But before she finished the passage she was rushing on unmindful of syntax or grammar, of which she was usually careful, "Knew his rights, and knowing sought to maintain them against me; while, in some respects, he was to me incalculably more than just." Time and again as Jane recounts an episode of their interminable conflict she interjects a qualifier. "But for" someone's intervention or influence the difficulty between them would have been resolved, or would have never arisen. It is as though neither she nor James was directly responsible for what happened to them. The finger of blame is always pointed outside the marriage.

The marriage went badly from the beginning and got no better as time passed. Apparently hopeful promises followed outbursts and recriminations, after which came attempts to patch things up, but the peace was always short-lived. Very quickly in *Half a Century* Jane lets it be known that the chief disrupter of the peace was Elizabeth Swisshelm, James's mother. There is a devastating sketch of her in the book, wiry, saturnine, "eagle faced," she is a domineering termagant.

Jane got on well enough with her aged father-in-law, and William, one of the younger brothers, who seems to have been a rather feckless, sweet-tempered young man, emerged as her open ally. Without a scrap of contemporary evidence it is impossible to do more than suggest the development of the relationships within the family, but it is evident that there was a lot of taking sides and some rather merciless undercutting going on from the beginning. In the course of time the Swisshelms divided into two warring factions, each of which struggled for the slightest leverage to use against the other.

Clues to the story are in *Swisshelm* v. *Swisshelm*. William Swisshelm incurred some large debts and defaulted on some promissory notes he had given to secure them. His creditors got judgments against him and were preparing to sue him. Jane bailed William out of his difficulty by lending him money to pay his creditors. In return William mortgaged to her his interest in the Swisshelm estate,

an equal share of which he would inherit with his brothers following his mother's death.

For some reason, it is not clear in the court record, William
either did not pay his debts or else he neglected to get back the
promissory notes after he had paid them. James secretly bought the
notes with the help of a conniving lawyer, who was the ostensible
buyer. Debtor proceedings were then initiated against William,
and the business culminated in a sheriff's sale, covertly arranged so
that there were no other bidders for the notes, the value of which
depended upon attaching William's future inheritance. In effect
James was bidding against himself for William's inheritance, which
was mortgaged to Jane. Behind James, as the court record clearly
shows, stood Elizabeth Swisshelm. Whether James plotted the affair with his mother's assistance or whether she herself conceived
the scheme with James being her henchman is a question that was
outside the judge's concern, so the court made no attempt to answer it. But from the fragmentary details the court record leaves
this much is certain: before Jane's marriage had run its course the
passions unleashed were so violent that a mother and son attempted to destroy another son's reputation and cheat him out of
his patrimony; and a husband, in league with his mother, skirted
the edges of criminal culpability in order to, using the the dis-
passionate phrase of the court, "strip" his wife of her property.
Beyond this the story is impenetrable, but it is no accident that the
most caustic portrait in *Half a Century* is Elizabeth Swisshelm's.
On the contrary, James is unfailingly presented as a husband who
"knew his rights and . . . sought to maintain them." So far as James
is concerned, the law is identified as the real culprit and oppressor;
it allowed him his "rights." He was neither worse nor "much better
than the average man." And Jane wrote this in the face of the
court's—the "law's"—own words in *Swisshelm* v. *Swisshelm*.

Before a year had passed, the Swisshelm marriage was on the
edge of disaster. James reneged on his promise not to interfere with
Jane's religion. He and his mother pressed her to convert to
Methodism, and they attempted to persuade her to become a lay
preacher. There were some furious sessions at Swissvale with
James, Elizabeth, and visiting Methodist preachers all belaboring

her with biblical quotations supporting their arguments. They pursued her like an "English parson did a fox," but she was, she said, like "granite." Of the Methodist preachers she wrote, "I believe there was not at that time a member of the Pittsburgh Conference who was a college graduate, few who had even a good, common school education, while two of those who preached in our meeting-house and were frequent guests in the family, were unable to read."

They are all presented as foils for her superiority, and the superiority of her own social traditions. It was she who introduced books into the Swisshelm family. Her minister, John Black, with his academic accomplishments, towers over the half-literate circuit riders. Her Covenanter ancestry is invoked—"my kith and kin died at the stake bearing testimony"—to support her in her refusal to "give myself to the Lord, help them save souls [and] preach [their] Mental Pablum."

The first year of marriage ended with the couple living apart. James stayed at Swissvale. Jane was established at Wilkinsburg in a little house where she provided meals for workmen in one of James's small businesses. He visited her once a week. The autobiography gives an account of bitter disappointment. "I shuddered to think that it had come to this in one short year."

Mary Cannon had at first stayed out of the controversy on the grounds that it was a "church-joining conflict" in which only God might guide and help her daughter, but finally she intervened and urged Jane to give up the marriage and come home to her. But this Jane refused to do. She told her mother that "all would be well." She understood, she said, the cause of her troubles. God was "scouraging me [for] making an idol and bowing down before it—for loving my husband." She gave her mother the same reason that they had used to explain the deaths of Thomas and William Cannon. As in the earlier instances when she had loved too much, Jane believed that she was suffering affliction from a jealous God. It was "all just," but she would not diminish her love for James.

Regardless of his faults and whatever disappointments he may have brought her, he was still her Black Knight. Her suffering was not "through any fault of his." God might "slay" her, but she would not give up her marriage. She bargained with James for a reconciliation. If he would allow her to remain a Presbyterian she would be like "wax" in all other matters. She told James she was now ready to "dig potatoes, pick apples and feed the cows like any common Pennsylvania farm woman," which she had earlier refused to do. "I must be the mate of the man I had chosen; and if he would not come to my level, I must go to his." She read nothing but the Bible, the only book James read. She stopped painting. She "resolutely crucified" herself.

The inevitable explosion came about three months later. Mary and Elizabeth Cannon moved back to Pittsburgh, leaving Jane alone in Wilkinsburg among the Swisshelms. As the winter wore on she became sick and bedridden. Elizabeth Swisshelm sent food to the little house, but Jane refused to eat it and returned the unopened hampers to Swissvale. In the spring of 1838 there was "a fearful crisis." Jane begged James to take her away from Wilkinsburg, and in June, 1838, they traveled down the Ohio River to Louisville, Kentucky, where James planned to enter a business already established by his brother Samuel. At Louisville, Jane hoped she and James would make a fresh start.

The Louisville account of the Swisshelm's life, two chapters in *Half a Century*, comes like a gratuitous anachronism. The narrative thread is almost broken. James virtually disappears, and Jane herself becomes more a passive reporter than an active participant in her own story. Written toward 1880, these two chapters are an antislavery tract, a brilliant epitome of the abolition indictment of slavery, yet at first glance curiously out of place in her autobiography. It is as though the old warhorse polemicist had had her memory stirred by the sound of muted trumpets and was returning once again to the battle.

She gets off to a contradictory start. After announcing that "Louisville was largely settled by Northern people, and was to prove an oasis in the desert of slavery," she and James step off the steamboat and are immediately plunged into a slave society.

Coming up from the docks on the way to their boardinghouse, she notices an inordinate number of men loafing on porches and street corners. Why were so many men "off work in the after-noon. . . ? How did they come to be standing around on corners and doorsteps by the hundreds, like crows on a cornfield fence . . . those fellows in shining black broadcloth, each with a stove-pipe hat on the side of his head, his thumbs in the arm holes of a satin vest, displaying a wonderful glimmer of gold chain and diamond stud, balancing himself first on his heels and then on his toes, as he rolled a cigar from one side of his mouth to the other?"

The rhetorical question is immediately answered. They were the "advance guard of a great army of woman-whippers which stretched away back to the Atlantic, and around the shores of the Gulf of Mexico. . . . They were out on duty as a staring brigade, whose business it was to insult every woman who ventured on the street without a male protector, by a stare so lascivious as could not be imagined on the American free soil."

Thus even before she and James arrive at their lodgings Jane has taken the measure of the slave society. Rich from the commerce of slave labor, and unsated by the dark pleasures they have taken among the slave women, the southern men are on the streets in their gold, diamonds, and satin offending chaste ladies. The only other signs of life are rickety wagons and spavined horses driven by ragged drivers. It requires three horses to pull every wagon, each of which, Jane said, could be put in a single-horse Pittsburgh dray and hauled away, load and all. Nothing else is seen on the walk from the wharves to the boardinghouse. Nothing else needs to be seen to set the stage and make the case. The air is heavy with violence and sensuality. The breeze slatting up toward the Ohio carries the odor of captive female flesh abused by lash and libido. The city wears a ruff of gaudy prosperity over an emaciated economy. The remain-der of the Louisville story is simply an illustration and extension of these themes.

Across the street from the Swisshelm's boardinghouse lives a "Northern mudsill." He owns one slave, a woman, who is less a housekeeper than a broodmare. She produces children, his own, whom he sells as they come to marketable age. Jane learns that the first time he sold a child he had to flog the mother because she "took on so." After the first beating she has become "reasonable" and makes no disturbances as the other children are taken off by slave traders.

Jane's landlady tells her the story of her bachelor uncle. As a young man he fell in love with his father's slave, Liza, a "tall handsome quadroon." But Liza spurned him because she loved another slave, Jo. Driven by his passion for Liza, the young master ordered Jo strung up and flogged, with Liza being forced to watch the bloody proceedings. "This was done three times, then Jo was sold, and Liza herself [was then] bound to the whipping post, and lashed until she yielded, and became the mother of . . . two beautiful boys.

Jane sees little boys on the streets wearing iron collars studded with spikes. A mistress nails her cook to a fence with a ten-penny nail. A father sells his "educated, refined" daughter and she is "lashed by her brutal purchaser, once, and again and again for chastity." And so on.

Although the greatest threat and violence exists for the slaves, Jane learns that she, too, can suffer at the hands of the woman-whippers. Outspoken with her own views on slavery—"I never thrust my anti-slavery opinions on any one [sic], but every Southerner inquired concerning them, and I gave true answers"—she is often led to the brink of trouble. In the boardinghouse parlor she is threatened with tar and feathers. A Mississippi planter gently cautions her, "Indeed, madam, it is not safe for you to talk as you do." She retorts that the Constitution guarantees the right of freedom of speech. The planter replies, "There is no danger in Pennsylvania from freedom of speech, but if people were allowed to talk as you do here, it would overthrow our institutions." She makes friends with a Negro family and tries to open a school for their children. Under the threat of violence it is closed after the first day. She finds that she is virtually declassed when she sets herself up as a modiste. "To a white woman in Louisville, work was a dire disgrace." On all counts she has become a pariah.

Before she is finished telling what went on in Louisville, Jane has touched all the bases of the abolition critique of slavery. The unbridled power of the slavemaster is exposed, the brutalization of the slave is illustrated, the pervading sexuality is revealed, the denigration of free labor is demonstrated, the churches are shown to be corrupt, the thesis of the slave power conspiring to take over the federal government is developed, and northern guilt-by-association is proposed. In the microcosm of Louisville she finds that there are no portions of American society that remain unsullied or unthreatened by slavery, and she in her own person has individualized most of them. Nothing is safe or sacred.

She is propositioned twice. "And old and wealthy citizen" offers her the use of his carriage and theater box. The liaison is proposed so subtly that she is not aware of what has been suggested. Her friend, a "Virginia Fitzhugh" who understands the ways of the proprietors in a slave society, has to come springing to her feet "with burning cheeks and flashing eyes" to tell her what really has happened. The second time, Jane is walking alone in front of her boardinghouse taking the night air. "A man overtook me, cleared his throat as if to speak, and passed on to the lamp-post, which had made one limit of my walk. I did not shorten my path, and when I came up to the post he again cleared his throat as if to speak, and next time stepped out, lifted his hat, and remarked:

"'A very pleasant evening, Miss.'
I stopped, looked at him, and said:
'It is a very pleasant evening; had you not better walk on and enjoy it?'
He bowed low, and answered:
'I beg your pardon, madam. I was mistaken.'
'Pardon for what, sir? It is a very pleasant evening; please to pass on.'"

There is a final episode that thrusts Jane directly in the path of a woman-whipper and enables her, true to form, to take his measure. She wants a servant. A "Kentucky gentleman" comes to tell her that he has a slave woman he will let out for hire: "'A good cook, good washah and ironah, fust-rate housekeepah! I'll let you have ah for two hundred dollahs a yeah; but I'll tell you honest, you'll have to hosswhipah youahself about twice a wekk.' While he talked I looked. His suit was of the finest black broadcloth, satin vest, a pompous display of chain, seals, studs and rings, his beaver on the back of his head, his thumbs in the arms of his vest, and feet spread like the Collossus [sic] of Rhodes."

Nowhere in her book does Swisshelm write better than in these two chapters. Some of the accounts are reminiscent of the free-swinging comic style of the great frontier humorists. Her moralizing slave vignettes are without a shred of distinction. The story of the flogged and crucified female slave is cut from standard abolition cloth, as are the stories about the father selling his daughter and the mudsill northerner who breeds his illegitimate children for the slave market. But when she takes the slaves out of her story and has the slaveholding gentry, especially the men, come in direct confrontation with her, that is, when she writes from personal indignation rather than from conventional pieties, she is superb. Before she can become truly effective, it is she, not the slaves, who must be in the transaction with the masters and mistresses. It seems that her contemptuous comic response to Louisville slavery is not so much in the slaves' behalf as it is for herself.

What actually happened to Jane in Louisville is almost impossible to say in any detail, for she provides only a few clues. The intent of the two chapters in *Half a Century* dealing with Louisville—"Habitations of Horrid Cruelty" and "Kentucky Contempt for Labor"—is to indict slavery after-the-fact. But it is doubtful that slavery was her chief concern while she was living there, or that she was an outspoken enemy of the slaveholders. She represents the fiery Virginian Fitzhugh as a personal friend, and both she and James worked hard to make places for themselves in the Louisville commercial community. Nor does her account of the Louisville period, the summer of 1838 to the summer of 1839, end with an expected and conventional pledge to strike slavery however possible. It concludes with a rebellion, but it was not against the women whippers; it was against her husband.

Jane had gone to Louisville in triumph. At last, it seemed, she had wrested James away from Swissvale and Elizabeth Swisshelm, but a heavy price had been exacted for her victory. She was in an unsettled mental and physical condition; perhaps she was on the verge of a breakdown. Regardless of her objections to slavery, they were not sufficient to give her pause to consider an alternative to Louisville. Her iterated phrase is "to the woods," or to the "poorest cabin," as refuges from Wilkinsburg and Swissvale. Whether "the woods" or "the cabin" was in a free community or a slave society was immaterial to her. Jane went to a slave society without any qualms about compromising what abolition principles she held.

What was at stake for her was her own freedom, and James's, and if that could be gained at the cost of living in the midst of slavery, it seemed a small price to pay. Any doubts she may have had on this score were removed by pretending that Louisville was "an oasis in the desert of slavery."

The Swisshelms went to Louisville expecting James to help expand his brother Samuel's trading business. But there was difficulty from the beginning. Deflation following the Panic of 1837 was deranging the economy, and business failures were common throughout the country. The economic pinch was intensified on the Louisville commercial operators because their rivals in Cincinnati were warring for hegemony on the Ohio and for portions of the Kentucky interior itself.[11] Furthermore, there was apparently some sort of difficulty between the brothers, because James soon left the joint venture and was in business for himself.

He worked from trading boats plying the rivers. His travels carried him as far as Little Rock, Arkansas. Jane was left to occupy her days and evenings as she was able, and to muse over the vagaries of life that took James away from his mother but brought him no closer to herself. But the economic squeeze forced her out of the boardinghouse. To help meet their expenses she took in piecework as a dressmaker. As James's business dwindled, Jane enlarged her operations. She opened a shop specializing in corsetmaking where (contradictorily) she found it "a joy to fit the superb forms of Kentucky women." Her business prospered, and soon she was hiring seamstresses to work for her. When she told James she could make a greater profit if she could buy her materials at wholesale prices, he sold some of his Wilkinsburg property in order to set himself up in the dry-goods business, from which he would supply Jane. But his dry-goods store failed, and with that they were dependent upon the corset and dressmaking trade. It was a sad denouement to the venture that had begun with such promise as they sailed away from the Pittsburgh docks on a June morning. Jane remembered the wispy ground fog swirling along the riverfront that morning, evanescent as the hope for the deferred fulfillment of her dream of the Black Knight and his Wax Doll securely established in their own home. It was thoughts such as these that she mulled over as she walked alone

one night and was mistaken for a prostitute. "I walked until I was tired, thinking of all the sacrifices I had made to be my husband's housekeeper and keep myself in woman's sphere, and here was the outcome! I was degrading him from his position of breadwinner. If it was my duty to keep his house, it must be his to find me a house to keep, and this life must end. I would go with him to the poorest cabin, but he must be head of the matrimonial firm. He should not be my business assistant. I would not be captain with him for lieutenant."

James's failure in Louisville was compounded by a bitter fight brought about by Mary Cannon's death. In the summer of 1839 messages came from Pittsburgh saying that she was dying from cancer and urging Jane to return. James counseled her to wait until more information came. What could she do now that could not be done several weeks later? Besides, he did not want her to leave him in Louisville with a useless inventory of dry goods, and he invoked the Scripture to support his arguments. "While he continued his comments, I buried my head in the pillows, saying, 'Lord what wilt thou have me to do.'"

They had a Scripture-quoting contest, both going to the Bible to support their positions. James threw at her, "'Wives submit yourselves unto your own husbands as unto the Lord. For the husband is head of the wife even as Christ is head of the church; therefore, as the church is subject unto Christ, so let the wives be to their own husbands in everything.'"

To which Jane countered, "'Honor thy father and thy mother.'"

As the debate wore on, James was making the better case. His passages, especially from Paul's letters to the Ephesians, were more telling, and Jane saw that she was being forced into submission by the authority she had always unquestioningly accepted. There were only two choices. She might accept the authority of the Scripture or "expunge" the threatening passages. She chose to expunge. "And thus," she said, "I unconsciously took the first step in breaking through a faith in plenary inspiration." Jane packed her clothes, walked to the wharves, "where respectable women were not seen alone," and took passage on the first boat bound for Pittsburgh. The fiasco was complete.

When she left Louisville, Jane Swisshelm carried the memories of a slave society with her. But they were stored away, the latent capital upon which she would draw when she emerged as an abolition polemicist. Some of her most biting phrases and savage stories would be drawn from her Louisville experience. One of the themes of her later writings is her claim of intimate knowledge of the slavemasters.

She never made a similar claim about the Louisville slaves. Their habits and character did not interest her. In *Half a Century* the slaves are almost immaterial except as they provide foils for the slavemasters. They are all clichés in the abolition biographical dictionary. One is struck by the fact that although most of the Louisville Negroes are given names they have no identity as human beings. On the contrary, the masters and mistresses, everyone of them nameless (only the "fiery Fitzhugh" and her brother are identified by name, and, significantly, they are declassed because they are bankrupt), are vital, believable people. The slavemasters, not the slaves, are the people who have stuck in her craw so that years after emancipation Jane lashed out at them with the same vehemence that characterized her attacks when she was an abolition propagandist. The slaveholders were as alive for her in 1880 as they had been in 1839. They continued to haunt her imagination and were resurrected with all of the power, comic invective, and irony that she had mustered against them thirty years earlier.

When James liquidated his business and left Louisville, he settled, as Jane disgustedly said, for "one panther, one deer, two bears, and a roll of wildcat money." He planned to tame Tom the panther and use him as a watchdog. The deer and bear were to provide whatever amusement that might be found in them, and the money was next to worthless. This tawdry menagerie and the worthless money were all James was able to show for his two years in Louisville and his trading operations along the southern rivers. The panther terrorized Jane. He "supplied memory with a picture." For years, Jane said, Tom was "a shadow on my brain"; "he never left me." In her dreams he stalked her, padding silently, waiting for the moment to attack.

Memory with a picture. It is a striking phrase, as applicable to

the anonymous *slavemasters* as it is to the Kentucky "panther."
Both are rooted in a common source and both serve the same function. Each is a nightmare terror. If Tom (and the bear, the deer, and
the wildcat money) were all the Swisshelms had to show for their
attempt to make a new life for themselves in Louisville, is it surprising that the panther—the savage failure—prowled in Jane's
dreams?

Tom was the living symbol of the Louisville fiasco, the city controlled by slave interests in which the Swisshelms had failed. How
different it might have been if James had not returned to Swissvale
trailing his pathetic menagerie, if he had made a success, if he had
been "captain instead of lieutenant," if he had become "head of the
matrimonial firm," if Jane has not fled Louisville in "rebellion."
How different the pictures of the slavemasters drawn out of
another memory might have been. But as it was, pictures out of the
memory of failure, they became the symbols and causes of failure.
What chance had free labor and individual enterprise in their
midst? When the Wax Doll and her Black Knight sailed away from
the Pittsburgh wharves, they sailed toward the fulfillment of a
dream. When Jane came back up the river alone in rebellion against
James and the Bible, she returned with imaginative desire and authority shattered. It is no wonder that toward the end of her life she
brought the old slave masters to life in such crackling, scathing
sketches.

At Pittsburgh, Jane nursed her dying mother. Mary Cannon suffered much pain. Her nerves screamed in protest against the
slightest sound. The tap of a spoon against a plate made her writhe in
her bed. Into the early winter of 1839 the house was muffled against
noise, against the sounds of motion, of life. It was a fitting resolution to the Louisville disaster. Withdrawal and silence in the midst
of pain. The world outside the house was shut off. Letters came
from James asking when she would return. Swisshelm in-laws
came to tell Jane that her duty lay with James, who was struggling
on alone in Louisville. They brought their Bible references with
them, and the interminable Scripture-quoting contests were resumed in muted voices. Jane heard them out, but she refused to
return to Louisville.

Subsequent to her mother's death, Jane introduces a curious and puzzling hiatus in her autobiography. There is an interstice of over two years about which she is exceedingly vague. She identifies the date of her mother's death, January, 1840; then the next reference point she gives is April, 1842, when she returned with James to Swissvale. During the interval she was at Butler, Pennsylvania, some forty miles north of Pittsburgh, where she taught in the Butler Seminary. How long she was at Butler she does not say, though she leaves the impression she was there for most of the period.

At least once, perhaps several times, James came up the river to ask, maybe to demand, that she return to Louisville with him. She adamantly refused. Then James made a shocking move; he told her that he would make a claim against Mary Cannon's estate for wages due her. Astounded, Jane listened as he explained her situation under the Pennsylvania law of "coverature." According to coverature a husband had the right to take whatever wages or fees his wife earned. James told her that although she had been paid nothing for her months of nursing service she should have been. Therefore, as her husband and protector he might recover what was owed her. Mortified by the thought of having a bill for her services presented to the executors of her mother's estate, Jane capitulated and ended her rebellion. "I could compromise," she said, "and I did." She agreed to return to James and live with him at Swissvale. At Swissvale they would live alone; this was James's part in the compromise. Elizabeth Swisshelm and William Swisshelm moved in with in-laws.

James sold out in Louisville, came upriver with his menagerie and wildcat bank money, and took Jane to Swissvale. He resumed his old job of managing the family's sawmill and supervising the farming of the Swisshelm lands. Jane kept house, gardened, and tramped across the rolling land with an eye open for improvements she intended to make. Back on his land and supervising the mill, James was captain rather than lieutenant. He was manager of "the matrimonial firm." The tame deer were turned loose to graze in the yard, the bear was penned beyond the house to amuse visitors, and Tom the panther, the picture of memory, was chained at the back door. The beast frightened Jane, but he had not yet invaded her dreams.

Jane recalled these months as pastoral and peaceful: The Pennsylvania summer ripened the land. She walked along the brooks, marking off places where she would plant willows. She dreamed of the future when the willows were grown and she and James would walk in the afternoon under their shade. Her days were long and full and happy. Her account of her return to Swissvale is a curious outcome of rebellion and compromise. Explosive self-assertion and challenges to authority and convention have somehow been resolved in the most conventional domesticity. For a woman whose tolerance for grievance was extraordinarily low and who, when she believed herself aggrieved, minced few words in her outrage, this placid resolution comes most unexpectedly.

In these few paragraphs of *Half a Century* that recall the return to Swissvale, Jane's recollection lies limpid and contented. It is not as though her rebellion had failed. Rather, the sense that she conveys is that she was a peace with herself, with James, and the world. She is extraordinarily happy. The reader finds himself out of turbulent currents and on the surface of still, quiet waters. One is reminded of the self-portrait Jane painted early in her marriage. The picture shows a young matron brought to soft curving ripeness. Seven years after the marriage, for the first time, the self-portrait and the self-description coincide.

After their return to Swissvale there was opportunity for Jane to write, perhaps with James's encouragement. She said that under the pseudonym "Jennie Deans" she published stories and rhymes in two Philadelphia newspapers, the *Dollar Newspaper* and *Neale's Saturday Gazette*. She said that she was writing in 1842 and implied that she began writing shortly after returning to Swissvale, but her memory played her false. The *Dollar Newspaper* did not begin publication until 1843, and *Neale's Saturday Gazette* was not begun until the following year. Therefore, if Jane is correct about the date of her return to Swissvale, then for eighteen months she was content and happy.

The fugitive pieces she published in the *Dollar Newspaper* are sentimental trivia, mostly conveying simple pieties about friendship.[12] There is no indication of the outrage or tormented unhappiness that characterizes her subsequent journalism. Her two poems,

"To My Cousin" and "Remember Me," would have been at home in *Godey's Lady's Book* or in the autograph memory books that women kept for their friends and visitors to inscribe with rhymed clichés. "To My Cousin" and "Remember Me," published toward the end of 1843, conform with the impression created by the self-portrait and made explicit by the memories in *Half a Century*. The portrait's imagined projection of self, the autobiography's remembered perception of self, and the two little poems' statement of sensibility may be brought into congruence and offered as an interpretation of Jane Swisshelm as she stood on the threshold of her career as a reformer.

Only once in her life did her imagined conception of self coincide with the realities of her life. Only once was she what she always dreamed of being, a thoroughly domesticated woman subscribing to the most conventional sensibilities, happily living with a prosaic husband. Her only stipulation was that her husband take his place as head of their household.

The *Dollar Newspaper* and *Neale's Saturday Gazette* were dissenting and reform newspapers. Most of their pieces on social issues discussed slavery and woman's rights. But neither followed the Garrisonian line, and they were especially hostile to the Garrisonian "anti-slavery No-Government Society." "Fanatic," the editors of the *Dollar Newspaper* and the *Gazette* called the celebrated Garrisonian resolutions to dissolve the Union, and when Abby Kelly, one of the more exuberant Garrisonians, was "forcibly ejected" from an antislavery meeting in New York they noted their approval.[13]

If the *Dollar Newspaper* and the *Gazette* offer a clue to Jane's thinking at the time, her mind was cast in the direction of those who were troubled about some of the conditions of American society and who raised protests about them, but who were not yet prepared to swim in turbulent streams of raucous minority protest.

Subscribing to the editorial positions of the *Dollar Newspaper* and *Neale's Gazette*, if indeed Jane did, was a passive, tacit, and thoroughly unexceptionable form of dissent. She had yet to make her move into the public life. We must look beyond the politicizing of the Covenanter conscience for the reasons that enabled her to move into the front ranks of dissent. For when she entered public life she had to abandon her pastoral life at Swissvale and give up her dream of those afternoons under the willows.

Elizabeth Swisshelm returned to Swissvale and ordered the willows uprooted and used to make baskets. Jane begged James to save them, but he gave in to his mother's demand. The compromise was broken, and the old rancor between the two women broke out again. Elizabeth accused Jane of stealing the butter money. Time and again Jane was in some conflict with her mother-in-law, and when she appealed to James for help and support he took his mother's part. During one of the bitter quarrels James "threw himself on the bed and poured out such a torrent of accusations as I had not dreamed possible." Echoing his mother, James charged her with stealing the butter money, stealing food, and spreading lies about the Swisshelms among the neighbors. "It was all," Jane said, "a blur of sound and fury. Livid with rage [James seemed] a mad man. . . . Earth seemed to be passing away." When she could stand it no longer, she ran away from Swissvale.

She only went to the house of a neighboring farmer, where she spent the night. She told the farmer that she was running away, because she knew that James would be told of her whereabouts. Next morning James came and persuaded her to return to Swissvale. Before he appeared she was reading the Bible: "I saw as by a revelation why this trouble had been sent to me, and a great flood of light seemed thrown across my path before me."

Jane was reading the twenty-fifth chapter of Matthew in which Jesus describes His millennial return and the Last Judgment. Surrounded by His angels He sits on His throne and asks the questions that separate the sheep from the goats. Were the hungry fed, the naked clothed, the sick ministered to, the prisoners visited? Suddenly it was clear to Jane that she was in mortal danger. Her "troubles" were a sign and a warning. A trial balance had already been struck for her, and she had been found wanting in her Christian duty. She rushes on:

Christ's little ones were sick and in prison, and I had not visited them! Old Martha [one of the maltreated Louisville slaves], standing before her judges, rose up to upbraid me! I was to have followed the Lamb, and had been making butter to add to an estate larger now than the owner could use. No wonder she [Elizabeth Swisshelm] thought I stole the money. I, who had failed to rebuke man-stealing, might steal anything. That meeting-house which I had been helping to build by entertaining its builders and aiding them about subscriptions, it and they were part of a great man-thieving machine. I had been false to every principle of justice; had been decorating parlors when I should have been tearing down prisons! *I*, helping Black Gagites. What was Peter's denial compared to mine.

Her predicament was revealed with crystal clarity. The man-stealers and the women-whippers lay at the root of her troubles. They were the cause of her difficulties with James and Elizabeth, and they would be the cause of her standing accused and condemned at the Last Judgment. It was they who had wrecked her "paradise." But there was time to rectify her errors. "I must attack that bastile [*sic*].'" The means for the attack were as yet unspecified, but the attack was now imperative. Both her marriage and her salvation depended upon it.

Brought back to Swissvale, Jane was put to bed for three weeks. A fever raged in her, and, apparently delirious, she saw "no one but my attendants and my phantom panther. He never left me. There was one corner of the room in which he stayed most, and sometimes there was not room for his tail to wag, and then he moved forward where I could not see his head. This troubled me, for then I could not hold him with my eyes. At night [his eyes] were two balls of green fire." Tom, the symbol of the Louisville debacle, for the first time invaded her dreams.

When she was strong enough to leave her bed Jane remained despondent, and "hope and pride [were] shut out." She could not sleep. She despaired because "there did not seem to be anything I could do for the slave." The days dragged on. Then she wrote a satirical verse arraigning some Pittsburgh Methodist preachers who had voted for the "Black Gag" at the Methodist General Conference in Baltimore in 1840.[14]

The published poem (which does not survive) was an indirect, long-after-the-fact assault on the "bastile." The Black Gag was no longer an issue in mid-1844 because the Methodist church had already split into sectional factions. Methodists of the Pittsburgh Conference were not bound by the 1840 resolution. Jane's first published attack on slavery is clouded with ambiguities, as is her sub-

sequent account of it. What seems to be the case is that the first
blow Jane struck against slavery was aimed more at the Methodist
Swisshelms than anyone else. Prisons and imprisonments pre-
dominate the account; and, as we shall see presently, the passage in
Half a Century that concludes the episode explicitly makes her the
prisoner.

After her poem was published, Jane saw "the vision of Glory,"
and she thought that "John's New Jerusalem never was so grand."
There is an exuberant memory: "Once more I took hold of life. I
organized a society at which we read, had refreshments and
danced—yea, broke church rules and practiced promiscuous dancing minus promiscuous kissing. Of course this was wicked. I
roamed the woods, brought wild flowers and planted them, set out
berry bushes, and collected a large variety of roses and lillies. . . .
My Patmos had been visited and I could dwell in it, work and wait."

Jane's "work" was writing occasional pieces for the *Spirit of Liberty*, a Liberty Party newspaper published in Pittsburgh. The paper
spoke for abolition's political wing.

Jane wrote for the *Spirit of Liberty* for almost a year, from the
fall of 1844 until the summer of 1845. In her autobiography she
dramatizes her entrance into public life as a political journalist. The
risks are presented as overwhelmingly destructive. As she surveyed her prospects it seemed that "If I wrote . . . I must throw
myself headlong into the great . . . maelstrom, and would of course
be swallowed up like a fishing-boat in the great Norway horror
which decorated our school geographies . . . and I could never again
hold up my head under the burden of shame and disgrace which
would be heaped upon me." She supposed herself standing alone at
some gulf. Her images suggest that she confronts some vast empti-
ness in her life. She had reached dead end. "No one," she said,
"could be better spared than I." She believed she would destroy
herself. "But what matter? I had a reckless abandon . . . and
would sell my life at its full value."

Yet for all her brave (and self-serving) words, the fact remained
that when she wrote for the *Spirit of Liberty* she did not sign her
pieces. They were published over the initials J. G. S., which did not
even suggest that the author was a woman. And the reckless aban-

don Jane attributes to herself in the fall of 1844 is better located in the summer of 1845 when she completed the transition from anonymous abolition publicist to outspoken advocate of woman's rights. It was only then, and on a different issue, that Jane was willing to sign her articles and risk the destruction that she supposed would be the consequence of her venture into reform journalism.

In July, 1845, the final settlement of Mary Cannon's estate occurred, with Jane and her sister Elizabeth equally sharing in the division of the property. As part of the settlement the trustees proposed to sell some Pittsburgh real estate, but the prospective buyers balked until the title was cleared from all possible encumbrances. They insisted that the husbands of the two sisters sign the deed to the property. Elizabeth's husband, Henry Z. Mitchell, willingly agreed, but James refused to sign unless he was given Jane's share of the money. He told Jane that he meant to use the money to improve Swissvale, which was owned by Elizabeth Swisshelm. It seemed an unconscionable demand to Jane. James's refusal to sign the deed hurt not only herself, but also the "only living" person "who had ever loved her," her sister Elizabeth. Jane decided that it was usless to "spend my strength quarreling" with James. Instead, she decided to "strike for the heart of that great tyranny." She began to study law, reading it under the direction of Samuel Black, John Black's son. She joined the campaign to revise the Pennsylvania laws relating to married women's property rights; and in the summer of 1845 the first articles bearing the signature *Jane G. Swisshelm* appeared in print. Their subject was the desperate legal position of married women.

Once Jane publicly supported woman's rights she severed her connection with the *Spirit of Liberty*. Male abolitionists were deeply divided on the issue of woman's rights. The backers of the Liberty party, unlike the Garrisonians, were no friends of sexual equality. One of the reasons for the split in the American Antislavery Society had been Garrison's insistence on an equal role for women, and as his opponents pulled off in the direction of political action they brought their ideas about women with them. With her penchant for overstatement Jane said, "The political action wing of the antislavery party had given formal notice that no woman need apply for a place among them." Yet as long as she wrote on abolition alone, the columns of the *Spirit of Liberty* were open to her. Furthermore, the sexual anonymity of the initials J. G. S. was her own choice; it was not forced on her by the editors. But when she moved to advocacy of woman's rights she thought she would embarrass the Liberty Party "with the sex question," and she had to find another newspaper to publish her articles. She considered making an alliance with the Garrisonians, but their arguments about the immorality of political action were no less "fallacious" to her in the summer of 1845 than they had been earlier. "I could not," she said, "work with Garrison on the ground that the Constitution was pro-slavery, for I had abandoned that in 1832 [1833], when our church split on it and I went with the New School," the schismatic New Light Covenanters.

If her own claim belied it—"I took pains to make it understood that I belonged to no party. . . . I was like the Israelites in the days when there was no king, and 'every man did that which was right in his own eyes'"—Swisshelm was, from her entry in reform journalism until she wrote the copy for the last issue of her ill-fated *Reconstructionist*, a political partisan.

From the summer of 1845 until December, 1847, Jane wrote for the Pittsburgh *Commerical Journal*, the city's leading Whig newspaper. The *Journal's* editor, James Riddle, was sympathetic to woman's rights. Furthermore, Riddle recognized the political benefits that would come from Jane's powerful invective against the Polk administration's expansionist policies, which the Whigs were opposing. In her occasional pieces published from the summer of 1845 until the spring of 1846 Jane sniped at the Democrats, taking the common antislavery line that the annexation of Texas and the pressure on Mexico for more territory in the Southwest were proofs of the slaveholders' conspiracy to expand slavery.

At the outbreak of the Mexican War, Jane Swisshelm became a regular writer for the *Journal*. Each of her Mexican War letters was announced in the preceding edition of the *Journal*, and although each was topical they all developed a common theme: As a result of the slaveholders' conspiracy a "great nation [was] engaged in the pusillanimous work of beating poor little Mexico—a giant whipping a cripple." In these articles her animus became increasingly personal and her *ad hominem* style was perfected. She made slavery "the synonym for the whole list of crimes" of which America was guilty, and in her pieces individual men were presented as the personification of the crimes. "Each one seemed to stand before me, his innermost soul laid bare, and his idiosyncrasy I was sure to strike with sarcasm, ridicule, solemn denunciations, old truths from [the] Bible and history and the opinions of good men."

In order to "lay bare" her victim she invented a "crooked telescope," her journalistic device that enabled her to "magnify" a person, bringing "his innermost soul" into sharp focus against the background of war and slavery. She spared no one. She applied her invective without discrimination or regard for personal friendship. With the same impartial remorselessness that she used on men on whom she had never laid eyes, she flayed Samuel Black, her law tutor and son of her beloved John Black, when he accepted a commission in the volunteer army. "Every man who went to the war, or induced others to go, I held as the principal in this crime," she said. She relished her articles, "direct, personal, nay almost unpardonable attacks upon many of the most influential citizens." She thought it was their savage quality that made her pieces so successful. Furthermore, she had no doubt about the source of her feral prose. It was the beasts that James had brought back from Kentucky. The panther and the bear were her schoolmasters, she claimed. At her writing table at Swissvale she could hear Tom, the "picture of memory," rattling his chain. She as much as says that as she wrote her Mexican War letters, the memory of the Louisville debacle was filtered into these pieces exposing the "conspiracy" that had plunged the nation into war. The leitmotif of the pieces was the "southern tiger." It was impossible for her to separate public policy from personal experience. Her indictment of the Mexican War, itself emblematic of "the whole list of crimes of which slavery was the synonym," was suffused with what she had suffered in Louisville. The memory of Louisville was a deep wound.

The woman's rights pieces that Jane Swisshelm wrote for the *Journal*—and her subsequent writings in her own newspapers as

well as the summation in *Half a Century* of her ideas on the subject,
are little more than elaborations of what she said in 1845–
1847—are clearly reflective of the situations that drove her toward
woman's rights. Her main thesis rested on a married woman's relationship with her husband, not on women qua women. She claimed
that marriage ought to be a true partnership, a "spirit union . . .
designed to make one out of two" (*PV*, November 24, 1849). Marriage should be recognized as such legally, especially in matters of
property. The estate should belong to the married partners equally.
Nowhere was the "spirit union" and the "partnership" more fundamentally demonstrated than in property. And it was, after all,
the Swisshelm's quarrel over property that drove Jane out in the
open as an opponent of men's oppression of women.

Her other leading ideas on woman's rights are consistent with
the circumscribed, qualified base on which they stood. "Educate
girls with boys, develop their brains, and take away legal disabilities little by little, as experience should show was wise; but
never dream of [women] doing the world's hard work, either mental or physical." Responding to James Riddle, her editor, who
urged her to greater boldness, she said, "Do not let your generosity
run away with your judgment." She was no friend of across-the-
board sexual equality, nor did she advocate—she borrows the abolition phrase—"immediate emancipation" for women. "Women,"
she said, "should not weaken their cause by impracticable demands. Make no claim which could not be won in a reasonable
time. Take one step at a time, get a good foothold in it and advance
carefully."

The fate that Jane had anticipated when she broke into the open
as a writer on abolition and woman's rights did not occur. Instead of
suffering shame and ostracism she was reaping "a crop of glory."
Instead of selling her life she was selling newspapers for James Riddle. In a few months she achieved celebrity and notoriety from
Massachusetts to Georgia.

But to find herself a survivor, even a success, did not relieve her
fears. There was more than self-serving hyperbole in her comment, "I [expected] to die." The clue to the nature of her fears is
found in the way her notoriety was developed by writers and
editors hostile to woman's rights. They made a lot of laughter at

her expense. The standard gambit was to welcome her into the "bohemian fraternity," then ask ribald questions about how she would fare in a profession that was celebrated for its rough masculinity. Invariably Samuel Johnson's comment about the woman preacher and the dog that walked on its hind legs was invoked. The idea lying behind the stale witticism was sometimes put explicitly, a woman journalist was "unnatural"; Jane had "unsexed" herself. It was not merely that she had strayed from home and hearth. To have strayed was simply to have been deflected from her proper course, to have become errant. At the end of the errant's path lay peccancy but not unnaturalness.

An interior dimension of the woman's rights movement that has never been properly explored rests with the meaning of the words *unsexed* and *unnatural*. For all the epithets hurled at the antebellum male reformers, loss of manhood or betrayal of "nature" were charges never made against them. Zealot, enthusiast, atheist, bigot, fairly well describe the outermost limit of screed aimed at the men. To their enemies they may have been enormously misguided, but however outrageous they may have seemed to their opponents, the men never ran the risk of being shorn of a fundamental identity given them by sex as well as by convention and tradition.

For a woman, breaking outside convention meant not only freeing herself from bondage but also abandoning her pedestal. If she was something close to ox and slave, she was also Diana and the Virgin, Rowena and Lady Jane Grey, and the cosseted creatures inhabiting the columns published by Alice Bradley Neal and Sarah Josepha Hale. The roles and functions were so intertwined that they could not be separated. Regardless of the social forces that enabled women to challenge law and break custom, the actual attempt to establish themselves as independent beings required desperate courage of individual women. As soon as a woman moved into an area that had been the prerogative of men, she was met head on with the condescension and the obscenity that conveyed the fundamental meaning imputed to her act: she had not only changed a social relationship, she had altered nature and had destroyed herself.

The destruction of self seems a paradoxical and incongruous consequence of Jane Swisshelm's quest for freedom. In order to appreciate the consequence, it is helpful to make an analogy that she and other pioneers in woman's rights made themselves, between white women and black slaves.

Other than being parts of a generic reform current, woman's rights and abolition seem linked in two rather obvious ways. It was abolition that brought women into the ranks of organized reform and conditioned them and society to the appearance of women in places that previously they had not entered: lecture platforms, newspaper offices, and agitator's stumps. Then having served their apprenticeship in the techniques of reform, women moved on in the direction of feminism. As they learned their trade they hit upon the tactical device of making common identification between themselves and the slaves.

White women and blacks, the claim ran, were victimized by law and custom and forced to serve out their lives in servility. The cause of one, therefore, was the cause of the other. This mutual identification, while eminently suitable for agitation, was nonetheless fundamentally flawed. [15] Negro slaves were never trapped by the same sort of dual role that society had defined for white women. For slaves the alternative to bondage was emancipation . The "protected" role that they gave up with emancipation was quite different from woman's historically idealized role that was being assimilated in nineteenth–century gynecolatry. As the slaves came to freedom they were not required to abandon a *role* from which they could draw dignity and nobility. But behind white women lay the stable at Bethelem, the Courts of Love in Aquitane, and the idealized sanctuary of the bourgeois home. Slaves would come to freedom sexually intact. On the contrary, if we are to believe opponents of pioneer feminists, women such as Jane Swisshelm had to repudiate not only their femininity but their sexuality. They would come to emancipation not simply sexual cripples, but as something approaching trans-sexuals. To embrace woman's rights was to willingly submit to an unnatural operation, to give up one's sexuality. Striking for emancipation in effect would be to destroy oneself as a woman. In a most profound sense the liberation of white women could be attained only through self-immolation.

The subject is one that women like Jane Swisshelm rarely tackled head on. Nonetheless the burden of proof was on them to show that they were not unsexing themselves. The charge against them was fearful, and it had to be met and answered, not only for those who made the accusation, but for the women themselves. One of the subtle themes running through the literature of woman's rights is the persistent reassurances that they give themselves on this matter. These women seem to have been interested in convincing themselves as much as their opponents that the "contemptuous word *mannish*" was in no way applicable to them as they undertook to remove the "disabilities and disadvantages, religious, civil and social" that hemmed them in. The reassurances were restrained and low keyed, but they were pressed with an insistence that leaves little doubt as to their meaining. These women were profoundly afraid.

Throughout her public life Jane Swisshelm was protective, perhaps obsessively so, of her feminity and her sexual nature. "We glory," she said, "in the distinctions of sex. . . . We should rather be whipped or traded off for corn, than be deprived of the protection and attention we claim in right of our sex." Her iterated claims of weakness, frailty and "nervous temperament" must not be interpreted only as calculatedly self-serving, but also as devices she employed to reassure herself that she had not unsexed herself. "There is," she wrote, "a very general impression that we are possessed of masculine, almost herculaean [sic] strength. This is a mistake." She insisted that she did not live in a man's world; nor did she ever expect to, and that she had left "our little world . . . which is very dear to us" with the greatest reluctance. Her repetitive references to her chronic bad health—"We have been ill, O, very ill, with a continued attack of quinzy and putrid sore throat [and] were much reduced before the disease was checked"—were offered as much as proofs that she had not become "mannish," as they were pleas for sympathy for an inexperienced woman political journalist who, she said, was simply responding to that "long tried rule of action, 'Do right and trust in God'" (*PV*, December 20, 1847; November 24, 1849). In a long editorial review of *The Scarlet Letter*, Jane came as close as she ever would to explicitly stating her ideas on woman's sexual nature and establishing a connection between female sexuality and behavior that implied her understanding of the goal of woman's rights.

"We never dreamed of anything so sublime," Jane wrote of Hester Prynne. She "is the most glorious creation of fiction that has ever crossed our path." "The moral force and grandeur of [Hester's] character" was a model for all women, and Jane scarcely needed to add that her "character" was released by a vital, uncompromising sexuality. Hester's only "sin" was her desire for a consummated "spirit union," a "uniting in a chemical affinity" with her lover. Her relationship with Arthur Dimmesdale was the perfection of female sexuality. The relationship led to disaster only because it was attempted outside marriage. If they had been married, they would have been "nearly allied to angels."

The review concludes with the observation that if Hawthorne had intended the moral of the story to be the rightful punishment for Hester's sexual misconduct, "his book is the most sublime failure of the age." "For our part," Jane said, "if we know there was such another woman . . . in Boston now, we should travel all the way there to pay our respects" because Hester Prynne "stands morally . . . head and shoulders taller than the tallest" (*PV*, June 22, September 28, 1850).

This admiration suggests a close identification with Hester Prynne which helps explain Jane's relationship with woman's rights. Hester's difficulties began with an incompatible marriage with Chillingsworth. Her revolt was grounded in her unfulfilled sexuality. Hester's marriage, like all bad marriages, was a legalized trap, within which the wife was doomed to remain woman *manqué*, loveless and barren. The only way to fulfill herself was to repudiate the marriage and the sanctions society had imposed upon married women. But the fulfilled woman was to be found in a conventionally romantic relationship with a man. Whenever she took a stand on an issue on woman's rights, Jane insisted on maintaining women's sexual characteristics. Her "opinion [was] that every attempt to destroy the . . . distinctions of sex is an outrage against the laws of nature and nature's God." Instead of being discarded she said, "these distinctions must be come more strongly marked [and] better understood." Draw sexual distinctions even more sharply, she argued. This was the real duty of reforming women; this was the way "to secure the largest liberty and most perfect life" for all women; and, it is clear, this was the way for advocates of woman's rights to protect themselves against being branded mannish and unnatural (*PV*, June 1, 1850).

This matter of her own sexuality, and the sexual nature of reforming women, seems to have concerned Jane for the rest of her life. In *Half a Century* she is at pains to say something about it. After her divorce, she says she accepted "the legal penalty—a life of celibacy." The comment is gratuitous except as a statement that she has remained intact as a sexual being, which must be the reason she made it. She has suffered a grievous penalty. She has been denied her natural function. But her impairment results from the "law," not from herself or her activities. She has the last word. It is the law of men that has forced her into an unnatural situation.

VI

The Visiter

"Shall I not visit for these things? saith the Lord: and shall not my soul be avenged on such a nation as this?"

In December, 1847, the first issue of the Pittsburgh *Saturday Visiter* appeared. Printed on James Riddle's *Journal* press, the *Visiter* was Jane Swisshelm's newspaper. Her name appeared on the masthead as editor and owner. No other woman in the United States owned and edited a political newspaper.

Founding the *Visiter* was the great event in Swisshelm's public life, and it was her public life's central point. If there is a focus in her discursive account of herself in *Half a Century*, it is on the *Visiter*. The lines of force in her autobiography converge on it and radiate from it. When she destroyed her personal papers, she saved her files of the *Visiter*. The paper was the contemporary record of her life that she meant to preserve. The *Visiter* and *Half a Century*, her gloss on the record, were the life documents she left behind her. It was as though she intended for the *Visiter* to be her monument and the autobiography her self-composed epitaph. She had complete control of the *Visiter*. As the founding of the *Visiter* represented the culmination of her movement toward abolition and woman's rights, a confirmation of her determination to fight in the open, and a compulsion to say, "what I please," regardless of the cost, then the reasons that lay behind her decision to publish the paper must excite our curiosity. With the appearance of the *Visiter* many of the strands of her life converge, and the making of a dissenter and a reformer was completed.

In her lead editorial Swisshelm confessed to the recklessness of her undertaking. "The world," she wrote, "was nothing to us, nor we to it; we did not live in it, nor ever expect to [but] now it must be different." What her editorial policy would be, she refused to say. "As to our course in [the] future, we can make no promise. Everything will be new to us in a great degree. The only assurance we can give to any [direction] is that it appeared *right* that we should make the strongest effort in our power to establish an anti-slavery paper in [Pittsburgh], in which a similar attempt has failed three times. . . . We cannot tell what [other] abolitionists intend doing . . . or what ground . . . Men will take; but we do know [what] one . . . Woman" will do. She said she believed that the only "proper mode" of abolition was through "Direct political action." There was "no [other] reasonable way except by a distinct third party. But excuse us gentlemen, do—for we could scarce keep from cracking jokes if we were dying—we had almost forgotten that we have not the honor to belong to any political party" (*PV*, December 20, 1847).

"Now it must be different." For Swisshelm the statement had a portentous meaning as 1847 came to an end. The Mexican War had run its course. American armies had been victorious at Buena Vista and Chapultepec. There was little question that a peace treaty would be written carrying provisions annexing Mexican territory. At hand was proof of the conspiracy to wage an aggressive war in order to guarantee Texas as a slave state and to acquire new land for the expansion of slavery. For those who were disposed to interpret

James K. Polk's policy as a response to the demands of an aggressive slavocracy the signs were manifest that old methods of opposing slavery had failed. It was only a step from interpreting the Mexican War as a consummation of the slaveholders' conspiratorial designs to inferring God's wrathful judgment upon a sinful nation. It was easy to look into the future and see imminent holocaust. Time was short; new methods must be adopted and new warnings carried to the American people. Now political power had to be wrested from the slaveholders if the nation was to be purified and God's wrath avoided.

Nurtured in the tradition of the covenanted state, Jane Swisshelm was led straight to this conclusion. By following John Black and the New Lights in the Covenanter schism of 1833, she could not escape complicity in the actions of the state. Since 1833 the fate of the nation and the New Lights had been inseparably linked, and in 1847 it seemed that the nation was in the hands of the slaveholders. Crisis was in the air. The covenant with God was broken, and His retribution was close at hand. The only hope for the nation was to bring righteous men to political power in order that the covenant might be restored. If the nation were to be saved, the righteous must leave their "little worlds" and come "live in *the* world." They must take up politics as though their lives depended upon it, as indeed they did. "Direct political action," Swisshelm wrote, was not the only "proper mode" of abolition, it was the only way to avoid the judgmental holocaust. "The elective franchise is a great moral lever, for the right use of which [voters] are accountable to God." If a man refused to vote, or voted wrong, he acted, Swisshelm said, "no less blindly than he who would reel drunk to a communion table to take an oath of allegiance to the King of Kings." In short, the failure to act morally through politics was blasphemy (*PV*, December 20, 1847).

There can be no doubt that the Mexican War helped shape Swisshelm's decision to publish the *Visiter*. She believed that the war came as a result of a conspiracy that drew the whole nation in sinful complicity with the slaveholders, and that the nation stood on the verge of divine punishment. She chose the name of her paper to make the point of the covenanted nation breaking its covenant and being confronted with the imminence of God's judgment.

The *Visiter's* name was taken from the motto flying at the top of the masthead, directly over Swisshelm's name as editor and owner. "Shall I not visit for these things, saith the Lord." The motto was from the Book of Jeremiah where the passage concludes, "and shall not my soul be avenged on such a nation as this?" The great message in Jeremiah is his demand that the chosen people repent for the manifold sins of the nation. Borrowing from Jeremiah and urging repentance, Swisshelm followed abolition's classic formula of claiming that slavery was not an evil but a sin. It followed that the individual and the nation must admit to the sin, repent, and free themselves of it by abolishing slavery. The doctrine had been common currency in the abolition movement for over fifteen years, and Jane was apparently following a well-worn path leading toward personal and national redemption. But unlike those who had adapted the formula to abolition, Swisshelm was sprung from a miniscule religious sect whose social definition and historical identity had been forged out of a stiff-necked commitment to the proposition of the redeemed nation of righteous people, and for whom the claim of the sinfulness of slavery had long been a key test of doctrinal purity.

But the schismatic accommodation of 1833 had placed a stain on that tradition. Whether they willed it or not the schismatic Covenanters were now part of a proslavery government. As this became clear the imperative to save the covenanted nation was all the greater. They had to save themselves from the consequences of their own action. They had to redeem their decision of 1833. By founding the *Visiter*, Swisshelm was attempting to save and reaffirm what she had been taught and had believed since she was a child. It was the recovery of the past and the reconstitution of the broken covenant that she desired when she created the *Visiter* in December, 1847.

But much remains unexplained.

It comes as something of a surprise to find Swisshelm drawing on Jeremiah for her paper's name when her "favorite literature" was John's *Revelations*. Surely *Revelations* yields ample texts for a person looking for a scripture in order to admonish a sinful people. Weeks before the first edition appeared she carefully considered alternative names and mottoes, and when she finally made her choice she settled on Jeremiah. There must be a compelling reason she went to Jeremiah for her paper's name and motto.

In the *Revelations* the end of the world is at hand. The holocaust John describes prefaces the final judgment of the world and the millenial reign of Christ. The carnage is fearsome and the judgment is altogether right, but no longer are there any alternatives for man. History has spun out to its end. The holocaust is the conclusion for all that has gone before. The fundamental message in *Revelations* is one of hope for the martyred righteous. It is the promise of redemption for those who have suffered unrighteousness. *Revlations* is no call to arms; nor is it a demand for a redoubled effort to bring about God's will on earth. For all of its violent motion, *Revelations* is passive. John's purpose is to comfort the remnant who have kept the faith as wickedness has triumphed in the world.

But there is nothing passive about Jeremiah. He insists upon action. There is still time to act. In fact action is imperative, and choices are still to be made. Jeremiah's purpose is to bring to arms and restore righteousness through repentant action. Furthermore, it is the chosen people not the remnant who concern—and infuriate—Jeremiah. They are the members of a particular nation. It is the chosen nation's fate that concerns him, not the world's, and the nation's fate hangs on the restoration of the covenant and the moral order. Jeremiah warns about God; on the contrary John comforts with God. John's message is hope for the remnant. Jeremiah's message is punishment for the chosen elite among mankind who have betrayed the divine compact.

In the Jeremiah text the meaning of *visit* is *punish*. The passage from which Jane drew her paper's name means "Shall I not *punish* for these things?" The phrase appears three times in Jeremiah. It is the prophet's iterated warning, a counterpoint to the catalog of sins he charges against the covenanted people.

How shall I pardon thee for this? . . . when I fed them to the full, they then committed adultery, and assembled themselves by troops in the harlots' houses.
They were as fed horses in the morning: every one neighed after his neighbor's wife.

Shall I not visit for these things? saith the Lord: and shall not my soul
be avenged on such a nation as this?

. . . .

They are waxen fat, they shine: yea, they overpass the deeds of the
wicked: they judge not the cause, the cause of the fatherless, yet they
prosper; and the right of the needy do they not judge.
Shall I not visit for these things? saith the Lord: shall not my soul be
avenged on such a nation as this?

. . . .

Their tongue is as an arrow shot out; it speaketh deceit: one speaketh
peaceably to his neighbour with his mouth, but in heart he layeth his wait.
Shall I not visit for these things? saith the Lord: shall not my soul be
avenged on such a nation as this?

Jeremiah has been called the most subjective of all the prophets.
His "personal experience and innermost feelings are more vividly
reflected in his words" than any prophetic writer.[1] Any number of
biblical texts would yield the approximate meaning of Jeremiah,
but Swisshelm went to him, borrowing from the one biblical writer
who like herself always permitted personal experiences to suffuse
his writings.

To find the Louisville slave masters, rich, sleek, and licentious in
these passages is not difficult. Nor is it difficult to see their northern
allies, speaking "deceit" and drawing the free labor portion of nation in the "conspiracy" to expand slavery. Swisshelm's enemies
shine through these passages. It is they who will be objects of the
visit, the punishment Jeremiah promises for the covenant breakers, those who have betrayed the compact made with God by failing
to use the state to create the moral order.

In her opening editorials Swisshelm's most severe words were
saved for northerners, "those poor, sniffling, whiffling, driveling,
pitiful sinners, the 'white slaves'" to southern ambition and power.
She set them off invidiously from the southerners. "Despite all our
hatred to [sic] their cause, there is something about the slaveholders we like . . . they stand fast by the cause they have espoused . . .
we cannot but admire the firmness with which they have maintained it." But, she wrote, the northerners have "basely suc-

cumbed, time and again, time and again—like whipped spaniels. If there is anything under heaven for which we feel a more unutterable loathing than for all other mean things," it is the northerners who have acquiesced to the demands of the slaveholders (*PV*, January 1, 1848).

Swisshelm threw the willful, proud slaveholders in the teeth of her readers. She often reduced the slaveholders to caricature but she never held them in complete contempt. For all of her hatred for them she nevertheless made "these insolent, bragadocia [*sic*], women-whipping ... beauties" (*PV*, September 23, 1848) models for her readers in one aspect. The southerners "stand fast" and bend others to their will. They are guilty of monstrous sins but they, possessors of "brute courage," have never been humiliated. Their pride remains intact. By acquiescing to the slaveholders the northerners not only suffer a bad conscience, they have been humiliated. Their disgrace is doubled.

In these opening editorials Swisshelm deftly separated the shame of bad conscience from the shame of wounded pride. When she did this she hit upon a formula she used as long as she wrote on abolition. The lineaments of the formula had appeared in her Mexican War letters, written for the *Journal* the year earlier. Now the informing ideas were made explicit. If the northerners had been whipped like dogs into supporting slavery and aggressive war, she took it as her mission to beat them back into the paths of righteousness and pride. She meant to shame them until they repented and gave up their "spaniel" ways.

Swisshelm's talent (and need) in bending a personal experience to polemical purposes is evident here. "I lived among Southern people too long," she claimed, not to know their "habits & character." And although she did not say it, she may have added, I knew humiliation and wounded pride at their hands. As elsewhere in her writings, her personal experience appears here as she developed the double thesis of the shame of bad conscience and the shame of the wounded pride. The cause of her double shame would not be revealed until she published *Half a Century*. In episode after episode in the Louisville chapters she fails to stand firm as she argues against slavery. She always slides into acquiescence with what the "women-whipping beauties" are doing. The intent of the episodes is to point out the murderous power of the slave masters, but she makes her case only by revealing herself as a tremulous, failed witness against slavery. Only once in the Louisville accounts does she lash out and sustain herself. That was when she was mistaken for a streetwalker and was courteously propositioned for her favors, and slavery was not directly at issue. As she wrote her opening editorials for the *Visiter* she seems to have been transferring the memory of her own humiliation to her readers, charging them with the shame of being a "white slave" that she herself had felt as the Louisville debacle had run its course. In these editorials there is much criticism of the self and perhaps anger at herself as she flayed her readers for acting like whipped spaniels.

There remains a final meaning to be drawn from Swisshelm's use of Jeremiah. In the prophet's baleful warning there is a lament for "the hurt daughter of the people" that repeats itself twice. Among the sins he charges against the covenanted people, Jeremiah adds, "They have healed also the hurt of the daughter of my people slightly, saying, Peace, peace; where there is no peace." In this passage Jeremiah promises retribution for three different malefactors: a society that wounded the "daughter," sleek sinners who abused her, and a "husband" and the "aged with him" who have given her "no peace." Conceding that an interpreter can find in scripture much of what he wants, and that many a specious case has been shored up with a selective appeal to it, to find the indictment of a "husband and the aged with him" in the biblical text from which Jane Swisshelm took her motto suggests a final element flowing into her decision to publish the *Visiter*. It is a grieviously hurt woman's retaliation against James and Elizabeth Swisshelm, who promised her peace but reneged on their promises.

"I am full of . . . fury. . . . I am weary of holding it in," Jeremiah wrote. It is a sentence that Swisshelm could have written. Surely she reflected on it as she read Jeremiah. There was much grim satisfaction there. Sometime toward the middle of December she chose the name of her paper and presently the first issue would come off the press. There is no doubt that she was full of fury or that she was weary of holding it in. She had held "it in" for ten years. "I will

pour it out," wrote Jeremiah. On December 20, 1847, Jane Swisshelm began to pour it out in the *Visiter*.

The external history of the *Visiter* is quickly told. It was published from December, 1847, until August, 1852. Within a year
there were over a thousand subscribers, and by the end of its second
year the paper's circulation rivaled that of Garrison's *Liberator*.
With pardonable exaggeration in her autobiography Swisshelm
claimed that she had six thousand subscribers. Probably the circulation never rose beyond three thousand, which was respectable
enough considering that the paper was published without organizational support or subsidy.[2] For most of its life the paper paid its way
with subscriptions and advertising, though toward the end it ran a
deficit that Swisshelm had to make up from the Cannon inheritance. In 1851 the *Visiter* hit the economic reefs. Perhaps there was
mismanagement on the part of William Swisshelm, who was the
paper's business manager; probably there was a heavy loss in reve-
nue because Swisshelm was then at the height of her anti-Catholic
crusade, and advertisers were withdrawing their patronage. The
reasons for the *Visiter's* financial difficulties are not at all clear. The
following year, August, 1852, Swisshelm sold the paper to her old
friend and advisor, Robert Riddle, the editor of the Pittsburgh
Journal. One of the stipulations of the sale was that he could have
her services as a writer for an additional two years. Riddle combined the *Visiter* with his *Journal*. The hybrid was published under
the name *Family Journal and Visiter*, and Swisshelm was an occasional contributor to it until she moved to Minnesota in 1857.[3]

The internal history of the *Visiter* is less easily disposed of. It is
more difficult because only the most fragmentary outline remains,
details are few, and most of them are useful only inferentially.
Many ambiguities surround Jane Swisshelm's relationship with
her own newspaper.

Although the *Visiter* was founded to promote abolition through
political action, from the very first Swisshelm complained about
the onerous task of writing the political pieces. She said that the
strain caused her chronic, "sudden and severe illnesses," and she
asked for men writers to relieve her of what she called "this harrowing attempt to write political columns" (*PV*, December 9, 1848).

She struggled on for six months, then in July, 1848, gave up her title as editor and became corresponding editor. In her place she substituted William Stevenson and J. W. Errett as coeditors. Recruited from the Free Soil political coalition, they had no qualms about working for a woman. The two editors were responsible for producing the political pieces and attending to the routine of getting the paper out each week.

The appearance of the Free Soil editorials brought a storm of criticism from the Liberty Party. Because Free Soilers aimed only at keeping slavery out of the western territories rather than striking at slavery directly, Swisshelm was charged with abandoning abolition. To these accusations she gave a characteristic reply. The *Visiter* was not any political party's "organ," she said. "The [Free Soilers] nor nobody [sic] else could raise a convention or a congress large enough, or wise enough to dictate to us in any matter of right or wrong." She said that she had defected from the Liberty party's general assault on slavery because she had come to believe that "the world is not ready for universal [abolition] . . . and won't try it. . . . They [the doctrinaire political abolitionists] got good too fast—put to sea in a hurry, without taking in ballast. . . . We tell folks just as much truth as they will pay us for, and not a word more, for if we did, we should not be able to tell any at all." She was willing, she said, to align the *Visiter* with the Free Soilers for tactical reasons, because restriction of slavery was the first useful step toward abolition. The Free Soil "Buffalo Platform is too low, but it is as high as the people are able to step at once, from the bottomless gulf into which they have sunk." "Checking the advance of an enemy [is] one step toward driving him off the field. . . . One dirty shovel [is] worth a hundred silver teaspoons in keeping back the waters." On the other hand, "the Liberty Party want to do everything, and do it all at once, and the attempt confines them to doing one thing— sitting like a city on a hill" (PV, June 21, 1851).

It was a masterful response. As she finished her defense against her apostasy, Swisshelm had not only taken her revenge on her critics, she had also skillfully augmented the portrait of herself as the undaunted, independent woman to whom "nobody could dictate." Far from being a deserter to the cause of emancipation, she became a greater proponent of it because she was determined to act. If acting, wielding a "dirty shovel," meant deserting her former allies, it was all to the good because she had discovered their true nature. They were impotent; even worse, they were fastidious. But she, a "frail" woman, meant to stay in motion; nor would she scruple to pick up "dirty" weapons in order to fight the battle. She served herself well in the exchange. Once it was over, Liberty party critics left her alone.

Freed from her weekly grind by the editorial arrangement with Stevenson and Errett, Swisshelm left Pittsburgh and Swissvale. She attended the commencement at Allegheny College from which William Swisshelm, her brother-in-law, was graduated, then moved leisurely on to Washington, happy to be away from the "harrowing" political journalism. Her contributions to the *Visiter* were travel pieces, descriptions of the people and places she was visiting. For six weeks she scarcely wrote a word on political and social issues. It was as though she did not care about the political assault on slavery that was coming to a head.

The split editorial arrangement lasted less than two months. While Swisshelm was traveling, an edition of the *Visiter* appeared with seven columns of "very indecent and obscene" material."[4] Inference suggests that it carried an explicit sexual content, the most damaging sort of material that could have appeared in the *Visiter*. The scandalous issue brought her racing back to Pittsburgh. She unceremoniously deposed Stevenson and Errett and tried to repair the damage. Week after week she wrote tedious apologies for the offending edition, always carefully skirting a description of the material that had caused the trouble. She begged her readers' forgiveness and explained with elaborate detail her version of how the offending advertising came to be published. Anxious and threatened, the extent of her fears indicated by her uncharacteristically profuse explanations and apologies, Swisshelm believed the future of the *Visiter* and her personal reputation were at stake. She feared that the *Visiter* of September 2, 1848, would be taken by her enemies and critics as proof of the consequence of her entry into the mannish world of political journalism. They would say that she had descended into a squalid sexuality, that she had lost her femininity.

In the aftermath of the "obscene" edition, Swisshelm increasingly complained of her "very severe illnesses," of her "frail hold on life," and she said she would rather edit a literary paper than continue her political journalism. She wrote, "We have felt our total unfitness to edit a party newspaper." The only reason she continued the political writing was because she would "not desert our political friends until they are able to support an editor." The appearance of the Pittsburgh *Chronicle,* a Free Soil daily, provided the excuse she needed. "The political antislavery movement . . . has gotten on its legs [and] it can dispense with our services." Pronouncing the movement sturdy and "running so fast we loose [sic] sight of it," she announced that she was retiring from political journalism and was revamping the *Visiter* (PV, December 9, 1848). She intended to make it a "Family Newspaper," carrying "Tales, Poetry, History, Biography, Essays, Farming and Domestic Receipts, General Intelligence, [and] the Best Market Reports." The prospectus for the new *Visiter* appeared early in December, 1848, and the first edition was published as the new year opened.

The new paper showed no appreciable difference from the old *Visiter.* Swisshelm's columns were as antic as ever, and political abolition and woman's rights still provided the core around which the paper's pieces were written. She might, Swisshelm wrote, have given up grinding out Free Soil editorials, but her "enemies . . . are mistaken about our 'fanatacism' [sic] being turned over to our surviving partners. As part of ourself, our fantacism must go with us. When we forget, or desert the slave, may our right hand forget her cunning" (PV, September 9, 1848). She would not, she promised, abandon abolition.

For four and a half years Swisshelm's writings in the *Visiter* covered a multitude of subjects. Advice to the lovelorn, essays on partisan politics, ironic accounts of her homelife, blazing social protest, everything was grist for her mill. Read sequentially, her columns seem to display less of an editorial line or fixed purpose than a kaleidoscopic personal commentary on events and issues. She gave herself free rein in "pouring it out," promising her readers that she would write on only what interested her. Issue after issue carried her readers willy-nilly to whatever was "the subject which ought to be thought on this week" (PV, December 9, 1848). Yet, for all of Swisshelm's discursiveness, certain patterns emerge from her writings that show a consistency in her thinking. Apart from political tactics, there is little that properly can be labeled expedient in her thought. Once she took a position she usually clung to it.

If Swisshelm's editorials are read topically instead of sequentially, many of her apparent ideological eccentricities dissolve. In the editorials there are unifying threads that bring the subjects "which ought to be thought on this week" into a fairly consistent unified whole, and which, for all of their pyrotechnics, are surprisingly temperate. "Prudence whispers," she said, that attacking slavery (or undertaking any social change) was not a license to dissolve all social institutions and relations and strike for some higher freedom. The structure of "the great [national] moral economy" was already established. The reformers' "service" to American society was to perfect it.

In the most sustained theoretical statement she wrote about the relationship between a reformer and the goals of reform, Swisshelm's conservatism is abundantly clear. The function of a reformer is to force the sovereign political power to exercise its authority rightly. "We will agree that this government ought to be all [the "universal reformers"] want it to be; but [they] are not the government. The reformers of this nation are not the constituted authorities, but only the reformers of these authorities." The reformers are forbidden the attempt to usurp sovereignty, or deny authority or arrogate it to themselves. The possibility of an illegitimate sovereign with coercive, destructive authority seems never to have crossed Swisshelm's mind. Abandoning an old political sovereignty for a new one was as unlikely for her as Jeremiah throwing over the ark of the covenant (PV, June 21, 1851).

The closest Swisshelm ever came to flying outside the bounds of existing political authority was when she applauded and eulogized John Brown and the Harpers Ferry raid. Even then she argued that Brown, "My Father in the bonds of Christ," had acted according to her theory of reform. John Brown was forcing "the General Government" toward "justice." He had not, she maintained, seized authority himself in the bloody attack on the federal arsenal. Im-

portant to understanding her conception of the proper role of the
reformer is that while she was praising John Brown she was in a
political campaign to bring the Republican party to power in Minnesota and in the "General Government." During the campaign
she was at pains to acknowledge "those Constitutional obligations
which unite [Minnesota] to the South." In the campaign she wrote
some splendid diatribes. Her metaphor for the Democratic
party—that "old rotten ship, lazily swinging in the lazy tide of success, her old hulk covered with the effluvia of offal, her effeminate
officers lunging away their useless hours"—presents Swisshelm at
her polemical best. But the aim of her rhetoric was to constitutionally displace possessors of political power who she believed were
abusing it. It was not her intention to reshape or displace the bases
of power, or to call power itself into question (*SCD*, May 19, October 13, November 24, 1859).

"*One thing at a time*," she said. "Every great reformer has carried out his measures by doing one thing at a time. . . . It has never
been given to any one man, or set of men, to do everything." The
consequence of Swisshelm's "one thing at a time" doctrine and her
distinction between reformers and "constituted authorities" gave a
conserving and practical quality to her ideas and clearly located
their source in her church's conception of the covenanted state.

Let us begin an examination of Swisshelm's ideas with her writings on slavery. In column after column devoted to the subject, she
said very little about slavery as a system. She made only a
rudimentary attempt at analyzing slavery. It becomes apparent
that she was not much interested in it as a social institution. She
denounced slavery as wrong, bad, evil, and destructive, but how
slavery operated to create these qualities was a subject about which
she seems to have cared very little. She had no general theory about
slavery. Her know-nothing boast, "Of slavery in the abstract I
knew nothing," supports the claim she made to George Julian
about her "long and careful study of the habits and character of the
Southern people" and underscores her writings on slavery. It was
the southerners, and especially a particular class of southerners,
not their peculiar institution that interested her.

Insofar as Swisshelm made an analysis of slavery, it proceeded along two lines. One is reminiscent of Tocqueville's description of the two economies on either bank of the Ohio River. To the north is prosperity. The land is bountiful and ripe, the farmhouses are solidly built and well maintained, the livestock is sleek and rippling with fat. Communities thrive. To the south the picture is altogether different. The land has a sparse, half-ravaged look about it, the countryside is littered with abandoned houses, the animals are spavined and gaunt. Communities exist.

More through descriptive implication than explicit analysis Swisshelm argued the thesis of the economic unprofitability of slavery, with the corollary about free labor's inability to flourish in slavery's midst. The gravamen of her critique was that slavery is incompatible with the economic health and development of the community, and that the nonslaveholder is doomed to a marginal existence. It was impossible for the nonslaveholder to succeed where slavery was established even "in its mildest form," as in Kentucky.

Her other critical thrust against slavery was framed in the most general *ad hominem* moral terms. Descriptive rhetoric served as analysis. Slavery bred a class of people who were insolent, arrogant, willful, overbearing and thoroughly immoral. They corrupted everything they touched. And, insolently corrupt—it is impossible to know which, in Jane's mind, was more heinous, the slave masters' insolence or their corruption—they were unfit to be members of a righteous community.

There is no program for abolition in her writings. Her "one step at a time" doctrine was invoked more to justify her espousal of Free Soil politics than the first phase of an unfolding plan for abolition. "I work for the Free Soil men because . . . I think they can and will reach the 'Old Bastille' sooner than any other force now aiming at that point. Their road is the shortest one . . . to . . . annihilation of the whole system." What the next step or the succeeding ones were she never explained. Assumptively, her idea was to choke off slavery's expansion, augment the free states' political power, and, by way of this power, somehow bring about abolition. The labored constitutionalisms such as those produced by Salmon Chase and Lysander Spooner justifying "the annihilation of the whole system" never appeared in the *Visiter*. Swisshelm's constitutionalism about slavery was splendidly simple, though it does, as we will presently see, stand on exactly the same base as did Chase's sophisticated version. According to Swisshelm, "The 'fathers of the Constitution' . . . not only opposed the *expansion* of slavery, but contemplated its *extinction* where it existed. . . . I believe slavery is unconstitutional on every inch of American soil. . . . The fact that [the Constitution] has been administered as pro-slavery no more proves it so than the practice of the American churches proves the Bible to be in favor of 'the sum of all villanies.'" Her ideas about the attack on slavery resolved themselves into the "first step," "building a high wall" around slavery, followed by a peaceful emancipation. Beyond that she had no plan to offer her readers except to vote for the political party that would take the first step (*SCD*, July 12, 1860).

What lay at the end of abolition? What were the new social relationships between the races to be? Were the freedmen by virtue of their common humanity prepared to move immediately into a secure place in a free society? Or were they, damaged by slavery, entitled to some sort of compensatory wardship? If so, who was to administer their estate and superintend their transition from slaves to accredited members of society? Would they be fully accredited members? Would they come to the suffrage, have political power? At the very bottom, underlying everything else, was the critical question, the question that divided abolitionists more than any of their quarrels over tactics and strategy: were blacks and whites equal? This question and similar ones that vexed the Reconstruction settlement were never raised in the *Visiter*. The closest Swisshelm came to suggesting anything like racial equality was when she compared female slaves with white women who also labored in "bondage," and there is little doubt that she was only scoring a debating point in favor of white women. The idea of a common human equality, not to mention an argument for it and a program to promote it, cannot be found in her journalism.

Does the trail end inconclusively with Swisshelm's equivocal silence? There is one further line of inquiry that may be explored to gain an answer to the question. To follow it, we must return to her rudimentary analysis of slavery because one important feature of it has so far been left untouched. What was the relationship between slavery and the slaves? As she answered this question did she say anything that suggested her conception of blacks?

As in the other parts of Swisshelm's crude analysis of slavery, this portion was allusive, metaphorical, and unsystematic. Reverse image-reflections of their masters' qualities, dark counterpoints of the "insolent, bragadocia [sic] woman-whipping chivalry," the slaves' relationship with the system was the obverse of the masters'. As the masters were willful, arrogant, omnipotent and corrupt, the slaves were complaisant, humble, powerless, and often corrupted. Both masters and slaves demonstrated the moral consequences of slavery. What the blacks were before they were enslaved, how the institution operated to change them, what changes were wrought on them, in short, the questions that might be asked of any social institution in an attempt to understand their human effects were questions that did not concern Swisshelm.

How slavery operated to create in the masters the qualities she attributed to them was also a question outside her needs and interests. For her purposes it was sufficient that both slaves and masters possessed the qualities with which she endowed them. Furthermore, the qualities were attributed on the basis of direct observation instead of theory. She had observed slavery in Louisville. But what had she actually seen? The masters. It was they who filled her eyes and her memory; it was they who had overwhelmed her: "There in Louisville we gained our ideas of slaveholders, and found the utter impotence of language to convey any impression of [them]" (PV, September 23, 1848). The masters framed Swisshelm's indictment of slavery; the slaves did not. She was not interested in the slaves except as they were the masters' victims, and as such the slaves never appeared in her newspaper writings except as documentation of the masters' perversion of the moral economy.

The problem of finding what Jane Swisshelm believed about racial equality cannot be resolved as long as the evidence is drawn from her journalism. Her newspaper writing was always accommodated to a political clientele. As she bluntly said, "We tell folks just as much truth as they will pay us for, and not a word more, for if we [told them more] we should not be able to tell any at all" (*PV*, June 21, 1851). If an answer to the question of what she believed about Negroes can be found, it lies in the pages of *Half a Century*. In the retrospective book she had freedom that she never had when she was writing for her newspapers. Now, at last, she was in a position in which she did not have to calculate the market value of the "truth," and serve up as much as the market would bear. When she wrote her book she could tell the whole truth.

Unlike her newspaper pieces, in her book blacks are often particularized, especially in the Louisville chapters. But the portraits are stereotypical and lifeless. The blacks are created (as they had been thirty years earlier in her newspapers) as comments on the slave masters; they never exist in their own right. Failing to elicit Swisshelm's imagination, they are not given personalities of their own. They are not human individuals.

Coming late to abolition, Jane Swisshelm had the choice of following paths already blazed by the pioneers. She might affirm or reject a particular wing of abolition but she could only subscribe doctrines and strategies already laid out. However, as a pioneer in woman's rights she was an original. There were no tracks for her to follow, and the choices she made were unconditioned by the existence of an organization giving structure to ideas. The first edition of the *Visiter* appeared six months before the call for the Seneca Falls Convention, and Swisshelm had already achieved national celebrity when the convention approved the Declaration of Principles that laid an ideological foundation under woman's rights. She was thus much freer in her choices in woman's rights than abolition, and as she made them it is easier to see the force of her own predicament in shaping the message she brought to her audience.

In Swisshelm's antislavery writings it was the slave masters who framed the issue. They, rather than an institution, were the enemy, and castigation of the masters served the place of analysis of the institution. In the case of woman's rights her enemy was the "law" and "Churchianity"; and in her attack on the law and the church she showed that she could undertake and sustain an analysis of social institutions. If antislavery brought forth her best talents as an imaginative writer, it was woman's rights that elicited her best efforts as an analytical critic. And, unlike her antislavery writings, her woman's rights writings reveal a carefully conceived, if somewhat narrow program for the "emancipation" of women. In 1844 Swisshelm began preparing herself for the task by studying law. In Samuel Black's office she pored over his law books. When his office closed she took books to Swissvale in order to continue her reading. Under Black's guidance, her studies led her back to English law, then to feudal law and custom in which she traced out, step by step, the devices through which woman had been turned into "property." Edwin Stanton, later secretary of war and then a rising young lawyer with an interest in changing some of the legal disabilities encumbering women, also helped Swisshelm sharpen her ideas about the way the law had been used to affect women. Along with her legal studies she read church history, weaving the two institutions—the law and the church—together insofar as they had operated to reduce women to "slaves," and make them docile as "a flock of sheep."

The central thesis that emerged from Swisshelm's analysis argued for a historic conspiracy against married women. Justified initially by a misreading of Scripture and supported by "Churchianity," the conspiracy was designed to despoil women of their property through the device of marriage laws. Her corollary was that marriage had been deflected from its "heaven appointed" origin and had become an "institution . . . which binds an old gander to his goose." Instead of being a "true partnership," with the "estate" belonging equally to the "partners," marriage developed into "mere legal conveniences" through which husbands gained control of their wives' "accumulations." In the final analysis, marriages were brutal economic relationships in which wives had no more rights or bargaining power than women off the streets. The whole weight of her analysis was laid on the historical and contemporary situation of married women, not women in general. Thus Swisshelm's stand on woman's rights was much like her polemic against slavery. Both were severely narrowed and were brought to focus on one particular group. In the case of slavery, it was the immoral slaveholder; in woman's rights it was the married woman insofar as she had been "robbed of 'love' and 'property'" (HaC, 139–46; PV, November 24, 1849).

This robbery and the destruction of the "spirit union" was the heinous crime perpetuated against married women; it was "the crucifixion of the spirit" and the "death agony." A woman's "heart [is] torn out" and she is "living in a state of prostitution." Only when love is lost does the legal-economic aspect of marriage become apparent. Then a wife's "poverty" and "beggary" is revealed, because only then is the husband willing to invoke the authority of "Churchianity" and the power of the law to reduce her to "slave," and taunt her that "her accumulations would [not] go to her heirs, [but] to her successor" (*PV*, July 27, August 3, 1850).

The plight of the loveless married woman, victim of the "grand mistake" of choosing the wrong husband, provided the starting point for Swisshelm's woman's rights proposals. "To commence at the root of the evil, we would have women so situated, and public opinion so remodled [sic] that no woman will be obliged to marry either for a living or to maintain a respectable standing in society." The implication was that if a woman married for love and that her marriage became the "true partnership," neither her situation in society or "public opinion" would have to be changed. A husband's love was sufficient for her. It was only the prospect of "mercenary matches" that necessitated the reformation of institutions and opinion.

In order for women to avoid mercenary matches, Swisshelm advocated two reforms. All girls must be trained for "some useful employment." What that employment was she never made clear, but it was evident that with the exception of light industrial and professional jobs she did not intend for women to invade the skills and professions that were traditionally the provinces of men. She "never dream[ed] of [women] doing the world's hard work, either mental or physical; and Heaven defend them from going into all the trades." The other reform Swisshelm advocated was a social morality and a law to make it "disreputable and illegal" for a girl to marry before she was twenty-one years old. Before that age a girl was "totally unfit for the great battle of life." She had not yet become "mistress of [her]self," and was therefore unable to "analyze [her] own feelings, faults, and foibles." In that unformed condition the girl could not know if she had "the right feeling" about her lover. She could not know if she had "got beyond [her] depth and

[was] attempting impossibilities," or whether a man's "love [was] sufficient . . . for bearing with many faults, for sticking to him through . . . crime, degradation, scoffing and insult." She might have added that before she became "mistress of [her] own soul" a young woman was unable to tell the difference between a Black Knight and a village sawmiller and farmer. And, failing to "know [her]self," she would make the grand mistake, the result of which was the death-agony. In place of domestic bliss stood a stark economic relationship between husband and wife, with a despoiled wife bargaining for her husband's favor. The Wax Doll had become a whore.

It was a terrible conclusion. Swisshelm drove toward it with her claim that a wife whose heart had been "torn out" was "living in a state of prostitution," and her anguish at coming to the conclusion is suggested by her use of the most agonized cry she knew: "Eloi, Eloi, Lami Sabacthani [sic]."

Tacked on to these two major reform proposals was a third. Swisshelm stood for "political equality" for women and proclaimed herself a "most strenuous advocate [of this] right." But her program for augmenting woman's suffrage was qualified, as was her claim for the political equality of women, which seems to have been limited to rather sobersided middle-class women. "Hills must be dug down and valleys filled up," she argued, "before the matter can be seriously talked about. To talk seriously about [the suffrage] for the dancing dolls that grace fashionable saloons, and the pale-faced, ignorant wretches that starve and toil in garrets, is positive evidence of lunacy. Suffrage in municipal election for [women] property holders who could read, and had never been connected with crime [is] the place to strike for the ballot. Say nothing about suffrage elsewhere until it prove[s] successful here" (PV, June 1, 1850; HaC, 146).

From 1848 until 1850 the Seneca Falls leadership tried to work with Swisshelm. During those formative years of woman's rights the organizational roles of the leaders were being perfected. "Lucretia Mott typified the moral force of the movement. . . . Lucy Stone was its most gifted orator, [Elizabeth Cady] Stanton its outstanding philosopher [and] Susan Anthony was its incomparable organizer."[5] There was a place for Jane Swisshelm with them, perhaps as chief publicist, or maybe simply as showpiece. She was, after all, an original in her own right, with strong claims for inclusion in the leadership.

Elizabeth Cady Stanton wrote Swisshelm a long letter inviting her to join the inner circle guiding the campaign for woman's rights. Swisshelm responded with a public letter in which she said that Stanton was "very wrong" in making the offer, for she was temperamentally unsuited for "leadership." But, she said, there was another reason for rejecting the invitation. She had no sympathy for the broad claims of sexual equality some of the pioneers were proclaiming. She "object[ed] to the entire principle." She thought that the Seneca Falls movement was leading in the direction of "an outrage against the laws of nature and of nature's God." It was an "attempt to destroy the social, political and religious distinctions of sex." She said that she was "a most devout believer in woman's right to life, liberty, and the pursuit of happiness—in her right to assist in making laws that govern her—to equal remuneration for labor, and equal protection in law; but [I] just as devoutly believe in the distinctive characteristics in the sexes. [I] want the distinction preserved."

"Verbose and irrelevant," was the Seneca Falls group's judgment of much of what Swisshelm wrote, but she was nevertheless too important for them not to try to bring into the fold. In October, 1850, the leaders thought that they had succeeded. For the first time they were able to get her to join in a call for a Woman's Rights Convention. Before, Swisshelm had scorned the women's conventions, arguing that they were "the old party machinery" attended by women bearing "whole armsful of Resolutions" that made them "look too independent. And that is ground which never can be maintained." The most objectionable characteristic of the conventions, she said, was that they were sexually discriminatory. Only women attended, "and that is apt to carry them too far, and open a door through which fools and fanatics will pour in" (*PV*, June 1, 1850).

Swisshelm's objection to the conventions was met when the Worcester, Massachusetts, meeting was planned. Men were invited to participate, and their presence, Swisshelm thought, would "modify" the sexual equalitarians' "madness." With men attending the Worcester meeting, she was willing to concede that the call for the convention contained "much good sense" and was "to the point." Once it was agreed that men would participate, Swisshelm permitted her name to appear on the list of Pennsylvanians supporting the convention. "Much is right" about the convention, she said. At last it seemed that she was willing to join the leadership.

But she kicked over the traces when the delegates attempted to link woman's rights with emancipation. She disgustedly wrote that it was a policy "altogether irrelavent [sic] and unwise." "This convention was called to discuss *Woman's* rights, and if it... paid right good attention to its own business, it would have had work plenty." Then, in one of the most brutal passages ever written by an abolitionist, Swisshelm proposed to separate emancipation from woman's rights:

The women of this glorious Republic are sufficiently oppressed without linking their cause to that of the slave. The slave is sufficiently oppressed without binding him to the stake which has ever held woman in a state of bondage. . . . Nothing can ever persuade us that the union of the two questions had not injured both. . . . As an individual we have done all we felt able to aid the colored man. We would still lend him an oar or show him how to make one; but we do not want him in our boat. Let him row his own craft! He is as strong and as large as a woman; and if we judge him rightly, he would prefer the exercise, and separate quarters, to getting into such very bad company. If he would not—if he is either so lazy or so selfish that he would peril the life of others for a poor chance of saving his own, he is not worth saving, and we would very cooly [sic] cut the fingers off such a loafer, throw him back into the water and see him go down (*PV*, November 2, 23, 1850).

"The call [for the convention] was explicit," she went on. It was to discuss the rights of *Sex*. We feel as if our name had been used for a purpose for which we did not give it. . . . It was a breach of trust, and one we shall remember when our name is asked for to another call [sic]."

After this outburst the woman's rights leaders gave up on Swisshelm. They invited her to speak at the next convention at Akron, Ohio, in 1851, where they judged her speech "far below the level of most of the others." Then they let her drift. Seeing what was happening, Swisshelm wrote, "We are a poor, unfortunate creature. It is almost impossible for us to take a step without getting in somebody's way." Even when "we determined to be very conciliatory and decidedly clever . . . we have a hornet's nest about our ears." As the woman's rights movement was now headed it "appears to us like [an] old maids' imitation of bachelors' hall. . . . It [is] more ridiculous than ridicule . . . more absurd than absurdity" (*PV*, June 1, 1850).

Amelia Bloomer, Elizabeth Cady Stanton, and Susan Anthony maintained a fitful connection with Swisshelm for the next thirty years, biding their time for revenge. When *Half a Century* was published a few of the old leaders praised it. A "coveted" book, one of them wrote Swisshelm, "*Glad you've done it*. . . . I thank God for your life & your brave woman-hero-soul."[6] But the true measure of their judgment came at the hands of the editors of the *History of Woman Suffrage*, the compendium history of woman's rights. The history amounts to the pioneers sitting in judgment of their own work, and that of their peers. In their official portrait of her the editors conceded that Swisshelm had been of much service to woman's rights, notwithstanding that she "has no just appreciation of the importance and dignity of our demand for justice and equality. . . . We can hardly blame any one for doing the work of the hour, rather than struggling a life-time for an idea. Hence it is not a matter of surprise that most women are more readily enlisted in the supression of evils in the concrete, than in advocating the principles that underlie them in the abstract. . . . On this ground we can excuse the author of *Half a Century*."[7]

The significant characteristic of the editors scoring her off lies less in their self-conscious judgment (in their estimate of her they remark that *Half a Century* "vouchsafes no words of approval for those who have inaugurated the greatest movement of the centuries"; that is, themselves) than in the fact that Swisshelm had offered it to them thirty years earlier. In 1850 when she rejected Elizabeth Cady Stanton's invitation, Swisshelm said that she was unsuited for leadership. She had, she replied to Stanton, "never at any time made any pretention [*sic*] to that calmness of judgment, and strength or reasoning that should have weight to any one's opinion. [I] talk and act from impulse, instinct, about as often as from well-considered plans." She was indeed, she might have said, doing the work of the hour.

"Principles . . . in the abstract" provide little access to this woman's ideas. Aggrieved responses to "evils in the concrete" provide better reasons for understanding why Swisshelm's woman's rights program was piecemeal and limited, and why, though she never hesitated to compare the condition of slaves with that of the white woman, she fought tenaciously to keep emancipation and woman's rights separate. Her woman's rights message was to the women "of Georgia as [well] as those of Massachusetts" (*PV*, November 2, 1850). All women were potential victims of the "grand mistake" that would plunge them into loveless marriages. As she fought to prevent that, the last thing Swisshelm wanted was an undifferentiated equality between the sexes or the union of woman's rights and emancipation.

The "fools and fanatics" that Swisshelm claimed were rushing into woman's rights were therefore recognized as a double threat. They might drive woman's rights in a direction that confirmed her deep fear that she had sacrificed her sexual identity and had become an androgyne so grotesquely misshapen that she could not live even in "a state of prostitution." Furthermore, there was the attempt to give organizational structure to the reformers' rhetorical linking of women and slaves in a common, indiscriminate slavery. To loosely use the rhetoric was one thing; to act on it was an altogether different matter. Swisshelm thought that such a policy could only wreck the women. It was not so much that both causes would be lost, but that women's chances would be sacrificed in a misguided attempt to help slaves. The alternative was to fit out the slave with his own "oar" and "let him row his own craft." Her savage metaphor of the "lifeboat" establishes Swisshelm's priorities as a reformer. Woman's rights came first; suffering women were more important than suffering slaves. In the final analysis slaves must fend for themselves.

The thesis of conspiracy, embedded in Swisshelm's ideas about slavery and woman's rights, informed another of those "subject[s] which ought to be thought on." As slaveholders had conspired to "nationalize" slavery, and as manipulators of the church and the law had conspired to enslave women, Catholics were also engaged in a conspiracy to undermine and destroy "liberty" in the United States.

Anti-Catholicism reached two peaks of intensity in pre–Civil War America, first toward the late 1830s; second in the mid-1850s. The diminution in the forties is characteristically attributed to the countervailing forces of the Mexican War and the intensification of the slavery issue, both of which drained off energies that otherwise might have flowed into anti-Catholicism. Swisshelm served as one of the connecting links between the two periods of greatest anti-Catholic agitation. She also illustrates the connection that often existed between abolition and anti-Catholicism.

Apparently she was set off by Bishop Michael O'Conner's proposal that Pittsburgh public school money be shared with parochial schools. As she seized it, the issue was the classic one of separation of church and state, and the *Visiter* opened its anti-Catholic war on this ground. But Swisshelm's fight with the Catholics was underlaid by labor unrest in the Pittsburgh metals industry, importation of "eastern workingmen . . . who [were] not fit for freedom" (*PV*, March 9, 1850), rapid growth of the Catholic community in Pittsburgh, building a cathedral emblematic of the new Catholic strength in the city, and the legacy of fear and malevolence left over from the first wave of anti-Catholic agitation. The situation was ripe for defenders of traditional values to display their own anxieties when they believe themselves and their institutions threatened.[8]

In late 1849 a semiliterate, anti-Catholic street preacher named Joe Barker was jailed after a brawl on the steps of the new cathedral. While he was in jail a mayoral election was held in which the preacher was put up as a candidate, more as a joke than anything else. Barker suddenly found himself the beneficiary of Whig party support that won the election for him. A gubernatorial pardon was forthcoming. On inauguration day a triumphant procession accompanied Barker from his cell to the city hall. In the mayor's office the judge who two months before had sentenced Barker to jail now administered the oath of office to him. Shortly after Barker became mayor the owners of the Pittsburgh iron mills announced a wage cut. The ironworkers walked off their jobs. The mill owners retaliated by importing workingmen, most of whom were Catholic. The stage was set for a vicious battle in the city known for "the bitterest of the labor wars [fought in] American industry between 1840 and 1860."⁹ It was in the midst of this upheaval that Bishop O'Conner pressed his demand for a share of the public school fund, and that Swisshelm discovered the Catholic menace to American "liberties."

With her tactic of "individualizing the sin," she struck directly at Bishop O'Conner. Following a tribute to the bishop's physical attractiveness—he was, she wrote, "one of those men by whose existence the Creator renders a reason for the continuance of the race"—she published her own version of the classic anti-Catholic screed, Maria Monk's *Awful Disclosures of the Hotel Dieu Nunnery of Montreal*, itself written by abolitionists. According to Swisshelm, Bishop O'Connor's sexual appetites were excited by a Miss Tiernan who lived in Pittsburgh. Luring her away from her family, the bishop persuaded the beautiful girl to forsake the world. Once inside a nunnery's walls she mysteriously disappeared, presumably to a mysterious death that "did honor to [the bishop's] manhood, however it may have affected his priesthood." The story concludes with the bishop, repentant for what he had done to the young woman, giving up his ring and crozier and immuring himself for the remainder of his life.

Once establishing Bishop O'Conner's character, Swisshelm transferred his crafty sexuality to the whole Pittsburgh Catholic clergy. Describing the priests in a procession at the consecration of the new cathedral, she wrote that "every head and face . . . were more or less stamped by sensuality and low cunning [they looked like] winebibbers, gross beef-eaters." The "most villainous-looking set [she] had ever seen," the priests were unquestionably fitted for the malignant, conspiratorial role she endowed them with (*HaC*, 150–55).

Swisshelm's first attack centered on Bishop O'Conner, his clergy, and his proposal for sharing the school fund. However, the bishop's request for a share of the school money was subsequently revealed as only part of a comprehensive conspiracy launched by all Catholics to "attack...the very foundations of civil liberty in America." As Swisshelm presented the case, the clearest proof of the conspiracy was the silence of the Pittsburgh press about the bishop and his scheme. The *Visiter* was the only paper to raise the alarm. Swisshelm said that the Democratic party newspapers refused to touch the story because they were all edited by Catholics. The Whig papers joined the conspiracy of silence because they were fearful of losing Catholic subscribers and advertising. With the party press muzzled, the politically independent *Visiter* had to carry on alone, though at a heavy price. Catholic subscribers canceled their subscriptions, and the paper lost advertising because Protestant businessmen feared retaliation from Catholic customers. As subscribers and advertising fell off and the other papers maintained their silence, Swisshelm became convinced that she had stumbled upon the key mechanism of the Catholic's "concerted attack" on "liberty." By muzzling the press all American Catholics, following in lock-step behind their priests, were able to work in secret in order to consolidate their political and economic power in America. "The secular papers of the United States, with a few exceptions, she said, are almost as much under the control of the Pontiff as the press of Austria.... Protestants do not carry their religion either into political or business relations, and so there is no offset to the religious, political and business concentration of Romanism." Hammering at the thesis of the Catholic conspiracy, Swisshelm took as the measure of her success her own claim that "I have seldom, if ever, met a Catholic so obscure that he did not recognize my name as that of an enemy." And, with obvious satisfaction, because it was a sign of the crucial role she was playing in unmasking the conspiracy, she said that she had become "the object of a hatred I had not deemed possible."

She argued that the massive concentration of Catholic power, though fearsome in itself, was not content to pursue its aims alone. The Catholics aimed at making an alliance with the other great conspiratorial power they so much resembled. Anticipating by thirty years the rallying cry of "Rum, Romanism and Rebellion," Swisshelm laid it down, "To be a member of the Roman church was to be a friend of Southern interests." Social upheaval in Pittsburgh might have provided the impetus for her emergence as an anti-Catholic agitator, but, she said, the events of 1849 were only the catalyst that drew her into the battle against the Catholics. Much earlier, she said, she had cast a wary eye at the Catholic community, seeing in it something sinister and threatening, not simply because it was alien, but because she was an abolitionist. Long before the Pittsburgh turmoil, she wrote, "abolitionists began to feel the alliance between Romanism and slavery."

As Swisshelm presented them, priest and slaveholder were cut from the same cloth. Her characterization of the Pittsburgh priests was as easily a description of the slave masters gorging themselves in her old Louisville boardinghouse. All that was needed to make the transformation was to divest the men "stamped by sensuality and low cunning" of their vestments and censers and equip them with ruffled shirts and whips, and the Catholics reappear as traveling Mississippi flesh-merchants. The priestly silencing of the Pittsburgh press was similar to the Louisville slaveholders' breaking up her school for free Negroes, and the intent of the priests and slave masters was the same. These "scoundrels" controlled "monster establishments." Their "monster establishments," weaving interlocking webs of "duplicity & trickery & fraud & chicanery & deceit," were aiming at, Swisshelm wrote, the destruction of "the genius . . . of our glorious American institutions" (*HaC*, 209–12).

It is not unexpected that Swisshelm, a rock-ribbed Protestant, would have a Catholic animus, but it is revealing that her attacks on the Catholics never presented religion as the reason for her hostility. Her reasons were always stated in secular terms. She made no case for religious freedom or for the freedom of conscience. Her claim was that the Catholics were using their church as an instrument to dominate the nation's "political and business relations." As she brought the slaveholders in partnership with the Catholics and assigned them the same motives and the same goals, she likewise made the slave tangential to abolition and shifted her animus against the slaveholder from one based upon religious doctrine and fortified by guilt, the self-claimed base of her abolition, to the most practical considerations of worldly power. Her portraits of the dual conspirators were indistinguishable so far as their morality and their social functions were concerned. Profligate and cunning, one the master of bond slaves, the other the master of the "slaves of centuries," they directed their "monster establishments" toward interlocking goals: the subversion of "civil liberty, the rights of property, and the right to labor or refrain at pleasure" [10] (*PV*, March 9, 1850).

It is a grotesque conclusion. After three years of sustained and "harrowing" effort at "pouring it out" to have come to this, the belief that slavery and Catholicism were inseparable in that they intended to crush a free labor system and steal private property. Furthermore, she wrote, the dual conspirators meant to go over society "like a 'header' over a wheat field [leaving] a deal level of stalks, all minus the heads, so that no tall fellows are left to shame them" (*HaC*, 209–12).

With her metaphor of some giant harvesting machine, Swisshelm's opposition to the Catholics and the slaveholders was reduced to the same terms as her quarrel with organized labor. The latter she feared and despised because "Their great Union rolling-pins flatten [workers] out like pie-crust, and tramps are not overshadowed by the superiority of industrious men." A diabolical trinity emerges. Labor unions, the Catholic church, and slavery were all in an interlocking conspiracy to destroy enterprising men who worked alone. The destruction of industrious men's "superiority" would result in radically shifting "that point which . . . define[s] one's form against the sky," the place where the "tall fellows" stood, which was a position that could rightly be achieved only by practicing "economy and industry" (*PV*, February 15, 1851). With their "slaves," either chattel or "of centuries" (or in the case of the unions, their "tramps"), the great conspiracies had institutionalized "indolence, extravagance [and] ignorance." If allowed to go unchecked, these monster establishments bid to keep a person from "occupying his proper station in the great social economy." In the final analysis, the enormous corruption (and subsequent destruction) of American society was prophesied out of a fear of the destruction of the individual workingman entrepreneur.

The plea for human freedom begun so boldly—she would "dare

the tempest," Swisshelm wrote in her first editorial, because she was compelled to "'Do right and trust in God'"—ended in a defense of economic individualism. The central theme embedded in her polemics against slavery, as well as those against Catholicism and organized labor, is that of the competitive marketplace and the ways it was abused. The marketplace was the arena in which the drama of the covenanted nation was enacted. In the marketplace, the "great social economy" (*PV*, February 15, 1851) and the moral economy were merged so that they became one and the same. Moral judgment was rendered on social institutions on the basis of the economic actions of their proprietors. Swisshelm's arraignment of the conspiracies concludes by bringing them to convergence in the marketplace where morality and economics are synonymous. When she put slaveholders with priests and union members in the marketplace the basic proposition informing her abolition becomes clear.

According to Swisshelm, a person's morals were demonstrated by his social standing. His moral worth, his capacity for "shaming" others, depended largely upon the amount of property he owned. Poverty and affluence were the most reliable measure of human affairs, and, most fundamentally, the gauge of a person's moral behavior. A man might come to "honest and honorable" poverty, but in America he was a rare exception. Uncharacteristically of an age in which poverty was rationalized by extolling its character-building virtues, Swisshelm bitterly protested the hymns of justification raised in behalf of being poor. She thought that her ideas would be unpopular because there "is much defense of these dear [poverty-stricken] fellows." Nonetheless, "poets may sing praises and philosophers may rack their brains to dignify and enoble poverty, but while their ink is running they fear and despise it." No hypocritical cant, she wrote, could hide the fact that in "most cases" poverty was not the hard testing ground of virtue, but was instead "the fruit of indolence, extravagance or ignorance." Therefore, she continued, "the world is just in visiting it with scorn. We can find no justification for any man's being poor, suffering, in this country, unless it is the result of accidents." Her case against the poor man was exactly the one she made against the habitual drunk. Except for certain unavoidable "accidents" a poor man came to his poverty precisely as an alcoholic came to his drunkenness, by individual action and moral failing. In an open, competitive society poverty was no more the result of social conditions than drunkenness was the result of "existing saloons, and non-existing bright hearths, smiling wives, pretty caps and aprons." As the "disease of opening one's mouth and pouring whiskey into it was under the control of the mouth-opener," so was the "disease" of poverty under the control of the poor man (*PV*, April 5, 1851). The poor man, like the drunk, was thus charged with the same moral failings with which she had indicted the conspiratorial slaveholders and priests, the proprietors of the "monster establishments" of slavery and Catholicism.

In the interchangeable moral flaws attributed to the drunk, poor man, slaveowner, and priest lies much of the core of Swisshelm's abolition and anti-Catholic messages. Slaveholder and priest and the poverty-stricken and the drunken were all guilty of idleness, wastefulness, and ignorance. But unlike the drunks and poor who lived passively on the margins of society, the slaveholders and priests had built complementary systems that protected and rewarded the fruits of immoral behavior. They had massed their power and were using it to threaten the "freeman" who was living morally by faithfully practicing "economy and industry." With "no offset" against their concerted attack in the marketplace, the priest and the slaveholder would crush "men accustomed to freedom." Then poverty, the scorned badge of immorality, would come to a person without the justifying "accident" which alone relieved the poor man of his burden of moral culpability. Consequently, society's "station of honor" would bear no relationship to a person's "proper station." Indolence, extravagance, and ignorance would displace economy and industry as the attributes characterizing the man who reached "the point where folks can see him." "Tramps" would indeed overshadow industrious men; and a man's social position would depend solely on "how much mud [he] wades through to get there." The competitive marketplace, the crucible in which morality was tested, would be completely sullied, and trails of muck would lead to all the prominent "places and stations." The moral economy would be thoroughly deranged.

One is reminded of the passage from Jeremiah from which Swiss-

helm took the name of her newspaper. Jeremiah charged the betrayers of the covenant with a catalog of sins reminiscent of her
indictment of priest and slaveholder. All of them were guilty of
"duplicity & trickery & fraud & chicanery & deceit," coupled with
the most unvarnished concupiscence. Nonetheless they "are waxen
fat, they shine . . . they prosper." In both Jerusalem and America it
was the corrupt who prospered. In ancient Jerusalem the prophet
was driven to the conclusion that "a wonderful and horrible thing is
committed in the land." The most reliable indicator of righteousness, the one that showed whether a man knew the way of the
Lord, was destroyed. Everything was askew when the wages of
immorality was "fat, shining prosperity." The most indisputable
evidence was at hand that the covenanted nation was careening
toward disaster.

At Swisshelm's hands the Old Testament moral indicator was set
inside the new covenanted nation whose canons were "civil liberty," "the rights of property, and the right to labor or refrain at
pleasure." These were the crucial clauses in the contract made between God and "the Fathers of the Constitution" in behalf of the
American people. These clauses were, as she interpreted them, the
bedrock guarantees in the Constitution to which the schismatic
Covenanters had subscribed in the church split of 1833. They were
the foundations of the moral state.

The implication in Swisshelm's understanding of the
Constitution-as-covenant is that "civil liberties" existed to nourish
and protect private property and free labor, the elements of "the
great moral economy." Embedded in the constitutional covenant,
they were the only constitutional guarantees responsive to "the
motives that influence common humanity." They were the ones
that expressed in constitutional form "the great mainspring that
keeps this world astir—self-interest" (PV, November 24, 1849).
Covenanted people demanded a moral content to secular activity.
They were thus provided the devices out of which came the proofs
of whether "men . . . have known the way of the Lord." For the
proofs to be conclusive they had to emerge from the competitive
marketplace where the "thou shalt nots were addressed to each individual." As long as the righteous prospered and the unrighteous

sank into poverty it was certain that the covenant with God was being kept. The moral state was flourishing. There was no reason to fear, like Jeremiah, that "a horrible thing is committed in the land." And there was no reason to raise an apocalyptic jeremiad against the slaveholders.

But, according to Swisshelm, the slaveholders (joined by the conspiratorial Catholics and unionized workers) had upset the competitive marketplace. They refused to act "fairly, openly and honorably" in the struggle to "get out from amongst the masses and be distinguished." It was not simply that the conspirators were guilty of "duplicity & trickery & fraud & chicanery & deceit" (the list of attributed "sins" is suggestive in itself, implying secular activity, misdeeds in the world of politics and economics, not assaults on the human spirit), but that they prospered.

In the Louisville sketches there is not one down-at-the-heels slaveholder. The Louisville economy might be as spavined as the horses dragging the wagons away from the river wharves, but the masters of the economy are gorgeous in their finery. Having laid society under their tribute, they want for nothing. Even their wives' and daughters' voluptuous bodies—the "superb forms of the Kentucky women" which Jane openly admired—were testaments to their wealth. Notwithstanding indolence, extravagance, and ignorance, the slaveholders as individuals and as a class were enormously prosperous.

The fact that they were prospering as a class must mean they were operating in concert. The "thou shalt nots were addressed to each individual," and as individuals the slaveholders were flouting them, but the retributive justice of poverty was not forthcoming. If all were immoral and none were poor, it must follow that the individual immoralities somehow had been translated through a vast conspiracy into a system whereby all escaped punishment. And this, Swisshelm claimed, was precisely what had happened. Without attempting to explain how the slaveholders' conspiracy had been perfected, she asserted that as a class "they stand fast by the cause they have espoused." The "Southern Tiger" had emerged with all of its "haughty insolence." The clinching proof of the "monster establishment's" existence was not found in voting patterns, public policy, or any of the divisive issues before the nation. It was found in what she herself had seen. As with Jeremiah's Jerusalem, the evidence was in hand in Louisville that the covenanted nation was close to disaster. The marketplace as mechanism of the moral order had stopped working.

With this conclusion Jane Swisshelm offers a profound insight into the values of American abolition and the meaning of "equality" that abolition helped impart to American society in the nineteenth century. Scarcely breaking with the past with her advocacy of the moral society, Swisshelm also anticipates the future in the way the moral society is to be achieved. It is only a matter of scale separating the values of her religious sectarianism from the victorious society's values, as it is only a short step from her scripturally sanctioned Manchesterianism to the scientifically justified laissez-faire of William Graham Sumner. For the Covenanter as for the red-tooth-and-claw Darwinist the free marketplace is the arbiter of man's moral worth, and the function of the marketplace is to produce a moral elite. Swisshelm's "men accustomed to freedom" diligently practicing "economy and industry" foreshadowed by more than a generation Sumner's exemplary "Forgotten Man." Swisshelm's man standing on the high places anticipates Sumner's millionaire. Each attained his position because of his incontestable ability, which is synonymous with shining virtue; and both "shame" the lesser fry beneath them. And if Swisshelm's man stood in close communion with God while Sumner's, whose science forced him to abandon anything that smacked of the supernatural, did not, there were more tender-minded men in Sumner's world who had not abandoned the old faith that God had indeed placed the watchcare of the nation's affairs (and the philanthropic nurture of certain of the poor whose poverty had descended by way of the horrendous historical "accident" of enslavement) in their hands.

VII

God and I against . . . a world.
JANE SWISSHELM

St. Cloud

In May, 1857, Jane Swisshelm left her husband for the last time. In *Half a Century* she leads her reader to believe that she made her decision in the midst of one of their interminable quarrels over money and property— about who must pay for clothes, books, china, and a piano. But as usual, behind the quarreling with James was Elizabeth Swisshelm. "After fifteen years in his mother's house I must run away or die," Swisshelm said. As was the earlier case, it was her revolt against James and his mother that propelled her into her second career as an abolition writer.

According to the *Half a Century* account, not only was she distraught by the soured marriage, she lived with bitter fears that the

Pittsburgh Catholics would abduct Zoe, her young daughter, either to kill her, or raise her as a Catholic, fates which she means her reader to understand were equally horrible. After she sold the *Visiter* she had tried to keep on with her part-time abolition and anti-Catholic writing, but she had come to the point at which she could no longer stand the tension. Her "strength utterly and completely failed." Her "hand and brain were numb." She said she wanted to die but hung on to life for the sake of Zoe. So she decided to run, flee the Catholics and Elizabeth Swisshelm. Ahead lay the long trip by steamboat and stagecoach that would take her to St. Cloud, Minnesota. There "on the confines of civilization" she planned to buy a few acres of land, farm it herself, and live in "the pine woods... in my cabin." She "looked at [her] hands, and thought, Once more you are mine. True, the proceeds of your... years of brick-making are back there in Egypt with your lost patrimony, but we are over the Red Sea, out in the free desert; no pursuit is possible, and if bread fails, God will send Manna."

She wants the reader of *Half a Century* to believe that as she left Pittsburgh she was heartsick and frightened, that she intended to live a subsistence life, trusting to farm labor and God to sustain her, and that she had severed all ties to her work and family. "My work was done." She had, she said, not only fled from an intolerable marriage and a fearsome threat to her daughter, she also had "run away from the irrepressible conflict... thinking I should see no more of our national curse." Therefore the intriguing feature of Swisshelm's life in Minnesota is the way she was brought back into abolition work. The examination of her return to the battle—an inquiry into the reasons why black slavery *"confronted me here as it had never done before"*—provides the focal point for this last portion of our inquiry into her life.

According to *Half a Century*, even before she arrived at St. Cloud she began to feel that she must once again be a witness against slavery. Evidence was accumulating that the slaveholders' conspiracy extended to Minnesota. In the stagecoach rattling toward St. Cloud she was told about "General" Sylvanus Lowry, the political master of northern Minnesota, who "was the embodiment of the slave power." Having immense wealth and influence, Lowry lived in semibarbaric splendor, held dominion over the northern frontier and was powerful in the territorial government which itself "was a mere tool of slavery." After arriving in St. Cloud, she said that she found all her suspicions confirmed. An "active . . . unscrupulous and aggressive foe" controlled Minnesota. The only identifiable abolitionists in the territory were a few Garrisonians and a remnant of the Liberty party, but neither would enter the battle against slavery. They suffered from "that moral dilettanteism [sic] which thinks first of his own hands." Everyone else she wrote off: "People had gone to [northern Minnesota] to make homes, not to fight the Southern tiger." It therefore fell to her to use "the voice of the pen in advocating the cause whose success appears to us necessary to the salvation of our country." "I have a mind," she wrote, "to start a paper myself." But, "What an uneven fight [it will be]. . . . God and I against . . . a world." Despite the odds, she was determined to take up the struggle again. On December 10, 1857, the *Visiter* was reincarnated in St. Cloud. Its front page carried the Jeffersonian credo of the equality of mankind. Linked with the credo was her doctrine that the Bible and the Constitution were authoritative statements against slavery. The *Visiter* was an "out-and-out Abolitionist newspaper."[1]

Beneath the surface of the story Swisshelm tells in *Half a Century* about her flight to Minnesota and her decision to revive the *Visiter* lie a tangle of motives and purposes. The impression she conveys of a headlong plunge into the unknown frontier, an act that, she said, caused the Swisshelms to threaten to "take out a writ of lunacy," is a patent contrivance. It is clear she meant to break away from Swissvale. What is less clear are the circumstances surrounding her flight and her subsequent reentry in abolition journalism. Unless those circumstances are explored it is impossible to reconcile the paradox presented by *Half a Century*'s account of the episode: She runs away from the battle over slavery but in six months reenters it in the face of the most overwhelming odds. She chooses to reenter the struggle because at St. Cloud, a frontier outpost in the northernmost territory of the United States where there were no slaves, where only in the wildest stretch of the imagination there ever could be, and where even the intractable

Garrisonians were quiet, slavery "confronted [her] as it had never done before."

The key to the paradox lies in understanding why the "confrontation" occurred in the first place, and why at St. Cloud the head-on collision assumed a magnitude "as it never had before." Unless these questions can be answered, her cry—"What an uneven fight. . . . God and I against a world"—as she swung into a brutal, violent fight with Sylvanus Lowry is reduced to the most self-serving fatuousness. We would be left with an incongruous, simple-minded "moral" explanation for "speaking with the voice of the pen" again, one that reeks not only of fatuousness but of hypocrisy, because the consequence of her fight with Sylvanus Lowry was a shift in secular power and the perfection of rival claims to social prestige and economic advantage. The difficulty is that the war cry "God and I" is indeed often invoked to justify precisely these things. However, to argue that a claim of God's will was a gloss Swisshelm employed to justify power and ambition makes her awesome God a mere convenience; it puts at a discount her profound need to propitiate the God residing in her. Furthermore, to summarily dismiss "God and I" as some sort of rationalizing screen denies us access to the intricate relationships connecting secular ambition and quest for power with a heavenly imperative that insists upon a moral people controlling a moral state. Unless the Minnesota phase of Swisshelm's life is approached with an appreciation for the subtleties that inform her situation at St. Cloud, the result will be to rob this bitterly unhappy woman, regardless of the fantasy she created about herself in *Half a Century*, of the courage and the gallantry that is properly hers as she made a new life for herself on the northern frontier. And we will fail to appreciate the profound meaning of her own painfully bought truth: that her soul was a warring army, struggling between her ambitions for the world and her desire for the annihilation of self in the embrace of her Covenanter God.

In the mid-fifties Minnesota was booming. Population doubled each year as immigrants poured into the territory. In 1854 there were 32,000 inhabitants in the territory; in 1857 there were

150,000 persons living there. Between 1855 and 1857 seven hundred towns were platted comprising more than three hundred thousand homesites for more than a million and a half people, exclusive of those who lived on farms. Minnesota was, in short, a speculative and entrepreneurial wonderland. In the race for land, timber rights, townsites, Indian trade, railroad charters, and other concessions for opening the frontier in mid-nineteenth-century America there were fortunes to be made. Agriculture may have been the mode of life for the Minnesota pioneer, but farming was not the way to wealth and power. The capsulated autobiography of George F. Brott is a summary of the realized ambitions of the successful Minnesota pioneer. Brott described himself as "farmer, wagon and carriage maker, sheriff, postmaster, real estate dealer, editor, townsite promoter, owner of flour mills, steamboats, steamships and sailing craft, wholesale and retail merchant, member of constitutional conventions, colonel of engineers, canal and railroad president and inventor." [2]

Brott had come to the territory as a New York carriagemaker turned sleighmaker. In ten years, from 1850 to 1860, he had engrossed most of the enterprises by which he described himself, and his subsequent story is a portion of an unwritten chapter in the history of the Civil War and Reconstruction. In 1862 he took the first merchant ship into New Orleans after the city fell. During those roisterous, freewheeling war years he tapped the commerce of the Mississippi River from St. Cloud to the Gulf of Mexico. Inside two years he made six million dollars; within another six he had lost it all. Meanwhile he would be important in bringing Jane Swisshelm to her second career as an abolition journalist.

In 1857 Brott married the daughter of Charles Stearns, one of the first pioneers on the northern frontier. Stearns was a territorial legislator and entrepreneur whose interests paralleled those of his son-in-law. Stearns County, of which St. Cloud was the seat, was named for him. At St. Cloud, Brott started a newspaper, the *Advertiser*, the front page of which carried a map of Minnesota with St. Cloud in the middle "with many imaginary railroads from all points of the compass centering there." He established the *Advertiser* in January, 1857, because he had large interests in St. Cloud

and other embryo metropolises in the northern part of the territory, and believed that a newspaper would aid in attracting new
settlers.[3] Brott's friend, the man who more than any other was in a
position to help him realize his dream of the railroads connecting
his "embryo metropolises" and converging at St. Cloud, was
"General" Sylvanus Lowry, who Swisshelm called the "Grand
Mogul, Czar, Bashaw with two tails and Dictator by divine
right . . . FFT [First Family of the Territory] and commander-in-
chief of all the women-whippers in North Minnesota" (*SCD*, August 5, 1858).

Sylvanus was the son of David Lowry. "A noble, big-hearted"
man, one of Minnesota's "foremost pioneers and one of the
strongest intellectually," the elder Lowry has been called.[4] A
staunch Cumberland Presbyterian, he is said to have responded to a
missionary impulse and an abolitionist conscience when he migrated from Tennessee in 1849. He accepted a commission as Indian
agent and undertook a double mission: to bring the Gospel to the
Indians on the northern frontier and take his slaves out of the
South in order that they might be freed. He moved his family from
Tennessee, settled in what was then the Wisconsin Territory, and
became a legend in his own lifetime as a practical, selfless
humanitarian. His son, Sylvanus, grew up on the frontier, was
raised as a Winnebago, spoke the language, was a full-fledged
member of the tribe, and succeeded his father to the Indian agency.
With the agency as a base, he capitalized upon his considerable
talents and his far-flung connections. All accounts make him a
witty, intelligent man as well as a man of considerable power;
though none of these accounts, including *Half a Century*, remotely suggest that he was a young man. When Jane Swisshelm
came to St. Cloud, Sylvanus Lowry was twenty-seven years old.
He owned 50,000 acres of land and held the commission as
commissary-general in the militia, the most lucrative position in
Minnesota's military establishment. Lowry was a business partner
of Henry M. Rice of the American Fur Company, who was also a
territorial delegate, the state's first senator, and the chief architect
of Minnesota's railroad land grants. A kingpin in Minnesota politics, Lowry was so agile in political maneuvering that he was able to

keep his fiefdom on the northern frontier faithful to the Democratic party in the Republican upheaval of 1858–1860. His influence was such that the Lincoln government tried to buy him off. During the Fort Sumter crisis the Republicans gladly paid his dubious (and maybe fraudulent) forty-thousand-dollar claim for supplies delivered to the Winnebagos that the two previous Democratic regimes had refused to honor. Beneath his charm and power there was mental instability that finally broke to the surface. In 1862 Lowry was committed to an asylum for the insane at Cincinnati. But in the late fifties he was a formidable opponent should anyone care to challenge his power. When Swisshelm arrived at St. Cloud, Lowry, Brott, and James Shepley, a lawyer who supplied the legal talent necessary for their operations, and who, with Brott, had made the original survey for St. Cloud, controlled St. Cloud, Stearns County, and the northern border. Ambitious newcomers might get ahead only on their sufferance, or by destroying them.

Jane Swisshelm and Zoe came to St. Cloud with Jane's sister and brother-in-law, Elizabeth and Henry Mitchell, and James Swisshelm's brother, Henry.[5] The year previous Henry Mitchell had left his store at Wilkinsburg to make a reconnaissance through the Northwest, scouting opportunities there. One of thousands of men responding to the lure of the Minnesota Territory, Mitchell decided that his prospects were infinitely better in the Minnesota boom than in the backwaters of Pennsylvania. He returned to Wilkinsburg determined to sell out and move to St. Cloud, where he thought his opportunity in the Territory was greatest. The town was newly chartered; Stearns County had recently been created; the bulk of Minnesota's undeveloped lands lay to the north; and the main channels of the Indian and the Canadian trade funneled through the little town. St. Cloud was the strategic spot for a new and profitable beginning. Everything lay ripening in the offing. It "was no time for timidity or even moderation in business ventures."[6] People coming now would be among the first to establish themselves and benefit from the transformation of wilderness to civilization. If being among the first meant standing in dusty streets with "a lot of Chippewas [who] played football with the heads of some Sioux, with whom they had been at war," such things would soon pass. And if it meant narrowing one's vision to "home necessities and home interests . . . in building towns and railroads, and bridging rivers" and thereby absorbing one's "surplus energies" in matters of "a local rather than a national character," it was a small price to pay in order to "establish homes of civilization and of plenty" (*SCD*, May 12, 1854). Such was Swisshelm's assessment of the St. Cloud venture and she had no quarrel with it. What was important was to stand toward the head of the line in the race for profits and power in St. Cloud, and be a "proprietor" of the northern frontier. Like other Minnesotans, she and the Mitchell-Swisshelm group were not going to the territory "to fight the Southern tiger"; they were migrating to "make homes."

Of crucial importance to understanding Swisshelm's life in St. Cloud is the timing of her rediscovery of the "Southern tiger," her reason for locating it in the person of Sylvanus Lowry, and her polemical transformation of the pioneers from self-centered home builders to western pilgrims who, carrying with them the "piety of the East," were laying the material foundations for the moral state. Much of the story relating to these matters remains hidden, but there are sufficient clues to piece portions of it together.

Winter lies bitter on the northern frontier. The land does not begin to stir until the ice breaks on the rivers in late spring. There was ample time between Henry Mitchell's return to Pennsylvania in the autumn of 1856 to call the family to council, close the Wilkinsburg store, pack the stock, order goods shipped on consignment, make business agreements with Henry Swisshelm, arrange steamboat passage, and study stagecoach schedules. There was ample time to have everything in readiness when the news came that the ice had broken on the upper Mississippi and that the roads were open to heavy wagons and stagecoaches on the roads north of St. Paul. There was also ample time during the winter of 1856 for Jane Swisshelm to realize that at last she had been presented with a splendid opportunity to wrest James from Elizabeth Swisshelm.

The Mitchells and the Swisshelms were working in close cooperation.[7] The migration was a joint enterprise supported by both families, and it recapitulated on a larger scale James Cannon's venture at Wilkinsburg at the end of the War of 1812, and James Swiss-helm's operations at Louisville in 1837. James himself was at first drawn into the venture, suggesting to the others that he and Jane join the immigrants. But for unknown reasons he withdrew. Although he backed out, he had helped create a situation in which Jane could try to force the issue between herself and Elizabeth Swisshelm. With her relatives, she could go to "the pine woods as [James had] proposed upon marriage" and wait for him to make the choice that she had pressed on him since their marriage: to live either with her or his mother. There is no reason to doubt the anguish behind her phrases describing herself as she came to St. Cloud, "my hand and brain were numb" and "I must run or die." But an impulsive daring flight to the frontier, the impression she created in *Half a Century*, is sheer invention. James "proposed" emigration to Minnesota "before I thought of going," she confessed. In James's absence she would be convoyed by her sister and two brothers-in-law. She would go to St. Cloud as safely as anyone could go to a frontier community, and she would make the journey with more support than many who undertook the journey. It begins to appear that her "flight" to the frontier was a carefully conceived strategem to pit herself and Zoe, who becomes almost a hostage, against Elizabeth Swisshelm in a desperate bid for her husband. Once she arrived in St. Cloud she waited for the mails, each of which she hoped would bring the news that James had at last broken away from Swissvale and Elizabeth Swisshelm. "Ah," she thought, "what a paradise it would be."

Meantime there was the matter of getting toward the head of the line in the business of exploiting the "confines of civilization at St. Cloud." There is no evidence suggesting that the Swisshelm-Mitchell group entered the political battle raging across Minnesota during the summer as Democrats and Republicans fought for control of the constitutional convention that would take the territory into the Federal Union. In this battle the issues of slavery and Negro rights played a prominent, if artificial, part, and some of the rhetoric was reminiscent of the struggle in Kansas: "But where shall these . . . outrages end? . . . Give this Republican party . . . power in Minnesota, and they will flood your Territory with the minions of their Emigrant Aid societies, armed with Sharp's rifles . . . and [they] will inaugurate scenes of violence and bloodshed."[8] In the midst of this battle Jane Swisshelm was absolutely silent. She had not yet discovered the "Southern tiger" in St. Cloud, or seen in the person of Sylvanus Lowry anything other than an imposing man having "all of the polish of a well-born gentleman," which was the usual impression Lowry made on visitors and new arrivals.[9]

Autumn came but the mails did not bring the expected letter from James. Instead, his letters asked for her to come back to Swissvale. With the approach of winter it was plain that even if James did relent he could not come to St. Cloud until the next spring when the rivers and roads were open once more. It would be a year before Jane could see him again. And his letters gave no sign that even then he would leave Swissvale. Increasingly it appeared to her that her challenge to Elizabeth Swisshelm had failed. Neither she nor Zoe could detach James from his mother. She reflected upon the last time she had seen James. Coming aboard the riverboat to bid them good-bye, he held Zoe on his knee and "wept over her." It was a promising omen. But James nevertheless had chosen to remain at Swissvale. She was driven to the bitter conclusion, "My husband [was] mine no more." Then, apparently, she collected James's letters and, in an act of significance of which she herself perhaps did not fully appreciate, burned them. Only then, toward mid-December, as the ice choked the rivers and winter's isolation began to close in on St. Cloud, did it come to her, "I have a mind to start a paper myself"[10] (HaC, 167; SCV, December 10, 1857).

Jane Swisshelm's reputation as a journalist, editor, and publisher came with her to St. Cloud. Hers were talents in short supply on the northern frontier. They were especially valuable at the time she arrived, because George Brott's Advertiser was about to fold. Already overextended and deeply involved in land speculation along the proposed route of the Minnesota and Pacific Railroad, Brott was eager to keep his paper publishing. If the Advertiser went under, there would be no newspaper north of St. Paul to herald the opportunities of the north country, or display the splendidly misshapen map of Minnesota with St. Cloud at the center, radiating the railroad network. During the best of times Brott was "continually under the harrow of debt," and if the *Advertiser* failed at this crucial moment he might "go under."[11] Surely his interests would suffer; so might those of Henry Mitchell, Henry Swisshelm, and their new ally and business associate, Stephen Miller.

Miller had arrived in St. Cloud seven months after the Swisshelm-Mitchell migration. Coming from Harrisburg, Pennsylvania, where he pursued a variegated career of lawyer, editor, flour miller and commission merchant, through which he had a business connection with James Swisshelm, Miller appeared in St. Cloud as a "confirmed invalid."[12] Apparently the bracing atmosphere in St. Cloud quickly cured his sickliness, because he was immediately in active partnership with Henry Swisshelm in various enterprises. They operated a general merchandise store, sold real estate, and were commission and forwarding agents for several eastern firms. In addition, Miller opened a law practice. Henry Mitchell rounded out the group's business activities as proprietor of another general merchandising firm, and he also sold real estate.

Economic rivalry developed between the Mitchell-Swisshelm-Miller group and the Brott-Lowry-Shepley interests. Being old Whigs, the former used the newly founded Republican party as a weapon to shoulder aside the entrenched faction. And if one took note only of the subsequent political history in which Stephen Miller and Jane Swisshelm, with Henry Mitchell's help, led the fight to organize the Republican party in the Minnesota north country, it makes more than a plausible case. The issues and methods they used in their struggle to break Lowry's domination of the northern frontier have an undeniable economic content. When the fight ended, Brott and his father-in-law, Charles Stearns, had gone over to the opposition; Lowry was insane; Henry Mitchell was entrenched as a local political magnate (succeeding to, among other things, Lowry's position as commissary-general of the state militia); Shepley remained with his law practice, but his partner, his brother-in-law George Barstow, seeing the handwriting on the wall, broke up the partnership and moved to California where he built a handsome practice and became speaker of the California house of representatives; James McKelvy, Jane's nephew, was established in local political office and would become a state judge; and Stephen Miller was on his way to the governorship and the dispensation of economic plums.

Power had shifted and with it profit and perquisite. But one follows this tack only by substituting a single-minded economics for the subtle convoluted relationships of a frontier town. Furthermore, to fit their activities into such an economic scheme one must misconstrue what Jane Swisshelm meant when, as the fight began, she said that she and her family group were excluded from the circle of "proprietors"—"that clique"—in St. Cloud (*SCV*, February 18, 1858). And, finally, in order to straighten these tangled complexities on the Procrustean bed of economic motivation, one would have to bypass a cryptic comment made by Sylvanus Lowry. After he was committed to the Cincinnati asylum Jane corresponded with him. Solicitously, she wrote to him as "a sick brother." In one of his replies Lowry said, "Your quarrel and mine was all wrong. There was no one in that upper country capable of understanding you but me, no one capable of understanding me, but you. We should have been friends, and would have been *if we had not each had a self which we were all too anxious to defend.*"[13]

In *Half a Century* Swisshelm said her chief purpose for writing the book was "to supply one quota of the inside history of the great Abolition war." Such a history was necessary, she claimed, because it was a common misconception that the "Anti-slavery struggle . . . originated in Infidelity and was a triumph of Skepticism over Christianity." Her aim was to save abolition for orthodox christianity, and her method was to show through her personal history—her "quota"—the true "motives which underlay [abolitionist] action." When she comes to the St. Cloud portion of the account nothing more than her Covenanter heritage of abolition is needed to explain motives. Swisshelm claimed that the fight at St. Cloud was a religious battle fought with political weapons whereby the moral order of the covenanted nation was achieved. Sylvanus Lowry is identified as the chief agent of slavery and the fight is on.

Subsequent writers have followed her and seem to have taken

her account at face value. They have made the fight in St. Cloud an episode in national antislavery politics. Only William Folwell has seen that the fight was a local one, but he presented it as a conventional partisan battle, a lamentable but illuminating part of the statewide Democratic-Republican strife. Whatever their interpretations, all the writers have agreed that from its inception the fight in St. Cloud was bitterly partisan in standard political terms; it was part of the Republican challenge to Democratic party hegemony. But Swisshelm laid a false trail for the others to follow. And her own desire to tell a good story in *Half a Century* begins the contradiction of this received version. The scene is a barroom, and the talk is about herself and Sylvanus Lowry. One of the hangers-on, Tom Alden, "rose, brought down his big fist, and with a preface of oaths, said: Now, boys, I tell you what it is. We're Democrats. This is a fight between her and Lowrie [*sic*], and we're going to see fair play. If she licks him, let him take it" (*HaC*, 183). Then there is the flat assertion of one of the participants in the fight. William B. Mitchell, Swisshelm's nephew, who helped her publish the *Visiter* said, "The . . . election [of 1858] was somewhat mixed, there being no political questions at issue, and the result turned on the personal popularity of the candidates." [14]

There are too many incongruous clues connected with the fight in St. Cloud to resolve it into a battle between outsiders and insiders for economic advantage alone; nor can pitting "freedom" against "slavery" be of much explanatory usefulness. "The cause whose success appears . . . necessary to the salvation of our country" struggling against "the Southern tiger" is more of a Swisshelm rhetorical embellishment than an explanation of what happened in St. Cloud. There is too much outside the two alternatives to accept either as a satisfactory explanation of why Swisshelm had to speak again with "the voice of the pen" in St. Cloud, and why she was compelled to say what she said.

The fact that he was a Buchanan Democrat did not prevent George Brott from approaching Jane Swisshelm with what seemed to him to be strictly a business offer. He wanted to save the *Advertiser* with its map of the railroads converging at St. Cloud. Not-

withstanding that she was known as an "out-and-out
Abolitionist," Brott offered the *Advertiser* to her on "the sole condition" that she would publish a paper. [15]

Swisshelm surveyed the prospects; they were not promising.
There was not much type and what she had was of poor quality.
There was not much paper, and she had "no more money than
Agur might have accepted with safety." [16] St. Cloud was over six
hundred miles from a type foundry or paper mill. The subscription
list was "shorter than the roll of Gideon's army," and, in the aftermath of the Panic of 1857, she doubted if she could extend the list
with cash-paying subscribers. More likely they would have to pay
in kind, "potatoes, corn, turnips, hay, beef, game, firewood, furs,
anything good to eat or wear, or use about the house" (*SCV*, December 10, 1857). She told Brott that the prospects for success were
slender. Brott added some town lots to sweeten his proposition. He
had many unsold because "you could not give away a corner lot at
that time." [17] With the real estate thrown in as part of the bargain,
Swisshelm accepted Brott's offer. Regardless, she wrote, of how
"strange" it might seem to those who thought that she was "settled" out of public life, she would edit and publish the paper.

Brott was pleased with the arrangement. He might have suffered
a loss in giving away his printing press, and the lots might have
future value, but the newspaper would continue. It did not matter
to him under what masthead the bold claim of being "*the* advertising medium for Northern Minnesota" flew. It was important to
him only that there be one. There was a carefree quality about the
man that enabled him to cut his losses without pausing to count the
costs. "Endowed with tireless energy, no amount of unfortunate
circumstances seemed to discourage him." Misfortune "seemed to
only wound him slightly before he was up and ready to go under
again." Brott was the personification of Swisshelm's Minnesota
pioneer whose energies were engrossed "in building towns, and
railroads, and bridging rivers." Moral ideology was as foreign to
Brott as stability in his own "patched up . . . shattered fortunes." [18]
It made little difference to him that Swisshelm had come to St.
Cloud with a reputation of having "in her soul a bitter burning
hatred of slavery," [19] or, as she warned him, "my normal state is

mutual [sic] antagonism to the superior sex; and contempt for their affectation of superiority." Brott had railroads and embryo metropolises on the brain. It made no difference to him that Swisshelm proposed to take editorial positions maintaining that "Slavery, Intemperance, Affectation, Ignorance, Idleness, Land Monopoly and Large Cities are the seven great evils which curse the Earth." Nor did it disturb him that the paper's masthead claimed that Bible and Constitution were unqualified abolitionist authorities. He perceived no conflict between his interests and the moral message Swisshelm proposed to bring to the northern frontier. And if he saw the possibility of conflict between himself as "upper country proprietor" and the little group of newcomers from Pennsylvania, it did not trouble him enough to call off the deal. Brott was an expansive, even-tempered man. If the wizened little woman to whom he offered his newspaper boasted of her reputation for "kill[ing] every man she has ever touched," he must have thought that the north country was large enough to accommodate them both. Surely, as he approached Swisshelm with his offer, Brott did not have a self that he was anxious to defend.

But Sylvanus Lowry did. Master of the northern frontier, he had not only power to protect but reputation as well. Lowry's position necessitated a different public personality than Brott's, for Brott did not suffer when his friends pointed out that his insouciant ebullience came close to harum-scarum buffoonery. Brott could stand in the dusty street in front of the Stearns House and boom out, "All aboard for Puget Sound! That is what [my] conductors will call out in a few years," and no one would think the worse of him.[20] But Lowry played the part of the grand signeur. He combined the lordly manner of plantation master with the style of frontier guide and host. Courtly and genial, he wore the habiliments of his role well. He was accustomed to deference from his neighbors. There must have been considerable vanity in the man. To refuse him deference was to strike him where he was most vulnerable. It was also an invitation for counterattack and reprisal.

Unlike Brott, who was interested in the newspaper only insofar as it supported his land speculations and town building, Sylvanus Lowry was concerned about the revived *Visiter* for a different reason. He could see what was lost on Brott, a newspaper was one of the most powerful weapons that could be wielded on the northern frontier. There were only six other newspapers in the entire territory; none except Brott's were north of St. Paul; and Jane Swisshelm's reputation, if nothing else, bid to turn the *Advertiser's* successor in support of the Republicans. Thoroughly upset by the brawling campaign of the spring and summer, Minnesota politics was in upheaval in 1857. Lowry had managed to keep his fiefdom under control, but the appearance of a hostile newspaper, the only one on the northern frontier, could only complicate his already difficult situation. He would have to try to entice the little woman editor to his side, and he would not be entirely without a chance of succeeding. Even in *Half a Century*, twenty years after she had established him as her archenemy, Swisshelm described Lowry as being "born to command—of splendid physique and dignified bearing, superior intellect and mesmeric fascination." She could scarcely help but be flattered by his attention and solicitations. There was a chance of persuading her to follow his lead by sheer force of personality. But more important, Lowry was in a position to help her. Her long-after-the-fact-observation that her newspaper "could not live without Gen Lowrie's [sic] assistance" was hyperbole, but there was no question that Lowry's support would be valuable. He could open many doors for her. The political patronage of the north country was at his disposal, and what that meant in printing contracts, advertising revenues, and increased subscriptions was incalculable. Certainly, at first, Lowry's patronage could be the difference between Swisshelm's publishing the *Visiter* on a self-supporting basis and using her own capital to subsidize it. And finally, there was the matter of her own politics. She was not yet a declared Republican. Even at the height of the 1859 campaign organizing the Republican party in the north country she said, "we are not and never were a Republican. Never held any connection with any political party except the old 'Liberty Party' and the 'Free Democratic Party'" (*SCD*, May 5, 1859). If in 1859 such a claim was enough to make one's head reel, it nevertheless was true in December, 1857. She had no party affiliation and was therefore free to move in any of several directions.

Her *Half a Century* recollection of her decision to pit the *Visiter* against Lowry and the Democratic party is fitted to accord with her identification of Lowry as prime target and enemy before she arrived at St. Cloud. While on the stagecoach one of the passengers told her that "them sentiments of yours won't go down [in St. Cloud]." Sylvanus Lowry, he said, "don't allow no abolitionists in these parts." To which, she remembers herself saying as she looked across the prairie, "This is a broad country: but if this be true, there is not room in it for [Lowry] and me." Then she remembers telling George Brott, as they were completing their negotiations about the paper, "There is one thing more. I feel that some day I will attack Gen. Lowrie [sic], who is your friend. He will set Shepley on me; I will make short work of him. Then we will have a general melee, and I will clear out that clique. Shepley is your lawyer, and I do not want to use your press in that way without your consent." She then reports that Brott told her, "'A lady has the right to be of whatever politics she pleases.'" His only concern was that she publish a paper in order to attract immigrants and sell land (*HaC*, 178–80).

After these preliminaries, *Half a Century* leads its readers to believe that the ordained fight moved rapidly to its climax. Lowry let it be known that he would become the paper's patron if the *Visiter* will support the Buchanan administration. However, if Swisshelm refused to follow Lowry's political line, there was no hope for the *Visiter*'s survival. "Such was his ultimatum," Swisshelm reports. Then, she says, she printed an editorial lampooning Lowry. "At first," she writes, "there was a laugh, then a dead stillness of dread, and men looked at me as one doomed." She had picked up Lowry's gauntlet and had flung it back in his face.

The difficulty with this version of the story comes on three counts. It was Jane Swisshelm who made the overture for support; Sylvanus Lowry did not make the first move. Second, it presents a picture of Brott being hand-in-glove with Lowry and Shepley, with their interests being interlocking. Last, the initial issues of the *Visiter* were not partisan. Swisshelm was nowhere near a confrontation with Sylvanus Lowry in these December, 1857, editions.

The editorial line of the *Visiter* changed in February, 1858, two months after Swisshelm began publishing the paper. She printed a long editorial (the lampooning one referred to in *Half a Century*) explaining why she was making the *Visiter* a partisan newspaper. This piece was the opening gun in the fight at St. Cloud, and it is an illustration of her ability to "cut them up as they deserve." But before she finished "cutting them up" she said more than she probably had intended. For that reason her editorial warrants attention in our attempt to understand why she entered the second phase of her career as an abolition writer, and why there is the interstice of silence from December 10, 1857, when she began to publish the *Visiter*, and February 18, 1858, when she turned it against Sylvanus Lowry.

She had come to learn, she wrote, that all the St. Cloud "proprietors" were Buchanan Democrats except herself and one other person. She was, therefore, selling out her principles and joining the Buchanan Democrats because she wanted to be a success at St. Cloud. Her lampoon was finished and her message was clear. Persons siding with Sylvanus Lowry were gullible fools or cynical operators, or both. And she pointed her finger directly at them. They are all St. Cloud "proprietors" except herself and one other person.

The intriguing question is who was the other proprietor outside the pale. The answer must come inferentially because he was never identified, either in the *Visiter* or in *Half a Century*. But he must have been Stephen Miller. It is Miller who helps explain why it took her from December 10, 1857, until February 18, 1858, to start the "general melee" with Sylvanus Lowry.

There is an enigmatic quality about Miller's presence in St. Cloud. Supposedly an invalid, he arrived in the dead of winter, probably in late January or early February, 1858, when travel along the northern frontier was exceedingly difficult for robust men. Once at St. Cloud, Miller recapitulated his old careers of businessman, lawyer, newspaperman, and politician, but with much greater success. As his public life ran its course he served as a brigadier general in the Union Army and as governor of Minnesota; and the foundation for his Minnesota career was laid with the destruction of Sylvanus Lowry's monopoly of political power at St. Cloud.

How Miller made his alliance with Jane Swisshelm is not clear. There is some evidence suggesting the contact was made through James Swisshelm with whom Miller had business dealings in Pennsylvania. Or maybe, since both were editors and political journalists, their paths had crossed in Pennsylvania. Perhaps there was some arrangement before the Mitchell-Swisshelm migration that entailed bringing Miller to St. Cloud. Or perhaps it was simple chance that brought him to a frontier town. But the speed with which the Mitchell-Swisshelm-Miller enterprises blossomed suggests something other than simple accident. When Miller appeared at St. Cloud, Swisshelm must have felt that she had been joined by a kindred spirit. An outsider, a man of talent but adrift, perhaps damaged but not broken in spirit, Miller in many ways was her male counterpart. Whatever their relationship, Jane Swisshelm did not put the *Visiter* on a collision course with Sylvanus Lowry until Stephen Miller came to St. Cloud.

William Fowell, the magisterial historian of Minnesota politics, apologetically relates the story of the fight in St. Cloud, deprecating it as "a local episode not worthy of recognition," and tells his readers that he presents it only in order to illustrate the bitterness of the political struggle in Minnesota as the Republican drive for power reached its climax.[21] But the localness of the fight is precisely what gives it its meaning. The "general melee" (*HaC*, 179) was a fight among St. Cloud's proprietors, between those who were established and those who wanted their places, between "that clique" and the rivals who stood outside the inner circle in the little frontier town. One can only conclude that it took two months, those howling winter-dead months, when life on the northern frontier is driven inside, and when people are driven inside themselves, for Jane Swisshelm to decide that there was a clique in St. Cloud and that she was excluded.

For there was more to being a proprietor in St. Cloud than possessing political power or economic advantage. Contrary to Swisshelm's remembered assertion of a fluid equalitarianism on the frontier, an easy accommodation of newcomers in which "the leaders . . . did not shrink from association with the rude forces," there was sharp cleavage between the old settlers and the newcomers at St. Cloud. To be a proprietor was to be a member of "the elite" and, if one chose to belong, to be part of "a gay crowd" whose "close intimacy endeared [them] to each other," and whose activities were often contrived to make invidious distinctions between themselves and the outsiders. During summer and fall when the northern twilight lingered over the land, the proprietors engaged light-draft riverboats and cruised the limpid water of the upper Mississippi. Aboard were bands, providing dance music and entertainment. As darkness settled over the river fireworks were shot off. Couples standing at the rails watched the rockets arching up into the night and wondered if they would frighten the Sioux into some sort of frenzy. And the languid nights dissolved themselves one after the other. In the winter the dancing was indoors, with card parties and dinners laid on like feasts. The dancing and eating went on deep in the night, after which the revelers turned out in the biting cold for rakehell sleighrides to clear the head and brace the body for another round another day. At the center of the proprietor's "gay crowd" stood Sylvanus Lowry, charming and gallant, lordly in his own fiefdom and ready to introduce his friends at the epicenter of Minnesota society in St. Paul.

No student of the frontier ever described these matters more lucidly than one woman who ran with the gay crowd, and who made such a summer steamboat excursion with Sylvanus Lowry. "When the restraints of an older and long settled community are thrown off, as they are to a large extent in newly settled districts, an unseemly indulgence is often a source of great embarrassment to those of stronger character." And, she added, when the waves of migrants broke in the territory in the late fifties the "older residents still kept our social compact, but the early custom of all citizens meeting together had to give away to smaller and more formal affairs." [22] Thus, when the Swisshelm-Mitchell group arrived in St. Cloud, clear sharp lines of exclusiveness were already drawn between "the elite" and the newcomers, and the newcomers were provided with a double grievance. Not only were they excluded from the "social compact," they could, if they were so disposed, find in the activities of the established residents an affront to their moral sensibilities. "Unseemingly indulgence" was a perquisite of the proprietors. Tolerant of freewheeling behavior in themselves and those who served them, the proprietors treated the northern frontier as a private preserve. They dispensed profit and office with an easy hand to those they favored. The instance of Christ Highhouse, the first sheriff of Stearns County, suffices here:

He was a tall, lank-sided customer, always ready for a quarrel if there was any chance for one and willing to fight if he could find someone to measure strength with him. He was ignorant, generous when in funds, a frequenter of saloons, and made himself popular among the early settlers of Stearns county by his hospitable regards at the bar, and his roystering habits when not engaged in disputes. He was elected first sherriff . . . and his position among wrong-doers was certainly unique. As a matter of fact in those days the judges themselves did not set too good an example of sobriety and court proceedings were often blent with scenes of mirth and gaiety, occasioned by a too free indulgence in ardent spirits. After having run his course here Christ went to Little Falls where he engaged in some alleged robberies and finally left the country.[23]

At St. Cloud in 1858 it was easy to find the unrighteous in "high places," especially if one were a new arrival herself, who found herself closed out by the elite.

Once Jane Swisshelm decided to remain at St. Cloud (and her acceptance of Brott's offer of the newspaper dates that decision as precisely as anything), she wanted and expected admittance to "the elite" and a place among the proprietors. Until then she had been a transient, asking nothing of St. Cloud except a place to stay and wait for James to come for her. But if James was lost, if the last desperate gambit for her husband had failed, and if she was therefore compelled to consign her old dream of the Black Knight and his Wax Doll to oblivion, there remained a portion of her pride and sense of self-esteem to be preserved.

No person at St. Cloud could approach her celebrity. Even Sylvanus Lowry's bailiwick went no farther than the legislative halls in St. Paul and the houses on Summit Avenue where the "bone and sinew" of Minnesota lived. But Swisshelm had had a national audience and clientele. United States senators had deferred to her demand to open the reporters' section of the Senate gallery to women; the nation's most powerful newspaper, Horace Greeley's *Tribune*, had solicited her Washington correspondence; and her arrival in St. Paul the previous summer was the occasion of a special newspaper interview. If Lowry was accustomed to deference in St. Cloud, Jane Swisshelm also had a powerful claim on it once she decided to stay there. Like Lowry she "had a self which [she was] all to anxious to defend." But the parvenues in a frontier town whose "social life was . . . a weird mingling of civilization and barbarism," shut her out. There were no invitations for sleigh rides, none for dancing or card parties presided over by the wives of Lowry and Shepley.

When Jane Swisshelm decided to publish the *Visiter* it was tantamount to claiming a proprietorship. She would be the public voice of St. Cloud and the northern frontier. Talent, celebrity, and deference as well as power were fused in the position. All of the claims of her public "self" would be recognized. Thus her overture to Sylvanus Lowry for support was scarcely an unqualified appeal for help; nor was it a request for admission to the elite. It was an assertion of her right to membership. If Lowry had agreed to support her, he would have stamped the imprimatur of the proprietors upon her. Notice would be served that she was one of them, and an opening into their circle would have been made for the entire Mitchell-Swisshelm group. But that was not the way the proprietors worked. St. Cloud was theirs, they had built it, and their writ ran—literally so, because the judicial district of which St. Cloud was the seat encompassed it all—from St. Cloud to the Canadian border. There was their pride also, the pride of having been first, of having survived, and in their survival having come to power. As Lowry told her, they both had selves that they were compelled to defend, perhaps too anxiously, too compulsively, but nevertheless vehemently. In the case of the old settlers it was as much place as privilege they were determined to protect. They were willing to share their prerogatives, but the sharing had to be on their terms. An act of deference, an explicit and unmistakable sign of submission was demanded of the newcomer whom they admitted to their circle. Lowry's ultimatum was a setting of their terms of admission by the proprietors. There was indeed an issue at stake when Jane Swisshelm made her bid to Lowry for his patronage, but it was not altogether the one she led the readers of the *Visiter* to believe. Because, as she later said of Sylvanus Lowry, he was not only the political master of the northern frontier, he was also "the man who stood ready to set me on the pinnacle of social distinction."

But there is still another dimension to the fight in St. Cloud. As this aspect is introduced the clarity of the division between old settlers and newcomers becomes clouded, and with it the simple social cleavages so useful for historical analysis are diffused. But the partial contradiction and ambiguity are welcome because it is in these grey interstices that most human experience lies.

There was a conflict between the proprietors and the newcomers, but there was also conflict among the proprietors themselves, with the newcomers taking sides in this battle. Two battles were being fought simultaneously in St. Cloud, one older and considerably more intricate than the other. But even in the ambiguities created by accounting for this other fight there is a gain. It is in the internal conflict between the old settlers that the economic and ideological characteristics of the "melee" in St. Cloud appear in their sharpest most indisputable forms. With their appearance the story of Jane Swisshelm and her St. Cloud abolition newspapers takes a remarkable turn.

The thread of the story is picked up with the Stearns County historian's observation, "When St. Cloud came into existence it was as a triplet." [24] In 1857 there were three St. Clouds—Upper Town, Middle Town, and Lower Town. Middle Town, the original St. Cloud, dated from July, 1853, when a land speculator, John Wilson, bought the rights to a half-section of land from Ole Bergeson, a Norwegian squatter. Two years later when the Minnesota boom began Wilson secured a town charter for his 360 acres. Nameless dreams in his head, Wilson baptized his speculation after the French royal palace, and, in February, 1855, began to sell lots to settlers.

Six months later George Brott appeared on the scene. Brott organized the St. Cloud Townsite Company, claimed a half-section of land adjacent to Wilson's, chartered it as St. Cloud City, and began to sell lots in the autumn of 1855. Brott's venture was Lower Town. Only a ravine separated the two St. Clouds, but the dreams of limitless profits separated Wilson and Brott. The rivalry between the two entrepreneurs was intense. Both were boomers, doing all they could to force feed the growth of their communities, and they fought for every advantage they could think of. They gave away lots to favored settlers, those who would establish businesses and industries stimulating population growth. They impeached each other's claim to the land, which forced Brott into a jangling legal battle in order to validate his original title, and embittered the Lower Towners. Then Brott made his masterstroke. He established the *Advertiser*. Brott's paper was not only "*the* advertising medium of Northern Minnesota," which was the claim Jane continued to make when she began to publish the *Visiter;* the newspaper "was devoted first, last and all time to advertising the interest of Lower Town. Very naturally this did not appeal to the people interested in the other parts [of St. Cloud], so their patronage [of the newspaper] was withheld."

By 1857 George Brott had forged into the lead; Lower Town had more inhabitants than either of the other communities, and it monopolized the industries in St. Cloud. Most commercial businesses were there, as were the main river landing and ferry crossing. Fearing that he would be overwhelmed by Lower Town, John Wilson made a countermove. He brought in a colony of German Catholics, settling them in Middle Town and on outlying farms. At one stroke he established the center of Catholicism on the northern frontier at St. Cloud. He also threatened the commercial hegemony of Lower Town because "the majority of the people in the tributary parts [of Stearns County] were German [and] they naturally preferred to barter and trade with businessmen of their own nationality."

The third part of St. Cloud, Upper Town, was Sylvanus Lowry's creation. In the summer of 1856 Lowry moved in from his Winnebago trading post to lay out a townsite north of Wilson's tract. Latecomer to the triple speculation, Lowry worked rapidly to populate his tract, drawing on sources neither Brott nor Wilson could tap. Using his political influence, he had the public Land Office, a plum both Wilson and Brott were seeking, moved from Sauk Rapids to Upper Town. The Land Office gave Upper Town its distinctive economic character. Most of the lawyers, moneylenders, and real estate dealers at St. Cloud clustered around the Land Office. The Indian traders located themselves there and gave Upper Town its raffish rough-and-tumble quality. Lowry also capitalized on his family's southern connections to attract settlers from Kentucky, Tennessee, South Carolina, and Alabama to Upper Town. Upper Town was distinctively southern. Soft accents from below the Mason and Dixon line predominated among the inhabitants. Their "houses were characteristic of the southern clime, low, one-story buildings, with wide verandas, in many respects better suited to Minnesota's summer than winter months." Here in Upper Town the gay crowd had its headquarters.

Middle Town was the most thoroughly immigrant of the three communities. Wilson's counterstroke had indelibly set the stamp of the foreigner on it. Overwhelmingly German and Catholic, the inhabitants of Middle Town were stolidly enterprising and thrifty. They knit a community of interest between themselves and the German farmers settled on the countryside. They had come to St. Cloud with sighs of relief because they had been met with blasts of hostility ever since they had landed in America. Even Maryland, where many of them first settled, proved hostile, though the state had a reputation for being a haven for Catholics. It did not take the Germans long to get their political bearings in the new land. Nativism had found its political home in the Know-Nothing party and with the rise of the Republicans had shifted there. Having been scathed in their passage westward by the nativism in the Republican party, the Germans were unswerving Democrats and were in Sylvanus Lowry's political pocket. Furthermore, the economic interests of the two towns were such that an accommodation could be made on that count. Upper Town was the preserve of the lawyers, real estate agents, moneylenders and Indian traders, all of which required competence and connections that the Germans did not have, nor could acquire until the second generation had matured. These occupations they conceded to the native-born. The Germans were a business and service community, interested in supplying the farmers, once the lawyers and real estate agents had settled them on the land. Therefore, more out of happenstance than anything else the economic functions of Upper and Middle Towns were mutually supporting, or at least they were not directly antagonistic, and they represented between themselves what was combined in Lower Town.

Lower Town therefore took on the characteristics of the common enemy. Not only economics but origins and sensibilities set the inhabitants of Lower Town apart from their neighbors. Brott's recruits were almost entirely from the New England and Middle States. Mostly Protestants coming from eastern areas where heavy Catholic penetrations had been made during the past decade, the Lower Towners found the Germans more provocative and threatening than the southerners in Upper Town. The Germans had already served notice that they would be staunch competitors for the farmer's trade, and their position was further strengthened because their land, the Wilson tract, had come with a clear title. Given the vagaries of land law it was possible that the Lower Towners would find their land suddenly swept from beneath them. The matter was so precarious that some of the residents of Lower Town were taking the precaution of buying quitclaims from John Wilson. Therefore, almost as soon as they had achieved it, the Lower Town settlers were faced with the danger of losing their hegemony. The Lower Towners and the rest of the people at St. Cloud were "like the Jews and Samaritans, [and] had no dealings with each other—at least none that could be avoided."

It was into this riven community that Jane Swisshelm and her Mitchell and Swisshelm relatives moved in the summer of 1857, and the strains and tensions became all the greater as the full force of the Panic of 1857 hit St. Cloud. It was in Brott's "St. Cloud City" that William Mitchell had stayed as he made his prospecting trip in 1856, and it was in Lower Town that the Mitchell-Swisshelm-Miller group opened their businesses. It helps clarify the nature of the fight in St. Cloud to read in the same issue of the *Visiter* in which she opened her assault on Sylvanus Lowry, Jane Swisshelm was puffing the virtues and supremacies of Lower Town: "Lower St. Cloud has all the machinery—a grist mill, a saw mill, a planing mill, a sash and blind factory, two churches, the Everett school and library, a large temperance hotel open and another to be opened in a few weeks, over a hundred dwellings and stores and a fine lyceum" (*SCD*, February 18, 1858). Jane Swisshelm had stepped forward to stir the witches brew at St. Cloud, and its inhabitants were at last at each other's throats.

Lowry's counterattack came swiftly. He struck with the same weapon Swisshelm had used against him, savage ridicule. He raised a public laugh at her expense; and he attacked where she was most vulnerable. He played on her haunting fear that she was indeed unsexed, unnatural, pulled up by her roots from the function that gave her meaning. The attack was especially brutal because it capitalized on a situation that had become painfully evident, that she had been abandoned by her husband. Only Lowry could have conceived it because in St. Cloud only he was "capable of understanding" her. Only he seems to have suspected that behind the public persona of the woman who bore the reputation of "kill[ing] every man she has ever touched" was the Wax Doll and her smashed dreams of the future.

Lowry's partner, James Shepley, the lawyer, one of the mainstays of the gay crowd in Upper Town, was selected to do the dirty work. Shepley gave a public lecture on "Women." It was understood that his performance was Lowry's response to Jane's attack. In his lecture Shepley developed four classes of women: coquettes, flirts, totally depraved, and strong-minded women. Although all of the categories were invidious, Shepley was able to find some "redeeming trait in all save the last" class, the strong-minded woman. As Shepley presented them, the four types of women all descended from the proposition that a woman found her fundamental meaning in her sexual nature. Coquette and flirt capitalized on their sexuality, the whore profited from hers; all demeaned it, but they remained intact as women and were in some way or other desirable to men. But the strong-minded woman was hopeless. She possessed no qualities that retrieved her from the ash heap. Aping men, she had willfully abandoned the characteristics that defined her as a woman, and if she had no shred of sexuality no man could desire her. Shepley made it obvious that Jane Swisshelm was a strong-minded woman. His description was carefully cut from a pattern that fit her. She was more of an affront to society than the totally depraved woman, the common whore. But more than that, and this was Sylvanus Lowry's message to St. Cloud, no man could possibly find Jane Swisshelm desirable. Even her husband had forsaken her.

After these opening blows events moved swiftly. In the next edition of the *Visiter* Swisshelm reviewed Shepley's lecture. She faithfully developed his four categories of women, then pointed out that he had omitted a fifth category, the frontier belle. Swisshelm described the belle. She was a "large, thick-skinned, coarse, sensual-featured, loud-mouth of double-fisted charm, whose entrance into a room appears to take one's breath . . . whose guffahs resound across a mile wide river, and who talks with an energy which makes the saliva fly like showers of melted pearls. . . . Her triumphs consist in card-table success, displays of cheap finery, and in catching a marriageable husband for herself and her poor relations." The frontier belle was a caricature of James Shepley's wife, who with Mrs. Lowry presided over the social life of St. Cloud. For all of its dimensions, the fight in St. Cloud had degenerated into a name-calling brawl in which Swisshelm settled scores for having been excluded by the gay crowd.

Before another edition of the *Visiter* went to press, Lowry, Shepley, and Doctor B. R. Palmer, another of the Upper Town social lions, raided the printing office. They wrecked it and threw press parts into the Mississippi River. They left a message, which Lowry wrote: "St. Cloud, March 24, 1858.—Editor of the Visiter: The Citizens of St. Cloud have determined to abate the nuisance of which you have made the Visiter a striking specimen. They have decided that it is fit only for the inmates of brothels, and you seem to have had some experience of the tastes of such persons. You will never have the opportunity to repeat the offence in this town, without paying a more serious penalty than you do now. By order of the Commander of Vigilance."[25]

Now the stage was apparently set for a reprise of the Elijah Lovejoy incident. Toward the beginning of "the aggressive phase of abolition activity" Lovejoy's *Observer* had been destroyed in Alton, Illinois. When he persisted in publishing his attacks on slavery Lovejoy was murdered, and abolitionist publicists seized the incident and exploited it for all it was worth. It was a heaven-sent proof of what the slaveholders were really about, and what slavery really meant. Slavery was not only the matter of holding blacks in bondage: it was an attack upon free men and their liberties, and most especially the freedom of speech and press. Lovejoy's murder and similar incidents of newspaper suppression and destruction were, therefore, signs of what the future held in store as long as slavery existed in America. Such incidents were splendid opportunities for broadening abolition's base.[26]

In *Half a Century* Swisshelm writes according to the Lovejoy formula, with some emendations to perfect her own part in the affair. She is frightened, perhaps terrified, by the destruction of her press and the vigilante's threat to her personal safety. But she remains undaunted. A mass protest meeting is held at the Stearns House, the largest public meeting place in St. Cloud. Despite warnings that she will be murdered, or assaulted, or set adrift on the Mississippi River with her hands tied behind her back, she plans to identify Lowry and his confederates. She writes her will and takes a friend as a bodyguard because she fears a riot. She instructs the bodyguard, "Save two bullets for me! And shoot so that I can see you." Knowing that her bodyguard is a "dead shot," and comforted that "he pledged himself solemnly to shoot me square through the brain, if there was no other way of preventing me [from] falling alive into the hands of the mob," she brands Lowry, Shepley and Palmer and speaks out against human slavery and the women-whippers' assault on classic American freedoms (*HaC*, 185–86). But the meeting does not turn out the way she feared. Public opinion is behind her. Parliamentarians took over, debated the issue, and named a committee to prepare resolutions appropriate to the "outrage." The resolutions deplored the destruction of the press, expressed the fullest confidence in her, and pledged all endorsers to support her "in publishing whatever she pleases on all subjects and on all occasions, against all opposition, force or violence, from whatever source it may come." The final resolution declared that "the St. Cloud Visiter shall be sustained and we will sustain it." Another committee was then named to oversee the reestablishment of the *Visiter*.

The upshot was incorporation of the St. Cloud Printing Company. There were twenty-eight incorporators. They subscribed the money to buy new type and repair the damaged press, and shortly the *Visiter* was back in business. But the travail was not over. In the first issue Swisshelm reprinted her review of Shepley's lecture along with her sketch of the Frontier Belle. Shepley brought a libel suit against the St. Cloud Printing Company and its incorporators. The suit never came to trial. The incorporators dissolved the printing company, folded the *Visiter,* and made over the printing plant to Swisshelm. She was now "sole owner" of the property. She changed the name of the paper to the *St. Cloud Democrat.* By changing the paper's name she met the terms of the agreement whereby Shepley agreed to drop his suit. He had demanded that the *Visiter* carry an acknowledgment that the destruction of the old press had occurred as an affair of personal honor and was not connected with public matters. After printing this confession the *Visiter* was never again to publish any reference to the destruction of the old press.

The dissolution of the St. Cloud Printing Company, the transfer of the property, and the appearance of the *Democrat* all occurred in a week's time. Under its new name the old *Visiter* continued without missing an issue. In the first issue of the *Democrat* Swisshelm reprinted the review of Shepley's lecture with its accompanying portrait of the Frontier Belle, but Lowry and Shepley left her undisturbed. She had beat them. According to her account she had beat them on the issue of a free press, with the aid of the stalwart citizens of St. Cloud who understood the issue at stake. At considerable risk to themselves they had backed her and the classic American freedoms of speech and press. "Almost to a man and without regard to party," they fought the issue through to victory; and during the battle they transformed themselves from a people "absorbed [by] home necessities and home interests" into citizens who understood that "principle itself underlies and forms the substratum of . . . society."[27]

If there is much community self-congratulation in the story of rebuilding the *Visiter,* it is understandable because it is a version of the story Americans love to tell about themselves. At bottom is the tale of social redemption and moral rejuvenation, with the inevitable triumph of righteousness once the issue is placed squarely before "active, intelligent and liberty-loving" people. Questioning the accuracy of the story verges on an act of social impiety. Even so, it is useful to look more closely at what happened in the Stearns House where the citizens of St. Cloud made their decision to join the fight for a free press and human liberty.

The Stearns House was not only the largest public meeting place in St. Cloud; it was Lower Town's social center. Charles Stearns, George Brott's father-in-law, was owner and proprietor, and he, like the inhabitants of Lower Town, took pride in its being a temperance hotel. Unlike the rackety inns in Upper and Middle Towns, no liquor or beer was dispensed there. It was on the street in front of the Stearns House that George Brott performed his act of the railroad conductor on the imaginary railroad, bawling out "All aboard for Puget Sound." Emblematic of the superior probity and morality of the Lower Towners, the Stearns House was Lower Town's bastion.

Once the meeting was underway two committees were formed. One drafted the resolutions protesting the press's destruction. The other was a "Ways and Means" committee whose duty was to rebuild the *Visiter*; from this second committee the St. Cloud Publishing Company emerged. As the business proceeded, something on the order of an interlocking directorate began to emerge. Of the five members of the Resolutions Committee, four became shareholders in the publishing company. Of the seven members of the Ways and Means Committee, six became shareholders in the publishing company. Thus, of the twenty-eight incorporators of the publishing company, ten were members of the two committees that led to its creation. All of which might mean nothing more than ten of the twelve committee members had the courage of their convictions, that they were willing to help pay for a free press in St. Cloud; it might mean precisely that, except for this singular fact: Every member of the two committees and every shareholder in the publishing company were residents of Lower Town. And insofar as their economic activities can be identified, every one of them had business, professional, or property interests that would thrive or wane according to the fortunes of Lower Town in its contest with Upper and Middle Towns.

The lines of force in the fight at St. Cloud had come to congruence. A frontier brawl over profit and deference, laced with religious intolerance, was shifted to a struggle over human liberty and constitutional freedom. Exploiting the issue of "press breaking" with the Germans, an opening wedge was driven by the Lower Towners in the alliance between Upper and Middle Towns and in Sylvanus Lowry's grip on the northern frontier. The way was prepared for a shift of power at St. Cloud.

Shortly after the press was destroyed the Lower Towners swept a Stearns County election. They won control of the county board of supervisors and the county clerk's office. This was an important tactical victory because it permitted them to move the Stearns County polls to Lower Town, away from Upper Town's liquor and Lowry's rowdies who, the Lower Towners claimed, intimidated the voters. How the Lower Towners controlled the polls once they captured them the sources do not disclose. It is sufficient to say that they dominated them, and St. Cloud became the political preserve of the new proprietors. But they could never completely break Lowry's power in the county because of the Germans.

Jane Swisshelm tried to woo the Germans, even going so far as to repudiate the party that called her *mother*. "We are not and never were a Republican," she wrote. "We are not the apologists of [sic] the Republican party. . . . Our doctrine is Democratic equality in its most enlarged and liberal sense. . . . We are . . . Independent Democrats. . . . The St. Cloud Democrat is [our] organ" (*SCD*, June 2, November 11, 1858). She railed at the Minnesota Republican "purists" who insisted on a "clean Republican ticket," but she saved her choicest invective for the Massachusetts Republicans who had changed the state election law to require a two-year residence after naturalization before a new citizen could vote there. The Massachusetts law aimed at controlling immigrants, and was, Swisshelm wrote, "a libel . . . and an insult to [our Minnesota] constituents." She wrote, "We are sorry the Old Bay State should have acted the fool. . . . As for Massachusetts it is very little matter what law she passes, she is only as big as a three cent piece and two thirds covered with rocks at that; and so far as we are concerned we would be glad if she would pass a law that no foreigner should live there; but that every mother's son of them should come out to Minnesota" (*SCD*, May 5, 1859).

Her polemics were futile. The "press breaking" issue worked in 1858, along with a fusionist politics that allowed the Germans to vote against the orthodox Democrats without calling themselves Republican; but in the consolidation of 1859 as Anti-Lecompton Democrats, Free Soilers, and Old Liberty partyites were welded into the Republican party in Minnesota, the Germans would not come along. In 1859 the Republicans swept Minnesota. St. Cloud itself returned a handsome Republican majority, but Stearns County was lost.

Despite her best efforts with the *Democrat*, Swisshelm could not bring the Germans into line. For months she hammered away at the twin issues supposedly dear to immigrants' hearts, homestead and free soil. But the Stearns County Germans voted the memory of the slights, the outrages, and the terrors of being alien in an inhospitable land. They kept Stearns County anchored to the Democratic party until the turn of the twentieth century.

As she surveyed the election results, Swisshelm searched for the reason for the debacle. It was very simple, it seemed. "The great mass of the people [in the county] were Catholics" (*HaC*, 186). This was explanation enough for her. The Stearns County Germans were thus woven into the web of conspiracy that she had seen earlier in Pittsburgh; and she found herself on the eve of the Civil War confronted with the old alliance of priest and slaveholder in northern Minnesota.

But the threat was not as desperate as it had been ten years earlier. The new proprietors controlled St. Cloud, and the Republicans controlled the state. Having wrenched power away from the Democrats they were eager to cleanse "this putrid and decaying carcass" (*SCD*, January 3, 1861). This daughter of the Covenanters had kept the faith. She had made no "hollow compromises" (*SCD*, May 2, 1861). She had done her part to redeem the schismatics of 1833. They had chosen the way of political action to restore the covenant between man and God. By 1859 they were succeeding. Surely in St.

Cloud the logic of events had proven the righteousness of their way. The immoral clique had been routed. According to George Brott, Swisshelm had "wiped the floor with Mr. Shepley, using [his wife] as a mop."[28] The gay crowd's "Bashaw," Sylvanus Lowry, was traveling abroad, attended by Dr. Palmer, hoping to find some relief from the maddening pains that were coming with increasing intensity in his brain. As for herself, shortly after the fight in St. Cloud, Jane Swisshelm found that "I am cured of my long-standing hallucination."[29] For the first time in almost twenty years she did not dream of Tom, the Kentucky panther.

In her home next to the *Democrat* office, she held bimonthly receptions. Her guests, she said, were "people . . . who would have graced any society." They danced, and she saw to it that they dined well. Republican celebrities shared her hospitality. Schuyler Colfax, Galusha Grow, the voice for homestead in Congress, and George Julian visited her when they campaigned in Minnesota. Minnesota's own Republican lights, Governor Alexander Ramsey and Lieutenant Governor Ignatius Donnelly danced with her. At her "fortnightlies" there was often a large delegation from St. Paul. She presided over these affairs—as her subsequent account of them was judged—"credulous" and "clothed with a glamour which her hardships probably led her to enjoy. . . . Whimsical in speech, alert, gifted with humor, and easily sarcastic . . . she seem[ed] never to have been conscious of a mistake."[30]

Enemies of the Covenant will always abound, conspiring against God and His desire for the perfection of the Covenant. Sometimes the conspirators might appear on the verge of capturing the world and thwarting heaven, but they will fail as long as the chosen elite remain true to their heavenly imperatives. The elite's God-given imperatives required that they never forget that the world and the flesh are delusive and that temporal affairs could never be ends in themselves. Thus chastened, they could, without fear of mistaking the desire to serve themselves for the obligation to serve God, seize the things of the world.

Jane Swisshelm's great truth about herself was that within her were warring armies in which her worldly dream for the Wax Doll was in mortal conflict with the heavenly imperatives of the

Covenanters' daughter. She was always forgetting what her God demanded of her. For years she had carried a bad conscience for "making an idol and bowing down before it," for desiring the world and the flesh over heaven. In Minnesota the conflict seems to have been resolved as much as it ever would be. There on the northern frontier the Wax Doll, now a middle-aged woman who "gave the impression of a bird," was shattered beyond repair; and her worldly dream was beyond any hope of retrieval. James never came to retrieve her. And the scourge of bad conscience, the hallucinatory panther, the emblem of the Louisville fiasco, and a young bride's attempt to possess an idol, was lifted. The picture of memory no longer haunted her. "I am cured," she said. Chastened, she might have said. Her conscience was at last clear.

Years later in the little house at Swissvale that she had wrested from James in *Swisshelm* v. *Swisshelm* the old woman lay in her bed waiting for the end. The cancer in her intestines had almost completed its work, and a merciful stupor had blunted the edge of her pain. Elizabeth Mitchell had come from St. Cloud to be with her sister at her last trial. She was joined by Zoe who had been summoned from her home in Chicago to be with her mother for the last time. At her bedside, with a newspaperman dispatched from the city to report the deathwatch of "Pittsburgh's most celebrated woman," the two women waited.[31] When it was over and the burying done, a stone was placed at the head of the grave. On it was the epitaph Swisshelm had composed for herself: "Speak unto the children of Israel that they may go forward."

Moncure D. Conway

Jane Swisshelm

Frederick Douglass

Henry C. Wright and daughter of a Scots friend

Salmon P. Chase

Thomas M. Cooley

Part Three

Frederick Douglass: Orphan Slave

VIII

Biography, Autobiography, and the Search for the Lost Past

This struggle may be a moral one; or it may be a physical one; or it may be both moral and physical; but it must be a struggle.

FREDERICK DOUGLASS

In the spring of 1894 Frederick Douglass was preparing for his death. He was now far beyond the years the scriptures accord a man. How far he had exceeded the threescore and ten he could not say with certainty because he did not know when he had been born. By his own calculation he was seventy-seven years of age. Correct or not, his self-given age was accurate enough to explain why the catlike somnolence—a cool torpidness until roused flashing into action—of his prime was now all the more characteristic. Whatever toll the years had taken on his big body, his strikingly handsome face and his voice, that superbly tuned instrument, his presence was still commanding, and there remained reserves of energy for him to draw on.

With the end in sight the tidying up of a life was being com-

pleted. Old scores had been settled by holding out the hand of
friendship to those who would take it: Oliver Johnson, the Garrisonian journalist who had delivered many hard blows when
Douglass had defected from the ranks of the Massachusetts Anti-
Slavery Society; Blanche K. Bruce, the sometime senator from
Mississippi who had fought him in a blistering struggle for power
inside the Negro leadership; Robert Purvis, who had fought him
first when Douglass became an apostate to Garrisonianism and
again as a rival for power after the Civil War. As Douglass made
peace he was also warding off new controversy by assuring men
holding positions of honor and power that he wanted neither for
himself. "I have been a long time in the world and a long time
acquainted with myself and I know just what I am fit for," he wrote
explaining why he was subscribing to a self-denying clause. The
accusations and "insinuations" of ambition that inevitably arose
whenever his name was mentioned were made of the whole cloth,
he claimed. He wanted nothing more from life than repose. His
mood was benign, his intentions irenic. His lifework was finished.
He had already divided his life into phases and this, the final phase,
was the time to "live and rejoice."[1] But his role must be played
out to the end. Exemplar for black Americans, so long as life was
left to him he would meet the obligations of the role he had assumed years before, and so, among other things, he faithfully attended the AME Metropolitan Church in Washington. He came,
he told the pastor, not because he was a believer but because, "I
believe it is a duty to set a good example. . . . Your church is doing
good to our people."[2] More of an institution now and bearing with
gravitas the title "Representative Colored Man of the United
States," Douglass placidly accepted the honors and testimonials
already coming his way, harbingers of the flood that awaited his
death. The ceremonial recessional had begun and, unlike most
men, it was given to Frederick Douglass to hear the music as it
struck up.

But for all of that, there remained something for Douglass to do
besides wait as a living monument for the end. There was a final
errand for him to make. On a March morning less than a year
before he died, Douglass left his Anacostia home and boarded a
train for the short trip from Washington to Baltimore.

At Baltimore he went to the home of a physician, Doctor Thomas Sears. How long he stayed with Doctor Sears is an open question. There was time enough to satisfy Douglass that there was no purpose in remaining longer, however hospitable the doctor may have been. His visit over, Douglass returned to Washington. When night came he was back in his home at Anacostia Heights. Next morning Douglass went to his study, took out his diary and wrote up the account of his trip to Baltimore. These were the last entries in his diary. For the few months that remained for him to live, nothing further was of sufficient importance for Douglass to write about in his little book.

Douglass' conversation with Doctor Sears had probably taken many directions. If there was not much that he and the physician held in common, there nevertheless was much that they had shared. Sears, a descendant of Douglass' old master, was the last contact Douglass had with the family that had once owned him. More important, Sears had some information about the old slavery days that Douglass wanted, and however much the conversation may have gone, Douglass must have been careful to turn it back to that point. He wanted, he said, as many "facts" as the doctor could give him about his old master and his family. Douglass wanted information about his lost past.

Douglass' concern for his past, the past beyond memory and recall, which brought him to the home of the Baltimore physician is one of the suggestive and unifying themes in his life. The short trip to Doctor Sears's home a few months before he died was one of the most revealing and one of the most significant acts of Douglass' life. Unmentioned by his several biographers, his trip to Baltimore is the starting point for our inquiry into the life of Frederick Douglass.

But first it is in order to raise the question of why all of the Douglass biographers have omitted the Sears episode in their accounts of his life. Even the two most careful biographers— Benjamin Quarles and Philip Foner—do not mention it, and apparently its implications have escaped them all, however aware they may have been of the connection between a man's private and public lives, between an inner emotional economy and the political economy he professes.[3]

The reason for the biographers' omission is obvious. The visit was intensely personal, quite out of the flow of his public life and therefore apparently unconnected with it, and consequently irrelevant to his biographers' purposes. They have all meant to portray the fugitive slave making his mark in a white free society, either as the courageous paterfamilias of a race, showing American Negroes the way toward a secure and equal place in that society, or as revolutionary prophet carrying a message not only of racial equalitarianism but also of a militant racial class consciousness. The Douglass biographers have used Douglass to illustrate and promote various social programs and ideals, all of which are variations on a single theme, moving American Negroes to a more desirable position in American society. They have turned Douglass to didactic social purposes, endowing him with an exemplary social role, a role Douglass was never reluctant to adopt for himself. But to use Douglass in this way is to accept the hazard of seeing him as he permitted himself to be seen, and consequently to accept his self-imposed sanctions and write an authorized biography, in this instance the authorization coming posthumously from the subject himself rather than from his heirs and executors.

There is no doubt that Douglass meant to preside over his biographers' work. No man more assiduously guided future biographers along paths that he wanted them to follow. The indispensable sources for Douglass' life are his three autobiographical writings. They establish the framework for anyone writing his life. *The Narrative of the Life of Frederick Douglass: An American Slave* was the first autobiography. It was followed by *My Bondage and My Freedom*, and by the *Life and Times of Frederick Douglass*, which appeared in two editions.[4] Written over a period of forty-seven years, the three autobiographies present a carefully painted portrait that Douglass intended to fix as part of the public record. The latter two books are essentially polemical narrative extensions of the preceding ones, coming to rest squarely on the first in which Douglass drew a picture of himself that with a few striking exceptions he never changed except by way of chiaroscuro.

Then a second difficulty intrudes. However much a personal statement the first autobiographical piece may be, and however vitally the self-portrait is drawn, Douglass' purpose, one which cast the mold for the successive autobiographies, was not so much to tell his life story as it was to promote a social program, abolition on the Garrisonian model. Writing for this purpose, Douglass diverted autobiography from its basic mode of revealing the writer, subordinated a conception of self to an ideology, and turned an art form into a tract.[5]

The special difficulty arising from the three Douglass autobiographies, and most profoundly from the first one, is not that Douglass himself gave his biographers the model for writing about him—using his life as a vehicle for a social program—but that he served as editor and censor for virtually every scrap of information connected with his life until it took on a public dimension and thereby became susceptible to cross-checking and substantiation. At his mercy for information, a biographer is obliged to rely upon Douglass and accept the hazards of deceitful memory, deliberate selection, and the prevaricating impulses of the unconscious as Douglass tells the story of the first twenty–five years of his life. Confronted by the problem of Douglass as the sole expositor of himself during these critical years, a biographer can do little but accept Douglass on his own terms. Douglass must be trusted for the *sine qua non* of the autobiographer, to truthfully tell how and with what results the inner self came into contact with the external world, and how he conducted the search for his "inner standing."[6]

If a biographer trusts Douglass to tell the truth about his quest for self, then his proper aim is not so much to recapitulate the autobiographical material, for, as Benjamin Quarles has aptly said, it would amount to a "rehash." Instead he must listen to Douglass with the keenest ear as Douglass talks about himself. He must listen carefully in order to understand what Douglass was saying about himself as a human individual, not as a historical presence. For only after Douglass has been heard as a human individual will he begin to be understood as a black American whose presence in American history has loomed so large and has been so compelling that he has been drafted into service as a personified social program by such widely divergent ideologues as Booker T. Washington and Philip Foner.

The paradox of Douglass' life is that it is indeed amenable to such disparate uses, which means in turn that there was basic contradiction as well as conflict in his life. The latter is self-evident. It would take a dull biographer not to exploit the conflict in Douglass' life, and none have defaulted on that count. But apparently they have not seen that the conflict is rooted in contradictions. Or if they have discovered the contradictions, they have shunted the knowledge aside, because to show the contradictions would result in the creation of an inconsistent Douglass that would take the edge off the social program the writers advance through the device of biography. A protean Douglass has not been desired by any of his biographers.

An examination of the two best Douglass biographies shows why a consistent Douglass has been necessary in order to promote a particular social program.

In Benjamin Quarles's biography Douglass is a black Ragged Dick. By luck and pluck Douglass broke free from the most humble of all origins an American can rise from. By dint of his already formed individual characteristics—he was, Quarles says, by the time he escaped slavery, "sensitive, intelligent and ambitious"— Douglass drove himself upward to a preeminent position in American Negro society, and as far toward the center of white American society as the fact of his being black permitted.

As his life ran its course Douglass achieved more than any Negro in America. The distance he moved from slavery can be gauged by the public offices he held. He was marshal of the District of Columbia, recorder of deeds for the District of Columbia, and United States minister to Haiti. In his movement from slavery to the highest appointive public offices a Negro might hold in nineteenth-century America, Douglass was quite like the boys of humble origin in Horatio Alger's stories—sensitive, intelligent, ambitious, and lucky fellows—who do indeed rise in the world. As they rose, inexorably so because they followed the formula whose provenance abounded in the society around them, they just as inexorably came to possess comfortable secure havens of respectable occupations and professions. "Comfortable" is Douglass' own word for his office as recorder of deeds. He had risen to it through his own efforts as a zealous Republican who gave no quarter to Democrats when election time came. He was quite happy with his office. Although he knew that it was a position "to which aspirants have never been few in number or wanting in zeal," he was not prepared to resign when the Democratic Cleveland administration came to power. He chose to wait it out, to see whether Grover Cleveland would keep his "implied" campaign promise to reform the spoils system and thereby enable him to keep his office.

Cleveland turned him out, but to Douglass it seemed that "President Cleveland did not appear to be in haste or to desire my resignation half as much as some of my Afro-American brethren desired me to make room for them." As he reflected over the loss of his position Douglass reserved his most ironic thrust not for the man who broke a "promise" but for other blacks who wanted the recordership. He had come to possession of his "comfortable office" by conforming to the social ideal of the mid-nineteenth century. He had worked, striven, achieved, acquired. Now he was denied the ideal's corollary: after acquiring, being left alone to enjoy the comforts that he had gained. Douglass was a bitter man when he was let out of the recorder's office. When he wrote his account of the incident for his *Life and Times,* he dipped his pen in gall.

It is precisely to the theme of luck-and-pluck that Benjamin Quarles wrote when he suggested that had not abolition fortuitously appeared, Frederick Douglass' life would have taken an altogether different turn. "Had quiet times prevailed," Douglass would have been led into the ministry. Superbly fitted for the "public platform"—Quarles couples Douglass' "logical mind, his air of sternness and rectitude, his imposing physique and the rolling thunder of his voice" with his "sensitive, intelligent and ambitious" character—Douglass would have made his mark in "the pulpit." He would have taken his place at the center of American Negro society and on the periphery of white society, secure and comfortable, where his personal ability and ambition would have been realized.

But Douglass was the great gainer through the luck-and-pluck formula informing Quarles's biography. Abolition broke at exactly the right time for him to ride the crest of its wave. In the crusade against slavery he found a higher platform than a pulpit from which he could display his brilliant talents, and the rest followed. In Quarles's *Douglass* the fundamental doctrines of two streams of American ideology are synthesized.

From abolition is drawn the doctrine of the radical equality of mankind regardless of color or heritage, with its accompanying corollary: to hold any other idea is a morally culpable act. Furthermore, from abolition comes the imperative to proclaim the equality of man in the face of bitter opposition. All of which was sufficient to set abolitionists at odds with the social order, and, paradoxically, allow them to draw support from the social order they were assaulting; for abolition rested on a generic commitment to dissent and to the more specific moral idealism born of the Enlightenment and radical Christianity.[8]

If abolition managed to maintain a connection with an existing society in this way, a much clearer and more tightly connected relationship was developed by taking on the propositions that ultimately found their summation in such statements as Andrew Carnegie's *Wealth*.

Carnegie's proclamation of the gospel of wealth, that the justified man was the man who most judiciously presided over his material talents, represented no new or alien doctrine for Douglass. "Douglass advocated the gospel of wealth," which for Quarles is the obvious conclusion to the observation, "His financial independence was another illustration of his preachments squaring with his practices."[9] Quarles thus not only achieves a desirable consistency between teaching and practice for Douglass, but he also brings Douglass straight, ideologically, to the mainstream of a social theory for which Andrew Carnegie, the Scottish bobbin boy, was the peerless model and exemplar. And if Carnegie found no fault with wealth so long as it was tempered with benevolence and had grown out of the moral discipline of hard work and self-denial, Douglass scarcely could do otherwise. "I hold it to be no sin," Douglass said, "to be rich, but, on the contrary, wish there were many rich men among American men of color." And like Carnegie, Douglass found that a man of substance was prey to "annoyances," in his case from the

numerous pressing and pathetic appeals for assistance [which] have come to me from colored people from all parts of the country.... These were no doubt honest people. . . . They are, however, of that large class of persons who are perfectly willing to subsist at other people's expense. . . . Though I could not exactly see how or why I should be called upon to pay the debt of emancipation for the whole four millions of liberated people, I have always tried to do my part as opportunity has offered. At the same time it has seemed to me incomprehensible that they did not see that the real debtors . . . are themselves, and that the absurdity of their posing as creditors did not occur to them.[10]

As neatly as any white proponent of the gospel of wealth, Frederick Douglass began with an unequal social situation and, employing economic metaphors, worked his way to a moral and self-justifying conclusion. These indignantly hard words are Douglass' from his *Life and Times.* Quarles gave their meaning an easier gloss by using Douglass from another passage, "Negroes would never be respected until they respect themselves, and that they would never respect themselves until they had the means to live respectably." But in order to prevent the point from being lost by the gloss, "'Aristotle and Pericles are all right; get that, too; but get money besides, and plenty of it.'" No one in the Gilded Age, not even Colonel Beriah Sellers, ever put it better or more succinctly. *Rentier,* moneylender and entrepreneur, "Douglass had a finger in banking and insurance" at the same time he was trying "to turn an honest dollar into manufacturing."[11]

If, during the freewheeling days of Reconstruction, Douglass turned his back on some of his less fortunate brethren, the fact that he did was scarcely inconsistent or unexpected. The doctrine of the radical equalitarianism of man presupposed not only a free man but an unencumbered man as well. Furthermore, if Douglass laid claim to the finest social ideal America had to offer, the claim of man's radical equality, it is no wonder that he also committed himself to America's regnant social ideology. If it happened that it was the gospel of wealth, or the earlier bold entrepreneurialship of Jacksonian times, both of which placed a premium upon individual enterprise, Douglass was happy to subscribe the doctrine. Douglass' "get money" was a ringing affirmation of a free-market society. His tuition in political economy, as in all subjects, he proudly said came "from Massachusetts Abolition University, Mr. Garrison, president." The lessons he learned from this faculty are best seen in the letters that he wrote his son Charles. They are a Chesterfieldian guide for getting on in Gilded Age Washington. [12] It should come, therefore, as no surprise that portraits of the collateral descendents of Benjamin Quarles's Frederick Douglass are to be found in the pages of Franklin Frazier's *Black Bourgeoisie.*

If Quarles's luck-and-pluck Douglass operated from a racially equalitarian gospel of wealth, Philip Foner's Douglass achieved his position and meaning in American history according to a different formula. Foner's Douglass was borne to eminence as a result of Marxian warfare between social classes, a war in which Douglass enlisted first to free the Negro "masses" from chattel slavery, then after emancipation fought to free them from an oppressive capitalism. There cannot be, therefore, as in the case of Quarles's Douglass, a coincidental conjunction of the talented ambitious runaway slave with a fortuitously emerging abolition. There is no place in Foner's biography for the sheer luck of history, the accident that "quiet times" did not prevail when Douglass escaped from slavery. Instead, Foner's Douglass must be foresworn while he was still a slave to undertake a mission that accorded with the design of history. He must escape slavery in order to lead a racially defined class struggle for freedom.

Foner located Douglass' motive of escape from slavery and commitment to abolition in a boyhood incident. While watching a slave ship being loaded at the Baltimore wharves Douglass pledged himself to the struggle, " 'I then resolved that whatever power I had should be devoted to the freeing of my race.' " [13] With his pledge made as a youth on the Baltimore docks, Douglass aligned himself with the black masses, and thus accepted a racial and a class identity for which the remainder of his life was the active confirmation. For Foner's Douglass such an identity and confirmation were natural enough while chattel slavery was inherent in American society. Indeed, there was no other way American blacks could define themselves. The simple fact of being black linked them with a slave class. Consequently, regardless of a Negro's particular circumstance he never forgot that the slaves' cause was his own.

As class identity carried Douglass into the Civil War, it was pursued beyond emancipation and Reconstruction. Foner's historical dialectic makes the Civil War and Reconstruction a way station, not a terminal. Therefore, in the postwar period Foner's Douglass cannot speak harshly about members of his own race except as they fall away from their true class interest; neither can he wittingly align himself with a social order for which Andrew Carnegie was the exemplar. Instead, Douglass must continue to represent the Negro masses. "Endeared" to them, he had a double function. He kept up his bold assaults on discriminatory racial practices as the rigor of Reconstruction dissipated; and he was the masses' best hope for escaping the "new alliance between northern and southern propertied interests," an alliance being "forged at the expense of the hard-won rights of the Negro people." But more than the blacks' loss of rights was at stake. This newly emergent union between northern industrialists and financiers and the old southern oligarchy, with the participants swapping economic for racial concessions, would provide the social apparatus for the "super-exploitation of millions of human beings through the oppression of the Negro people." In such a situation the blacks become the crucial instrument by which all "people's movements" were to be crushed by the masters of capital. The end of the scheme does not come with handing over the Negro masses to the southern oligarchy whereby they "would practically be restored to slavery"; it comes with semislavery for "labor, farmers, and small property holders" throughout America.

With this turn of events, the unfolding of the classic ruination of the petty bourgeoise and the increased oppression of workers, Foner's Frederick Douglass is endowed with a critical historical role to play. If the reactionary class-sectional alliance was to be consummated, it must be transacted with the Negro masses as the medium of exchange. All else hinged on this. And Douglass, "endeared" to the black masses and thereby capable of swinging them as he wished, becomes the pivot point on which history will turn. At this time, 1876, as the great sectional compromise was in the making, Foner's Douglass becomes the most important man in the United States. The responsibility for saving not only the "hardwon rights of the Negro people" rests squarely upon him; he is a potential secular Messiah set in the framework of a class dialectic.

To respond to the challenge, to play the role that history demanded of him, Douglass must first appreciate the mutuality of class interests. He must understand how the fortunes of American Negroes were linked with those of white Americans, except the northern masters of capital and the southern oligarchs. In fine, as the critical year 1876 approached, Douglass must understand that history was rushing on, that American society was bending under the threatened consummation of a reactionary alliance, and that the only way out was to advocate the mutual interests of a biracial agricultural and industrial proletariat and petty bourgeoisie.

Douglass' opportunity to speak out came in April, 1876, when he delivered an oration at the unveiling of the Freedmen's Memorial Monument to Abraham Lincoln. As he came to the rostrum where Ulysses Grant and his cabinet sat with the justices of the Supreme Court and a flock of senators and congressmen, he, according to Foner, "had a unique opportunity 'to trouble the American people.'" Never before had a Negro "so great an opportunity to reach the American people with his message." But something went awry. Instead of sounding the alarm, Douglass "dealt with the past." He spoke of Lincoln's movement to emancipation and the Lincoln achievement. Instead of delivering himself of "stirring words," Douglass gave a "disappointing" recapitulation of the past, a past that Douglass previously had said warranted no attention except insofar as it was "'useful to the present and the future.'"

Had Douglass misunderstood the situation and the processes of history? Had he consequently misconstrued his own role? Foner acknowledges that in his declining years Douglass sometimes did not fully "understand the class character of the struggle in which he was engaged." But his failure to respond to the challenge in the spring of 1876, only a month after he, "embittered by the turn of events," staked out the thesis "'that there is no middle ground for us. . . . We [can never] cease to trouble the American people,'" came from no failure to appreciate the class struggle. Foner lays reason for Douglass' missing the mark in the freedmen's memorial speech to another cause. As principal orator, Douglass was "overwhelmed by the honor bestowed upon him, [and] remained silent."

The following year when the compromise was transacted and

Rutherford Hayes, fulfilling a portion of the sectional bargain, ordered federal troops withdrawn from their last southern posts, Douglass once again "voiced no opposition." If on the occasion of his previous "silence" Douglass was guilty of inconsistency induced by a benumbing honor, with this second silence he came close to apostasy. Critics arraigned him for having been bought— "a fat office gagged him"—when he accepted Hayes's appointment as United States marshal for the District of Columbia. Even though, as Foner admits, "the evidence does not entirely support Douglass" in his claim that he always opposed the Hayes policy of conciliating the South, he maintains that Douglass wore no gag. Instead, the fact of Douglass' officeholding was an encouragement to Negroes and a testament "to a large class of the American people of all colors and races" that racial change was possible. "He had made a contribution toward the progress of his people."

When all is said and done these silences were minor aberrations. One was understandable, the other justifiable, and neither appreciably deflected Douglass from his lifelong mission. His only real fault resulted from his inability to understand the changing relationships of economic interests with politics. He did not see that "the big-business interests which dominated the Republican Party had long since receded from their advanced position during the early stages of Reconstruction when they had championed Negro civil and political rights." With this failure excepted, Foner's Douglass was safe in the doctrine of social class identification and was sound in his commitment to "the struggle." Even as he clung to his outmoded political loyalties, he never defaulted on the pledge he made on Kinnard's Wharf in Baltimore to free the black masses. Toward 1875 he may have lost his bearings on the economic orientation of the Republican party and the class interest the party now served, but within that limitation he was sound as a dollar. He knew that a predetermined war must be waged between blacks and the forces of reaction. The only way out was to organize and "'Agitate! Agitate! Agitate!'" The descendants of Foner's Frederick Douglass are currently found in "a powerful movement . . . with the working class, women and youth playing an ever more important and leading role . . . uniting, as never before." They and "their progressive white allies'' carry on the class struggle with Douglass' benedictional sanction.

For all their apparent differences Quarles and Foner have created a similar and consistent Douglass. To be sure, he emerges within the framework of two different conceptions of history and two divergent social programs, but although these differences place additional dimensions on the biographical problem they do not change it. The differences between their two Douglasses lie no deeper than a biographer's prerogatives of selection and shading, in their case with the manipulation of Douglass' paper trail in order to create a character compatible with their histories and social programs. The consequence is that their Douglasses differ only in particulars, not fundamentally. In each biography there is never any doubt that Douglass knows exactly and precisely who he was. His conception of self was rooted in the double fact of being a slave and a Negro, and as such he identified himself all his life. All of his actions and all of his motives for action stemmed from his refusal to be a slave, either under the law or to racial prejudice, and from his proud willingness to be a Negro. In both biographies Douglass' conception of self—his self-given identity—is perfected by the time he was an adolescent in Baltimore, if not earlier. When he fled Baltimore, Douglass knew who he was, and for the rest of his life he consistently confirmed his conception of self.

With the creation of a consistent character for Douglass the biographers have written in the classical biographical tradition that resolves the problem of human unruliness not by grappling with it but by avoiding it. Rather than attempting to pierce the mysteries of the hidden springs of human action and reconcile the cross-purposes and paradoxes that exist in every life, biographers sought a complemental cluster of traits which provided the key to personality. Around that cluster the biography was organized. Thus the data were chosen, arranged, and emphasized in order to create a consistent personality. The effect was to produce a person who moved without any deviation through chronological time, with his subsequent life providing the certification and amplification for the established personality traits. The Victorian's elegant phrase for the personality core by which the consistency was achieved was the "moral harmony," and it answered the aesthetic problem of biography, the need for thematic unity in life, as well as the social conventions of the era which demanded moral instruction from a biographer.[14] Writing in this tradition, both Quarles and Foner have employed the technique of the consistent personality in creating their Douglasses, though in their case the moral harmony— the core of personality traits and the fundamental motive for action—is lifted out of its Victorian meaning and restated in terms of a racial morality. But with this difference they accord with the nineteenth-century formulation. As Douglass' life unfolds a consistent personality is blended into a consistent moral statement. Both rest on Douglass' conception of self, his knowledge of self, his firm conviction that he knew who he was from the first time he acted to make a moral statement.

Surely in Douglass' accounts of himself there is little to suggest that his biographers have gone astray in developing the consistent personality. In the final summary of his life Douglass brought together succinctly the traits that composed his moral harmony. He had "suffered," he had "endured and risked," he had "battled," and he, finally, could "live and rejoice." Douglass' strong, active verbs imply the personality traits that the biographers have used to provide the thematic unity for his life. And Douglass helped them even further as he neatly paralleled these traits with the various stages of his life. First he was a slave, during which time he suffered; then he was a fugitive from slavery, and he endured and risked; next he lived a life of "conflict and battle"; and finally there came the vindication and victory, which if not complete was at least unquestioned, a time for rejoicing.[15] Consistency of personality is blended with a lineal consistency of purpose and action. The life experience is a pleasing progressive whole.

The difficulty arising from following Douglass in his summary conception of self comes not so much from the fact that a person often does not see himself as he is, but from the contrary fact that Douglass spoke more for black Americans than for himself. His recapitulation of his life is less an analysis of self than it is a history of American Negroes restated in personal terms. For, as he said, the time was fast approaching when the survivors of "this special period," the era of slavery, would be gone. Shortly, all former slaves and slaveholders would be dead. Although the old masters would scarcely want for their "narrators" and apologists, and consequently would continue to enjoy their day in court, the old slaves were likely to find themselves without an advocate or historian. For this reason Douglass undertook to keep the Negroes' side of the ledger from being blank. "My part," Douglass said, "has been to tell the story of the slave." [16] Thus he wrote the story of his life as an extended historical metaphor. The final version of his autobiography is more a forensic history than the story of a life, and as such Douglass' self-given personality traits and the successive stages of his life are transposed to become common to all blacks who came out of slavery.

Unless one is willing to unblinkingly follow Douglass in this assessment of personality, and in so doing subscribe to an archaic biographical method, a biographer must separate Douglass' personal statement from his historical argument. It is necessary to recognize Douglass' metaphor for what it is and understand that his self-given consistent personality was a device employed by an advocate as he stood before the bar of history pleading his case for millions of black clients. But, as we will presently see, when the separation is made a consistent Frederick Douglass is dissolved.

The closest any biographer comes to imputing inconsistency to Douglass is Foner in his account of Douglass' equivocation as the 1876 political bargaining was consummated, and this is quickly glossed and explained away in order that the cluster of traits already attributed to him will not be deranged. Only when there is no risk of impairing the core of personality does Foner indulge himself in a criticism of apparent inconsistency. This he does in his account of Douglass' oration at the dedication of the Freedmen's Monument to Abraham Lincoln. For that episode Foner chastens Douglass because "the bulk of his oration dealt with the past" instead of the threatening future. Foner counterpoints his criticisms with Douglass' earlier statement, "We have to do with the past only as we can make it useful to the present and to the future." But instead of catching Douglass in an inconsistency, Foner inadvertently points out that the functional past is one thing for himself, another for Douglass. That is, by reminding us of Douglass' need for a functional past, Foner suggests a way the autobiographies may be read so that Douglass emerges from their pages as a human being instead of a metaphor.

In the Lincoln oration, instead of uselessly laboring over the past as Foner criticizes him for doing, Douglass was putting it to a specific purpose. He was using the past in an attempt to define himself as a person. For, as he told his audience, he had come out of the past as a fatherless orphan and his identity had been forced on him by "circumstances and necessity." The imperatives of the Civil War had at last given him a social identity. He was Abraham Lincoln's stepchild. War had brought him into the family of American citizens. An adopted child, having come into the family through the back door, he was nonetheless pleased, even happy, to accept that identity. The oration is an eloquent illustration of Douglass' conception of a double-functioned past, one that served both as a vehicle for a social program and an instrument and arena for self-definition. Yet within the definition of a social identity there was still the question of a personal identity. He remained, after all, an orphan, literally, and he was never able to put the haunting questions surrounding his lost past out of his mind. Had it been otherwise he would not have made, years after the oration, the trip to Thomas Sears. It was a search for a usable personal past that took him to the home of the Baltimore physician. As he talked with Doctor Sears he made his last attempt to find out who he was. He was pressing back into the obscurity surrounding his origins to a time from which not a consistent but a divided conflict-torn Frederick Douglass emerges.

Long before his visit to doctor Sears, Douglass had struggled with his past. It would not be stretching the point to say that for most of his life he wrestled with his past in an attempt to shape it into some coherent and satisfying meaning. The intensity of his struggle can only be surmised, but of its continuation there is no doubt. The clues for penetrating the meaning of Douglass' concern for his past are found in the autobiographies. On their face the successive accounts seem to be fleshier extensions of the previous versions, becoming more rhetorical as Douglass found and mastered his style. The anecdotal form is perfected; the sparse narrative framework of the *Narrative* is embellished with pirouetting asides and arabesques of description, but they rarely fall off the point in the subsequent *My Bondage and My Freedom* and the *Life and Times*. Douglass remained in full control of his technique. The books are a platform style set in type. They are oratorical efforts. Their aim is to move, justify, and persuade. They do not propose to tell. But they do tell. They reveal far more about himself than Douglass intended.

While autobiography may proceed on three levels, the historical, psychological, and spiritual, at its best it ceases to be either a historical or a psychological document. Instead, it is the story of how the writer conducted his search for his "inner standing," how he came to terms with himself, how, finally, he came to see himself. It is the revelation of the writer's "spirit." Fine autobiography tells the story of the life's journey less in terms of how the journey was made (the personal history) or why it was made (the self-analysis); rather, it concerns itself with the unfolding of self-awareness in the course of the journey. By way of autobiography itself the writer comes to terms with himself. At the end of his autobiographical journey he stands face to face with himself, revealed and reduced to his essence.[17]

Under this rubric, a severe and austere one that is intended to establish autobiography as an art form, Douglass' self-writings stand at a discount. Douglass' autobiographies were written as forensic historical statements, intended to be "complete" vindications of American Negroes against the charge that they were inferior to white people.[18] It is necessary to remember that considered as psychological documents most of the autobiographies' psychological statements are also forensic. They were intended to support Douglass' indictment of slavery and racial discrimination by showing how the systems operated to disturb Negroes' psychic stability, and, conversely, to demonstrate blacks' power to withstand stress and tension and maintain their psychic stability. Committed to play the advocate, Douglass made no attempt to move to the higher level of autobiography in which the "inner self" is revealed. Had he contented himself with only one autobiography he would have produced a lopsided personal history and a social tract that answered the intended purposes but in which the self-portrait was static, and there the matter would have rested. But Douglass' desire to make the strongest historical case for blacks—and for himself—forced him to become a better autobiographer than he intended. As he continued his narrative through the successive versions, he unwittingly told the story of his self-awareness unfolding. More by accident than design Douglass moved toward the higher level of autobiography in which his static self-portrait dissolves and his revealed essence emerges winnowed from the personal, tractlike history.

Paradoxically the emergence of Douglass' "essence" is seen most clearly in his sections on his lost past. Unlike most autobiographies in which the writer's conception of self is revealed as the life story progresses, Douglass presents his conception of himself in the opening chapters of his books. His strategy was to use his slave past as a matrix out of which he came as a formed man. He would have us believe that he knew who he was at the very moment he disguised himself as a free sailor and bought his train ticket for the trip north, and the rest of his life is the progressive unfolding of that which he had become when he fled Baltimore.

Douglass' strategy of emerging from slavery as a fully formed man is crucial to the intent of the autobiographies. This strategy simultaneously serves two purposes. It establishes the former slave as a functioning member of a free labor society; that is, it argues that the slavery experience, regardless of its brutalities and deprivations, did not inhibit the development of a slave's essential characteristics as a human being. As soon as he is free he can participate in a free society. He is not psychologically crippled. Second, it permits Douglass to move straightaway to attack social conditions in the free society that inhibit the former slave from being what he already is. In short, the story of the development of a man is broken off in favor of social criticism. Except as it suits the purpose of social commentary an account of further personal change and development is abandoned, and with it the purpose of autobiography.[19]

But if Douglass' autobiographies are read comparatively, something else quite different becomes strikingly apparent. It becomes clear that Douglass used his lost past not only as a matrix in which he was formed but also as a stage on which the drama of his continuing modification of self was enacted. Instead of being frozen his past was continually revised (Douglass changes the stage sets and actors), and with the modification of his past his self-portrait was also changed. The past became the mirror of Douglass' ongoing life, reflecting his contact with the world which necessitated his redefinitions of self and the unfolding of self-consciousness, and resulted in the better, more revealing autobiography.

This revelation did not occur by conscious intent. It happened because Douglass rewrote his story,[20] and because an autobiographical carte blanche was given him. The absence of a verifiable past was a license to make much of his past exactly what he wanted it to have been. Douglass' past waited for him to invent and use as the setting in which he created the person he was (or seemed to be) at the time he was writing. With his strategy of emerging from slavery as the formed man, the self-created past was a representation of the present. Therefore, whatever adjustments Douglass made in his conception of himself will not be found when they occurred but in the sections about his childhood and young manhood where he transposed them, and where he attempted to authenticate himself.[21] This authentication Douglass never achieved. But his struggle to attain it is the essence of his personal story— and the heart of his biography—once his story is separated from his social tracts.

IX

Nantucket: Confirmation, Betrayal, and Rebirth

I suspect he also felt accused by his own people for the increasingly conscious desires he felt to leave their company, to spend his time with white people, even to be white. After we had known one another four years he told me that some of his friends in college deny ever having thought of what it was like to be white. I no longer record our talks on tape, but he spoke words to this effect: "I would never have admitted to you two years ago that I wished I was white when I was at school with whites. I never really could admit it to myself. The thought would cross my mind, and I'd try to forget it as quickly as it came."

ROBERT COLES, *Children of Crisis*

Only since his Editorial career has [Douglass] seen to become a colored man! I have read his paper very carefully and find phase after phase develop itself as in one newly born among us.

JAMES MCCUNE SMITH

When he visited Thomas Sears and asked him for information about his ancestors, perhaps Douglass had a premonition that this would be his last opportunity to penetrate what had always been a blank wall of time surrounding his past.

The blankness of time was the subtle but pervasive characteristic of the slave culture from which Douglass was sprung, for slavery had a time with its own logic and rhythm. There was sidereal time for the sailors and watermen on the Chesapeake who marked their nights with the rising and waning of the evening star. There was seasonal time for the landbound on the eastern shore whose lives were regulated as much by planting time and laying-by time as by the customs and laws of slavery which held that no slave needed a calendar or records to support the very fact of his existence. Enumerating a nameless slave for the census was enough. Beyond that, whatever records there were depended upon the accounting practices of the master, which were rudimentary enough to give credence to Douglass' observation that genealogical trees did not flourish for slaves.

Slavery's time was a factless, recordless time. Its quality was memory, which is to say, the past was remembered personal experience, nothing more, nothing less. For the slaves, time and history blended together and were changed to psychology, *tabula rasa* as it were. Existence, then, other than the split-second moment of the present, depended upon memory. Memory alone fixed things in time and gave connection and coherence to being itself. Such a time system was splendidly suited to a slave culture for it made the slaves prisoner to themselves, to their powers of recall, and gave them no fixed reference points except the stars or the running of the shad or tasseling corn. And what dangers lay in these things? For the slaves the past was memory without support, without the paraphernalia of the masters' records with which recollection can be tested and purified, purged of treacherous recall; or better yet, used to fill lacunae that memory has forgotten; and best of all, to take one beyond conscious memory into that time from which there comes no recollection. To provide that paraphernalia— "facts," Douglass called them—was to shift reference points, and the consequence was to change being, which was the one thing the masters were desperate to prevent. Once they conceded that, everything else was given away.[1]

Douglass had moved toward this conclusion while still a slave. He never put it precisely that way, but slavery's system of time is implicit in the second sentence he put in print after he escaped from slavery: "I have no accurate knowledge of my age, never having seen any authentic record containing it." He said that being ignorant of his birthday was a "source of unhappiness" when he was a child. He wanted a birthday and could see that white children had them. If this was not the first experience establishing that he was

different, that he lived under a different imperative, it is still significant that being without a birthday is the reason for his first
declaration of grievance appearing in Douglass' personal indictment of the slave system /The other reasons came later. The stock-
in-trade deprivations and brutalities are described, but the depriva-
tion of a past beyond remembered experience comes first, and it
haunted him. The childhood unhappiness of having no birthday
was never overcome. To the end of his life the mystery of his birthday was "a serious trouble," [2] and it puts into a kind of shorthand
both slavery's system of time and the reason for Douglass' determination to make the trip to Baltimore to visit Doctor Thomas
Sears.

Surely the conversation with Sears was important for Douglass,
because he went to the trouble to find his diary and make an entry
about it the morning after he returned from Baltimore. It was his
first entry since he made a hurried note in it while he was at London
six years earlier.

I called yesterday while in Baltimore . . . upon Dr. Thomas Edward
Sears, a grandson of Thomas and Lucretia Auld and learned the following
facts:

    Capt. Thomas Auld, was born 1795
       Amanda Auld, his daughter was born Jan 28 1826
    Thomas, son of Hugh and Sophia Auld was born Jan: 1824
    Capt Aaron Anthony, Died Nov 14 1823" [3]

Here were coveted "facts." Whether Douglass was disappointed
by them, whether he had hoped he would find more, he did not say.
But this was more information than he ever had about matters
connected with his childhood and probably was as much as Doctor
Sears was able to find in his Bible or whatever books and papers
comprised the family archives. The doctor had gone to some pains
to oblige Douglass, to search his records for what information he
did have, for Sears was indebted to Douglass, and to find a few birth
and death dates was a cheap repayment for favors Douglass had
granted him.

Almost ten years earlier Thomas Sears had asked Douglass to
lend him five hundred dollars to secure a mortgage on a farm on
which his sisters lived. The young doctor was only beginning to

establish himself in his Baltimore practice, and since their father's death there had been more debts than income. Would Douglass help, the doctor asked, even though, of course, the Searses had no claim on him except his goodwill and Douglass' "regard for their mother"?[4] The request was a longer chance for Doctor Sears than for most of Douglass' supplicants—"numerous and persistent beggars" he called them—because Douglass was Sears's grandfather's runaway slave. But since the war they had made their peace. The grandfather, Hugh Auld, said that if he had been in Douglass' place he would have run away, too. Douglass in turn apologized for some harsh statements he had made about his old master's callousness. And Douglass said that he held a deep affection for the doctor's mother, the daughter of the woman who had treated him compassionately when he was a slave boy.

Whether Douglass loaned Thomas Sears five hundred dollars is not revealed in the fragments of the correspondence. Whatever Douglass' response, the next year Sears asked again for help. Would Douglass this time find a job for his sister, Annie Sears, in Washington? The doctor believed Douglass had access to many clerkships in government bureaus and agencies. "Any kind of employment" would be acceptable to Miss Sears because her need was great. But if the doctor were optimistic about Douglass' ability to find places for his friends in the government service, he did know Gilded-Age Washington. He knew it was the spoilsmen's province and that any request must be accompanied by a certificate of party fidelity. So he reminded Douglass that he was "a true Republican," and he added that his "heart echoed" the party principles that Douglass had recently proclaimed in a speech commemorating the abolition of slavery in the District of Columbia.[5]

Within the week Douglass replied, and he must have written an encouraging letter because the doctor thanked him for it in more than a perfunctory way. With this exchange the correspondence ceased, and Doctor Thomas Sears seems to have disappeared from Douglass' life for eight years.[6]

Perhaps Douglass found a job for Annie Sears, or at least opened a door for her, and with his sister provided for and his own medical practice growing there was no longer any need for Sears to ask

Douglass for help. Or perhaps upon learning that Douglass had been turned out of office as recorder of deeds in January, 1886, the doctor understood his inability to help. Whatever the reason there were no more letters from him.

Douglass probably helped Thomas Sears and his family. When he chose to be he was a magnanimous, generous man, and though he never intimated it to Sears he, a master of irony, scarcely could have been insensible to the ironical situation. Born to serve, he was now able to oblige.[7] But more than that, Thomas Sears was one of the few people who had access to a portion of Douglass' lost past, the cause of his first declared unhappiness about being enslaved.

Another person who could help in his quest was Thomas Auld, the "Tommy" of Douglass' youth. To serve Tommy was the reason he had been sent across the Chesapeake to Baltimore. In the manner of convoluted southern family relationships, he had come up from Maryland's eastern shore as a gift from his first master, Tommy's grand-uncle by marriage. He was to be Tommy's companion and playmate, a relationship Douglass happily embraced, "I had . . . fallen in love with the dear boy."[8]

It was through Tommy that Douglass achieved his freedom, for Baltimore was the key that opened the door to freedom for him. If he had not got to Baltimore, he probably never could have escaped slavery. By being in the city he was half-free, saved from the stupifying existence of Tuckahoe plantation. The commerce of ideas flowed around him, however dimly he perceived them. Baltimore's free Negro community gave him tangible proof that, contrary to the scriptural exegeses delivered by the plantation preachers, the color of his skin had not foreordained his status as slave. Tommy's mother, Sophia Auld, began to teach him to read, and then, forbidden more lessons by Hugh Auld, Tommy's father, Douglass took Tommy's discarded spelling books and secretly labored through them on his own.

"Viewing it in the light of human likelihoods," he later wrote, "it is quite probable that but for the mere circumstance of being thus removed [to Baltimore] I might have continued in slavery until emancipated by the war."[9] Therefore if Thomas Auld had once been the agent of his freedom, he might now bring him freedom from the ignorance of his lost past. He turned to Thomas Auld before he made his visit to Doctor Sears.

But before he was able to contact Auld, Douglass became involved in the last of the four great controversies of his life. Earlier he had found the break with the Garrisonians, his complicity with John Brown, and his connection with the failure of the Freedman's Bank galling and necessitating elaborate explanation and justification, and he now found himself obliged to go to similar lengths to defend his conduct in Haiti.[10]

Resigning his position as consul general in protest against American naval and maritime policies that he claimed exploited the Haitian people, he returned to the United States. His action brought accusations that he had put the interests of foreign black people ahead of the national interest. It was a difficult charge for Douglass to combat in the early nineties as racism and imperialism moved to congruence, and as far as the American public was concerned the burden of explanation lay with him. The Harrison administration was not inclined to help him. His resignation had been accepted without any sign of regret, and he was on his own to defend himself. But occupied as he was through the summer of 1891 making his defense he could not put from his mind his lost past and the help Thomas Auld might give him.

In August, 1891, Douglass wrote to Auld. It was the first letter he wrote after his resignation that did not have to do with the Haitian controversy.[11] But Thomas Auld had recently died. His brother, a Baltimore police captain, replied to Douglass' letter, and he answered some of Douglass' questions. Douglass responded: "You tell me much that I wanted to know." Captain Auld's answers sparked his memory: "In those days the [Fells] Point and town boys often spent their Sundays in pitching cents and fighting near the old Drawbridge. I am sorry to say that I . . . was often with them as bad as the others." But however pleasant the evocation of those ancient Baltimore Sundays, there were no "facts" there. He wrote again. Captain Auld's "kind good letter . . . embolden[ed]" him. "Can you," he asked, "tell me in what year your father entered into partnership with Edward Harrison and began shipbuilding on the City Block? Can you tell me in what year he quitted work on the

'frigate' in Beacham's shipyard and went to work in Dorgan &
Bailey's?—I had not begun to notice dates at that time and a
knowledge of these dates will help me to fix other dates and events
about which I wish to be accurate. . . . I am especially desirous to
know in what year Mr. James Beacham built the frigate."

The questions poured from him, and he wanted to ask even
more, but he hesitated to impose further on a busy and important
man on the police force. Nevertheless, Douglass nudged him a bit:
"Perhaps there are those within your acquaintance who can help
you to this knowledge." He enclosed the proofs of a new biographical sketch of himself with the request that the captain return them.
It was one of his most artful letters, engaging, entreating, and set
with a subtle trap to force a reply. [12]

The "fact" Douglass wanted especially was the year he had come
to Baltimore. That was why the frigate was so important. The ship
was finished shortly after he had come to the city; that much he was
confident he could remember. But when was it finished? As early as
1881, when he wrote the first version of the *Life and Times*, Douglass had decided the ship was completed in 1825. "I know that it was
in the year 1825 that I went to Baltimore, because it was in that year
that Mr. James Beacham built a large frigate at the foot of Alliceana
street, for one of the South American Governments." [13] But what
Douglass really knew was that his unsupported memory provided
no guarantee that he was correct, and ten years later in the middle
of the Haitian controversy he was forced back to Captain Auld.

With his letter that "emboldened" Douglass to ask for more information, Captain Auld disappears from Douglass' correspondence. Perhaps a reply never came. Maybe the captain of
police thought he had answered enough questions about those
early days in Baltimore. Certainly he, unlike Thomas Sears, was
under no obligation to Douglass. Quite possibly he laid the whole
business aside and forgot it. If it had been otherwise, there would
have been no reason for Douglass, two and a half years later, to
have concluded the diary entry that recorded his visit to Doctor
Sears as he did: "The Death of Aaron Anthony makes me to fix the
year in which I was sent to live with Mr. Hugh Auld in Baltimore,
as 1825." At last he had his "fact." Aaron Anthony had died

November 14, 1823; and if Douglass had to somehow extrapolate the year he arrived in Baltimore from Anthony's death he nevertheless was satisfied because the extrapolation did rest on a fact. Then having established the year in which he came to Baltimore, Douglass closed the gap even further. "I know that it must have been in the summer of that year that I went to live in Baltimore because the Spring lambs were big enough to be sent to market, and I helped to drive a flock of them from Smith's Dock to Fells Point on the day I landed in Baltimore." With his memory of lambs in the summertime the last entry in Douglass' diary ended, and so did his lifelong attempt to find the coveted information to support the hazy recollections of his childhood. Beyond Baltimore there was no recoverable information to purify memory.[14]

If the Douglass autobiographies are read with an eye for the rather inconspicuous and subtle but profoundly significant changes Douglass made in the pre-Baltimore sections of his past, another dimension of his life is exposed. The autobiographies' surface accounts of remarkable courage and splendid achievement remain, but beneath them there are glimpses of a wracking story of conflict within Douglass himself, a conflict that in the manner of great autobiography is the continuing story of a man searching for his inner standing. Intended to demonstrate the triumph of a man and vindicate a race, and in the fashion of nineteenth-century self-help manuals to offer a model for those who would follow,[15] the autobiographies in fact tell the story of the anguish of a divided man.

To move to this deeper level and illuminate with the greatest clarity the question of why Douglass, through the modification of his lost past, was shifting his conception of himself, it is first in order to consider the still unsatisfactorily answered question about him: why he became an abolitionist. This is necessary because in "choosing" to become an abolitionist Douglass provided unmistakable clues to his first conception of self. It was from this original conception that he subsequently moved, and as he moved he readjusted the autobiographical past to make it consistent with his movement. The Garrisonian convention at Nantucket is the great reference point in Douglass' post-Baltimore life, not only because it was at Nantucket that he entered the public life, but because it was there that he was first able to become the person he believed himself to be.

Almost incidentally his biographers take up the question of what moved Douglass to become an abolitionist. For both Benjamin Quarles and Philip Foner the aim is to place Douglass on the public platform as quickly as possible in order that he may speak out against slavery and racial inequality. Both biographers rapidly dispose of the pre-Nantucket phases of Douglass' life: growing up enslaved; his successful escape and fetching up at New Bedford with his bride Anna Murray, a Baltimore free black who followed him north, where they made their first home. But however much the biographers rush through his earlier life in order to establish him as an agitator and spokesman, they nevertheless are obliged to consider the problem of explaining why Douglass came to the abolition platform. Antislavery agitation is not synonymous with fleeing slavery, nor are the motives informing them the same. Therefore it will not suffice to supply Douglass with motives for escaping slavery and imply that these carried him into the ranks of abolition, especially since he, however remotely, risked the slavecatchers once he entered public life and openly acknowledged that he was a fugitive.

Quarles, after producing the motives that drove Douglass to escape slavery, move through New York, and settle in New Bedford, introduces Douglass to abolition. At New Bedford he "became aware of the abolitionist movement." He subscribed to the *Liberator* and began "to attend the abolition meetings held by colored people. Gradually he rose to leadership among his fellows" and in June, 1841, was chairman of a meeting that censured the Maryland Colonization Society "for threatening to remove colored people from that state by coercive means"; that is, Douglass surfaces as a leader for the first time. In August, 1841, he attended an antislavery meeting at which William Lloyd Garrison spoke and was "impressed [and] awed" by Garrison. Next day he joined the Garrisonians on a boat trip to Nantucket for an abolition convention, and the following day he was "unexpectedly called upon to speak." After his performance he was asked to take an agency by which he could proclaim the wrong and suffering of three million slaves. Given the invitation to become an abolition field worker, Douglass was able to give voice to his "great hatred of slavery," a hatred that transcended his "personal experiences" as a slave because, Quarles wrote, "what portion of his hatred of slavery may be traced to the experiences of his days in bondage is difficult to determine." According to Quarles there were motives other than the fact of his own enslavement that led Douglass into abolition. These motives complement each other. Douglass' "great hatred" for slavery is harnessed with his "psychological make-up"—his sensitivity, intelligence and ambition, which in turn are focused in his "urge to speak."

This "urge . . . had been upon him from his first purchase of a book on elocution. Fascinated by those with the gift of tongue, he sought out debating societies and gained experience in self-expression among church groups. Had the abolition movement not offered an opportunity—had quiet times prevailed—Douglass' abilities would doubtless have led him into the pulpit. His logical mind, his air of sternness and rectitude, his imposing physique and the rolling thunder of his voice had fitted him for the public platform."

Quarles's solution to the problem of why Douglass came to abolition thus proceeds in a linear manner. As a young slave Douglass learns the anguish of being enslaved, but he somehow develops an enormous hatred for slavery that is not explicable in terms of his own experience. Simultaneously he becomes consumed by an urge to speak. Then after a time (and fortuitously) the speaking platform is provided by the Garrisonians, and desire and opportunity are brought together.

The Foner solution, unlike Quarles's, does not proceed sequentially from slavery to freedom to abolition; it fuses the stages and has Douglass committed to abolition before he made his break for freedom. Still a slave in Baltimore, Douglass is acquainted with the abolitionists through the newspapers and by hearing Hugh Auld, his master, talk of them. He then declares, "There [is] hope." Whether it was hope for personal freedom or freedom for all slaves is not clear. In either case Foner then introduces the episode in which young Douglass is at the wharves watching a coffle of slaves being herded aboard a ship bound for the Gulf, and, following Douglass' later statement, the sight provided the first thrust toward abolition: "I then resolved that whatever power I had should be devoted to the freeing of my race."

After settling in New Bedford, Douglass subscribed to the *Liberator*. Garrison's newspaper "'became my meat and drink. . . . My soul was set all on fire. Its sympathy for my brethren in bonds—its scathing denunciations of slaveholders—its faithful exposures of slavery—and its powerful attacks upon the upholders of the institution—sent a thrill of joy through my soul, such as I had never felt before.'" But Douglass was "not satisfied to sit at home and thrill to the paper. He now began to attend the Abolitionist meetings held by the Negro people of New Bedford." He "became more and more involved in the Abolitionist activities of the New Bedford Negroes [and] gradually assum[ed] a position of leadership," and appears chairing the meeting that censured the Maryland Colonization Society. Subsequently at an antislavery society meeting he saw William Lloyd Garrison for the first time. "It was a red-letter day in the life of the young Negro, barely twenty-four years of age and but three years removed from slavery, because on that day, he saw in the editor of the *Liberator* the mission for his own life." The following day he sailed with the Garrison party to Nantucket and was soon on the public platform.

There are difficulties in either solution, though fewer in Quarles's because he refuses to accept Douglass' long-after-the-fact claim about the pledge made on the Baltimore wharves and he is willing to consider the matter of blind luck in establishing a talented, ambitious man in a particular enterprise. The capital difficulty with the Quarles solution comes with harmonizing Douglass' great hatred of slavery, a hatred that transcended his own experiences, as a primary motive that impelled him into abolition with the speculation that had quiet times prevailed Douglass would have been led to the pulpit where, presumably, his "rolling thunder" would have been unloosed to save man's soul, not his body.[16] Stipulating the luck of timing, the question must be raised as to whether this powerful motive might be adduced to help explain

why the runaway slave chose to come out into the full glare of
public notoriety, or whether, instead, Quarles indulges himself in
a bit of *post hoc, egro propter hoc* reasoning.

The Foner solution to the problem of why Douglass became an
abolitionist is considerably more troublesome. It rests on Douglass'
1870 claim that he pledged himself to abolition as well as personal
freedom while he was a young slave watching the coffle, then dou-
bles back on itself as Foner has Douglass "see" in William Lloyd
Garrison the mission for his own life. Even if the Baltimore pledge
was made in nonspecific terms and if Douglass, watching the slave
ship load its cargo, took all slaves' cause as his own, it nevertheless
remains inexplicable that he should be obliged to wait until he had
seen Garrison in the flesh before he "saw" his own mission. As a
reader of the *Liberator* he had already learned the Garrisonian
methods. "I had not long been a reader of the 'Liberator,' before I
got a pretty correct idea of the principles, measures and spirit of the
anti-slavery reform. I took right hold of the cause."[17]

Human motivations remain the despair of biographers. Elusive
and unfathomable, they will never fully yield to investigation and
analysis. But they provide the hard kernel the biographer must try
to break unless he is willing to default on his obligation to get,
according to his lights, as close to the truth as possible. Quarles
labored to crack the kernel. Foner permitted Douglass to supply his
own after-the-fact motive, then attempted to improve on it and
consequently tangled himself with Douglass' previous testimony.
In both cases one must wonder whether they appreciated the nature
of the question they attempted to answer. It is the most important
question that is raised about Douglass' life. For once he stood before the audience at Nantucket and found that he could speak out
(and his listeners decided that he would be a useful instrument for
their purposes), he not only found his life's work, but, insofar as
motives for action provide clues to a person's conception of himself,
Douglass in his decision to accept the abolition commission made a
clear statement about himself.

Lacking a month, Douglass was three years out of Baltimore,
beyond Hugh Auld and the easy accommodations of urban slavery,
and even farther beyond the Eastern Shore and "indigent and

spiritless" Tuckahoe. His world was New Bedford, "clean, new and beautiful," where even though he was denied work at his craft by white ship's caulkers who permitted no black competition and as a consequence had to take day labor—"new, dirty, and hard work"—he nevertheless "went at it with a glad heart and a willing hand. [For, he continued] I was now my own master. It was a happy moment, the rapture of which can be understood only by those who had been slaves." [18]

Excepting the remote possibility of capture, Douglass' enslavement was now behind him. If he could not make his living at New Bedford shipyards, common labor was still better than Baltimore where Hugh Auld waited at the end of each payday to take his wages. Suffering gratuitous prejudice was a cheap price to pay to be out of slavery. He knew the "rapture" of being his own master, of "freedom." But how "free" Douglass considered himself was revealed three years later as he joined the Garrisonians for the trip to the Nantucket convention. There was a row on the boat about separate accommodations for the Negroes that was not settled until all the abolitionists, black and white, agreed to share the weather deck. Here for the first time the Garrisonian doctrine of racial equality was put to the test before Douglass' eyes, and the assay proved that the doctrine was pure. They seemed to mean what they said. At the convention, Douglass "felt strongly moved to speak," but he hesitated. The idea of addressing the convention "was a severe cross." Because if the orator in him was clamoring for release, and if he at last was before an audience that would permit him to witness not only for himself but for the "great hatred of slavery" that compelled him to speak in behalf of millions of slaves, he nevertheless was obliged to speak before "white people." Before them he quailed and his metaphor was the cross. "The truth was, I felt myself a slave." [19]

Although he had been welcomed by the Garrisonians at New Bedford and encouraged by them to come along to Nantucket, though he had shared the *Telegraph*'s weather deck with them and was called by them to speak, Douglass could only look at them and think that regardless of the miles and the years he had put between himself and the Maryland slave code he was still a slave. He was defined not by the New Bedford ship caulkers or the *Telegraph*'s captain or any of the countless men from whom he had learned to expect the sting of blind animosity, but by the encouraging, receptive white people who sat before him.

It is impossible to know with any certainty what Douglass said at Nantucket other than that he "told his story." The abolitionist reports attributed "eloquence" and "great power" to him. And, in the manner of the day, claimed that "flinty hearts were pierced, and cold ones melted," oblivious to the howling inconsistency of having such hearts at a convivial meeting of kindred spirits, the object of which was to enthusiastically belabor slavery with whatever weapon came to hand. About his speech Douglass himself said only, "It was with the utmost difficulty that I could stand erect, or that I could command and articulate two words without hesitation and stammering. I trembled in every limb." But once he got underway he "felt freedom" and spoke with "considerable ease." Whatever shackles he had borne across Nantucket Sound were struck off as he talked. He no longer felt himself a "slave."

He was asked to speak again at the evening session, and when the meeting was over the proposition was put to him; would he accept an agency? Would he join the public workers and share with them the responsibility of spearheading Garrisonian abolition? When Douglass accepted the offer he was confirming that which he had already experienced. He had found his tongue while speaking to white men. His powers of speech had given him freedom from being defined by the others' whiteness.

All of Douglass' biographers treat the Nantucket meeting as a climacteric in his life, and rightly so because only then does Douglass' life assume historical dimension and significance. For Quarles the movement is so abrupt that he changes the mode of his biography, shifting from an "essay in interpretation" to straight line narrative. Foner rings down the curtain on the first phase of Douglass' life as the meeting ends, and the other biographers have made the same turning point though not with such marked emphasis.

The characteristic biographical interpretation has Douglass taking the first dramatic step that led to his emancipation from white leadership and domination. At Nantucket he ceased to be intimidated by white people. His motives for accepting the abolition agency all point to his conception of self. He was a proud ambitious black man, who by the power of his tongue, that is, by his innate, born-in-slavery powers, found a way to break clear of the stigma of color.

In all the Douglass biographies there is a consistent progression. The boy comes to understand that he is a slave; as he grows up he yearns to be free; he strikes for freedom; after escaping slavery he casts his lot with the Garrisonians and devotes an extraordinary ability and talent to the freeing of other slaves. As the progression unfolds there is never any question raised about Douglass' conception of himself. He is a slave and a Negro. He undertakes his abolition mission as a black man, and it is a black man he remains throughout his life as he pleads the cause of American blacks. The history of the man runs parallel with the history of the race in the double movement from slavery to freedom and from freedom to equality. His name is a reproof to those who have accepted some easier way and a virtual eponym for black people who have refused to suffer accommodation and compromise. It must be such if Douglass' fundamental meaning and significance is that of the archetypical black claiming a free and unfettered place as a black in American society. Nantucket, then, is the confirming experience of both identity and vocation. And the rest followed.

However desirable such an interpretation may be, it becomes possible only by disregarding Douglass' several accounts of his Nantucket experience. The closest Douglass came to a *cri de coeur* in either *Bondage and Freedom* or the *Life and Times* is the passage he wrote describing his feelings as he accepted the Garrisonian agency. There was ample place for such a description in the *Narrative*, which was written about three years after the Nantucket meeting, but here the *Narrative* is silent as Douglass trials off in a vague wish that his abilities will be sufficient to his task. But the latter autobiographies are pointedly explicit about what he "wished." First written for *Bondage and Freedom*, the passage puts the Nantucket episode into a lengthened perspective of experience that was impossible when the *Narrative* was written, and Douglass must have been satisfied with the way it stood because when he reviewed his story for the *Life and Times* he left every word untouched. This passage is Douglass' enduring summary statement about the way he felt as he entered the abolition enterprise, once he was able to see what that experience had really meant for him. Almost hidden in the story of his life, it rests like a crumpled forget-me-not in the two later autobiographies: "Young, ardent and hopeful, I entered upon this new life in the full gush of unsuspecting enthusiasm. The cause was good, the men engaged in it were good, the means to attain its triumph, good. . . . *For a time I was made to forget that my skin was dark and my hair crisped.*"[20]

Joining this passage with the "slave" passage in the *Narrative* puts an altogether different but brilliant shaft of light on the question of why Douglass accepted the agency and committed himself to the role of abolitionist agitator. As he spoke at Nantucket he became free. He no longer felt himself a slave, and he entered a new life. But he was scarcely freed from white people. Instead, for the first time in his life he was able to repeal the Maryland slave code, "The children of slave women shall in all cases follow the condition of their mothers."[21] He was "made to forget" that he was Harriet Bailey's son. He was divested of his dark skin and crisped hair. He had ceased to be a Negro. The agency, the "good cause," was the literal escape from his physical features and from everything that tied him to his black mother.

But it is the passive, not the active, voice that speaks in this keening passage. Douglass makes a striking shift in his narrative style that always drives flashingly forward in active engagement. All of a sudden, and very briefly, he becomes the passive participant in his own drama. Power over self was lost and control over his life—the very definition of self—passes to others in this case the Garrisonians.

Between the writing of the *Narrative* and *Bondage and Freedom* Douglass had come to know that in those heady days at Nantucket he had been permitted to forget. He had not *become*. And in the passage with its shift to definition by others, there is also the muted cry of deception and betrayal that Douglass glossed with his characteristic ironic humor: "I found full soon that my enthusiasm had been extravagant."

The extent and duration of Douglass' freedom from his blackness, a desperate game of self-delusion that he was encouraged to play, must remain speculative. As late as 1845 Wendell Phillips was maintaining, "He never thinks of his color and we never do."[22] But Phillips did not speak for all the Garrisonians. Only two months after the Nantucket meeting Edmund Quincy, reporting impressions of Douglass, said that he was suitable modest for a "nigger," and other Garrisonians were exchanging reports in which their condescension was apparent.[23]

It is easy to detect signs of tension between Douglass and the Garrisonians long before the open rupture in 1847. The quarrel and break have been interpreted as an evidence of the "emancipation" of the black leadership from white tutelage, a confirmation of Negroes' own sense of self as Negroes.[24] But in Douglass' case the evidence indicates that he protested actions, and, it may be supposed, subtle moods that belied what he took to be the "promise" given to him at Nantucket. Certainly as the post-Nantucket period unfolded the Garrisonians could never come to terms with Douglass or understand his refusal to play the part they had assigned him. There is no doubt that he was meant to play a particular role in their establishment. He was intended to be a specimen. He was told by the Garrisonians, "Give us the facts [about being a black slave]. We will take care of the philosophy." Furthermore, he was advised to leave "a little of the plantation speech" in his accent. "Be yourself" was their instruction.[25]

Douglass, of course, was trying precisely to do that. But the man he wanted to be was not that which suited the Garrisonians; nor was it a man that accords with the interpretation that has him moving toward a rejection of the Garrisonian leadership because he was preparing himself as a black leader.

The clearest insight provided into this matter, and most specifically into the problem of Douglass' relationship with the Garrisonians, came from Isabel Jennings. Douglass' "Dear Isa" was an Englishwoman and his lifelong friend and confidante. Trying to smooth out a misunderstanding between him and the Garrisonians, she told Maria Chapman that Douglass "could bear to have fault found with him if it was not taken for granted he *must* be wrong."[26]

The fragmentary evidence relating to this period in Douglass' life—*circa* 1841–1847—must be handled with care and not be abused in an effort to make it say too much. But it must be read as sensitively as possible in order to understand what was happening between Douglass and the Garrisonians and what was happening to Douglass himself. The theme running through these materials is the fear, and in some instances the direct charges, of betrayal. In the case of the Garrisonians, it is Douglass' betrayal of their confidence in him to play his assigned role. In Douglass' case it is the Garrisonians' refusal to make good the promise he believed they had given him at Nantucket, that he could now live without the attributes of blackness. Both defaulted, as they must have, because the premise from which they proceeded meant inevitable "betrayal." The role the Garrisonians assigned Douglass was incompatible with the promise he believed they had given him. All that remained was for time to do its destructive work, for Douglass to come to understand that the few people he had trusted to let him be what he desperately wanted to be had failed him.[27] No more so than the New Bedford shipyard workers or the Maryland slave-owners were the Garrisonians prepared to permit Douglass to "be himself."

Of the biographers, Foner has most clearly described what was happening to Douglass. But what he does not say is *why* it happened:

From the day he made his first Abolitionist speech in Nantucket until the time he founded the *North Star* he had moved almost exclusively among white Abolitionists and only occasionally had he discussed issues confronting the Negro people other than the abolition of slavery. Now (c. 1847–1848) he began to build a closer relationship with other Negro leaders and with the Negro people themselves, to examine the whole range of Negro problems, and to pry into every facet of discrimination. Barely eight months after the paper had started, James McCune Smith commented: 'You will be surprised to hear me say,' he wrote Gerrit Smith, *'that only since his Editorial career has he seen to become a colored man!* [sic]. *I have read his paper very carefully and find phase after phase develop itself as in one newly born among us.* The Church question, the school question, separate institutions, are questions that he enters upon and argues about as our weary but active young men thought about and argued about years ago, when we had Literary Societies.[28]

Newly born among us. Only now has he seen fit to become a colored man. These are striking, penetrating phrases. And if James McCune Smith loaded them with irony it probably was less to punish Douglass than comment on his hopeless secret desire to be white and the absurdity of selecting abolition as the instrument to blot out his blackness.

X

Exiled from [your] native heaven
Oh, might I live to see thee grace
thy birthright place.
The Lady of the Lake

Genealogical trees did not flourish
among slaves.
FREDERICK DOUGLASS

The Highland Chief, the African Queen, and the Garden of Eden

If when Frederick Douglass wrote *Bondage and Freedom* he knew something about himself and the Garrisonians that he was unable to understand when he wrote the *Narrative*, if he was in fact changing his conception of himself—or was being forced to change it—there should be corresponding clues to the shift in the autobiographies. With his method of showing adjustments in his conception of himself in his past instead of the contemporary present, Douglass' redefinitions of self should appear in the sections of the autobiographies in which he created his lost past, the portion of his life over which he had the greatest control, and from which it was his strategy to emerge as the formed man. Most specifically, the redefinitions should appear

248

in the passages that relate to his mother and father, the autobiographical matrices from which he came. In all the autobiographies there is nothing more illuminating about Douglass' continuing struggle with his past and his attempt to come to terms with himself, to "authenticate" himself, than the sections he wrote about his parents. In these passages about his father and mother, to use his own metaphor, Douglass tried to grow a genealogical tree in the bitter earth of slavery.[1]

In *Bondage and Freedom* and the *Life and Times* Douglass expanded and embellished the outlines already established in the *Narrative*. In only one particular did Douglass deviate from his method: when he took up the account of his father. Here instead of expansion there is contraction. In quantitative terms he had less and less to say about his father in the later versions. But not only did he diminish the earlier emphasis he placed upon his father, he also changed his mind about him. The lead sentences with which Douglass introduced the subject provide unmistakable guides for charting his changing ideas. "My father was a white man," is the simple, unequivocal statement in the *Narrative*. Some ten years later, 1854, as he wrote *Bondage and Freedom*, he equivocated. "I say nothing of *father*, for he is shrouded in a mystery I have never been able to penetrate." About twenty-five years later, 1881, as he wrote the *Life and Times* he took the position that he let stand in the subsequent edition of 1892. He returned to his first, firm position, but he turned it inside out. Without qualification he said, "Of my father I know nothing."

Using these introductory sentences the successive positions Douglass took on his father may be plotted. He moved from certainty to hesitancy and doubt to certainty again. But it is an inverted sort of certainty. In the *Narrative* he *knows*; in *Bondage and Freedom* he *says nothing*; in the *Life and Times* he *knows nothing*. In the *Narrative* he knows that his father was a white man: "he was admitted to be such by all I ever heard speak of my parentage." It was "whispered" that he was his master, Aaron Anthony.

In *Bondage and Freedom*, Douglass first gave his father up to mystery, but after he worked his way through an ironic statement

about Anglo-Saxon blood purity, he reversed himself and seemed
to return to the position he had taken in the *Narrative*: "My father
was a white man." But he stopped short of the earlier unequivocal
assertion and qualified, "or nearly white." He also removed the
sexual animus that appeared in the *Narrative*. The man now may
be master and father and guilty of selling his own children, but he is
no longer sensual, ridden with lubricity, always ready to "administer to [his] own lusts." Still given over to race pride and willing to
take a profit behind the protection of the law that freed him of
responsibility for his children, the father was now cleansed of unbridled sexuality. Even as he becomes less distinct, the father becomes more acceptable, less culpable, and less white.

When he rewrote this passage for the *Life and Times*, Douglass
was ready to repudiate the white father: "Of my father I know
nothing." The remainder of the section stood substantially as it
appeared in *Bondage and Freedom*, with the striking exception of
the abrupt reversal he made in the latter when he returned to the
father and identified him as a white man, or "nearly white." This
sentence was expunged, and with it the paradox of Douglass' lost
past is enlarged. Even as he extended and widened his past by his
rewriting, he consistently reduced one sector of it so that when he
completed the final version of the story of his life he had sealed it off
altogether. As an identifiable man his father had ceased to exist.

The more obvious and striking shift that Douglass made in the
course of his autobiographical redefinition relates to his mother. In
the *Narrative* Harriet Bailey is a hazy, unrealized woman. There is
scarcely an outline for her portrait. All Douglass said was that she
was "quite dark." But she becomes the tall, splendidly proportioned, glossy-dark, regular-featured woman in *Bondage and
Freedom* and remains so in the *Life and Times*. But more important
than the changing description is a changing relationship and emotion. In the *Narrative*, Douglass implied that his affection for his
mother was stunted. Maybe it was even destroyed by separation;
or perhaps it was never developed in the first place. In *Bondage and
Freedom* the quality of the relationship is changed to one that was
not "very deeply attached." And in the *Life and Times* an explicit
statement of his emotional relationship with his mother is dropped

altogether, though he leaves the impression that however tenuous the connection between them might have been, his feelings about her, like the memory of their physical contacts, were vivid and imperishable. In the *Narrative* as he is told that his mother has died, he accepts the news with the same feeling he would have experienced had a stranger died; he suffers no distress. In *Bondage and Freedom* he learns of her death without "strong" sorrow. In the *Life and Times* the precise nature of his reaction is dropped, but the event of her death is handled with great poignancy, and Douglass gives his reader to understand that her death was a deeply felt experience for him.

In *Bondage and Freedom* the Aunt Katy passages—the episode that brings Harriet Bailey into sharpest focus—is added, and it remains much the same in the *Life and Times*. When out of the night his mother suddenly appears and brings cruel Aunt Katy to book, the little boy at last learns that he is "somebody's child." He sits regally on his mother's lap savoring his deliverance from the "virago." And in *Bondage and Freedom* there is an inconsistency between the episode in which he discovers that he has a mother who can make him feel like a prince and the statement that he learned of her death without feeling powerful sorrow. This discrepancy is removed in the *Life and Times*. In the final version, glossy, dark Harriet Bailey sweeps her son into her "strong, protecting arms." Enfolded by her warmth and security he finally experiences the full flood of maternal love. This love is displayed in a scene (which in *Bondage and Freedom* he introduces rather clinically as "instructive as well as interesting") so overwhelmingly powerful that it is beyond his ability to describe, he says. And the breaking of the mother-son tie because of Harriet Bailey's death is a continuing "grief" for him.

Although the matter of Harriet Bailey's literacy (and, by implication, intellectual prowess) is never brought up in the *Narrative*, it is introduced in *Bondage and Freedom* and continued with only one subtle but significant change in the *Life and Times*. Whatever talent he may have in the language is, in both versions, attributed to his mother. In *Bondage and Freedom* Douglass is "willing and even happy" to locate his "love of letters" in Harriet Bailey. In the

Life and Times he does not equivocate; "willing" is abandoned and the hesitant "even" is dropped. He is simply "happy" to acknowledge his debt to his mother. Should there be a genetic transmission of characteristics and abilities, the one Douglass prized above all, the only one he mentioned specifically in the entire passage, his talent with the language, is derived from his mother. When he wrote the *Life and Times*, Douglass subscribed no genetic or racial Salic law. Any "love of letters" he possessed he "fondly and proudly" believed he had inherited from his mother, "sable, unprotected, and uncultivated . . . who belonged to a race whose mental endowments are still disparaged and despised."

Rewriting for the *Life and Times*, Douglass removed a final double inconsistency. In *Bondage and Freedom* there are discrepancies in the striking portrait he first drew of Harriet Bailey, the concluding description of the sorrowful, toilworn, downcast woman, and the way she saved her son from Aunt Katy's clutches and brought Aunt Katy to terms. In the final version the woman of sorrow whose appearance and manner reflected her sadness ceases to exist, and no longer must the queenly Harriet Bailey deal with Aunt Katy by threatening to appeal to their master. In the *Life and Times* she forces her own will on the virago. With these changes Harriet Bailey's metamorphosis was completed. The dark woman who in the *Narrative* passed through Douglass' life almost literally a stranger in the night becomes the sable, tall fine-featured, impressive dignified mother who imposed her will by her own overwhelming force of character. She becomes a mother who made him feel like a prince, and who endowed him with the preeminent quality of language. It was she alone who enabled him to become a writer and speaker; she gave Douglass his "voice." No factitious reading of these passages is required to understand what Douglass was doing. Through the continued development and refinement of the autobiographical mother, Douglass was also developing and refining his own conception of self. He was driving himself deeper and deeper into a proud identification with Harriet Bailey who above all else was a black slave.

Having no picture of her, Douglass turned to a standard illustrated international anthropology, James Prichard's *Natural His-*

tory of Man, for a picture of Harriet Bailey. Finding an acceptable likeness in Prichard's book presented no great difficulty because there were dozens of pictures to choose from. Furthermore, Douglass said, he could go to these pictures confident that he remembered how his mother looked. When he wrote *Bondage and Freedom* he had convinced himself that her features were "ineffaceably stamped" on his memory. He found in Prichard "the head of a figure . . . the features of which so resemble those of my mother, that I often recur to it with something of the feelings which I suppose others experience when looking upon the pictures of dear departed ones."

The striking feature of the matter of Harriet Bailey's "picture" does not come from the question of whether it actually resembled her. That Douglass claimed it did from the first time he saw a copy of Prichard, when he was in England in the midforties, to the time he wrote the *Life and Times* is not at issue. According to him, for close to fifty years he took up his copy of *The Natural History of Man*, opened it to page 157, and studied the engraving there. He must have spent hours musing over the picture that "so resemble[d]" Harriet Bailey. What is striking is that, according to Prichard, the picture is of the "head of a statue supposed to be that of Rameses. It is thought . . . to resemble the second Egyptian type . . . which approaches the Hindoo." This second Egyptian type, the description says, refers to the "Indian." Therefore searching for a likeness of his "dark, glossy" mother, Douglass chose a picture in which the color was not specified and which according to the ethnological categories of the time was "Indian-Hindoo." Prichard's description, "the general expression is calm and dignified," accords with Douglass' "remarkably sedate and dignified," but beyond that the picture raises more questions than it answers. As he contemplated the picture Douglass surely must have read the descriptive passages that accompany the engraving. Furthermore, in order to find this particular picture Douglass was obliged to skip the entire section which, with abundant illustration, was devoted to various "African races." These are illustrations that might be termed "sedate and dignified," and that established beyond question sex and the "dark, glossy complexion." And, most remarkable of all, sometime during those years he must have read the passage describing the head as that of a man.[2] So for most of his life Frederick Douglass apparently found his black mother in the form of a princely man who, as far as the picture showed, may have been white.

Seemingly driving himself closer and closer to his mother in whom he was confirming his own blackness, Douglass was also leaving telltale clues to the continuing conflict within himself. Try as he might to perfect a definition of self that was rooted solely in Harriet Bailey, it remained *manque,* underlaid and forever shattered by the primal fact of his life. Within him there were two people and two imperatives: Harriet Bailey, carrying that which was brought out of Africa through a slave culture to her son, and Aaron Anthony the master, heir to the "Anglo-Saxonism" which Douglass scathingly arraigns in *Bondage and Freedom* and the *Life and Times,* but does not mention in the *Narrative.* In the *Narrative* the father is a licentious betrayer, taking economic profit and sensual pleasure while hiding behind a terrible law that permits him to repudiate the rightful claims of his children. The father's repudiation is the crime for which the son indicts him. The indictment is brought against an individual who is a participant in a brutal system. The father is not, as he is subsequently in *Bondage and Freedom* and the *Life and Times,* accused of being a member of a race and culture whose overriding characteristic is complacent arrogance, fit only for ironic contempt and rejection. The distinction is profoundly significant because his father as much as Harriet Bailey was the instrument with which Douglass shaped his autobiographical conception of self, and in the *Narrative,* written during the Nantucket period of his life, Douglass, regardless of his harsh words about his betraying, perfidious father, levied no attack against the father's race.

Nantucket was a climacteric, but not only in the sense the biographers have accorded it. There is an inner meaning for Nantucket which rests on the basic fact of Douglass' life—he was half white, not simply a white man's offspring. Two cultures, and the claims of each, as well as two persons lived inside Douglass. Born into one the other was forbidden to him, but the fact that Douglass recognized the existence of the other, and felt its claims, can be seen in the distinction he made in his attack on his father. In the Nantucket period he attacked a man and a system. He was not yet ready, or not yet forced, to broaden his attack to include his father's race and culture. They were, after all, his rightful portion and had been since he was "whisperingly" told who his father was.

Douglass developed the theme of a lost patrimony twice in his autobiographies. In *Bondage and Freedom* he contrasted the life of a white child, his "brother," with that of a slave boy, whom he explicitly identified as himself. The episode is based upon an allusion to the "white son" and his slave "brother" in the *Narrative*. The slave boy is allowed to lead an idyllic, uninhibited life. He is a black Huck Finn. He runs with the clouds and the animals and is "as happy as any little heathen under the palm trees of Africa." Douglass almost lost control of the episode, saving it only at the last moment from being a charming description of an idealized natural child in nature by making the point that the slave boy was denied the "restraints" and discipline, the attributes of "Anglo-Saxon" culture, imposed on his white brother. In the *Life and Times* this episode was expunged as Douglass perfected his claim for springing from the "uncultivated" Harriet Bailey.[3]

The matter of a lost patrimony also seemed related to Douglass' name changes. Certainly as one changes his name he is making a choice and a statement about whom he believes himself to be. One of the easiest magical tricks to play, and one of the few magics freely practiced in a rationalistic world, as a man changes his name his fantasy and desire are invested with a reality as unimpeachable as a bank account or a physical presence. Without a satisfying name, a name that places a man in a satisfying relation with the world outside him, there is an unsatisfying world inside him. Such a man without an "identity," Douglass said, the word is his, was "like the confused waves of the sea." He suffered from "a sense of loneliness and insecurity" because he knew that he was not yet truly "free or . . . safe."

Even before he escaped slavery Douglass shed the "pretentious and long" name his mother had given him, Frederick Augustus Washington Bailey. In Baltimore he renamed himself Frederick

Bailey. When he fled Baltimore it was as Frederick Stanley, and in New York he called himself Frederick Johnson. In New Bedford he changed his name again, and for the last time. He assumed Douglass from the Douglas in Scott's *The Lady of the Lake.* Through all of these changes he refused to give up his first name. "I must hold on to that, to preserve a sense of identity," he said. But it was identity as "Frederick," not "Frederick Bailey" that he felt compelled to preserve. He finally found a suitable "identity" in the Scottish hero Douglas, in whom he "found some peculiar fascination and destiny."[4]

The basic characteristic of Scott's Douglas is his unflinching fortitude in adversities brought about by the wrongful loss of his patrimony. Yet for all of the loss of his honors and wealth, he never is embittered or vindictive. Nor, of more importance, is he the leader of a cause. That role is given to the unhappy Roderick Dhu. And the *Lady of the Lake* ends with Douglas' patrimony being restored to him. He was, Douglass said of his namesake, the poem's "great character."[5]

Not only did Douglass identify with Douglas, he also internalized him. Much of the time of his British trip in 1845–1847 was spent in Scotland, some of it traveling alone unengaged in antislavery work, which was the mission that took him to Great Britain. While in Scotland, Douglass extended his trip beyond what was originally planned, and he immersed himself in Scottish ballads and songs, which he sang and played on his violin for the rest of his life. Reveling in the Highlands, he wrote William Lloyd Garrison, "If I should meet you now, amid the free hills of old Scotland, where the ancient 'black Douglass' [*sic*] once met his foes . . . you would see a great change in me!"

Nine years earlier at New Bedford as he assumed the name Frederick Douglass, Douglass entered his claim for his lost patrimony. At Nantucket three years later he certified his claim. There at the Garrisonian convention, where he found his voice, the other person, the father, and the other culture, the "Anglo-Saxon," that Douglass carried in him was confirmed. But the confirmation carried a heavy price. It occurred simultaneously with Douglass' denial of Harriet Bailey. He had already shorn himself of the long and pretentious name that she had given him. Now he believed it was possible for him to "forget" the physical appearance she had bequeathed him.

When Douglass escaped from Baltimore he was not only fleeing the world Harriet Bailey bequeathed him, he was also fleeing Harriet Bailey. She and her world were inseparably linked under the fatal law of slavery and race which held that the child must follow the condition of the mother. From the law there was no appeal, except to those who claimed they denied the law's efficacy, the Garrisonians. The law's imperative ran not only in Maryland but followed Douglass to New York and New Bedford, where the white caulkers drove him from the shipyards, and where such cold comfort as Negroes might find came in the separate pews that had been set apart in the white churches for their use. Beyond that, the defining restraints of crisped hair and dark skin, Harriet Bailey's legacy, denied Douglass the usufruct of the father. Finally at Nantucket, at the end of what must be understood as sustained flight and escape from Harriet Bailey, the restraints seemingly were removed, and Douglass supposed himself free of his blackness.

Toward 1847, as the Nantucket phase of his life came to an end, Douglass was not only established in the historical role he would play for the remaining portion of his life, he had also learned the lesson that confirmed him in his role. There was no alternative for him. Wendell Phillips' claim notwithstanding, the Garrisonians were scarcely color-blind. There was a point beyond which their rhetoric and their acts of being at one with him could not proceed. In the fragmentary correspondence that survives between Douglass and the Garrisonians what one vainly searches for is a sense of trust, a willingness to confide, to be vulnerable, to meet on equal terms. Instead what one finds is the studied, mannered responses of a man who has learned his lessons well. Douglass writes what is expected, but his guard is up, and on those occasions when he goes on explosive expostulations, what he protests is the Garrisonians' failure to give him the benefit of the doubt, a fair chance, the opportunity to be taken on his own terms.[6] Rarely did he permit himself to "write freely." And then it was to people outside the Boston coterie. On these outside correspondents he unburdened himself about "the miserable and contemptible prejudices—too common even among those who claim to regard [me] as a brother."[7]

From the first the Garrisonians were wary of Douglass. They suspected him of some sort of double-dealing, and were never sure that he might not jump the traces and bolt the path they had marked out for him.[8] On the eve of the open break with Douglass, Garrison, with genuine puzzlement, wrote his wife about Douglass' plans to strike out on his own and edit a newspaper. "Such conduct," Garrison said, "grieves me to the heart . . . impulsive, inconsiderate, highly inconsistent with his decision in Boston. What will his . . . friends say of such a strange somerset? . . . Strange want of forecast and judgment!" And then later in what must be the most revealing comment Garrison ever made about Douglass, "His assurance seemed to me excessive. Confidence is a plant of slow growth, and in his case will be particularly so with me."[9]

What myopic Garrison could not understand was that he was underscoring Isabel Jennings' earlier observation to Maria Weston Chapman that the Garrisonians were prejudging Douglass according to the role they had selected for him. In their own way they too, like the southern slave masters, had reduced him to an object, a creature of the passive voice. Above all the Garrisonians wanted Douglass to be black; indeed to be literally blacker than he was. Some of them "wished" that he was a "full blood black [without any of] the white blood that is in his veins."[10]

The open rupture between Garrison and Douglass occurred when they were on a tour in the Midwest. The break was painful for both. They became physically ill. Garrison was laid up for weeks with his "brain terribly oppressed." Douglass suffered what seems to have been a more obvious psychosomatic ailment. As the Nantucket phase of his life opened with him learning that his way with words gave him access to the one group of white people who promised him that he could be white, it ended with him no longer being able to say the words that had once freed him from his blackness. As the full force of Garrison's "betrayal" descended on him, Douglass lost his voice. He was literally dumbfounded as he came to understand he could neither escape being a "weary" young black nor "rebirth" as "a colored man."[11]

The Garrisonians' determination to keep Douglass where they wanted him, as a supplicant black man, was demonstrated a few years later. When the breach between them was beyond healing, the Garrisonians brought out of their armory all the well-worn epithets they hurled against defectors. In their exasperation (and maybe vindictive determination to destroy him) they went the further step and unleashed the weapon *ne plus ultra* of whites against a Negro man. Accepting the hazard of confirming one of the most explosive and damaging charges made by the abolitionists' opponents, they claimed that Douglass had a sexual relationship with "that double-and-twisted worker of iniquity, Julia Griffiths," the Englishwoman who had followed him from England and who played a major part in stabilizing his newspaper enterprise. [12]

As the Garrisonians were raking outrageous scandal on top of apostasy, Douglass had already accommodated himself to his fated place in American society. He had become one of the young men that James McCune Smith described when he observed that Douglass was "newly born among us." He educated himself to the thought and ways of the free Negro community, assimilating them with the same rapidity and facility with which he had earlier internalized the highland chief who had lost his patrimony. The Nantucket "promise" had been long since laid aside. But it remained in the depths of his mind and found expression in that striking passage that was yet to be written in the autobiographies, "For a while I was made to forget."

There remains a final piece of evidence to be fitted into place. It is a poem that has lain unpublished in the Douglass manuscripts. Undated, the poem was probably written when he was courting Helen Pitts, the white woman who became his second wife, and it most certainly was written for her.

"What Am I to You" is susceptible to two different readings. It may be read as Douglass no doubt consciously intended Helen to receive it, as a proposal of marriage qualified with his admission that all sorts of difficulties lay in store for her if she accepted him, and provided with an easy out for her. In the poem he told her that he would understand if she refused to submit herself to the "bruises" and "wounds" that surely must come as a result of the marriage; if she rejected his proposal, he would content himself with admiring her from afar and treasuring the memories of the happy times they had shared.

"What Am I to You" also may be read as Douglass' statement about himself that sweeps from his origins (the "old plantation" and its deprivations) to the present. The poem's simple transparent imagery provides further clues to Douglass' conception of himself at the time he wrote it, probably 1883. And it should be borne in mind that in 1883 he had completed the autobiographical revision of self. The first edition of the *Life and Times* had been published. In it Douglass had varnished his portrait of the queenly black Harriet Bailey, and he had denied the existence of his white father. For the public record he had become the black Douglass, completely identifying himself as a Negro.

Many stanzas long, the poem is Douglass' variation of the Garden of Eden story, adapted to him and Helen Pitts. Douglass imagines himself as a sort of masculine Eve, and Helen as the apple, "in size and form and hue divine." It is "that same old story often told." However, each "new generation" must retell the old story in its own way in order to tell "the truth," which is what Douglass binds himself to do in the poem. He places himself under oath to hold nothing back from Helen.

Douglass enters the edenic garden as a result of his powerful "wish to make it mine / without a fair condition." He wants the garden to be unqualifiedly his. And it is critical to "the truth" Douglass is telling that it is the entire garden that he "wishes" to possess, not only Helen, the forbidden fruit. Alone in the garden, he makes a one-man assault on the vast deep-rooted tree holding the apple, trying to shake loose the "precious gem of Eden." The tree is impervious to his "puny" strength. He gives up, backs off, leaves the garden, and puts the best face he can on his impetuous, feckless efforts. "Reason" tells him that he has no claim on this primal, "enchanted" place, or any of its fruits. Aberrant desire—a "thought fell somewhat out of line"—has brought him into the garden; anyway, he has no "means to gain possession," conditionally or not. It is himself against the world, and no "reasonable" man would place himself in such a situation. For a moment he has lost control of himself, but he is now back "in line" as he retreats from the garden. [13]

In January, 1884, in the face of public outcry and over his childrens' bitter objections, Douglass married Helen Pitts. He maintained that the marriage was emblematic of the doctrine he had always proclaimed; he and Helen Pitts Douglass lived the ideal of racial equality. But the marriage was also a partial redemption of the old Nantucket promise. Douglass had at last entered his father's garden. He had reclaimed a portion of his lost patrimony.

Beyond that, Douglass played out his fated part to the end. He accepted the definition that the Garrisonians and all the rest had forced on him. "I shall never get beyond Fredk Douglass the self educated fugitive slave," he complained. This "Fredk Douglass" was the one that blacks and whites supposed him to be, and he would, he said, do his best to meet their "expectations." [14] In time he found that he could "rejoice" in forever being the self educated fugitive slave; and because he found that he could play the part proudly and with dignity and because his heart was courageous, he almost successfully covered the conflict that once raged within him, a conflict that was never laid to rest. Only traces of it remain, but the record is plain and unequivocal though it demands drawing together the raveled skein that runs from Harriet Bailey's transmogrification to that springtime trip to Baltimore when Douglass made his final attempt to pierce the darkness surrounding his origins, to find out who he was, to come to terms with himself.

Douglass himself pointed the way for following the raveled skein. A stanza in his poem for Helen Pitts is a guide and an admonition for any person who writes the story of this divided man who lived in a divided world:

I venture now to say in verse
And beg you not to think the worse
Of some things I would fain rehearse
    In friendly conversation.
For heart of man though mainly right,
Hides many things from mortal sight
Which seldom ever come to light
    Except upon compulsion.

Part
Four

"The Great
Things"

The starting point . . . is the birth of nineteenth century civilization, [but] it is not its economic and social effect that we have exclusively in mind, nor even the determining influence of these effects upon modern political history, but the fact that, our social consciousness was cast [then]. . . . A world was uncovered the very existence of which had not been suspected, that of laws governing a complex society. Although the emergence of society in this new and distinctive sense happened in the economic field, its reference was universal. . . . Its amazing regularities and stunning contradictions had to be fitted into the scheme of philosophy and theology in order to be assimilated to human meanings. The stubborn facts and the inexorable brute laws that appeared to abolish our freedom had in one way or another to be reconciled to freedom. . . . With the finality of an elemental event, a new set of ideas entered our consciousness.
KARL POLANYI, *The Great Transformation: The Political and Economic Origins of Our Time*

It is the [nature] of our people . . . that they cram everything under the head of morality. Morality is the cant and crack word of the place. If you go to our fashionable churches, you will hear the fashionable clergyman preach "morality"; if you visit a private gentleman's house, he is sure to entertain you with "morality"; if you attend a public meeting, the "moral" speaker will address his "moral" fellow-citizens on the subject of "public morals"; if you listen to the partisan harangues of our professional politicians, they will conjure the people "in the name of morality" to outvote the profligate antagonist faction. Morality seems to be the great lever of society; the difficulty only consists in findings its fulcrum.
FRANCIS J. GRUND, *Aristocracy in America*

XI
Self-Creation and Social Imagination

Biography, Claude Levi-Strauss has said, is low-powered or anecdotal history. Richest from the point of providing information, biography is the least satisfactory mode of history for providing explanations because it is incapable of rising above the particular. Of course he is right. Biography cannot tell us much about the past unless the life stories are, as he says, "dove-tailed" with a higher-powered history, and even then the explanation is circumscribed.[1] In the following pages I have undertaken some of this dove-tailing. This is what Moncure Conway, Jane Swisshelm, and Frederick Douglass did when they wrote their own life stories. I have followed their lead, first letting them guide me as they made the gambit themselves, then leaving them and pursuing some of the themes they have developed into

the lives of Henry Wright, Salmon Chase and Thomas Cooley. As I
have made these connections I have not shifted the mode or the
"power" of my inquiry. I have not tried to write a higher-powered
explanatory history; I have simply attempted to make some relationships between my subjects and some larger matters having to
do with nineteenth-century American abolition that provides more
information about them and the content and meaning of their abolition work.

Conway, Swisshelm, and Douglass were creative writers. Although all of them wrote fiction and even tried their hands at verse,
their imaginative achievements as writers were themselves as rendered in their autobiographies. But their imaginative impulses for
self-creation were held in check by two limits: what they knew
about themselves, and the background against which they were
obliged to define themselves, *quorum magna pars fui* Conway
called it. They understood that they got their historical meaning
and were given their social force from "the great things of which
they have been a part." Their impulses for self-creation therefore
had to operate between two boundaries, and their mutual problem
as creative writers was to obtain as large an area as possible in which
the act of self-creation might occur. Their imaginations flickered
against each of the two limits, constantly testing them and bending
them in order to give themselves the maximum room for self-
creation.

The first three sections of this book are inquiries into their imaginative explorations of the boundary established by what they
knew about themselves, particularly before they became part of the
"great things." These sections show them engaging in considerable
self-creation and account for its impulses. The burden of the book
lies there because I have interested myself in individual origins.
Quorum magna is "history," another subject altogether, and I
have so far dealt with them only as it seemed helpful in understanding why each of these people became part of them. But we must
come again, at least briefly, to the "great things" and face them as
directly as a biographical confrontation allows, which never can be
more than obliquely and elliptically.

In order to have the largest area possible for their self-creating powers to work, Conway, Swisshelm, and Douglass also had to deal with the other boundary impinging upon them. Their imaginations had to play along the edges of the great things, arranging them in ways that were satisfactory for the purposes of self-creation. At their hands abolition was therefore not only a social undertaking; it was an imaginative act designed to yield them the greatest possible "freedom" both at the time they took up their life work and in their subsequent autobiographical accounts of their work. On the evidence there is ample reason to believe that as they were compelled to seek their own freedom from intolerable "enslaving" circumstances they found the means and the justification for satisfying this compulsion by freeing other enslaved people. It is here that a crucial relationship was made: what they imaginatively desired for themselves was stated socially, and personal needs were given substance by a social enterprise. Inasmuch as they defined themselves (at the time and retrospectively) by their social cause, they were also commenting on their own imaginative limits. Therefore as they described abolition they were defining the contents and limits of their social imaginations. In these next pages I have followed them as they employed abolition in their self-creating impulse and fitted it to their imaginative social desires.

Let us begin with Jane Swisshelm who wrote an unvarnished apology for abolition. She never doubted that from God's hand ensued the great things. She was entirely satisfied with them. When she wrote her account of abolition her only concern was that it be protected from the slander that abolition had emerged from religious infidelity and skepticism.

Excepting her capacity for putting a personal grievance into a brilliant journalistic polemic she was a rather unexceptional person. Her imagination never plunged her into dazzlingly unfamiliar areas or blazed startling new paths through uncharted territory. Even on the subject of woman's rights she only strained against conventions, and her ideas about abolition are but part of antislavery's protean claims. When all of her pyrotechnics are cleared away a simple commonplaceness remains about her. And therein lies her great instructiveness. On close inspection there is a remarkable prolepsis about her path. She had already traversed the ground when the theme of the illegitimate, immoral government was beginning to tincture Garrisonian abolition.[2] She thus anticipated by a generation the radical abolitionists' acceptance of the state as the instrument whereby a righteous people waged the wars of the Lord, and she was prepared twenty years before the event to believe the self-demonstrating proposition that violence was a judgment on the unrighteous and that the Civil War was an apocalyptic holocaust out of which the redeemed nation emerges. In short, in the 1850s the radicals began to catch up with her, and once war broke out their paths became indistinguishable.

When the war began she went east where she served as a nurse, first in the field with the Army of the Potomac, and subsequently in the military charnel houses at Washington.

It is with the blood and horror of war that she seems to have relished that we get a firm purchase on Jane Swisshelm's understanding of abolition as well as an accurate measure of her own imaginative limits. At the center of the great things is the broken covenant and the holocaust, prospective, imminent, and finally *visited.* The reason for the bloodbath is that the moral order has broken down. American society is topsy-turvy. No one seems to be getting their deserts. The nation is errant and God's retributive cleansing is upon it. The story is as ancient as the prophet, it suffuses the history of the old Covenanters, but at Swisshelm's hands it is adjusted to accommodate the libertarian politics and economics of the nineteenth century. Her social vision was of the nation as moral marketplace which man entered as a free agent and flourished or perished according to his moral choices and strengths. A bundle of colossal contradictions and inconsistencies—the God-predestined is free to shape his destiny, free moral choice is the social right of every individual but ethnic origins forever determine the capacity for it, complete equality is the birthright of all blacks but their only social function (other than for the males to help the Republican party at the polls) is to allow the moral temperature of the republic to be taken, the state is laissez-faire and arbitrarily paternalistic and coercive, its powers simultaneously wielded to subsidize transcontinental railroads and break labor unions, to free black slaves and summarily execute Sioux warriors—her vision was impeccably consistent on one point. The writ of individual freedom must run to the meanest and most depraved person, otherwise the market becomes deranged and the covenant perforce broken. Her vision is filled with a raging personal need for revenge. It is doubtful that any abolition writer invoked the retributive holocaust more persistently or with greater intensity than she, but her vision's lineaments go far beyond any individual need. They catch the lines of national development that her life itself followed: from the speculative little hamlet of Wilkinsburg that was planned to batten on the migrant tide bursting through the Alleghenies after the War of 1812; to the Minnesota frontier at St. Cloud, the jumping off place for the fur trade and timber domains, and the junction of five speculative railroads, the terminus of which was the Pacific, with the Orient beckoning beyond.

When the war ended she remained at Washington where she established herself as a self-appointed ombudsman for blacks, a leader in the early Radical Republican mobilization for the assault on Andrew Johnson, and a claimant for abolition's right to set the terms of Reconstruction. In 1865 her *Reconstructionist* opened the attack on Johnson's doorstep in Washington.[3] Excepting its style, the copy for the *Reconstructionist* might have been taken from the *Commonwealth*, the *Independent,* and the *Anti-Slavery Standard,* abolition's big guns in Boston and New York. Their message was "Equality Before the Law." The slogan was, like generic abolition itself, ambiguous and protean. In its most expansive sense "Equality Before the Law" synthesized a moral law of radical human equality with constitutional and statutory law; but it also bid to establish abolition on legalisms, channel abolition's broad claims into narrow questions that were susceptible to legal adjudication, and make, as was the case for the old Covenanters, litigious disputants of moralists.

As abolition flowed into the postwar settlement, the grand outline of public policy for a social mechanics and a social morality, both of which were expressive of Swisshelm's social imagination, became apparent. She and other abolitionists supported the Thirteenth Amendment, the Fourteenth Amendment, the Fifteenth

Amendment, and "the 'crowning work' of reconstruction," the Civil Rights Act of 1875, the posthumous achievement of Charles Sumner, whereby he succeeded in pressing federal power beyond the expressed (and disputed) limits of the amendments themselves. "'I know,'" Sumner said of his bill, "'nothing further to be done in the way of legislation for the security of equal rights in this Republic.'"[4]

Insofar as it dealt with bond slavery and race, abolition's legal achievement may be summarized: Slavery was abolished; Negroes were declared citizens of the United States and of their respective states, and as such they were guaranteed equal protection of the laws in such classic freedoms as speech, worship, assembly, and security of person and property; Negro males were enfranchised; and Negroes were given equal access to public transportation, theaters, and "other places of public amusement." Except as a commentary on the intensity of racial prejudice and animosity it is almost beside the point to observe that Reconstruction guarantees were grudgingly given, compromised in the circumstances of their enactment, and ineffective from the moment they took on the life of the law.[5] The point is that collectively these laws (including their lacunae) marked the outermost limits of abolition's imaginative thinking about "freedom." It was within these limits that blacks were now free to find what destinies they might choose. Blacks were—and it does no damage to abolition's racial constitutional achievement and Charles Sumner's "crowning work" proposition to put the matter this way—admitted to legally equal participation in the moral marketplace.[6]

When the Civil Rights Act was declared unconstitutional in 1885 and as it became apparent that the reconstruction settlement was being undermined and that the blacks were in for bitter times, Swisshelm believed it unnecessary to carry social policy beyond the limits that had already been staked out by the law. The right must be rejoined, but the battleground had already been fought over. Shortly before her death she delivered her last abolition exhortation: "Our Samson is asleep on the lap of Delilah. . . . Wake Samson! Compel him to make good his pledge of freedom to the Southern slave! Give him no rest until the black man has the ballot tendered him not in mockery! . . . Keep Samson stirring until [he is] back on the ground selected by [Charles] Sumner."[7] The moral law, she said, had been stated and already enacted into secular law. The covenant had been consummated and its instruments perfected. The "great things" had run their course. Thereafter the task of the righteous will be to keep the nation true to the covenant, not tamper with its provisions. For Jane Swisshelm abolition had occasioned no radical transformation of aspirations nor a seismic shift in ideas or values. Abolition was the efficient cause of the realization of the national potential and destiny, and her own fulfillment as an agent for God's great works.

Frederick Douglass' books are also apologies for abolition. Of our three imaginative writers, he was most completely defined by the great things. The anticipatory *Narrative,* then *Bondage and Freedom* and the *Life and Times,* where the floodgates of activity are opened, are much fuller accounts of the antislavery crusade than are Swisshelm's *Half a Century* or Conway's *Autobiography.* And of the three writers the relationship between Douglass' self-creating impulse and abolition was most critical and is most easily seen.

Abolition stopped Douglass dead in his tracks and forced him to reinvent himself. When he wrote *Bondage and Freedom* he had learned the hard central truth about abolition. Once he learned what that truth was he was compelled to tell it even if it meant giving away the most secret truth about himself. From then on he accepted abolition for what it was and rode the fates, the cold destiny of pure chance he alludes to in the *Life and Times,* with raw courage and a sharp eye open for the main chance.

The truth he learned about abolition was that it was a white enterprise. It was a fight between whites. Negroes joined it only on sufferance, remained in it on sufferance and then at their own risk. It was a hard truth bitterly bought. How much bile Douglass had to swallow before he could reshape the enormity of the truth into the delicately ironical statement about being permitted to delude himself into believing that he was a white man is a question the answer to which was buried under his pride and artfulness; they made forbidden luxuries of certain human traits. One silently cuts his losses, stifles the wild bellow of rage even as it is welling in the throat, and turns a pleasant face toward his betrayers. William Lloyd Garrison hounded him for years. "I regard him," Garrison said, "as thoroughly base & selfish. . . . He reveals himself more & more to me as destitute of every principle of honor, ungrateful to the last degree. . . . He is not worthy of respect, confidence, or countenance."[8] But Douglass for the rest of his life permitted himself that single subtle retaliatory shot. His "out of line" thoughts were reshaped into velleities or were subdued entirely. There were always the masks to keep up.

Then to be irretrievably black in a white world? Where then does imaginative freedom run if the great things are white-begotten? We may safely suppose that Douglass resolved never again to risk himself to duplicity and betrayal. As firmly as any man can he resolved to find guarantees, bastions behind which he was secure against the hypocrisy and the perfidy that he now knew lay awaiting him along the path he had to follow.

He made his way with what amounted to the applied ideas of Alexis de Tocqueville and Francis Grund who were writing at the time Douglass made his break for freedom and his bid for whiteness. And it is important that these expositors of American society were concerned with a social type defined less by ethnicity or color (though of course they presume whiteness) than by function. Grund and Tocqueville were celebrants of the "new men," the "self-made" men who were breaking through old proscriptive restraints—deference, monopolized privilege, restricted franchise, circumscription of the main chance—to make their way in the world under the aegis of individualism and autonomy. That Negroes were confronted by the most vicious deadly restraints any new men had been compelled to face in the United States presented horrendous but not insurmountable odds. For in brilliant prophecy Tocqueville had read the auguries. Should the whites fall out among themselves, then, and only then, did the blacks in America "have a chance of salvation."[9] The blacks might then make allies (but not common cause) with one of the disputants in the fight and exploit the alliance to yield guarantees of access to the devices of power and mobility the new men had historically sought. Here, then, were Douglass' political strategy and social goal.

When civil war broke out Douglass' political activities were undertaken to make the alliance whereby the social goal might be achieved. Negroes were mortised into the structure of the national state. Raising the free black regiments for service in the Union Army was a policy intended to give Negroes a sturdy claim on the state and to undercut the dictum in *Dred Scott* that they were not citizens of the United States. Enlisting former slaves in the army gave the once-enslaved similarly powerful, but undefined, claims on the nation. In the Reconstruction melee these claims on the nation were honored by the Thirteenth, Fourteenth, and Fifteenth amendments, and, but for the omissions of unencumbered access to public schools and cemeteries, were rounded out by the Civil Rights Act of 1875.

Once he learned his bitter personal truth from the Garrisonians, Douglass never deluded himself by thinking that Negores were anything but the nation's "step-children," taken into the "family" as a result of accident and necessity. But they were no longer there on sufferance. Although they were not of the nation, they were in the nation; they were "fellow citizens" and they were on "equal" terms. The laws of the national state guaranteed that.

Toward the end of Douglass' life new waves of violence and proscription were unleashed on black Americans. It was in these savage times that Douglass delivered himself of his celebrated advice to blacks: "Agitate! Agitate! Agitate!" But for what? If it is to make any sense his war cry must be set in relationship with his understanding of the Reconstruction guarantees of the national state. The guarantees have been broken; it was not that they were insufficient. He was altogether like Jane Swisshelm. Douglass' best counsel was to get *back* to the ground occupied by Charles Sumner and the other architects of Reconstruction. It was there that Douglass' social imagination had found its limits, for it was there that the moral economy had been harmonized with the political economy, and it was then that the new black men had had their equal chance.[10]

Abolition also stopped Moncure Conway dead in his tracks. It betrayed him, too. But unlike Douglass he did not have to reinvent so thoroughly himself after the blow. As he presented abolition, it was one of the succession of religions he had to shed during his lifelong journey toward the outer reaches of illusionless "freedom."

Conway's stated case against abolition, another instance of his "youthful visions turned to illusions," he said, was precisely that, the "cause was a religion." Abolition had, he claimed, a canon, a creed, and a catechism by which it set limits and enforced them. Abolition was therefore a denial of freedom instead of being freedom's cause or its agent. But because of its "Calvinistic accent" it was more lethal than any of the other religions he had shed. In abolition "lurk[ed] . . . that creed about the 'covenant,'" with its "consecration of the sword" whereby things of the spirit were reduced to affairs of state, and wherein the social condition of man was forever a war between the chosen and the condemned. Garrison was "the inspired axe-bearer . . . the adamantine judge parting to [the] right and left the . . . good people [in] both [North and South]." From its origins, he claimed, abolition was coercive. It waited only for the occasion to engage in the worst of all coercions, making war in the name of the state, "the great prizes of [which] are bestowed for successful manslaughter." Under the banner of human freedom abolition mustered the finest impulses of the nation and rushed them in a holy nationalizing bloodletting. Even his friends the gentle Maryland Quakers were consumed in the conflagration. Conway developed his theme unsparingly. It coils through his book with an obsessive hold on him. He kept returning to it as if repetition itself might mitigate his own complicity in abolition.

Having expatriated himself, Conway was not directly involved with abolition's thrust into the post-Appomattox period. He followed the Reconstruction racial program through a correspondence with Charles Sumner. Sumner's civil rights bill he considered sufficient (he approvingly, though out of context, quoted Sumner) in its guarantees to kill "'any relic of slavery'" and to prevent the "'perpet[uation of] an Oligarchy of *the skin.*'" But it mattered little to him that the bill was enacted without the public school provision or that the law itself was subsequently ruled unconstitutional. Nothing really mattered once abolition handed "reform" over to the Union war. From then on the great things were hopelessly corrupted. All they had amounted to (this judgment is at the turn of the century) was that the blacks "might be freely lynched," while the "North and South [were] united to lynch also Spaniard, Filipino, and Chinaman."

Now in all of this there is considerable self-justification, and the bleakness is compounded because when the old man wrote it he was, as he said, "broken by personal bereavement, filled with horror by the reign of terror suffered by negroes in the South, [and] alienated from my countrymen by what seemed to me a mere lynching of Spain." But there is nevertheless in his arraignment a cold probing of one of the most sensitive of the roots of the modern American empire. He had caught sight of something that eluded his contemporaries, and he was determined to report it: the nightmare horror of his country as a fatuous self-deluded imperial power of which abolition was the handmaiden and the justification.

With his critique of American imperialism Conway's self-creating impulse seems to have carried him into a new realm of social imaginativeness.[11] The question we wish to put to him, then, is: what if abolition had not saddled "reform" with the onus of a nationalizing war? If reform had somehow managed to keep its purity, if it had not been betrayed by abolition into the "great catastrophe," and instead had run its writ across American society, what then?

We expect to enter some extraordinary world because Conway has broken through barriers inhibiting his old abolitionist colleagues. His social imagination may run to previously uncharted limits. With his analysis of American expansion he went far beyond anything any other abolitionists could conceive. Surely he will exceed them here. Some dazzling, shimmering social setting for human freedom must await us as he answers the question.

His answer was derivative and he forthrightly acknowledged his debts. "Two small books," Von Humbolt's *Sphere and Duties of Government* and Mill's *Essay on Liberty*, provided the basis for his understanding the "principles" of "the just law" on which his ideal society was based. What he learned from Humbolt and Mill he augmented from Herbert Spencer, "One of my earlier friends in England."[12] Conway's imaginary ideal society was one in which "human laws" were in perfect congruence with the "principles" so

that there was "freedom of individual difference to develop itself."
Once the principles were established by "charters, bills of rights,
[and] constitutional guarantees" all subsequent law is negative. It
"existed only to prevent one from injuring another, or others; that
is, from violating individual rights or public order." With the exception of intervention, "albeit cautiously," in the areas of public
schooling and health measures, the state's sole duty is "the defense
of personal liberty."

According to Conway, insofar as the Reconstruction racial program related to these matters it was worked out along lines consistent with his principles. The Thirteenth, Fourteenth, and Fifteenth
amendments, and the Civil Rights Act of 1875, excepting the public
school omission, was "just law." By these devices black Americans
were set at liberty and were protected against "actual injuries,"
which were the only ones the law comprehended for citizens. "In-
ferential and incalculable injuries," those torts against the human
spirit, were not admissible to the courts of the just law. But,
claimed Conway, the Reconstruction guarantees of liberty were
hopeless even before they became law because their principles were
forfeited when abolition carried reform into civil war. The foundation upon which these just laws rested was the coercive state, which
was also a capricious and expedient state that was bound to make
"encroachments upon . . . personal liberty," and which only waited
the occasion to renege on its promises and to license and condone
"lynching."

By an altogether different route Moncure Conway came to the
ideal society we have already observed informing Swisshelm's and
Douglass' social imaginations. In Conway's version it is shorn of
any providential apparatus and is thereby freed of any hint of the
hateful covenant which linked the state with a preordained favored
social group, and it has an elegant consistency that Swisshelm's
lacks. Conway abstracted the brutal grubbing—"'Aristotle and
Pericles are all right; get that, too; but get money besides, and
plenty of it'"—that characterizes Douglass' Black Ragged Dick setting out to make his way in the world. But the lineaments of the
three are the same and the results are identical. Conway's, Swisshelm's, and Douglass' social imaginations strike precisely the

same limits: the world as an unfettered marketplace in which the moral order is palpable. The moral order is achieved through a political economy that sets at liberty every individual to make his way in the marketplace where moral behavior is vindicated materially.

The only substantive difference between Conway and Swisshelm and Douglass is that the latter two were certain that abolition had almost flawlessly achieved the moral marketplace with the "equalities" of the Reconstruction Amendments and the Civil Rights Act. Conway was sure that abolition had been instrumental in destroying it forever. As they grew old they all stayed in the battle ranks and fought on: Douglass and Swisshelm to regain their whilom world, Conway, like a valorous Confederate, for the cause that was lost even as it was being born.

XII
Henry Wright: Abolition, Sexuality, and "The Great Day Coming"

This biographical (and ellipti-
cal) inquiry into "the great things" is not yet completed. It needs
extending because Conway, Swisshelm, and Douglass were all on
the peripheries of the attack on slavery, and with a mutual social
imagination that finds its limits in a morally justified classical economy and a legalistic equality, they may therefore bring a suspect
commentary on the social meaning of abolition.

To the contrary, Henry Wright's witness is unimpeachable. He
was out of the marrow of New England dissent, and as a longtime
Garrisonian he was more royal than the king. So perfectly was he
the radical reformer that the received version of his story is almost
a larger-than-life parody of what we have been accustomed to believe about them. Even the ordinarily clear-eyed Henry Thoreau

278

succumbed to the stereotype and did his part to perfect the parody. Wright was one of a trio of reformers Thoreau wrote up in a notorious passage in his journal. It is, a Thoreauvian has said, "one of the few pages of pure disgust he ever wrote." [1]

Here have been three ultra-reformers, lecturers, on Slavery, Temperance, the Church, etc., in and about our house . . . the last three or four days,—A. D. Foss, once a Baptist minister . . . Loring Moody, a sort of travelling pattern-working chaplain; and H. C. Wright, who shocks all the old women with his infidel writings. Though Foss was a stranger to the others, you would have thought them old and familiar cronies. (They happened here together by accident). They addressed each other constantly by their Christian names, and rubbed you continually with the greasy cheeks of their kindness. They would not keep their distance, but cuddle up and lie spoonfashion with you, no matter how hot the weather nor how narrow the bed. . . . They lick you as a cow her calf. They would fain wrap you about with their bowels. [Wright] addressed me as "Henry" within one minute from the time I first laid eyes on him, and when I spoke, he said with drawling, sultry sympathy, "Henry, I know all you would say; I understand you perfectly; you need not explain anything to me"; and to another, "I am going to dive into Henry's inmost depths." I said, "I trust you will not strike your head against the bottom." . . . I do not like the men who come so near me with their bowels. It is the most disagreeable kind of snare to be caught in. Men's bowels are far more slimy than their brains."

Wright was, he said of himself, "a man of one idea. I have lived for one object, and one only. . . . This has been my life-long object of pursuit. . . . THE ELEVATION AND HAPPINESS OF MAN." [2] We therefore come to Henry Wright with considerable expectations. "The most anarchistic of antislavery radicals" and "an extreme case" he has been called, Wright was "the exemplar of the vagaries of antislavery." [3] As such he is a useful counterpoint whereby we can approximate the pervasive qualities of Conway's, Swisshelm's, and Douglass' social imagination.

Wright was also from another New England tradition. He was the beneficiary of the peculiar kind of primogeniture practiced there for generations. A concerted family effort lifted the chosen son out of farming or an apprenticeship in order to send him to college and thence to the professions, and thereby gave him a leg up in the world. In Wright's case it was a matter of being raised from hatmaking and being sent to Andover Seminary. "My parents and brothers," Wright said, "offered to assist in furnishing the means, if I would study and become a minister. This inquiry, then, was before me. Shall I be a minister, or a hatter? I determined to go to school a few months, and then go to work again at my trade."[4] Wright attended a private school, where, "I was . . . conscious that my success depended solely upon myself; and that I could be wise, good or great, only by my own efforts. . . . I felt that my time was short, and that I had not one moment to spare. I wanted to discipline my mind to think, and to write out my thoughts in an intelligible manner, so that as I pursued my work in after life, I could apply my mind to acquire knowledge by myself."

After satisfying himself that "I accomplished my end" he left the school and set out as a journeyman hatter to ply his trade. Business was bad, his prospects worse. British-made hats glutted the American market during these years directly following the War of 1812, and he wandered about "seeking work and finding none, till I saw it was hopeless to go further at that time. So I returned once more to my father's home. . . . Now, once more the question came, Shall I be a priest, or a hatter? This time I decided for the ministry."

His family subsidized him for two years of private tutoring to prepare him for Andover Seminary, which had been founded as a bastion of New England Congregationalism once Harvard had slipped away from orthodoxy. He came to Andover in 1819 when he was twenty-three years old. At Andover he was "determined to pursue a course of investigation and conduct, and to dispose of my time, and use the opportunities afforded for study, without any reference to the opinions and practices of the students or professors, except in so far as the settled studies and duties of the Seminary required a given line of conduct." To this end he drew up several self-disciplining rules:

That for sixteen hours a day, I would give my undivded attention to the prescribed studies of the Seminary, and to such others as I saw fit.

That, on all subjects of theology that should come up for investigation I would, as far as possible, put my mind into a posture of neutrality.

That I would have as little intercourse with the students as possible; not calling at their rooms, nor seeking their intimacy.

That I would avoid all intercourse with the people of the town and vicinity.

This regimen he augmented by a diet of crackers, milk, and water, the object of which "was to provide nourishing and easily digested food [that would] enable me to devote the greatest possible amount of time to study—with the least sleep and exercise."

The Andover years, three of them, were not pleasant for Wright. He had come to the seminary "totally ignorant of the feelings and habits of young men, when brought together in college, [and] wholly destitute of the training which they get there . . . . Nor had I any idea of the importance which young men attach to the fact that they have been through college, and obtained the degree of A.B. or A.M. Of these things and many other things, a knowledge of which might have been desirable, I was," he said again, "totally ignorant." He took some rough, rankling knocks at the hands of his fellow seminarians who "expected deference and supposed [it] to be due."

As one might suppose he got his revenge, marking down these callow, overbearing "A.B.'s and A.M.'s" as "puny men in minds." They were, he said, "far short of what I expected and wished. . . . They did not study . . . for love of study . . . They seemed to me to have no enthusiasm in their object, but just did as little as they could do and get along. . . . I imbibed a strong feeling of contempt for the abilities of most of my classmates. . . . If they had any time to spare it was fooled away in chit-chat, and in things that could not add to their character and power in society."

As for himself, "I abandoned myself to the work as if this was all I had to do on earth." Wright immured himself at Andover. Once, during his first two years there he made a trip that took him five miles away from the school. For the remainder, "Vacations and term-time were alike consecrated" to his studies. He devised a desk at which he studied standing up, and, he said, "I did not lose one day, nor scarcely one hour, of my prescribed time of sixteen hours per day, from my studies." Wright pursued his "consecrated" studies while sharing a room with a man who must have been the opposite of everything he had supposed a seminarian to be.

He ate and ate and ate, without intermission or limitations. . . . Chairs, desks, and beds, converted into tables at once! Even the floor ever strewn with edibles, and the refuse; bones, crusts, potato-skins, clam-shells, oyster-shells, &c. Closets converted into pantries, and store-houses for food; and drawers ever filled and daubed with cheese, butter and animal fats in various forms. . . . He was ever groaning in agony from indigestion, and ever loading his poor goaded stomach with what the stomach of a wild elephant would groan under. . . . He exercised, and was obliged so to do. To this end, he bought a saw, axe and saw-horse, or hod, and quite a number of planes, chissels [sic], hammers, and other carpenter's tools, and converted our room into a work-shop, as well as a provision, cook and eating shop. Such a litter and din as I studied in. . . . But I confirmed a habit that has been greatly useful since, that of fixing attention on any given subject I chose, amid the utmost confusion and uproar. I learned to think, to study and write amidst that din and litter, as in utter solitude. My concentrativeness must have been rapidly developed during that time, and it has been growing ever since, for I can live in silence and solitude, whatever or whoever may be around me. This power has been of great service to me.

When Wright finished his second year of study he took leave in order to teach school at Newburyport, Massachusetts. Probably he went to work because he needed money. His father died the following summer; perhaps there was an extended illness, and expenses at home straitened the family and made it impossible to continue the Andover subsidy. He taught at Newburyport for a year, "glad of the opportunity to . . . get out of myself," and he reduced his consecrated study time from sixteen hours to ten hours a day. The next fall he returned to Andover for his senior year, which he did not complete. Halfway through the senior year he "made up my mind to leave . . . and return no more." "I procured a letter from one of the professors, attesting to my having been there, and how I conducted &, left."

Much of the while he was in the seminary Wright thought himself an atheist. An early journal entry, written when he was living in the clam shells and sawdust, and his roommate's hammering and "heavings and tossings and groanings at night," reads:

He is happy those circumstances suit his temper; but he is the more excellent who can suit his temper to his circumstances. . . . It is the lot of some to pass through life in circumstances similar to those in which they passed their childhood. . . . Others, being called to move amid scenes and influences totally different from those which gave the first impulse, must experience great revolutions in their modes of thinking. . . . I feel deeply this change going on in myself. I am sad and desolate in spirit. Where are the notions which, as a child, seemed so sacred to me? . . . I am in a revolution, and where I am to land, God only knows. . . . I am floating on a sea of doubts, having but one thing settled, i.e., *my own existence*. . . . All else seems darkness and death-shade to me. The deep foundations of my soul have been broken up. . . . I am lost; I know my soul was not made to be ruled by authority, only by conviction; yet how to solve the difficulties in my path, I know not. I am in chaos; darkness broods over the moral universe.

I now loathed the thought of being a minister, and, in my present state of mind, was sure that, come what might, the thing could not be.

Wright left Andover with his faith in God restored. None of the proofs offered in the lectures on the "Existence and Attributes of God" had satisfied him. But in a passage that might have come from William James's *Will to Believe* he told how he worked himself out of his atheism. He described how he drove self-consciousness into autonomy and toward the verge of solipsism, which prepared him to believe that he was constrained by no authority except himself.

I was alone—the usual feeling came over me: I EXIST, THAT I KNOW, AND IT IS ALL I KNOW. The inquiry arose, and for the first time with vividness, How do I know that? The answer returned, emphatically, was—I am *conscious of it*. The thought returned, Have I not the same evidence that there is a God?

Long did I turn this thought over in my mind, and the more I reflected on it, the more definite, clear and tangible it appeared. What reason could I give for a belief in my own existence? Not one; except that I was conscious of it; and no matter how I came by it, I knew it was there, and that by no possibility could it be eradicated. On a belief thus founded in reference to my own existence, I acted from moment to moment. Why not rest satisfied with a belief in the being of a God thus founded, and act upon it? My mind became composed; I knew that I had the same consciousness of the being of a God that I had of my own existence; the one was no more clear, distinct and indestructible than the other; and though I could not tell how either came into my mind, I had the same certain knowledge that they were both there; that my faith in both was founded on precisely the same consciousness; and that no reason existed why I should not act upon the one as confidently as upon the other. . . . I am—therefore God is.

Wright left Andover in order to marry. About his wife Wright is intriguingly reticent and uninformative in his autobiography and the published portions of his journal. She is never identified by name, nor is she or her brood of children more than rarely mentioned. It seems Wright met her during the year he taught at Newburyport, where in church and community she was known as a woman who was "zealously, earnestly, and consistently devoted to what she deemed her religious duties [and] was noted for her benevolence and humanity." She was a widow, apparently of some means, with four children. The youngest child accompanied the bride and groom on their wedding trip, a three-month tour that wended its way from Saratoga Springs to Niagara Falls, then on to Montreal and Quebec, and finally back to Newburyport, where, in the fall of 1823, Wright "settled down with my family . . . to pursue my studies."

"In this pursuit," he says, "I was . . . interrupted by an invitation to officiate as a minister [at] West Newbury, five miles up the Merrimac River from Newburyport." He pleased the tiny congregation. They "gave me," he says, "a *call* to settle among them permanently, as a minister to perform divine service for them. . . . They offered me a definite price for a certain amount of labor; I accepted the offer, and thus became a paid minister. . . . Then came the Ordination; for, as yet, I had no power to baptise, to marry, or administer the supper." Wright's examination by neigborhood Congregational ministers and his subsequent ordination was, he says, a "miserable mummery. . . . It was a solemn farce, and I ought not to have subjected myself to it. . . . Yet I was willing to go through the operation in conformity to common custom, and to avail myself of whatever advantages it might confer."

The Sunday following his ordination Wright preached his first sermon as "a paid minister." The sermon could not have taken more than a few minutes to deliver, and in it there is none of the oily bonhomie that Henry Thoreau attributed to him. Wright's text was "Am I become your enemy, because I tell you the truth?"

Some Ministers spend a great portion of their time in visiting the people, and in talking praying with them in their houses. I must frankly say, that I do not think myself qualified . . . to be so useful in this way as most others; having for years been exclusively devoted to books, I am not qualified to enter into the feelings and sympathies of a people. . . . It is in the pulpit that you must judge me. . . . My habits of study I never wish to shake off. It is necessary that I have a large portion of my time to devote to study, and to a preparation for Sabbath and pulpit exercises. . . .

So far from being my duty to make you think well of yourselves, it is my duty and wish to make you odious in your own estimation, so long as you live in the practice of evil. I would strip off the mask, and let you see yourselves as you are. . . .

Do you wish me to give assurance that I shall always hold and preach my present sentiments? I can give you none. I acknowledge no creed, and I must interpret the will of God for myself, without reference to the opinions or practices of others. . . . I may change all my present views; and should I do so . . . you shall be the first to know it.

Should I see faults in anyone, I shall not whisper them behind his back; I will meet him face to face, and tell him what I think. Will you do the same? By so doing, we can live in peace.

For seven years Wright performed his duties and collected his money before he decided to leave West Newbury. His journal says, "Our connection has been a pleasant one. Their treatment of me has been as kind and friendly as I could wish. . . . It has been a trial to settle my mind to leave them." As he closed his West Newbury house, he wrote, "This day left the room and the house where, for seven years, I have enjoyed much domestic happiness. With a sad heart I left our pleasant house, where I had spent so many pleasant hours, and where my wife and her children had done so much for the good of the people, and for all good objects. They have been deeply interested in the Anti-Slavery movement; far more so than I have been. Mrs. W. was more beloved among the people as a pastor, than I was; she had a peculiar way to speak to them. . . . She had done much among the children and mothers, in a maternal association."

The room to which Wright refers as being the place in which he enjoyed so much domestic happiness was his "sleeping-room" and study, a combination arrangement, tucked under the eaves of his house on the third story. It was a "dear spot," which he had to stoop to enter. He kept doves there for company, "till one died and the other flew away to get a mate." "There the children came to recite; there friends came to chat. . . . There I had loved and been loved." His precious books were there, as was his "writing apparatus," and it was there that he "journalized."

"This writing a journal does me good. I can let off my indignation. . . . I am far happier when I write a little every day. When I journalize I am a happier, better, and more useful man. It saves me from many dark hours to write what I . . . feel. . . . My soul would turn in upon and consume itself, if I did not thus let it out in my journal. . . . It has been my salvation."

In his journal Wright disclosed his sustained attempt "to dissect my own character" and gave the theme around which his reports of the dissection are woven.

I am often annoyed to think I have no control over my[self]. . . . I often think I may as well attempt to tame a tempest. . . .

Two characters seem natural to me, i.e., that of a daring, joyous, romping child of nature, and that of a staid, sober, severe priest! I often think that I would engage in something bold and spirit-stirring, or in nothing at all. Let me dash ahead, or let me sleep. . . . There is that in my nature that sympathises with anything terrific, daring, desperate, and energetic. At the same time, I love to mingle my spirit with the bounding joy and playfulness and gentleness of little children. But probably the world would be better and happier, if I were out of it. It is hard to discipline my spirit into the staid and necessary rules and practices of this world. . . . I do not know where I shall end.

Then, after reading Seneca in his bedroom-study, Wright "journalized," "He strikingly observes—'when a man cannot get what he wishes, he can gain the same end by not wishing to have what he cannot get.'

"I would so regulate my passions, habits of eating, drinking and sleeping, *and all my appetites,* that I shall not be made unhappy by every little privation. I would not be the slave of any appetite, and would take the loss of any little comforts pleasantly. . . . 'Whatever I ought not to have, I will supply to myself by not desiring [it].'"

In order to "regulate" himself, Wright rose from his bed at two in the morning and ran for miles along the banks of the Merrimac

River. These lung bursting jaunts were concluded by drenching, cold baths in the dark, after which he settled in his solitary bedroom-study with his books. He gave up all "stimulants," coffee, tea, and alcohol. The 1828 Thanksgiving was celebrated in the West Newbury house by smashing the family's wine glasses. Thereafter Wright drank only water.

Finally, the journal reported this conclusion: "Total abstinence from all that intoxicates is the only safe rule. Freedom from all sin, or indulgence to all, is the only law under which man can live."

Here, it appears, are the seeds of Henry Wright's "perfectionism." By 1828, two years after he and "Mrs. W., and her four children" had moved to West Newbury, and four years after his marriage, Wright committed himself to live without sin. He was now embarked on a sustained campaign to "tame" himself, an undertaking which was nothing other than a systematic attempt to annihilate one of the two "characters" he believed lived within him, the "child of nature," the creature of passion, appetites, and "all that intoxicates," of "sin."

In the summer of 1833 "Mrs. W. and her children" moved back to Newburyport. Wright once again set out on his solitary wandering. This time, however, it was not, as it had been in 1824, as a catch-as-catch-can supply preacher. He had been commissioned as an agent of the American Sunday School Union. His assignment was to travel about New England soliciting donations for use in establishing Sunday schools for southern slaves. As an agent of the Union, he was strictly instructed "to let slavery and abolition alone," an order he seems to have faithfully complied with. He worked for the Sunday School Union for a year and a half. Toward the end of 1834 he gave up his agency and moved to Boston. He came to Boston to conduct a "chapel" for children and the poor. The chapel was sponsored by the orthodox clergy, whom he despised, and with whom he had been at war with since he was at Andover. Shortly before he accepted their invitation to come to Boston, he "journalized" them and their religion: "Imposing, pompous, soul-crushing... they stifle and crush... turn their backs on men... defraud, oppress, enslave, and slaughter their fellow-beings, and convert them into fiends." There was a vast rage in the man on the eve of his coming to Boston. In Boston, Wright lived alone and "boarded with . . . several young clerks and others." His family, he said, "lived in Newburyport."

In the spring of 1835 Wright joined the Garrisonians. He came to their Washington Street Office and, according to his journal, asked the secretary "to put my name on the Constitution [of the society]. I ought to have done it before; but my prejudices against Garrison, and my fear of being censured by those who are opposed to him, have kept me back. . . . I ought to have done so . . . long ago, but my position in society, as a minister, was against me. Henceforth, my voice shall be heard among abolitionists, come what may to reputation or life." He met Garrison, told him about living free from "sin," and began to tutor him in the doctrines of "perfectionism" and "Non-Resistance." And until he died in 1870 Wright was a free lance for radical reform.

If Henry Wright was not the most incisive critic of American society that abolition raised, he was surely one of the most persistent and comprehensive. For almost forty years he wrote, talked, preached, and published on "'the redemption of man from the dominion of man,'"[5] and he early established himself as a leading expositor of Non-Resistance, which was the most rarefied of all the successive stages an abolitionist might attain in the journey toward human freedom. In its pristine form Non-Resistance seems to have meant throwing overboard all human forms of social control and authority and submitting to nothing other than the laws of the "government of God." And until the government of God came into existence one bore stoically what iniquities and evils the world laid on him. "Let the injured party suffer and die," Wright said, "and leave the whole business of punishing evil-doers to Him who alone knows how to do this strange work—to adjust penalties to crimes and execute them." The difficulties such a doctrine presented in bringing about the end of slavery simply illustrate the snares abolition sometimes laid for itself. It is more to the point that Wright, after the Confederate attack on Fort Sumter, supported the Union side in the Civil War.

But it is in another connection that Henry Wright interests us here. In the abolition polemic, aberrant, evil sex runs through it like a scarlet thread. As it verged on pornography, abolition's sexual propaganda was saved from sheer prurience by employing pornography's "aesthetic" whereby salaciousness is used as a device to present in graphic metaphor "the bestial backdrop against which man's moral image must always be projected"; therefore the key feature in this writing is the moral image and its contents, not the moral anarchy that is served up as eye-catching stage setting.[6] The perverse cruelty of the slaveowners best met the need of the polemic, but when taken as a whole abolition sexual propaganda portrays the entire South as some vast libidinal pit.[7] Jane Swisshelm's Louisville fairly drips with sexuality. Wendell Phillips' famous phrase about the South being a great brothel epitomizes abolition's notion of southern culture as well as the abolition sexual polemic; it also provides access to an important portion of the moral image that abolition projected against slavery's backdrop. "Brothel" fuses sex and economics. Wrongful profit as well as unbridled sexuality lie in the whorehouse. Harem or seraglio, words much in fashion in the nineteenth century, that Phillips, a master of diction, might have used are sufficient to convey an immoral power; but neither convey an immoral profit. One is reminded of Swisshelm's lubricious Catholic priest and licentious Mississippi planter as social types that are functionally interchangeable, and whose immoralities converge in the disruption of the covenanted marketplace.

An excellent example of the sustained sexual theme and its connection with an economic order was produced by Austa French in her *Slavery in South Carolina and the Ex-Slaves*. The book purports to be an eyewitness report of what Mrs. French found when she came to the South Carolina Sea Islands as a missionary in 1862. The relationship between perversion and economics is developed axiomatically. On the plantations "it is torture, torture! torture! scientifically used, TORTURE! the ONE SCIENCE OF SLAVEDOM. . . . There is no escape from it, but to let everything go to wreck upon [the] plantations, OR HAVE FREE LABOR." Graphic tortures abound in *Slavery in South Carolina*, most of them descending upon women, as does an uninhibited carnality. According to Mrs. French, slavery's primary objects are economic profit and the gratification of perverse sexual desires. The South is nothing but a

profit-seeking sexual lunatic bin in which the moral order is inverted. "Qualities which . . . were virtues, all shrivel into vices. . . .
Frugality becomes avarice. System, order, punctuality, become
tyranny, despotism, barbarity. . . . Chastity becomes beastly sensuality, self-respect, towering madness at any restraint." Slave
women are "martyrs to chastity." Slavemistresses are brutalized as
much as their female slaves, mostly by their husbands who abandon them in favor of sexual relationships with the slaves. Of the
mistresses Mrs. French says, "Did not the grave open for many,
many, such, this land would be filled with lunatics. To pray for
DEATH, is most common, FOR LADIES AT THE SOUTH. . . . Vice
rules." "Sanity," or moral order, is "projected" and restored with
the appearance of the Union Army and the institution of the free
labor system under the guidance of the abolition "evangels."[8]*

Some of Henry Wright's work was part of this propaganda, but
his major writings went far beyond the confines of an attack on
bond slavery. By the outbreak of the Civil War he was abolition's
chief sexual theoretician; a position he buttressed by his claim of
"many years" of investigation, in the course of which he apparently was a pioneer in the use of the sexual questionnaire.[9] He was
the expositor of the "new [sexual] conscience" and the self-
proclaimed prophet of the sexual "good time coming." As he addressed himself to the subject of sex he could not have announced

---

*The ease with which these themes could be converted to riotous hardcore pornography is
illustrated by the *Memoirs of Dolly Morton: The Story of a Woman's Part in the Struggle to
Free the Slaves; an Account of the Whippings, Rapes, and Violences that Preceded the Civil
War in America with Curious Anthropological Observations on the Radical Diversities in
the Conformation of the Female Bottom and the Way Different Women Endure Chastise-
ment* (Paris: Charles Carrington, 1899).

Dedicated "To the Brave Men and Women of the 'Underground Railway,'" the *Memoirs*
takes its abolition heroine across the spectrum of southern society that is little different from
Mrs. French's. From aristocratic "Woodlands" to poor white shanties, Dolly Morton is
victimized by all sorts of explicit "spread-eagling," "futtering," "bottom-blistering," and
"'the usual thing[s].'" She and the slave women live in an ambience of "sighing, squeaking
and bucking." Even elements of the moral economy informing the abolition conception of
the righteous world are sketched in the *Memoirs*. As the Army of the Potomac encircles
Woodlands, and as the slaves melt away into what is now a free labor economy, Randolph,
the master of Woodlands, salvages vast amounts of money and jewelry and flees to New
York. He stays in New York only long enough to learn that his wealth itself is not sufficient to
provide for his corrupt desires. With some libertine friends he sails for Europe where the
social system is much like the slave South's.

with greater clarity his priorities as "a true Reformer." "Compared
to the power of sex," he said, "the power . . . of . . . the Church . . .
the State . . . religion, government, priests and politicians are nothing." And when human sexuality was abused and perverted, not
even the "crimes of slave plantation [and] slave . . . ships would
surpass" the consequent "corruption and ruin."

According to Wright, the core and the nexus of all human relationships was "the sexual element." Sexual activity between a man
and a woman was the foundation of society, and individual sexual
relationships were the determinative factor in all social activity and
institutions. It was therefore the world's great tragedy that there
was "such . . . blind . . . bewildering ignorance" about sex and the
proper sexual relationship between men and women. Wright took
it as his mission to lay open sex's "mysteries," "give the scientific
facts" about sex, and expound "the laws" that "governed" sex. His
iterated motto was "Let there be Light!" "Calmly . . . earnestly
[and] without anxiety" he set about his task of bringing light to the
benighted. He would do his part to help supersede "the Age of Fiction" with "the Age of Fact." He might, he said, encounter difficulties in "the Present," but he was certain that he was writing for
"the ages." His vindication would come when the "good time"
arrived. His major published works on sex are *The Unwanted
Child: The Empire of the Mother over the Character and Destiny
of the Race*, and *Marriage and Parentage: or, the Reproductive
Element in Man, as a Means to his Elevation and Happiness*. The
latter book went through five editions, two of which were abridg-
ments published in England after Wright's death in 1870. And
doubtless his work, as he hoped it would, remained to "be found on
the tables [and] in the hands and in the hearts of all who are able to
appreciate and to obtain it" as the twentieth century opened.

As a true Reformer of sexual relationships, Wright's one great
insight—it rings familiarly in our ears—had to do with woman's
rights. "So long as [the issue] is confined to woman's political,
pecuniary and social rights, it will not conflict, materially, with
[men's] selfish passions. . . . The discussion [therefore] cannot stop
here." And he laid it down unequivocally that "It is a woman's
right, not her privilege, to control . . . her [body]."

In order to pursue the discussion Wright created an epistolary dialogue between an Ernest and a Nina that runs on for almost two hundred pages in *Marriage and Parentage*. Their correspondence amounts to a mutual catechizing through which are revealed the elements necessary for the good time coming, of which the equality of women is but one portion. This model couple instructs each other thus: Ernest, "As a husband, my nature is complete in thee. . . . I can desire no honor, no station, no heaven, apart from thee. . . . We are one in love, in will, in purpose, in destiny. Be it ours to eternize this oneness." To which Nina responds, "The husband is to the wife the ideal actualized. No other man is like him or ever can be. . . . [Because he] has given the deepest depths of [his] nature . . . she is set apart to fulfill the highest office of her being." As they finish investigating such subjects as "The Mission of the Sexes," "Variety in Love, or Polygamy," "Love and Passion," "The Reproductive Element: Its Expenditure Governed by Fixed Laws," and "Home and Its Influence," Ernest and Nina have not only responded to each other about the "facts" and the "laws" of sex, they have also concluded that "the love which has made us one for life and death, cannot be measured by common rules; nor shall its manifestations be copied from a common standard." It may be, Ernest tells Nina, that they will have to "stand alone in all the world," but they nevertheless shall have "satisfi[ed] the utmost capacity of our natures for enjoyment."

This is a brave conclusion. Unfortunately it is not sustained by the text itself. And the fact that in coming to it Wright succumbed to the demotic of romantic love only tips his hand that he was purveying a conventional sensibility and morality. Far from being a guide for sexual liberation, Wright's work is a justification for the gynecolatrous domestication of woman; and the love that "cannot be measured by common rules" is a human relationship freighted with sublimations and repressions that are associated with the Victorian middle class. So far as the sexual act itself is concerned, it is obvious that Wright is trapped by the genteel conventions of diction, and he cannot avoid euphemistic circumlocutions. As he strove for a scientific vocabulary to present his facts and laws he was obliged to resort to "the true office of love" or "passional relations" when he came to sexual coupling; even the Latinate, medical coitus seems to have been too strong to be borne. When he dealt with women Wright simply omitted the sexual act and finessed physiology with embryology: "It would not be pertinent to notice her connection with the germ, till it comes into the position in which its existence and growth depend on nourishment derived through her system." The medical illustrations in *Marriage and Parentage*, which was his major effort, are consistent with the text. There are several plates showing the growth stages of a fetus. There are no pictures giving a scintilla of information as to how the growth may have been originated.

As theoretician Wright was confronted with a dilemma of the first magnitude. For not only was coitus necessary for propagation, it was, he believed, the crucial device for the "progress and perfection" of the race. But coitus was likewise the act of greatest violence and cruelty and was consummated in the onrush of a "'state of wild delirium'" that overrode all other desires, instincts and training; in short, it overwhelmed any controls known to man and society. The sex act was quite literally a running amok. Wright was never able to resolve the dilemma. The best he could do was force it into an uneasy ambiguity, and his attitude toward sexual intercourse was perforce ambivalent. It was worse than "intemperance, war [and] slavery"; but it was also "refined, noble, pure and lovely." The woman's "natural" role in the proceeding was dutiful acquiescence; but there is a passage in the "Mission of Man to Woman," a chapter in *Marriage and Parentage*, that is nothing other than a rapturous prefiguration of behaviorism's current doctrine that an orgasmic woman moves through several defined coital phrases from passivity to resolution. Except when sex was employed for the triple functions of propagation, progress and perfection, it was forbidden. Serving these ends it was subject to extraordinary sublimations and repressions.

Case histories were adduced to illustrate the laws governing the "Reproductive Element [and] its Expenditure." There are the horror stories, instances in which the husband and wife go at it hammer and tongs, with the results being their mutual physical illness (Wright provided a catalog of the attributes of clichéd nineteenth-century sexual debilities: "dyspepsia, rheumatism, gout, apoplexy, paralysis, consumption, and diseases in various other forms") insanity, and the production of the most loathsome, crippled children. On the other hand there are the reports from couples who have rightly understood one another's "nature," and, likewise understanding the great sexual laws, have done their sexual duty to each other and for the race.

Before we began to live together as husband and wife, we often conversed on . . . the laws . . . govern[ing] passional intercourse and the expenditure of the Reproductive Element. . . . We moved to our log-cabin. We cleared and fenced our homestead. We toiled steadily and happily together three years. . . . But we had no child. Our neighbors began to ask us, jokingly, why. We assured them the child would come when we were ready for it, and wished for it. Meantime we put up a pleasant cottage house. . . . Our cottage home seemed to us an Eden of God, for in it, in anticipation, we blended our souls. . . . On the fourth year, we raised wheat and corn to supply us for two years. We sold off our stock, and so arranged our affairs that we could devote the fifth year to . . . the creation of a child. . . . Before the sexual union was consummated . . . we endeavored, for some months, to get our bodies and souls into a healthful, happy condition as possible.

This blessed couple, in short, deferred the sex act for five years. In preparation for its consummation they subjected themselves to the most intensive spiritual, physical, and economic exercises in order that, when they at last did come to the conjugal bed, there was not the slightest chance that they would be transported into the state of wild delirium, wrecking themselves and contributing to the wreck of society.

One comes to Henry Wright's work with considerable trepidation. Certainly his ideas are not inspired prophecies leaping beyond contemporary constraints and aspirations. Nor, once beneath their iconoclastic surfaces, are they imaginative plunges outside convention or sweeping, out-of-hand rejections of tradition. They are in fact ideas with an entirely different purpose. They were intended to accommodate Americans to a new and often terrifying society and save the "richest legacy" of the past in a world seemingly unhinged. If his several books were not part of the standard writings on sexual behavior in nineteenth-century America,[10] their obsession with repression and control might have no meaning beyond

what biographical light they cast on a tortured man who was driven
to "tame the tempest" raging inside him. But inasmuch as they are
part of the canon establishing normative behavior for nineteenth-
century American men and women it is possible to read them as
epitomies of a general attempt to tame the tempests that were rock-
ing American society during much of Wright's life.

Unlike most of the notable abolitionists involved in the last phase
of the attack on slavery, Wright had grown up in pre-War of 1812
America, was comfortable in it, and was on his way toward establishing himself in it when the war ended. He was directly impinged
by the postwar dislocations that forced him to give up his chosen
craft and come to the seminary a fish out of water, a mature man in
the midst of teen-agers, feeling himself declassed by his "puny"
privileged classmates. And as a man approaching middle age he had
to absorb and rationalize the shocks of the social changes trans-
forming the United States that made him "conscious that my success depended solely upon myself."

In 1835 when Wright, thirty-nine years old, joined the Garrisonians, the full blast of social change had struck America. A people
penned up on the Atlantic littoral for nearly two hundred years had
burst through the Appalachian barrier with such explosive energy
that before the century was out they had carried the continent before them and had established themselves in the Orient. This
energy release was fueled by massive land acquisitions, heavy infu-
sions of immigrants, a forced labor draft on millions of blacks,
technological innovations that seemed to pour from an illimitable
ingeniousness into an insatiable maw of adaption and use, and a
factory system that was imposing a new industrial discipline upon a
people newly off the land. A new democratic politics was shaped
accordingly, and a new economics; for the old systems could not
carry such massive burdens that were now placed on them. The
new politics and economics were the practical tokens signifying the
full emergence of democratic man, who was likewise a marginal
man, without roots, prescriptively defined purpose, and the com-
forting sense of *place* in the world and its affairs. In this new world
of cut and thrust, boom and bust, of what could a man be certain?
The future was as evanescent as the past; the present was but a way

station on the trunk line of contingency. The distressing question
descended far beyond the traditional matters of making a living and
getting on in the world, or even finding a place in heaven. It came to
the matter of *being* itself. What did it mean to be a man? Or a
woman? How did one define himself (and consequently act) in a
world so apparently hostile to received ideas of belief and conduct?
Within a generation the nature and conditions of American society
seemed as different from those preceding it as the parched arroyos
of the Cimarron were different from the lush pastures of the
Shenandoah or the rich textures of the Connecticut Valley. And if
the new carried much of the old with it, and if in fact the old gave
the new much of its shape and substance the difference of scale was
itself sufficient to unhinge and disorient. In the old Appalachian
society the very smallness of the world seemed to make it manage-
able, its verities certain, and its conflicts negotiable. But in this
transmontane world, in time as well as place, everything was *out-
landish,* proportion was lost and the familiar landmarks seemed to
have had vanished. The prairie traveler navigated precisely as the
sailor. Both steered by the compass, for there was nothing on the
horizon by which the voyager might take his bearings.

At West Newbury, Wright watched the old Appalachian world
vanish before his eyes. New England, he wrote in some of his earliest social criticism, is becoming "little else than a manufacturing
village. . . . The people are collected into small [industrial] villages
[and] crowd[ing] into cities." All of this, he wrote, is "Somehow . . .
connected in my mind with vanity, effeminacy, luxury and de-
bauchery . . . a compound of . . . impurities." The "richest legacy"
derived from the old world into which he had been born was being
engulfed by "putrid[ness] and impurities. . . . Factories [Wright is
referring to textile mills and their paternalistic methods] train up
men and women to habits of dependence . . . and unfit them for
self-government; they . . . deeply affect domestic order and discipline, and they have a demoralizing influence. . . . [people] . . . lose
character [and] habits of industry and economy."

At Buffalo, when the Erie Canal opened and the city became the
gateway to the upper Midwest, he wrote, "I am boarding in a hotel.
Rose early, and came down to . . . watch the movements of these

human beings, and look into their bosoms with intense and melancholy interest. . . . They [are] prepared for almost anything, having lost all respect for property or persons. . . . It is indescribable! Not one cares for another; each is for himself alone. . . . Why are they such brutes. . . ? They are utterly regardless of decency. . . . I have traversed the streets of Buffalo from end to end . . . to see my fellow-beings, and read what is in them. I have witnessed a melancholy development. . . . One would think they were a set of famished wolves tearing at a carcass." But what, Wright asked, "are houses, towns, cities, ships, agricultural, manufacturing and mechanical operations and implements, Railways and Electric Telegraphs . . . [this] intense . . . human energy . . . when our domestic, social, ecclesiastical, political and commercial relations and associations [have] become corrupt and inharmonious [?]" This is a comprehensive description and indictment of an America in which things were not, as Emerson said, in the saddle, but, infinitely worse, had run out of control.

It begins to become clear that it is certainly not slavery or even sex alone that was informing Wright's ideas. It is the "state of wild delirium." He is describing America as it was assuming its modern shape, and sex was his metaphor for American society, as well as his device for bringing it to heel. The problem, then, was to restore social order, which more than anything else meant rationalizing this pell-mell, for attempting to truly control it was beyond the power that Americans of the nineteenth century dreamed of permitting any agency. But the new postmontane world had to be "moral," with the predictable and unequivocal dispensation of just deserves as they traditionally had been understood and defined. Wright insisted that this new world had to yield the fruits of "self-government, order and discipline, honesty and integrity," all of which he claimed characterized the world in which he had grown up, and which had exploded before his own eyes.

It was Henry Wright's genius of "suiting his temper of his circumstances," or maybe the torment of trying to "tame the tempest" during the West Newbury days, that took him closer to the core of the rationalization of social order than anyone else. Among abolitionists there was no more brilliant expositor of the free man in the moral marketplace than he; nor a better publicist. He staked out as his preserve for the rationalization the most personal and the most enticingly forbidden of all possible grounds for exploring the subject: individual sexual behavior.

Wright followed individuals to the deepest recesses from which they had come. As he emerged with his findings Wright had in his possession the "facts" about a social cosmogony that provided the "laws" for a social cosmology that splendidly met the needs of his era. He pursued the individual to the time of conception, to the split second when spermatozoon and ovum locked in their own sexual embrace. From that moment on the individual was nothing more (and nothing less) than the sum total of individual choices and constraints. The intrauterine individual was the product of individual action, "the mother, aided by the father, acting through her." It was the mother's "blood" that provides the "materials of which the child . . . is composed," both its body and "soul." Now Wright was not certain about the composition of the mother's blood. Perhaps it was a synthesis of "light, heat, air, water, earth, vegetable or animal food." But it is not his quaint hematology that is significant. Rather, it is the absolute separation of the mother's blood elements from any social source or process. Her blood is, as she is herself, the product of a series of individual choices and actions; her own, her husband's, and her parents', and so on. Wright thus laid the base for the most rigorous individualism and the most thoroughgoing social atomism. He was on his way to projecting something close to a solipsistic world. But, paradoxically (and here is, of course, the necessary condition of the great rationalization), it is a world in which social laws and controls prevail. If they are flouted, the comeuppance is certain and severe, as the sexual case histories abundantly demonstrate.

It is an easy task to make Wright out as nothing more than an apologist for a straitened capitalistic economics. Certainly there is an unmistakable economic content to his ideas. It is significant that on his roster of sexually caused debilities "failure in business" is listed among gout and paralysis. His notion of sperm as fixed sexual capital lends itself to a convenient economic application; and his entire system can be turned into an orrery for the scrimping, calculating private accumulator of worldly goods. But to leave Wright's work in this way, so that he comes out having done nothing but follow economic man into his bedroom is to misinterpret what he attempted and underestimate his achievement. He replaced *homo economicus* with *homo sexualis*. By relocating mankind's basic motive impulse it followed that the very definition of man would be changed. It presumptively followed that man's "corrupt and inharmonious" social relationships and institutions would also be changed, and the tumults—the state of wild delirium—of the nineteenth century would be brought under control. For what Wright grappled with was a changing culture, not simply a changing economics. The nineteenth century altered traditional patterns of family relationships and child nurture as well as changing a labor force; and it impinged the time-tested ideas of what it meant to be a man and a woman as well as shifting the ways in which they worked, and the conditions under which they worked.[11] Wright's solution to the problem of a changing culture was to confirm it, not breast its currents. He accepted the nineteenth century's basic premise and relentlessly drove it to its logical conclusion. Subject to the great "laws" let the individual be free and solely responsible for his fate. Wright's achievement was to locate individual freedom and responsibility where it was guaranteed that no external agency would intrude: in "the most sacred penetralia" of a person's life: in sexuality. And Wright's choice of a device for dealing with the new society is the one that most exactly implies his desire to preserve the idealized qualities of the old one: Sex=Reproduction.

Even at his boldest, when he was on the freedom of women, Wright affirmed the needs of his century and social class. His splendid insight about driving the matter of woman's rights beyond the vote, equal pay, and legal equality together with his proposition of a woman's right to control her body, dissolved into the conventions of American Victorian domesticity.[12] The "thorough regeneration" of women's place in society will result—this is Wright's exhortatory conclusion to *The Empire of the Mother*—in "mak[ing] them what God designed they should be, *healthy mothers of healthy children!*" There is no sturdier advocate of the dictum that biology is destiny. A woman's womb was her destiny, and her fate lay in the hands (and "heart") of her husband alone. For Wright, it was almost unthinkable that sex could occur outside of marriage, and the fact that it did was simply more unfortunate proof that the great laws governing the expenditure of the Reproductive Element were being violated. But by far the greater abuse of the laws were occurring within the precincts of marriage. So for all practical purposes Wright devoted himself to marital sex, and the domestic relationship between husband and wife. Therefore, inasmuch as monogamous marriage was the "natural" relationship of men and women, his work in effect was an attempt to define American men and women in their nineteenth-century world because it was only in marriage that men and women could bring themselves fully in accord with the sexual laws.

The laws were never codified. One was left to infer them from the illustrative case histories and from the expositions, particularly those turbid ones having to do with "Organization" that occupy much of *The Empire of the Mother*. Of the latter it is difficult to make much sense because when Wright has finished with "Organization" his reader has been whirled willy-nilly from infant mortality rates in New England to a theory of childhood that claims the newborn appears as homunculus and simultaneously lays the strongest stress on postnatal nurture and training of both body and "soul" to bring them to completion, through comparisons of "THE PASSIONS AND APPETITES" of assorted "Mormons, Yankees, Chinese, Russians, Laplanders, Bedouin Arabs, Presbyterian[s], Universal[ists], Hindoo[s]," and past a consideration of "whatever influence, material, domestic, social, political, ecclesiastical, commercial and literary surroundings may have on human character and destiny." But lest the reader lose his bearings, Wright developed his basic point in a loose syllogism that was easily grasped. "DESTINY IS DETERMINED BY ORGANIZATION—ORGANIZATION IS DETERMINED BY MATERNAL CONDITIONS. So far as human agency is concerned [only] THE MOTHER MAKES THE MAN.... If the prayer, 'Thy Kingdom come,' is ever to be answered on earth, it must be answered, not by the church, nor the state, but by the Mother."

Embedded in all of this is the alternative to the shattered community of the Appalachian world of pre–War of 1812 America. In community's place is substituted individual relationships. But these are of the most severely restricted sort. They exist only between two people, a man and a woman, husband and wife, who do indeed "stand alone in all the world." They are isolated and exclusive, as is their home. This home, the "Eden of God," is nothing more than a bastion, the chosen defensive position in which Americans are to make their stand against their own world raging outside. It is a world into which the men venture for their livelihood, but from which the women have withdrawn to be wives and mothers. In the home, the wife-mother is the preserver and transmitter of the old cherished values that have been endangered by the state of wild delirium.[13]

Wright anticipated the objection to such an atomistic stance. "It is said," he has Ernest tell Nina, "that exclusive[ness] and isolati[on] necessarily engender selfishness. . . . This is true, when ambition, avarice, vanity or desire for sensual indulgence, creates and maintains [a] home. It is founded in selfishness, and can engender only that. But, in a home created by conjugal love, the single object of each is the happiness of the other, and every pulsation of such love, and every manifestation of it, expands the heart, and fills it with a more active sympathy with all of humankind. That such results are so seldom seen is not attributable to the fact that the home is *isolated*, or that the love that creates is *exclusive*; but to the fact that it is the creation of sensual passion."

This ideal couple have only two social responsibilities. They are very clearly stated. First, by "reserving The Reproductive Element [until] it may be expended for just and natural purposes," is to make "perfect" babies. Second is setting a visible example of domesticity. On the latter point Ernest instructs Nina at some length: "Man needs a home for the body as well as for the soul. It is natural and right that a man and a woman, living in the conjugal relation, should seek to surround themselves with material beauty and elegance, as well as comfort. . . . I have no sympathy with that feeling which forbids men and women to seek and enjoy such elegancies, while others are destitute of the necessaries of life. I would help every husband and wife to a beautiful, elegant, healthful, material home. The best way to do this is to show them, by example, that such a home is possible, even to the poor, and how it can be attained. . . . To know how to create it honestly, and to use it wisely, is a talent that should be and will be better cultivated and more highly appreciated, when men and women come more fully to understand the bearing of their material surroundings on the refining and ennobling influences of home." With this statement of social responsibilities Wright came to the limits of his social imagination. After meeting these two responsibilities, his couple had no further social duties. They live in a world in which, as Nina says to her Ernest, We "depend upon ourselves." It is a world in which they "owe . . . allegiance to nothing [that] conflicts with [their own] perfection and happiness."

Wright could dream of nothing better than an America being populated with replicas and descendants of his Ernest and Nina who knew the "facts" and lived in accord with the "laws." That this should come about, he seems never to have doubted. "We can," he wrote in the middle of the Civil War, "never estimate too highly our nature and our destiny."

Surprisingly for this man who was "an extreme case," and almost too neatly, Wright slips into complementary congruence with our other three abolitionists. Their ideas mutually resonate. Wright's laws are functionally indistinguishable from Moncure Conway's principles. Neither can imagine a more desirable world than one in which an individual makes his choice alone and, consequently, bears the sole responsibility for it. Both accord with Frederick Douglass' *principled* objection to slavery: "To make a man a slave was to rob him of moral choice. Freedom of choice is the essence of all accountability." They all agree on the conditions of the endless social preterition from which Jane Swisshelm's self-electing Children of Israel emerge as the proprietors of the redeemed nation.

And if Conway, Swisshelm, and Douglass were likewise extreme cases, all of them—the black, the southerner, and the frontier woman—like Wright, on the several peripheries of abolition, what then of their allies and coadjutors who lay inside them? To chart the limits is to imply the middle, where the currents of abolition ran full and deep.

In this connection it is useful to reflect on Karl Polanyi's proposition that nineteenth-century civilization had to be assimilated to human meaning. This civilization, the "origins of Our Time," was founded on the contradictory premises that man is free and that man is imprisoned by laws governing a complex society. These antithetical premises imparted to nineteenth-century society what seemed to be "its amazing regularities and stunning contradictions," and established as one of the century's great tasks the harmonizing of the contradictory premises so that the "stubborn facts and inexorable brute laws that appeared to abolish our freedom [were] in one way or another . . . reconciled to freedom." [14] In the United States the premises had to be reconciled so they could coexist as fundamental conditions of society and as satisfying explanations of what was happening to a people who in the living memory of a single generation swept from the Appalachians to the Pacific. The achievement of this generation of nineteenth-century Americans was threefold: the creation of the "democratic" national state, the augmentation of a semi-laissez-faire industrial society of imperial scale, and the moral rationalization of their conditions which had burst in upon Americans with such sudden savageness.

If the ideas of Moncure Conway, Jane Swisshelm, Frederick Douglass, and Henry Wright partially box the compass of abolition's social imagination, then it begins to become clear that the achievement of American abolitionists was to contribute to all of these American achievements, particularly to the rationalization, that assimilation to human meaning Polanyi speaks of. It was a contribution that in its implications went far beyond their attack on the southern slave system, the destruction of a bonded labor force, the creation of a national system of racial "equality before the law," and even their labors after Reconstruction, particularly in privately supported education for Negroes that James McPherson has recently documented.

Seen this way, much of the task American abolitionists performed was accommodating and synoptic. There is reason to believe that they were more assimilators than root-and-branch icon breakers. The content of their social imagination suggests that they were less men and women desperately drumming up a coterie of true believers than they were the nineteenth-century American middle class writ in bold relief. It also suggests that they were less tories sourly displaced from social niches of deference and respectability than they were secular paracletes offering a means for achieving self-esteem and social respectability in a marketplace society characterized by its amazing regularities and stunning contradictions. And certainly the content of their social imagination suggests that instead of being illuminators of timeless universal truths they were expositors of certain "truths" peculiar to their own circumstances and the origin of *their* time.

In the following chapters I pursue Polyani's theme of assimilation in order to show why it was that two enterprising young men, obliged to live in this "amazing" world, helped reconcile themselves to it by taking up the cause of abolition.

XIII

Salmon Chase: Abolition, Union, and "The Great Moral Revolution"

Texas v. *White* is celebrated by reason of one memorable sentence—the most enduring thing Chase ever said: "The Constitution, in all its provisions, looks to an indestructible Union, composed of indestructible States," CHARLES FAIRMAN, *Reconstruction and Reunion*.

In the preceding two chapters we have moved from foreshortened biography to some straitened history for the same reason Conway and the others made a similar move. They knew that their life stories were not worth telling except as part of the great things.

We have also seen that American abolition might be approached as the work of imaginative writers whose main achievement was self-creation because it is in their imaginative writing about themselves that their social imagination was free to run to its limits. As an imaginative act abolition was able to take on the undisturbed clarity and purity of a visionary *ought*. The writers could have abolition the way they wanted it to be. It was safe from being thrust into the expedient and happenstance *is*, the world of men and events that equivocates and compromises and consequently makes an understanding of abolition such a bedeviling task, which is precisely the reason why Conway, when he told his story, separated "abolition" from "reform"; that is, abolition represented the corruption of his vision, and he was able to retain its purity only by making abolition itself the casualty to men and events—to history.

What is abundantly clear in the uncompromised visions is that generic abolition reached out and touched such a range of affairs that when the enterprise was at flood tide its agenda amounted to a "remarkable [and] sometimes mutually exclusive" shopping list of which the following is an abbreviation: abolish the post office monopoly, the army and navy, and all secret societies; protect secret societies; institute woman suffrage, deny women the vote; give all adult men the vote, restrict the ballot to the "wise"; promote internal improvements; abolish the tariff, raise the tariff; and so forth.[1]

It is small wonder, then, that the contemporary literature of abolition is as much a record of quarreling and infighting as it is a polemic against slavery and the South. But with such apparent cross-purposes the greater wonder is that common purpose and unanimity could finally emerge from abolition. The event signaling the unanimity was the Confederate artillery assault on Fort Sumter, the consequent "about face" of abolition's irreconcilables, and the unequivocal establishment of the first item on abolition's agenda: preservation of the Union.

Supposedly biography should not help in explaining why the agenda was set with such unmistakable unanimity and firmness. The decision to prosecute the Union war was a historical event of such magnitude that individual life histories are swallowed up by it. But perhaps an interpretive mode more usually applied to biography than history is useful for understanding what happened to abolition in the spring of 1861, why unionism was so deeply embedded in abolitionists' social imagination and why, as we have seen earlier, the Garrisonians repudiated Moncure Conway when he proposed to swap emancipation for Confederate independence.

During the first decades of the nineteenth century when abolition began to mature—in the words of Quentin Anderson, "in the generation of Emerson's youth"—Americans appear to have suffered a punishing psychic blow. Anderson is more suggestive than conclusive, but his ideas about the existence of a deeply traumatized generation have the merit of pressing us toward a conception of post-Appalachian America that carries beyond "the Marxist notions [or] the positing of sheer acquisitiveness" that have predominated the analysis and interpretations of antebellum America.[2]

When Americans burst into the post-Appalachian world, and as it imploded on them, they found themselves without the emotional supports of the preceding generation, the Revolutionary fathers', and they were compelled to find alternatives. Revivalism, the whole range of antebellum reform with its remarkable catalog of contrarieties, and the creation of what Anderson has called the Imperial Self testify to a massive search for alternatives. What is implied here for the Americans of the generation of Emerson's youth is more of a lostness than a rejection, and more of a generation time-warp than generational combat. One has only to turn to Henry Wright, that "extreme case," for the basic clue. Wright's quarrel was with his own world, not the world of his father. The portrait drawn by Wright of his father is warm with affection and respect. Excepting his religious ideas, the elder Wright, the old Revolutionary veteran, is presented as a paragon. He was literally a progenitor of the "richest legacy" of the individual and social virtues that his son believed were being destroyed as much in the paternalistic New England factory towns and in wild-woolly Buffalo as by the slaveholding South.

It is possible, then, that the more exuberant and volatile portion of the generation of Emerson's youth were less rebellious children than they were sons and daughters who had been emotionally orphaned by the assault of post-Appalachian America on their father's world. What makes the idea more than plausible is what happened in 1861. When we recall that the fathers' preeminent emotional "fact" was the nation, that the nation was their creation and the most prized portion of their richest legacy, then what better way was there for the emotionally orphaned children to reconstitute the link with the fathers than by literally saving the fathers' greatest creation and legacy. Radical abolition's swinging in support of the Union war might then be interpreted as the filiating affirmation of the most emotionally depleted of all the children whereby they attempted to regain the sustenance they imagined had been afforded the fathers: the self-satisfaction, the sense of well-being, of order, stability and control, the confidence that a received private and social morality prevailed—the emotionally sustaining belief that they were indeed a moral people in a moral society of which the Union was the framework and foundation.[3] If radical abolition's "about face" describes an arc turning the most volatile abolitionists back toward union, then it follows that "moderate" and "conservative" abolitionists lay inside the arc, and that their commitment to Union was no less strong. We deal here with an enormously powerful emotional charge, the one Lincoln appealed to when he evoked the "mystic chords of memory" in his first inaugural. Quite possibly it was stronger than the guilt and empathy often ascribed to abolitionists, and surely it is an emotion of which an account needs be taken as we extend our inquiry into some of the strands woven into abolition. Henry Wright having provided the basic clue to pursue, we now come more directly to another abolitionist, one of these "children," a member of the generation of Emerson's youth who seems to have sustained the punishing psychic blow Anderson postulates and who responded to it as I have suggested.

Salmon Chase was litigious abolition's stalwart. He was its leading constitutional theorist and one of the founders and chief strategists of abolition's political wing. He was abolition's first senator; he was also governor of Ohio, chief justice of the United States and five times a candidate for a nomination for the presidency of the United States. During the Civil War, Chase was secretary of the treasury. He bore the burden of arranging the financing of the war, and the fiscal and monetary policies established under his administration set the direction for the next fifty years. Chase came into the Lincoln cabinet as the representative of political abolition. He was the inner-council advocate of the "radical grounds" it occupied. In the cabinet he was always at the forefront pressing for abolition, and he was "the mainspring" of the South Carolina Sea Islands experiment in the ways and means of black freedom that has been called the rehearsal for Reconstruction. It was Chase's editing of the final passages in the Emancipation Proclamation that gave the document what moral force it has, linking justice, Constitution, military necessity, and Almighty God as the authorities for the act.[4]

Indefatigable in his labors for abolition—one reads his papers and watches his meticulous script fill pages with plans, schemes, calculations, exhortations, entreaties, and pieties and appreciates the ponderous force that energized him; "Sometimes," he confessed to Charles Sumner, "I feel as if I could give up—as if I *must* give up. And then after all I rise and press on. . . . I should faint certainly if I did not believe that God in heaven . . . orders all things well, and will not suffer those who trust in Him through Christ to be utterly cast down"[5]—Chase appears never to have faltered in his abolition faith.

Chase committed himself to abolition when it seemed nothing more than a motley, splintered enterprise of a few eccentrics, malcontents, and enthusiasts. From the first his analysis struck to the heart of the matter as he proclaimed his "hostility to slavery as a *power* antagonist." And in this original analysis he explicitly identified his goal. He intended to force "the system of slavery to be stripped of her [protective] veil, to be exposed in all her monstrous deformity, and to perish amid [destruction] of them whom she has so long deluded & betrayed."[6] What makes this identification of goal important (and it is crucial that Chase says it in 1841) is that he surrenders the distinction political abolitionists insisted on for the next twenty years and of which he himself was a primary formulator: the claim that they aimed only to "denationalize" slavery, confine it where it was established by "local law" where it would perish at the hands of "local" lawmakers. But this sentence may be read not as a rhetorical conceit but as a metaphor, *veil* being the metaphor for *Constitution*. Thus: once abolition has the *power*, it will strip away the constitutional protection of slavery where it exists under local law and carry the attack directly to the slavemasters, who themselves as well as their "system" will be destroyed. This is a declaration of total war, not limited war. "So must it be," said Chase.

Chase proposed to secularize abolition, to take it out of the realm of a struggle for men's souls and plunge it into the arena of social combat. He was not the first to make the proposal to politicize abolition, but he was without doubt the most sustained and systematic of political abolitionists. For over twenty years he worked to organize northern politics on an abolition base, and his political odyssey is both an encapsulation of abolition's search for a constituency and an illustration of its protean qualities. In the course of his partisan career Chase was a Whig, a Liberty party man, Free Soiler, Independent Democrat, Radical Republican, and Democrat. His undeviating message, the one he staked out when he first went into abolition politics, was that "free labor" was locked in a mortal struggle with slavery. For Chase, free labor was more than a system of labor; it was a system of ideas expressive of the aspirations of the small independent entrepreneur. In the final analysis free labor was a powerful ideological device that provided much of the moral sanction for the social behavior of the emerging middle class.[7] At Chase's and his fellow political abolitionists' hands free labor was insinuated to the heart of abolition, giving a systematic theory to the conception of the nation as moral marketplace that such nonpolitical abolitionists as Henry Wright had crudely outlined. Free labor also splendidly served the needs of political abolitionists who had the task of recruiting a constituency from a people for whom the question of enslaved blacks (and their subsequent situation in a free society) was at best a matter of indifference, and for whom the nationalizing of the contract-competitive system of labor would serve self-interest. Chase was aware of the hazards that recruiting such a constituency posed. In seeking votes the moral content of abolition might be diluted. He was therefore careful to keep his political discourse on the level of moral and religious obligation to the enslaved, and he was in firm agreement that it was critical that "the opposition to Slavery" must be organized so that "whilst the money-policy may be made to follow close as it is possible on religious duty, the latter . . . ought always to be allowed precedence."[8] Were it possible for one person to engross abolition's varied strands, Chase would come as close as anyone to containing them. As he proudly said of himself, "What I shall ... do will depend on circumstances; but you may depend upon it I shall protect my own honor and allow no detriment to the cause I revere. ... I can tell no lies, wear no double face."[9]

Like many abolitionists Chase flirted with the notion of breaking up the Union in order to promote abolition. For over ten years he said he would have "no hesitation in supporting" disunion abolitionists if they somehow were able to put their idea to the test of action, a position he claimed to hold as late as 1855.[10] But the bona fides of his unionism were established during the Great Secession Winter. Confronted by the prospect of real disunion Chase professed to "abhor the very idea of a dissolution of the Union." Furthermore—this is on the eve of South Carolina's secession—"*If I were President [I would crush disunion] by all necessary means. The question of slavery should not be permitted to influence my action, one way or the other.*[11] With South Carolina's secession an accomplished fact he appealed to Winfield Scott, the service chief of the army, to "preserve the Union which [the fathers] established." He reminded Scott that he held "a commission which no other American, save Washington, ever held." He urged the general—here Chase is almost frantic—to set aside his "deference to civil authority" and on his own authority order the army into action against South Carolina. He begged Scott, "Permit no obedience ... to any order of President or Secretary [of War] to deflect [you] from "the higher and holier duty" of suppressing secession.[12]

What is most suggestive in Chase's response to secession is not that he anticipates the last-ditch disunionists coming full circle, but the means he was willing to use to keep the Union intact. Chase's public career was based on two foundations, constitutionalism and abolition. But in December, 1860, in order to crush secession he proposed to rip the Constitution to shreds and jettison the attack on slavery. The question we desire to have Chase answer is, What lies at the heart of Union that is so overwhelmingly powerful that you are willing to turn the army loose and scrap twenty years of abolition work in order to keep it intact? What is evoked when the mystic chords of memory are struck?

Chase was never so obliging to directly answer the question. Or, more accurately, he answered it any number of ways. There is an eellike quality to Salmon Chase; he was always slipping away. He slid from one position to another, ripe with distinctions and justifications that a close examination of the record simply will not sustain. He was always pressing others to take firm stands on political and social "creeds," but he dodged firm stands himself, saying he had "no faith" in them.[13] Just to pin him down on a definition of abolition and get him to commit himself to it (or reject it) is an arbitrary act. And his long-standing association with abolition disunionism is a caution to anyone who tries to make neat categories among the abolitionists.

Many of his contemporaries thought Chase was self-interested duplicity personified. His sometime friend and biographer said, "Chase had [a] wonderful idealizing faculty. He could idealize the most prosaic character. He could neglect his truest friends to win the doubtful friendship of weak men. Bad men as well as good men saw the weakness. . . . He was, indeed, sought less by strong men and good men than by weak men and by bad men." His enemies were harsher, calling him "a political vampire . . . a sort of moral bull-bitch."[14] Chase often did not strengthen his own case, as in the instance of Edward Pierce. Pierce was Chase's protégé, and subsequently Chase handpicked him to direct the civilian side of the South Carolina Sea Islands experiment. In the late fifties young Pierce was trying to establish himself in Massachusetts politics and journalism. Solicitous of Pierce's budding career, Chase offered to help him buy a newspaper and support him in other ways. He also offered his young friend this equivocal advice, "Make it seem & felt that you act from conviction and you will be strong."[15]

If we stipulate Chase's alleged duplicity, rapacious ambition, and bad judgment there is still the problem of his explosive reaction to secession. His impulse was to lay on the altar of unionism the two things that (if we wish to be tough) enabled his disreputable qualities to consummate themselves in fame and power. Had he somehow been able to act on his impulse, Chase would have been thoroughly discredited and his career destroyed. Not only would he have been instigator of the highest sort of constitutional crime, he would have been exposed in the most enormous hypocrisy. In

mentioning Chase's dark side we have simply deepened the curiosity of his response to secession and his commitment to union. We
wish all the more to know what "Union" meant for him. In pressing on for an answer Chase's commitment to constitutionalism is a
useful lead to follow, initially.

Regardless of the exotic interpretations that sometimes flower
under its claims, constitutionalism is by nature conserving. It seeks
to keep in touch with origins, hold on to roots, and affirm the qualities of the beginning, because it is there that authority and security
lie. A constitutionalist's final appeal is always to the founders and
their intent. He is filiating, both in the strict legal meaning of the
word and in the broader sense; his fathers are sought, invoked,
affirmed.[16]

From his first venture into abolition Chase strove mightily to
keep in touch with the fathers. He would never relinquish his grasp
on them even though in order to sustain it he had to invent an
imaginative history about the making of the Constitution, particularly regarding what the framers intended to do about slavery
through constitutional action. He also had to deliver some fanciful
interpretations of the Constitution itself, especially the Fugitive
Slave clause that at his hands was pretty much expunged from the
text. The result was to make the Constitution a charter for abolition
and the Founding Fathers, especially Thomas Jefferson, dyed-in-
the-wool abolitionists. At the heart of Chase's constitutionally justified arraignment of slavery is this plea: Let the Fathers' will be
finally done. Let us be true to them and their charter for the original Union.

But why was Chase so insistent on the fathers; what was so be-
guiling about them and the fantasy document and "world" he invented for them? This is not "lawyer's history" with its obligatory
appeal to the framers he was creating. Chase had a profound emotional investment in the original Union. Had it been otherwise his
remarkable response to secession would be inexplicable. After all
he cast everything, even the Constitution itself, to the winds in
December, 1860, in order to "preserve the Union which Washington established."

Now if Chase were willing to tear up the Constitution in order to save the Union, it is clear that Union was not dependent upon the Constitution. Therefore it seems when Chase talked about Union he was not thinking of something that a constitution describes and implements: sovereignty, government, even "rights." He was onto something else that was "higher and holier." What was it that Washington and the other fathers, particularly Jefferson who was Chase's special hero and authority, personified that was so ineffably precious for him? Answering this question puts us on the final track leading to an illumination of the nature of the psychic blow postulated as having been sustained by a generation of Americans in the first part of the nineteenth century and the way the wound is likely to have been connected with abolition.

Chase himself suffered a punishing blow when he was young. This personal blow perhaps made him all the more susceptible to the generational one that followed close on its heels. The Chases were minor gentry with their roots in New Hampshire and Vermont from which they had branched out into some prominence. One of Chase's paternal uncles was a national-level politician, being a congressman and senator. Another was a bishop who carried the burden of establishing the Episcopal church in the Mississippi and Ohio valleys immediately following the War of 1812. Chase's father, Ithamar, was a businessman and entrepreneur for whom the end of the War of 1812 meant ruin. He had invested most of his money and his wife's dowry in the glass industry which was badly crippled in the postwar economic dislocations attendant to renewed British penetration of the American market. Ithamar Chase lost his glass factory and was "embarrassed" in his other business operations. The Chases were already on the edge of genteel poverty when Ithamar unexpectedly died in 1817, and the settlement of his estate left his widow with "but a remnant" to provide for her eleven children.

Salmon, who was nine years old when the death occurred, seems never to have recovered from the shocks of Ithamar Chase's failure and death. His father's death haunted him when he was a young man, and on into midlife he referred to his orphan-ness and his belief that the world remained unfair to him. He complained that his life was truly a "vale of tears." He had been dogged by misfortune and death, against both of which he must constantly struggle in order to achieve serenity of mind and "the accomplishment of great things"; and his financial security was a constant worry to him.[17]

His bishop uncle brought him to the Ohio frontier for several years, apparently to ease the family's burdens and to attract young Chase to the ministry. Subsequently he was shipped back to New Hampshire where family scrimping and his own off-term school teaching supported him at Dartmouth College from which he graduated in 1826. Chase ranked toward the undistinguished middle of his class, a position he promised himself he would never occupy again. Hereafter, "I shall strive to be first wherever I may be," he vowed as he left Dartmouth. Never again, he said, would he be "an idle goose."[18]

It is at this time that the copybook maxims and moralisms begin to flood Chase's commonplace book, his correspondence, and his diary. A few examples suffice to establish their tenor. "I have perhaps singular views of life. Certain it is that I regard this world not as a place of leisure—not as a place of selfish exertion. . . . I do not regard myself as at liberty to make any disposition of my time that may suit my inclination but I esteem it as a sacred trust to me by my God every moment of which ought to be devoted to a diligent preparation to discharge any duties which He may call me to perform. . . . 'Tomorrow and tomorrow and tomorrow creeps in.' How precious a treasure is time and how I have lavishly squandered it. . . . Yet even now there is time if I will but resolve and resolutely act to do much. Future scenes of triumph may yet be mine . . . and golden reputation." Throughout his life Chase never departed from his simple belief that it was incumbent for him to "struggle earnestly for the prize of well doing and leave [everything else to] the great Arbiter of all Destinies."

Chase left New Hampshire and went south where he hoped to open a school for boys. His first stop was at Frederick, Maryland, where he failed to attract any students. He moved on to Washington where he failed again. Desperate now with his money running out and all of those tomorrows creeping in, he turned to his senator-uncle for help. He asked his uncle to get him a government job. His uncle heard him out then closed the interview by saying, "I once procured an office for [another] nephew of mine, and he was ruined by it. I will lend you fifty cents with which to buy a spade, but I cannot help you to a clerkship."

With this brutal offer ringing in his ears—Chase remembered it verbatim thirty years later—he tried again to set himself up as a schoolmaster. This time he was successful. An elderly established schoolman wanted to divest himself of his boys' department. He arranged for Chase to take it over, which Chase thought was an act of God's special intervention on his behalf because he was "almost destitute." For the next three years he presided over twenty boys at his Select Classical Seminary. In addition to the set-piece curriculum he prided himself in giving special attention to the moral training of his students, which included severe whipping at the slightest provocation.

From the first, Chase detested "the drudgery and thanklessness of schoolkeeping." The school itself was "a yoke to be borne," and there was the larger matter; at Washington teachers were given "but little real respect." He desperately wanted "to cultivate [the] noble, commanding... dignified" people in Washington, but he was "restrained by bashfulness." He dreaded the reception that might be given him by these luminaries. "How," he asked, "can a man expect to be pleased when his *profession* ranks him with a degraded caste?" His Select Classical Seminary "is a trial. . . . It is a test—a criterion of strength—energy—power." For three years he looked forward to the moment "I . . . shall be released from it."

While "bearing the yoke" and "testing his strength" Chase lived in cheap boardinghouses inhabited by "the Goths" whom he despised, and who elicited from the young man with "an unmanageable mouth" the most biting condemnations. Scorning these boardinghouse denizens and their "congressional" equalitarian ways, he made a few friends, "young adventurers" like himself, ambitious, talented, with vague literary aspirations, hanging on in hand-to-mouth jobs waiting to move on to "executive" superordinate things and escape what Chase emblazoned in his commonplace book, "The Scandal of being one *whom* nobody knows." [19] Chase and his few friends were moralizing, self-righteous, rather priggish young men, quick to draw exclusive lines to shut others out and confirm their own recititude. Chase wrote off one couple he met: "He seemed to be a rake and she seemed to be an idiot and I took little notice of them." Another occasion found him at a party at which liquor was served and, "As soon as propriety allowed I took my leave." Sometimes Chase was compelled to exceed his friends in this mutual self-conscious moralism. He reported a conversation with a friend about the propriety of comparing women with statues. The point was that statues were "generally naked." "Whereupon," said Chase, the friend undertook "a learned discussion, the particulars of which I do not remember and if I did should not . . . deem them worthy of relation." Some of his friends he slandered, and his sister reproached him for his arrogance by calling him "His Lordship."

Tall, rawboned, and "uncouth," young Chase, unlike the sleek portly Chase who is recorded in his later daguerreotypes, had "a terrific temper" and a streak of uncontrollable violence in him. He whipped the boys in his school as a matter of course, a practice that had gotten him in trouble with the patrons of his first New Hampshire school and that led to the withdrawal of some students from the Select Seminary; and there are at least two instances in which he "severely thrashed" and "kicked downstairs" "burly, powerful" men for what Chase considered "unprovoked insults" and "base proposals." There was enormous energy and force in young Chase; there was an enormous rage, too. He was constantly lashing out against those "unprovoked insults" even when they came from that poor couple whose offense was that Chase did not like the way they looked and they happened to be in his neighborhood. Of this time in Washington, Chase later said, "I made much too little use of the advantages which a residence [there] afforded. I became slightly acquainted with a number of prominent characters, but was too diffident to put myself into notice; possibly too proud to ask for recognition, and preferring to wait for it. . . . I was poor and sensitive; a young teacher, needing myself to be taught and guided."

Chase never supposed his school was more than a stopgap and a means to prepare for his chosen profession, the law. He came to the law by the process of elimination. Philander Chase, the bishop-uncle, had urged him to take up the Episcopal ministry for his life's work. But Chase's elder brother warned him against a career in the church. Any minister, his brother told him, ran the risk that he might "disgrace the Christian church"; then, pointedly to his younger brother: the disgrace results from "pride, lust of power and hypocrisy." A career in the church was vetoed, though Chase remained, from those early years in Ohio with his uncle, a "zealous" Christian and Episcopalian churchman. A prospective career in medicine was examined and ruled out. "After all [there was] the ridicule which has been cast upon the profession in all ages." This historic prejudice would have to be overcome if a physician was to become "a practitioner of eminence . . . and [be] held with great respect." Which left the law. Above all professions the law was responsive to "an ambition to be extensively usefull [sic] to your species by being advanced to rule over them and be known and distinguished as a *MAN*. If you wish for wealth, become an honest conscientious and moral lawyer." Chase chose the law. He staked out his future. "My plan of life . . . is this. To pursue the practice of my profession undeviatingly until I have accumulated a little—enough to render me independent of the world and then to run a political career. I think in this way I may be more extensively useful than in any other and therefore I wish to pursue this course." [20]

Chase studied law with William Wirt. Wirt was a patron of the Select Classical Seminary in which his son was a student and through which the connection with Chase was made. A habitual preceptor and a sort of Polonius, Wirt agreed to supervise Chase's legal studies and "to cheer and encourage the young and inexperienced traveler," as Chase called himself, "on the paths of life." In Wirt, Chase found the teacher and guide he craved. Chase's impulse for filiating that we have earlier observed was consummated in Wirt. Wirt became his surrogate father and was the channel by which Chase was led to the world of the Revolutionary fathers.

Young Chase heaped on Wirt all of the affection and admiration an idealized father could have elicited from him. Immediately upon meeting Wirt he said, "I feel for him the highest respect and shall omit no endeavour to gain a place in his confidence and esteem." Of all those "prominent characters" Chase hungered to associate himself with in Washington—and with Wirt's patronage he entered the homes of many of them—Wirt himself was, in Chase's adulous eyes, the most "polished and fascinating" of all, including Henry Clay, John Quincy Adams, and Daniel Webster. Wirt reciprocated in the relationship. He gave Chase the run of his home where he became a combination protégé and factotum. Wirt also unwittingly placed Chase in an anomalous relationship with one of his daughters. Young Chase seems to have resolved this tempting but frightening situation by writing some mooning poetry, complaining that he was poor, and wishing that "happier stars had shone upon me [and] it had been my lot to possess a sufficient portion of wealth [to attempt] to win her affections."

Chase also was Wirt's social deputy. He was given the duty of making such "drawingroom" appearances as Wirt chose to avoid, an assignment Chase relished because it permitted him to "shine a little by reflected light." From these affairs he drew the conclusion that "success . . . depends quite as much upon the *Savoir-Faire* as upon the Savior." He made vain attempts to curb his sharp tongue. He also tried to copy Wirt's "popular and winning address," but he was never able to free himself of his ponderousness, and it took years to shed even his bumptious "uncouthness."

Given the freedom of the house Chase soon found his favorite place. It was Wirt's study. In Wirt's absence he would go there and sit and dream about his patron, "where in his 'midnight vigil . . . he had evoked Fame' and she had come at his call."[21] Chase's biographer adds, "In the delightful family of Mr. Wirt, and among the friends of the family, Mr. Chase found all of the social life that his heart desired, and was happy in it." At the close of his tenure with him, Chase said of Wirt, "I *love* him." And to Wirt directly he promised, "God prospering my exertions, I will imitate your example."[22]

Now at the height of his fame and power, the man Chase chose as his mentor and exemplar had achieved almost exactly the goals Chase had laid out for himself, and whose early life approximated that of Chase's. The orphan son of a tavernkeeper, sometime schoolmaster, and protégé of Thomas Jefferson, Wirt had managed to qualify for the bar, had made a handsome legal reputation for himself, and then had "run" a political career. When he took Chase under his wing Wirt was toward the end of a twelve-year tenure as attorney general of the United States, and was, in addition to being a wheelhorse in politics, a famous litterateur and orator.

A child of the Revolution, a Marylander by birth, and a Virginian by cultivation, Wirt was the sedulous ape of the revolutionaries. He was the self-appointed custodian of the original republic and the celebrator of its creators and their putative virtues.

A southerner, Wirt was never a sectionalist or a defender of slavery. His first criminal case involved two men accused of whipping a slave to death in which he argued that slavery is a "foul disgrace to men who affect to glory in the hallowed name of liberty [and is] the guilt of the nation." But once he could afford to buy slaves Wirt bought and traded them, and when Chase came to him there were a dozen slaves serving the Wirt household. Wirt's legal reputation was founded on the part he played as a young government attorney prosecuting Aaron Burr for treason against the United States. Following the Burr trial he established himself as a constitutional authority in *Hunter* v. *Martin's Lessee*. This was a case in which he hammered away at "the doctrine of national supremacy . . . in a manner prophetic" of Marshall and Story. In the twilight of his career Wirt labored to clear the memories of Jefferson and Madison of any taint of secessionist tendencies connected with the old Kentucky-Virginia Resolutions affair, and he straight-forwardly denounced the South Carolina nullifiers as smugglers and pirates.[23]

Wirt's literary reputation was secured by his *Sketches of the Life and Character of Patrick Henry* which he claimed was "history, too." The *Life of Henry* was part of Wirt's larger plan to write the biographies of all the Revolutionary worthies in order, he said, to keep the historical record straight and prevent the heroes from altogether falling into the hands of hagiographers. But his work was in fact part of the patristic writings of the first post-Revolutionary generation who were attempting to persuade themselves of the Founding Fathers' "perfection" in order to assimilate this perfection and thereby "gain a sense of personal stability and national pride."[24] Wirt got no farther than the *Henry* with his "great object," but the ideas that might have informed it are suggested by his later set-piece oration eulogizing Jefferson and Adams. The oration was delivered as a state occasion, with Wirt speaking before the Congress, government dignitaries, and the diplomatic corps. For all practical purposes Wirt was speaking for the nation. Subsequently his *Discourse on the Lives and Character of Thomas Jefferson and John Adams, Who Both Died on the Fourth of July, 1826* was published and distributed wholesale by Congress "for the encouragement of learning" in the United States, and it may be taken as the authorized synoptic history of the making of the nation and a certified description and analysis of the early republic.

The *Discourse's* self-congratulatory nationalistic bombast—a xenophobic shot is taken at the British minister seated in the diplomatic gallery, and "with reverence" Wirt has Jefferson and Adams ascending to heaven like twin Christs—comes as no surprise. But as Wirt warmed to his task he wove into his nationalistic message a complementary social theme. The "matchless skill and talent" of Jefferson and Adams and all the revolutionary fathers consummated itself in brilliant leadership because certain social conditions prevailed at their time. A superb balance, order, and restraint characterized the early republic. There was no popular confusion between a Napoleonic-Jacksonian leader who inevitably led a nation to excess and "crime," and the father-heroes who lived "under the check of strong virtues," and enjoyed "the happy poise of . . . character." In "those attic days" only virtuous men were allowed to come to power. What Wirt ascribed to the early republic is a complementary relationship between a self-regulating social order and self-regulating men. Unfailingly, the formula for success was "rectitude and aptitude." But, Wirt lamented, those days are gone. It is as though a social system has died with Jefferson and Adams. And, Wirt asked, "what heart does not sink at the prospect of the future?"[25]

The *Discourse* is also an autobiographical statement. "An orphan, and a poor one too,"[26] Wirt believed he had made his way to the top of the heap by engrossing the qualities he ascribed to the fathers. He was able to escape the "accidental position" of his origins because the fathers' system prevailed as he was coming up. He was the beneficiary of those attic qualities he imputed to their world wherein "virtue" chastened raw ability and provided moral leadership in the United States.

Wirt was a casualty to the post-Appalachian world that shattered the fathers' world. The 1828 political upheaval turned him out of office. In the wake of the Jacksonian victory portending the "threatening storm" that he feared would soon engulf the nation Wirt returned to private life. He closed his handsome Washington home, leaving young Chase alone in it as the caretaker. Chase wandered about the desolate rooms and walked in the empty garden, the favorite place of Mrs. Wirt, a noble woman, Chase characterized her, with a "tincture of aristocratic feeling." He sat in the garden with his books, where, he said, "I found a melancholy pleasure reading passages which I used to admire with my absent friends." He recalled "the unbroken felicity here," picked a flower, and walked back into the house. He climbed the stairs to Wirt's study where his "sorrow Beguile[d] itself" by pondering Wirt's fate and his own future, for the two seemed woven together.

Chase's first response to the collapse of Wirt's world, the one, slaves and all, he had appropriated as his own, was partisan. He spouted some anti-Jacksonian cant about the "misled people" and the onset of "the Millennium of the Minnows." He "looked with abhorrence and indignation" at "this modern Robespierre" and his followers who were "utterly incompetent to the discharge of [the] smallest duties." He compared invidiously "the purse proud, vulgar and affected" people swarming into Washington for Jackson's inauguration with the "pure and gentle and refined and cultivated circle" to which Wirt had given him access. And he faithfully allied himself with Wirt and the rest of the dispossessed "prominent characters" who were victims of Jackson's "system of relentless and unsparing proscription." "For me I would prefer to fall with the fallen than rise with the rising," he vowed.[27]

But Chase's reference to the aftermath of the 1828 political upheaval carried far beyond partisan politics. He tried to practice what Wirt taught. "You must," Wirt was fond of saying, "take a wider horizon. You must be continually awake and alive to all that is passing around you, and let nothing escape your observation. You must depend on your own lynx-eyed observation [and] vigilance that nothing can escape." "[Imitate] Mr. Jefferson [who] was only sixteen years of age when he began to keep regular files of newspapers and pamphlet[s] on any public subject, whether of politics, arts or sciences. Thus he was continually master of all that was passing in every quarter of the world." Chase came to believe, no doubt with Wirt's encouragement, that something deeper and infinitely more unsettling than partisan political change had occurred in American society. A profound dislocation had happened directly around him of which political realignment was only symptomatic. His phrase is striking: "The Alleghenies are annihilated." Something had been pierced, old boundries had been destroyed and roots severed. There was a deep rupture. He was being hurtled into a "savage" world and "a new society" in which "space [itself] is almost annihalted [with his variant spelling, the word became a favored descriptive for Chase]." New, unprecedented relationships were forming while old ones were being sundered. Even the cities seemed to turn and face in new directions, as was the case for Baltimore, which, in Chase's mind, pivoted from the northeast and turned toward the west and the "annihalted" mountains. Chase was convinced he was now living in a world in which old arrangements will be discounted or stand for nothing. "Strangers will succeed." And they will succeed, Chase said, in an ambience in which "distrust has come in place of confidence and reserve instead of frankness." "How long," Chase asked himself, "will these things be?"[28]

The empty house and Mrs. Wirt's garden beginning to go rank was only "the discordant prellude [sic] to . . . ruin." Wirt's fate was a "prophecy of what is coming upon [all of] us." A profound unease and anxiety seized Chase. He was "miserable." Dark, apprehensive thoughts descended on him. His law studies were coming to an end. Presently he would stand the bar examination and begin his professional life. But his carefully laid plans were now qualified and trailed off in references to "the *new* society," "baleful influence," "licentiousness and anarchy," and "pestilential influence corrupting everything it touches." Chase thought he was living on the brink of disaster. With Wirt gone he was adrift again, an orphan once more, precisely as he had come to manhood and was preparing to embark on his life's work: "My birthday. I am twenty-one. I have *now* no guardian save him whose wards we are thro life."[29]

Here, of course, is a fledgling standing on the threshold of his chosen life's work stricken by fear at the thought of failing at it. But these are not the anxieties of a driven, ambitious young man setting out in a familiar hospitable world which wants only from its beginners what Chase called "energy, industry and resolution," all of which he assured himself he had in abundance. He was hagridden by the blackest fears of failure, his manifest and self-certified abilities notwithstanding. He was obsessed by the fear that "strangers" to the qualities and abilities he possessed and strangers to his "circle" would push him aside.

Surveying his dubious prospects Chase tried to arm himself against the possibility that it would be *his* fault should "extensive attainments" elude his grasp and go to those strangers. In this arming, which came from desperate needs, we are able to see how Chase had so completely assimilated William Wirt and the "attic" qualities of Wirt's mythopoeic world of the fathers, and in so doing engrossed a reference that suffused his ideas for the rest of his life.

First, Chase blamed his crimped chances on his "defective education" and his "superficial" preparation for the law. However, on reflection he thought that "this is but a miserable comfort." "Let me no longer deceive myself, [these reasons are] miserable pretense[s], nothing more than apologies . . . or cloaks" of self-deception. For Wirt, too, he reminded himself, had had a "miserable education"; in fact Wirt's schooling was considerably more haphazard and foreshortened than his own. Nonetheless, Wirt had transcended his marginal origins and defective preparation and had "evoked Fame." But Wirt was toppled, and if Wirt, already at the top of the heap and in full possession of his powers, could not survive in this *"new* society" of "minnows" what chance was there for young Chase who was only beginning to make his bid for fame and power?

Chase stopped his "miserable pretense" and self-apologizing and came to the second of his attempts to arm himself against a

threatened future. This second arming was successful and enduring. He found a satisfying explanation for exculpating himself if he
failed to make good on his promise to Wirt to "imitate your example" and achieve those "extensive attainments" he had set his heart
on. Once perfected, this explanation established the base for his
subsequent career in abolition, and illuminates the reason for his
startling response to South Carolina's secession thirty-two years
later. It is here in this second arming that Chase consummated his
filiating with the world of the fathers; furthermore, Chase enables
us to see with great clarity why the consummation occurred. We
are also able to understand why it was, when he was in the bosom of
Wirt's family and had already appropriated Wirt as his surrogate
father, on his twenty-first birthday Chase asserted his orphan-ness
and threw himself over to God's guardianship.

Taking "the wider horizon" as Wirt had taught (using young
Jefferson as the example), Chase tried to "observe" and "master all
that was passing." In the upheavals of 1828–1829 the critical thing
Chase "observed"—and what confirmed his orphan-ness—was
this: "The day has past, I fear forever past in this country, when a
man will be rated according to his intellectual strength, extensive
experience [and] moral excellence."[30]

Here is the weapon Chase selected to defend himself against his
terrifying fears of failure. It is a precise echo of what Wirt formally
stated in the Discourse, which eulogized a dying social order as well
as the dead fathers. This is the graveman of Chase's case against the
world in which he was "now" compelled to live as an orphan. The
formula for success that provided the recognition of "matchless
skill and talent" was a casualty to this new America just as the
Alleghenies, "space," and William Wirt were casualties. The loss
was almost overwhelming but not altogether irretrievable. There
were, Chase told himself, "amid the gloomy clouds which over-
hang our future destiny faint revealings of a mighty moral revolution." The effect of the revolution will be the restoration of the
splendid qualities of the early Republic with its attic order and
equilibrium, the core of which is the rating system that dispensed
rewards according to ability chastened by virtuous character. In the
crisis of being "orphaned" as he was coming of age, young Chase

found his solace in a historical scheme of lost perfection, degeneration and restoration that he employed, restated as imaginative constitutional history, when later he helped equip abolition with its redemptive free labor ideology.[31]

Presently at Baltimore, Chase passed his bar examination. It was arranged, probably with Wirt's assistance, and much like Wirt's own admission to the bar, that Chase did not have to satisfy the requirement for the length of time a candidate was to have studied the law. Chase wanted to follow Wirt to Baltimore, settle there, and begin his law career. But he was stopped by a three-year residence requirement that had to be fulfilled before he would be permitted to practice in the civil courts; "thus," he said, "confining me during that time entirely to the criminal court" and blocking him from business and corporation law which was the path he wanted to take. Not even with Wirt's influence could he get the residence rule "suspen[ded] in my favour." Disgruntled and vexed, he had to find some other place to make his plunge in "the wild ocean of futurity."

Chase considered, maybe even intended, beginning his career at New Orleans or somewhere else in the booming Southwest, which he planned to "survey" on a long, looping trip in the spring of 1830.[32] That he would be headed straight where slavery was entering its flush times was of no concern to him; even there the bar was being reshaped in ways agreeable to Chase. The freewheeling frontier lawyers with their sporting life, and raffish "unprofessional" behavior were losing out to austere professionals. And in the Deep South as elsewhere the practice of the law, Wirt said about the time Chase left Baltimore, "is much changed. . . . The age of ornament is over; that of utility has succeeded. Go [Wirt advised] for strength and not for beauty . . . *rough, abrupt strength*."[33]

Embarking on his trip to the Southwest, Chase got no farther than Cincinnati where the new legal "commercial, corporate system [based on] the city" was already establishing itself. Its "inflexible and rigid" style suited him and was congruent with his austere personality traits. "Here," he reported to a friend, "is the future scene of my professional labours and here, if anywhere, must I build up my reputation. And indeed I see no great reason for dis-

couragement. The lawyers here are far from being a very talented
or highly educated body of men. . . . I am still of [the] opinion that if
you are a man of popular and winning address, and withal of a
happy gift to exhibit all you know in such a way, as to make fools
(of whom the number is infinite) stare, you will succeed here.
Perhaps you will succeed at once: perhaps it will be a work of
time. . . . Since I have been here the citizens have treated me with
great attention. . . . I think I shall succeed." Furthermore, he said,
making a virtue of necessity, "I would rather be first in Cincinnati
than first in Baltimore, twenty years hence."[34]

Within the year Chase's career was blossoming. After a business
trip which brought him east, he reported that at Boston "I was
highly gratified by my reception. . . . I received a great deal of attention from the best quarters. At Philadelphia, New York & Baltimore also I had no cause of dissatisfaction." Now back at Cincinnati, "Everything goes on smoothly enough if I could make a little
more money. . . . I have I believe a pretty strong hold on the respect
and regard of the community and look forward to golden days."
Shortly, Chase was established in the city and made his reputation
as one of the most successful lawyers of the state. And before he
was thirty years old he had, as he had planned, begun to run his
political career.[35]

Meantime he found the "mighty moral revolution" he had been
seeking since those dark days when, alone in William Wirt's house,
he had armed himself against an instable, unpredictable world.
First the revolution appeared as the temperance crusade which
Chase joined and zealously supported by trying to outlaw Cincinnati's roistering taverns and *biergartens.* But in the aftermath of
civic disorders, national economic collapse that plunged him in
debt, and a stunning series of harrowing personal tragedies the
"faint revealings" were clarified. Chase became "fully persuaded"
that the revolution was being conducted under the banner of abolition. "The movement," he said, "no doubt, must be in the beginning unpopular. But it will go on and gain friends constantly. In a
little while multitudes will come out of their hiding places. . . .
There is a large amount of genuine antislavery feeling in this city.
It does not show itself principally because it is believed to be un-

popular, but partly because ministers and Party leaders denounce abolitionism. The time will soon arrive, however, when this feeling will find a voice and a head."[36]

After some hesitation and temporizing—and only after suffering the "absolute despair,"[37] the similar feelings of vulnerability, and being adrift in a hostile world that he had felt when William Wirt's world collapsed in 1828—Chase took it as his "clear duty" to "obey the call" to provide abolition (and the moral revolution) its "voice" and "head." As Chase helped lead abolition into politics his methods and tactics changed as he predicted they would, according to "the process of events." But throughout his career he never loosened his grip on the fathers, particularly Jefferson, to whom he had been led by Wirt, the only man he ever said he loved. During the next twenty years as abolition enticed those multitudes out of their hiding places, it was Chase's belief that the "fathers' intention regarding slavery" would be consummated and "our Government [will be restored to] its true scope and end." With the consummation would come the retrieval of the vital quality of the fathers' society, the quality Chase had learned from Wirt, whereby men find their social destinies solely on the basis of their "poise of character, their intellectual strength, extensive experience and moral excellence."

Such an evaluation of individual characteristics splendidly meshed with the demands of a free labor economy and admirably justified its human consequences. But in Chase's case the roots of the social justification of character lay less in economics or the aspirations of an emerging entrepreneurial class as in an orphan boy's need to find a father and protect himself in the post-Appalachian society being created by the very forces his subsequent abolition ideology augmented. As for free labor's religious roots, other men might have found justification in their understanding of heaven's blessings on worldly activity; but Chase, "whose religion darkened his mind and made him far from happy," was never able to satisfy himself that he was worthy in his God's eyes. He always judged his life to be "exceedingly sinful." Instead of worldly rewards, Chase believed that his heavenly Father offered only forgiveness for his sins and "the perversities and guilt of my heart."[38] It was his "almost superhuman"[39] worldly fathers who offered him the rewards of the world on the condition that he would strive to emulate them and preserve the greatest of their legacies for their children. Chase's God could never be satisfied; but the fathers might. The power of Chase's need to satisfy them was revealed by his frantic response to the South Carolina secessionists, the latter-day "pirates" who were trying to wreck William Wirt's and Washington's and Jefferson's Union. In December, 1860, Chase proved his fidelity to the fathers. He acted as a fiercely loyal, self-sacrificial son. He was prepared to jettison everything he had proclaimed in "the new society" in order to save the fathers' original creation, slavery and all.

Chase was chief justice during much of Reconstruction. He assigned himself the task of writing the leading opinion in only one of the Court's more important decisions, *Texas v. White.* This was the occasion at which, as Charles Fairman has observed, Chase delivered himself of the most enduring thing he ever said. The Union is indestructible. In the final analysis everything else gave way to preserving the Union. With the Union assured the Chase Court rarely disputed a Congress that was, as George Clemenceau said, sailing the abolition sea. With his capacity for blinding himself to distinctions that more sensitive jurists might see, Chase drafted one of the supplemental congressional Reconstruction acts, and he had a hand in the congressional "tailoring" of the United States judicial system in order "to suit better the demands and needs" of the proponents of free labor.[40]

Toward the end of Chase's tenure as chief justice the first test and interpretation of the Fourteenth Amendment arose with the *Slaughterhouse* cases. *Slaughterhouse* is one of the most celebrated and notorious of all Supreme Court decisions, particularly because the opinions laid the foundations for the constitutional crimping of federal protection of Negroes' rights and the constitutional justification of a national laissez-faire economy. For the latter the principal warrant was found in the Declaration of Independence and the *Wealth of Nations.* Three weeks after concurring in the opinion laying claim on Adam Smith and Thomas Jefferson in behalf of constitutionally protected human liberty and equality, Chase died.

XIV
Thomas Cooley: Abolition, Law, and "The Day of Better Things"[1]

That was how it was in Western New York [around Attica]. Something about the land, or the York State land as it used to be—the near horizons lifting up their high-angled screens between folded valleys, the days full of clouds forever drifting, ominous and beckoning, sliding past green-grey summits and throwing their shadow from the straightedged slopes. "Stand up and seize," the land said: "or rise and prophesy, cock your ears to the invisible."
JOHN GARDNER, *The Sunlight Dialogues*

Following "the great things" full post-Appomattox course and showing the augmentation of abolition's social imagination and social mechanism in any detail is beyond the competence of biographical interpretation and therefore outside my main purposes.[2] But portions of this larger subject may be briefly suggested by Thomas Cooley and his work whereby abolition's vision of the free individual and the national moral social preterition became incorporated in the law of the land.

A standard observation about American constitutional history is that for generations following the Civil War it amounted to an exegesis of the Fourteenth Amendment, and that the exegesis itself, beginning with *Slaughterhouse*, amounted to a sustained dis-

330

tortion of the amendment so as to hand over the law of the land to an unparalleled materialistic rapacity. Particularly, the use of substantive due process and "the development of the [doctrine] of the liberty of contract as a limitation upon the powers of both state and national governments was a judicial answer to the demands of industrialists in the period of business expansion following the Civil War."[3]

According to the received interpretation, the crucial connection between the Fourteenth Amendment and the judicial response to the demands of the industrialists was made in 1868, the same year the amendment was ratified. Congruently with ratification, Thomas Cooley, a teacher at the University of Michigan Law School and a justice of the Michigan Supreme Court, produced his *Constitutional Limitations*. Published as America entered the industrial and business boom of the last part of the century, *Constitutional Limitations* "precipitated," "crystallized," and "implemented many . . . elements of theory . . . where legal and economic thought merged," and laid the groundwork for shaping the Fourteenth Amendment into a license for the predatory and materialism of the Gilded Age.[4]

In his preface to the second edition of *Constitutional Limitations*, published in 1871, Cooley remarked on the "unexpected favor" with which his book had been received by "an enlightened and generous profession."[5] The book went through four editions in ten years, an astounding success in legal publishing, and was established as the most cited commentary on constitutional law in the latter half of the nineteenth century. Cooley himself "came to have the reputation of the greatest authority on constitutional law in the world, being 'the most frequently quoted authority on American constitutional law.'" And as James Bryce was preparing his *American Commonwealth*, the *fin de siecle* counterpart to Tocqueville's *Democracy in America*, he turned to Cooley for advice and help. The result was that Cooley wrote manuscript sections that appear "almost verbatim" in the commentary, and thereby he alone, of all post–Civil War legal writers, "exerted a direct influence upon political science." But according to his critics, Cooley's foremost achievement was "almost single handed[ly] delivering the legal

ideology" for the constitutional interpretation whereby "liberty"
was shifted from its old protean meaning to a new narrow definition of economic activity.[6]

Some five hundred pages of sustained disquisition on personal
liberty, *Constitutional Limitations* systematically developed the
thesis that "every man will possess [liberty] in proportion as the
laws, while imposing no unnecessary restraints, surround him and
every other citizen with protections against the lawless acts of others." "Without mentioning the words 'liberty of contract,'
[Cooley] expressed the contents and the pattern of that doctrine as
it was developed" by his fellow jurists. Cooley's thesis on personal
liberty was applied to the Fourteenth Amendment's guarantee of
equal protection so as to reshape the guarantee in order to serve
purposes altogether different from those intended by the amendment's framers. In "this backdoor fashion" an era of entrepreneurial liberty was judicially sanctioned, and the doctrine of "natural
entrepreneurial rights" entered the Constitution. Cooley has,
therefore, been made out as one of the chief corrupters of the antebellum values that had guided American growth and had set the
moral tone of the free-labor portion of the prewar republic; and he
was without doubt the leading legal writer who supplied American
business enterprise the constitutional justification for a free hand in
the United States. Written concurrently with it, Cooley's *Constitutional Limitations* was "almost . . . a direct counter" to Marx's
Das Kapital.[7]

According to his critics, it was almost inevitable that Cooley
should have produced the "counter" to *Das Kapital*. "It was inevitable in 'a government of laws, not of men' that political issues
should merge with constitutional interpretation." This comming-
ling of constitutionalism with politics had informed a class struggle
between "the aristocratic planters and the industrialists of the
North . . . during the first half of the century." When Cooley published *Constitutional Limitations* "the political issue was settled in
favor of the capitalists by the Civil War." Now

the vital conflict changed to one between the increasing economic power of
the capitalistic "classes" and the political power of the agrarian and laboring "masses." The battle was transferred from legislative halls to the

courts, where it was given the appearance of a contest between lawful private rights and unlawful interference. In that contest the lawyers as such came into their own, for they were the necessary intermediaries between capitalists and the Court.... Socially and professionally the leaders of the bar were the natural allies of the propertied classes, for they lived among them, sharing their ideas and representing their interests. Hence the lawyers were the front line of defense of the property right against the threat from popular sovereignty and majority rule. The Constitutional lawyer . . . is at the top of the profession and is therefore more than representative; he sets the tone of bar attitudes.

And Cooley having the reputation of the greatest authority on constitutional law stood at the pinnacle.[8]

Cooley has thus entered our histories as the grand architect of a system in which the whole apparatus of the law was set in motion to sustain and protect private property by outlawing majoritarian political power; to impinge upon individual economic enterprise in any "unnecessary" way was, Cooley laid it down, "the difference between freedom and oppression." The linchpin of the system was the doctrine of liberty of contract whereby personal liberty was defined in material terms, and under whose aegis "freedom" was nothing other than the condition of grubbing and getting under "equal" conditions established by the law.

But Cooley's most able hostile critic concedes that he has "perhaps painted a rather one-sided picture" of the great legal expositor of untrammelled liberty and the way "laissez faire capitalism was supplied with a legal ideology."[9] It is to an alternative picture that we now turn.

Early in his career Cooley practiced law inauspiciously in Adrian, a county-seat hamlet in the Michigan frontier backwaters.

Practically everything on the contemporary record about Cooley was produced to memorialize him, which in itself is a sufficient caution to approaching his life, but there is an extra caution about dealing with his early life because these scant materials have not only been shaped in view of commemorating him but also to celebrate him as an exemplary self-made man who began his career "without property and without friends to assist him." He "could not be conquered by poverty" or "crushed by unyielding opposition." "Against every discouragement he set his indomitable will [and] a determination to succeed in spite of many obstacles which must have seemed insurmountable." His posthumous memorialists were hard put to exceed what was written about him while he was living: "Mr. Cooley exemplifies in his life his own ideal, being pure, courteous, faithful and just. His whole life has been characterized by incessant labor, and the untiring devotion with which he has applied himself to his work has made his name immortal." [10]

Not only had his social origins dealt a hard blow to the young man with "unquenchable ambition," but nature itself seemed to conspire against him in his chosen profession. Cooley spoke poorly. His voice was thin and his manner unprepossessing. He was scarcely an advocate that inspired confidence in a client, or in a jury that his client's case was worthy of their votes. Nor was he "regarded as a strong advocate on the trial of an issue of fact." Cooley's "strength . . . was on an issue of law," which gave him the opportunity to bring together the fruits of his legal studies and his fascination for shaping the law to his own ends. "Judicial authorities were his guides and helps . . . [but] not his master." Cooley would find and make his own law. If "facts" stood in his way, so much the worse for them. He was, even in these early days at Adrian, seeking eternal truths and universal principles as expressed by the law, which he himself made.

An imaginative legal scholar, Cooley spent years trying petty cases in petty courts. So it is altogether understandable why these Adrian years were marginal ones for the ambitious young lawyer. Such success as he had as an attorney came only after he abandoned practicing by himself and entered a partnership with Charles Croswell, a genial affable man, easy with people and instinctively inspiring confidence, who later became governor of Michigan. Croswell kept the law office, drummed up clients, and convinced them that Cooley could argue their cases successfully. Meanwhile in order to make ends meet Cooley had been obliged to edit the Adrian *Watchtower*, farm part-time, serve as village recorder for the pittance it paid, and sell real estate, which he gave up upon discovering that he was no good at it. For years he "could not get a foot hold."

Cooley was nineteen years old when he came to Adrian. He fetched up there in the autumn of 1843 because his money had run out; he was unable to continue to Chicago where he was bound except as a hand-to-mouth beggar.

Cooley's odyssey began on his family's farm in western New York near Attica in Wyoming County. His father, Thomas Cooley, Sr., was part of the immigration that swept whole communities from the Berkshires section of Massachusetts in the trans-Appalachian thrust following the War of 1812. Thomas was the tenth of fifteen children in the family. The Cooleys' circumstances were not easy, and all of the children worked, as soon as it was profitable for the family enterprise. But the "crushing" situation alluded to by Cooley's memorialists must be taken with a grain of salt. His father was one of four brothers who settled in Wyoming County. The brothers all "became substantial farmers and men of considerable influence in the neighborhood"; and Thomas Cooley, Sr., himself enjoyed the reputation of being "an upright man . . . respected as a citizen and neighbor." Young Cooley's father was a county political chief, an uncle was a sometime congressional candidate, and an older brother was an editorial writer for a local newspaper. All these elder Cooleys were connected with the radical loco-foco politics of New York State. The memorialists say that the family's grinding circumstances forced the precocious, ambitious boy, buried down in that pack of offspring, to become an autodidact in the Lincoln manner. "It is a tradition that as a boy [Cooley's] evenings were spent [after the day's labor] by the light of the open fire where he would absorb such standard historical authors as good fortune might throw in his way." But the fact is that Cooley regularly attended the district free school, and when he was fifteen years of age he entered the Attica Academy where he was a student for three years, apparently with the family's support. When he was eighteen years old he went to Palmyra to study law with one of the prominent local lawyers, still apparently with his family's blessing, if not their support. Then "suddenly," and according to all the memorialists, inexplicably, young Cooley pulled up stakes and headed west. There is another tradition that there was conflict with Thomas Cooley, Sr., over going to college, which the son dearly wanted to do and which the father opposed. Or maybe it was a matter of young Cooley's "unquenchable ambition." The West beckoned. By the mid-1840s western New York had already passed the flush of growth in which an ambitious young man stood the greatest chance of bending the world to his own desire. At any event, after working for a few months in the Palmyra law office, Cooley struck out for Chicago. He landed in Adrian where, despite being "known as a most intense and rapid worker" and a man who "would work for very little rather than not work," he struggled along for years in his obscure practice.

Finally things began to go in Cooley's favor. Within seven years he moved from the wretched little county courthouses to a seat on the Michigan Supreme Court. In 1857, probably by way of Croswell's political connections, he was commissioned to compile the state laws. He finished the staggering job in a year. He was rewarded by being appointed reporter for the state supreme court, which gave him the opportunity to display his talent for lucid legal expository writing. Two years later he was appointed to the faculty of the new University of Michigan Law School where he took the assignment of teaching constitutional law, the lectures for which provided the basis for his great book. In 1864 he was appointed to the Michigan Supreme Court, a seat he held in conjunction with his professorship for twenty years. In 1868 the first edition of *Constitutional Limitations* appeared. Late in his life Cooley accepted several public service appointments. He was the first chairman of the Interstate Commerce Commission; he also acted as receiver for the bankrupt Wabash Railroad. In the latter instance "his brilliant management of the Wabash system was a revelation in the line of the control of railways. . . . He evolved order out of chaos." Undoubtedly, wrote one of his memorialists, if "a desire to study law [had not] possessed him," Cooley would have made his name and fortune as one of the great financial-industrial barons of the nineteenth century.

But we must come again to origins and to another portion of the world surrounding Thomas Cooley, the only world that he knew for the first nineteen years of his life. In that world, in the almost impenetrable mists surrounding Cooley's beginnings, we may find a substantive thread leading to *Constitutional Limitations* that helps change the "rather one-sided picture" of Cooley and his work that has been given us, and establishes an abolition connection with Cooley's counter to *Das Kapital*.

Attica and Wyoming County, where Thomas Cooley, Sr., settled and where young Cooley was born and grew up, were at the center of New York's Burned-Over District. The peculiar name made reference to the remarkable events that occurred there, to "the fires of the spirit" that blazed through the populace during the second quarter of the nineteenth century and which made the district the epicenter of the "driving propellants of social movements important for the whole country."[11] The district comprised a belt of counties bounding the Erie Canal, the terminus of which was Buffalo where Henry Wright found conclusive proof that wild delirium reigned in America. The canal was the new highway to the West over which swarms of immigrants poured, and along which Cooley traveled as he began his trek that landed him in Adrian.

The district was also America's "psychic highway." It was the well-traveled road of the inhabitants of the district themselves as they made their way toward purification, regeneration, perfection, salvation, all of which were expressive of a social imagination exploring new boundaries of human freedom. As such the district was the "storm center" of the demotic attempts of the first post-Appalachian generation to find alternatives to the shattered world of the fathers. The most extravagant religious revivalism, antimasonry, abolition, millennialism, prohibition, spiritualism, woman's rights, the Mormon church, the Millerites, either in their origins or in their first significant manifestations converged in the Burned-Over District.

According to its historian, anyone growing up there could hardly have escaped the tumults unleashed in the district. The currents of dislocation flowed over all of them and swept them up in a "series of crests in zeal that formed the crescendo phase of a greater cycle [that] reach[ed] a grand climax between 1825 and 1837." "It mattered little [what a person] was nominally"; in the final analysis "the same techniques, the same habits and mannerisms" permeated the many "liberties" being proclaimed on the psychic highway. The central proposition informing the variant forms of the liberterian imagination nourished in this national storm center was that the world is a moral battleground, and the rewards of the world ought to be commensurate with the merits of the spirit. Exposed to all of this, there must have been times when a sensitive, impressionable boy believed the world was swinging from the verge of apocalypse to the threshold of Utopia. In either case, for this was the common lesson taught in the district, the outcome depended upon the actions of autonomous man, and man's free capacity to make choices, which were fundamentally moral choices.

Growing up as these crests in zeal reached their grand climax, and coming of age precisely as the harvest of these whirlwinds of liberterianism were being reaped, young Thomas Cooley could hardly have escaped a consequence of living in the Burned-Over District. He seems to have been prepared to become a rather self-righteous, broad-ranging reformer whose mission was "detect[ing] and right[ing] the wrongs which others do." Some of Cooley's early poetry expresses the ideas being proclaimed in the district. His verse may be read as a Protestant auto-da-fé, with regenerative fires looming in the offing. He evoked populist revolutions that "scourge the land . . . when the People rise and . . . cast the old abuses down." The effect of these old abuses was to make people "paupers" through no fault of their own; and the result of the revolutions is a "pure, and bright and new world" in which there is "room and bread for all" who have freed themselves from "corruptions."[12]

More particularly, growing up in the district young Cooley could hardly have escaped being seared by abolition. In his case there is ample reason to believe there is the strongest connection between a youth moving toward his life work and the work itself, and that *Constitutional Limitations* has deep roots in the abolition fervors surrounding Cooley for the first nineteen years of his life. All of those "driving propellants of social movements important for the whole country" roared through Wyoming County, Attica, and Palmyra. Of the several "movements" left in their wake abolition was especially powerful. Wyoming County was distinguished as an antislavery stronghold in the region that was notable for being abolition's national bastion, and the comparative suggests the intensity with which abolition raged in the county.

Thomas Cooley was born and grew up in the stronghold. For years he must have had abolition's message of human equality drummed into his ears. The abolitionists carrying the message—the itinerants among whom, perhaps, were Henry Wright and the grass-roots locals—were, Cooley later said, "the pioneers in the wilderness of public morality." It was easy for him to believe they were writing a contemporary chapter of the histories that he loved to read in which "his sympathies were always with those struggling for individual and political liberty." The extent to which he associated himself with "the pioneers" is evident in his mature work and was made explicit late in his life. At the flood tide of his career Cooley identified his forerunners, his generation's champions in the historic struggle for "liberty" and "equality." They were the early abolitionists in the District. It was they, Cooley said, who "prepared the way for a day of better things." As he began writing *Constitutional Limitations*, his contribution to the day of better things, the struggle was coming to a climax. When it was over Cooley said of the old abolitionists who had "burned" his community when he was a boy, "We honor them all the more." [13]

The formal structure of Cooley's equal rights ideology with its comprehensive laissez-faire was yet to be erected when he left the District,[14] but the foundation was laid, as was his commitment to an abolition-infused moral politics. The 1848 national election was the first in which Cooley was old enough to vote. From then on he was partisan in the accepted tradition of political abolition. For the 1848 election he was an organizer for the Free Soil party in Michigan. But however promising Free Soil was to strike at the expansion of slavery, it did not propose to drive the attack home. Nor was the party a friend to comprehensive equal rights. Cooley abandoned Free Soil as soon as he had the opportunity. He was involved with Salmon Chase in an abortive attempt to organize an Independent Democratic party that was tougher on slavery and stood squarely on equal rights. He wound up as an early member of the Republican party when it appeared to him that Republicanism offered the best means to strike at slavery and carry an equal rights program nationally. Cooley's entrance into the party coincided with his meteoric rise from obscurity to a position from which he was able to write *Constitutional Limitations*.

Before coming directly to *Constitutional Limitations* it is useful to take some account of the broader context of American law from which Cooley's work emerged, bearing in mind that his work is acknowledged as a crystallization and implementation of "many inchoate elements of theory . . . where legal and economic thought merged," and was the first major attempt to restate American constitutionalism after Appomattox.[15]

When Cooley began his legal study in the Burned-Over District, American law was being transformed, and when he published *Constitutional Limitations* the transformation was virtually complete. An earlier "instrumentalism" was being attacked and displaced by the proponents of a new jurisprudential "style." This instrumentalism was characterized by flexibility; it accommodated antagonistic interests and compromised divisive questions in order to achieve expedient, short-term results. Instrumentalism was a freewheeling jurisprudence, admirably serving some of the pressing needs that accompanied the first rush into post-Appalachian America. But its chief merits were also its greatest liabilities, and by midcentury instrumentalism was particularly vulnerable on two counts. Insofar as it attempted to keep a national legal system operating it had to accommodate slavery, and it was therefore susceptible to being held in complicity with the "slave power." And because it required flexibility, instrumentalism could claim no consistent legal foundation or universal truths in its behalf without stumbling into deep anomalies and contradictions. It had, its detractors claimed, no authority. Instrumentalism was, in short, the antithesis of "formalism," the legal style that was used to attack it and displace it.

Formalism's greatest strength was that it was considered authoritative; it rested on universal truths. Law derived from these authorities was susceptible to uncompromising application. As a rival jurisprudential style, formalism discredited instrumentalism in the prewar fight over slavery, broke its back with the Union victory in 1865, and was regnant in American law until the turn of the twentieth century.

At formalism's heart was an abolitionist constitutionalism. This core of formalism was an expression of human rights stated in legal language. In turn, the matrix of abolition's constitutionalism was not the law but a combination of "lay ethical and moral opinions." It had to be because the law itself simply could not carry the burden abolition placed upon it. The law overwhelmingly supported slavery. Judges hostile to slavery "really squirmed" under the pressures the law placed on them when they were compelled to try slavery cases, chiefly those having to do with fugitive slaves.[16] Abolition lawyers squirmed too. Advocates pleading abolition cases were forced very quickly to shift the grounds of their cases from the authority of the law to the authority of "the higher law," usually expressed as natural rights. Abolition legal theorists were obliged to make the same move. The matter is conveniently illustrated by Salmon Chase, a long-time abolition trial counsel as well as one of abolition's chief constitutional theorists. In the *Mathilda* case, Chase attempted to prove that the Fugitive Slave Act of 1793 was unconstitutional. He began with a constitutional argument which was quickly exhausted, then shifted his ground. "There is," Chase argued, "such a thing as natural rights, derived, not from any constitution or civil code, but from the constitution of human nature and the code of Heaven. [These rights are the same] in all ages . . . and destined to no change. . . . [One of them is] that all men are born equally free." "Interpretation," observed a sympathetic student of abolition's attempt to equip itself with a usable body of law, "is far too dull a word" to describe the "inventive process" by which these theorists served up their "hearty fare of great moral, political, [and] constitutional truths."

Once these "great truths" were invoked the deeper implications of abolition's constitutionalism began to become apparent. Natural rights, "the constitution of human nature and the code of Heaven" apply to all people. By definition, universal authorities extended far beyond issues relating only to blacks, bond and free, they attached to whites as well. As it emerged, abolitionist constitutionalism was encompassing. Its stated aim was to give all

Americans equality before the law. As it matured at the hands of skillful judges "the final product was an extraordinary consistent body of immutable rules" that were applied with "single-line inevitability" to create this legal equality. With the delivery of the final product after Appomattox the achievement of abolition jurisprudence was revealed: the use of the law to impose moral order by "provid[ing] 'final solutions'" to a whole range of problems besetting American society. The legal device employed by the judges was "separat[ing] the public and private sectors into fixed and inviolable spheres." The effect of this separation was to achieve the widest area of human activity in which individual actions would reveal their moral content, and in which the national social preterition would occur. This is also, as Charles McCurdy has said, "the stuff of laissez-faire."

When Thomas Cooley began his law career, advocates of antislavery were beginning to fill both state and federal judicial posts; and, as William Nelson has stated, toward 1870 their ascendancy was almost complete. They were ready to consolidate the victory of the new jurisprudential style. These judges were the ornaments and interpreters of the "enlightened and generous profession" to which Cooley addressed the first edition of *Constitutional Limitations*, and they had, as he modestly said in his second edition, received his work with "unexpected favor."

Constitutional Limitations is prima facie a triumph of the formalistic style; it is also an exposition of abolition's matured constitutionalism. The latter is embedded in the book, and is arrestingly apparent in Cooley's chapter on the "Formation of State Constitutions." Probably written before the Fourteenth Amendment was drafted, this chapter is as expansive a description of equal rights as any abolitionist could have delivered.[17]

The chapter is an examination of what provisions a constitution must contain compelling a state to act unswervingly to serve its citizens. There are five provisions. Four of them having to do with the establishment of representative government are stated briefly and summarily dismissed. It is Cooley's fifth provision that is arresting. Unlike its predecessors, the fifth provision is long and specific. Furthermore, there is a staccato intensity in these passages that distinguish them from the rest of the book, which proceeds at a magisterial leisure. Cooley is hammering here, nailing something down, and clinching it tight. These few pages on the formation of state constitutions is the heart of *Constitutional Limitations*. Everything else—the massive subsequent chapters on protection of persons and property, protections of personal liberty, protection of property, liberty of speech and of the press, religious liberty, and such—hang on what Cooley says here.

This fifth provision is the "declaration of rights for the protection of individuals and minorities" that "not even . . . the largest majority" can overturn. The three sections in the declaration are packed with "general principles," "fundamental rights," and "principles of morality and virtue" that must be constitutionally guaranteed. Twenty-three of these various rights and principles are itemized, but each section ends with the expansive phrase, "the like," which is Cooley's license for constitution-makers to go beyond his list in order to achieve what the declaration strives for, the absolute equality of all "freemen" before the law, with all of these principles, rights, and "the like" placed in the protection of the "iron grasp" of a constitution. Furthermore, in this section there is the clearest signal that abolition's constitutionalism swept far beyond matters of bond slavery and race. Cooley links the rights of individuals with the rights of minorities so they are inseparable. Both individuals and minority collectives, that is, whites and blacks, stand in precisely the same relationship to "exclusive separate public privileges" and "absolute, arbitrary power," of which bond slavery and racial proscription were only two portions. Conflation. The rights of whites and blacks are blown together here, with Negroes' rights being part of a larger realm of rights protected against discriminatory actions by the state.[18]

There is a second feature of this declaration of rights for the protection of individuals and minorities that distinguishes it from the rest of the book; it connects with both Cooley's memorialist's observation that he was less masterful with the "facts" than the "law," and antebellum abolition constitutionalists' general problem. The law not being on their side, they had to resort to other means to support themselves. There is a prodigious scholarship in *Constitutional Limitations.* The corpus of English and American law is laid under tribute, as well as such commentators as Locke, Franklin, Jefferson, Adams, Tocqueville, Bancroft, and Bentham. Practically every page is loaded with citations, the bristling authorities protecting Cooley as he expounds. But in the declaration of the rights for the protection of individuals and minorities the citations dry up and Cooley wings it. He nonetheless remains confident that he is expounding "the settled principles of American constitutional law." In his own language he is "interpreting," not "constructing," the distinction being that interpretation proceeds directly from the text, whereas construction "is the drawing of conclusions respecting subjects that lie beyond the . . . text," from "elements known . . . in the spirit, not in letter." But when Cooley comes to the heart of *Constitutional Limitations* where the rights of individuals and minorities are hammered out, there is no text. He is in the realm of the spirit. He is drawing from his imaginative desires. In his own words, he is at the fountain of law, at the source of all "the latent powers which lie dormant in [the] nation, and [which] are boundless in extent, and incapable of definition." A social vision is being described in the language of the law.

As chief justice of the Michigan Supreme Court, Cooley once found himself at "the fountain." In *People* v. *The Township Board of Salem* he tried a case for which there were no precedents. Unencumbered by the "embarrassment" of any guiding or controlling decisions, he was, he said, able to decide the case solely on principle. Here Cooley could run free and make his own law.[19]

Ostensibly the case was about the state's power to tax. The question was whether, under the authority of state law, the residents of a township had the power to tax themselves in order to float bonds to support railroad construction and thereby use public money for a private profit-seeking enterprise. But Cooley meant to sweep beyond that question. He had his villains, separate public privilege and arbitrary power (in this instance wielded by the majority of the voters in the township), in the dock and he intended to try them and judicially kill them. The case was argued twice, and Cooley subsequently said that he devoted more attention to this case than any he ever tried. Before the reargument Cooley directed a volley of questions at the lawyers that pointed the way he intended to carry the case. He told the lawyers to go beyond the question of the taxing power and study such seemingly irrelevant matters as making treaties, raising armies and navies, and protecting religious freedom. Pulling the other judges along with him—and their opinions show their profound unease with what Cooley was compelling them to confront—Cooley was boxing the compass of the powers of government. But more than laying the ground for establishing the limits of governmental crimping of individual action, Cooley was undertaking the definition of the basic conditions of American society and moving to a law that was descriptive of those "latent powers" in America that previously had been thwarted by special privilege and arbitrary power.

In *Salem* Cooley slid in and out of interpretation and construction with the same ease that distinguishes "the declaration of rights for the protection of individuals and minorities" from the remainder of *Constitutional Limitations.* The "text"—the disputed tax law and the Michigan constitution—barely appears, but Cooley marches serenely on, "interpreting" all the way. Page after page he proceeds, laying down *his* law and interpreting it: "The State can have no favorite." The corollary to his law is likewise succinctly stated and interpreted: the "most urgent needs of society are relegated exclusively to the law of supply and demand." The state's duty is to permit this law "its natural operation." Each instance of the state's proposed impingement of the law of the marketplace must be examined with penetrating care, particularly with an eye for those "convenient fictions" and "fanciful" sophisms that are invoked to justify upsetting the market mechanism, because invariably "discriminations by the State . . . is an invasion of that equality of right and privilege which is a maxim in . . . government. When the door is opened to it, there is no line at which we can stop." Therefore, lest these delicate balancings and "proper proportions" become upset, there must be "inflexible and absolute . . . restraint" against discriminations by the state even if they come at the hands of the political majority.

It is almost beside the point that Salem township could lawfully tax itself in favor of the Detroit and Howell Railroad Company. Cooley was after bigger game than a majority of voters in a township who believed they might benefit themselves by helping a railroad. What Cooley did was canvass from every angle he could imagine—he even managed to bring in racially "impartial accommodations" in public transport—the way people must make their own way in the world, and how "individuals as such" must earn their own "benefits" and rewards. Cooley's opinion in *People* v. *The Township Board of Salem* is a celebration of a social system and a description of the mechanism actuating the system presented as a judge's decision on a contested law. More than a judicial gloss on the social vision described in *Constitutional Limitations*, *Salem* is a work of imaginative writing. Cooley created characters, supplied them with motives, and set them at work. Street scenes in the nation's cities spring to life with bustle and clangor; the wilderness is peopled and brought under cultivation. No one is poor who has not brought it on himself. The day of better things has dawned.

The companion case to *Salem* is *People* v. *The Board of Education of Detroit*. [20] The year before he laid down his comprehensive law about the discriminatory state and the inequalitarian political majority in *Salem*, Cooley struck down racially segregated public schools in Detroit. The Detroit Board of Education claimed it had the authority to systematically segregate the races under a state law permitting certain school districts to organize their schools as they saw fit. Furthermore, the board did not evade the question of why segregation was desirable. A "large majority of the white population of Detroit [has] a strong prejudice or animosity against colored people." This hostility was "transmitted to the children in the schools," and if black children came to white schools there would be "quarrels and contention" and, consequently, the impairment of "the good government and prosperity of the free schools of [the] city."

Cooley would have none of that; he swept aside all of the board's arguments. In his decision he did not equivocate. He applied a variant of those inflexible and absolute restraints against a discriminatory state to which he was committed. Detroit children have "equal right to all the schools, irrespective . . . of race or color, or religious belief, or personal peculiarities." This was, Cooley said, the general application of the Michigan public school law. But it is the specific nature of the case that shows Cooley reaching the limits of his understanding of the meaning and purpose of equality.

The suit was brought to admit a child whose father was "more than one-fourth African"[21] to one of Detroit's graded schools, all of which were exclusively white. Cooley ordered the child admitted. But it was a conditional admission. The curriculum of the graded schools was different from the ungraded schools. The work was stiffer, the pace was swifter, the examinations harder. The graded schools were more a simulacrum of the competitive world outside. Cooley said the black child must "submit to all the rules, examinations and regulations" that were peculiar to the graded school. On condition that the child submitted and survived, he may attend the graded school. Nothing less than equal access to a competitive education was his right. But nothing more. In the final analysis the black child was on the same footing before the state as those "individuals" living at Salem township. They all must make their way by themselves.

As Cooley conflated the rights of whites and blacks in *Constitutional Limitations, People* v. *The Township Board of Salem* may be conflated with *People* v. *The Board of Education of Detroit.* The two cases are variants of the same text, Cooley's law that the state cannot play favorites, and the conflation is further evidence that the goal of abolition jurisprudence extended beyond securing blacks' legal equality.

It is right to read *Constitutional Limitations* as an attempt to consolidate the victory achieved by the Civil War; surely it is the legal implementation of many of the elements that fed the conflict and produced the victory. But to read the book as the legal *summa* for an unrestricted industrialism, or as antimajoritarian capitalism's response to Marx's *Das Kapital,* is to mistake what Cooley was after and to miss how the work was intended to be a contribution to the "better things." Like *Das Kapital, Constitutional Limitations* is informed by a dialectical process. Both Marx and Cooley presume historical social warfare with the possession of property being a vital ingredient in the conflict. Throughout *Constitutional Limitations* "liberty" and "equality"[22] collide against "exclusive separate public privilege" and "absolute arbitrary power." In each instance the strength and authority of noxious privilege and power are crimped, and the gains made by liberty and equality are consolidated within a constitution's "iron grasp." In effect, *Constitutional Limitations* described a battleground that was constantly shrinking as Cooley's protagonists moved toward their final victory, the climax of which came with "the liberty [Cooley] valued most . . . being achieved on the battlefields of the Civil War."[23]

Foremost, *Constitutional Limitations* is an ethical and moral tract. It is a meditation written in legal language on human freedom and the connection between human action and consequences. What Cooley did was use the law in an attempt to guarantee freedom in order that action and consequence would be brought into an unsullied relationship. Never before in human history had such a condition existed. Now for the first time—and with "single-line inevitability"—people would get what they morally deserved. This was the end to which the struggle for individual and political liberty was directed, and it was to this end that the abolitionists had pioneered in the wilderness of public morality. Now the wilderness was burned out. The land was ready for the new planting. It remained only to keep the tares from the fields.

Coda

The elements of abolition that Cooley crystallized came to their full-blown constitutional implementation in *Lochner* vs. *New York*. Lochner, having to do with a state regulating the number of hours bakers might make bread, came before the Supreme Court toward the turn of the century. Characteristically the case finds its way into the history books as a stalking-horse. The court majority striking down the New York bakers' law is set up for Oliver Wendell Holmes, Jr.'s dissenting apothegem: "The Fourteenth Amendment does not enact Mr. Herbert Spencer's *Social Statics.*" Holmes said, "A constitution is not intended to embody a particular economic theory, whether for paternalism and the organic relation of the citizen to the state or for laissez-faire. . . . I think that the word 'liberty,' in the 14th Amendment, is perverted when it is held to prevent the natural outcome of a dominant opinion."

With *Lochner* it seems that the trajectory of Cooley's "Day of Better Things" reaches apogee. Holmes's dissent is much like a gravitational pull that is at last overcoming velocity, anticipating the last straining toward outward limits before course is deflected and arc develops. Or, to shift metaphors, *Lochner* signals the end of post-Appalachian America. The fathers have now been transmogrified into the founders. Their emotionally orphaned children have been forgotten or canonized, and their psychic wound has become incorporated in mythopoeic history. There are new wounds, and the Holmes dissent prescribes the programmatic lenitive. Or so it may be made out to be.

But on close inspection Holmes proves to be a dubious guide. Before he finished his dissent he had become so equivocal that it is obvious he was on something deeply troubling, something that defied his own analytical powers and his resourcefulness with the language. *Lochner* was not, Holmes said, simply an "economic" decision; even if it were solely that, he said, he "should desire to study it further and long before making up my mind." What was at the heart of *Lochner*, Holmes said, was "a judgment or intuition more subtle than any articulate premise." He as much as said that he was groping toward something beyond the competence of the law, something lying beneath the threshold of consciousness, something outside rationality itself.

Lochner turns on the question of what a people might legally do. But in his dissent Holmes was trying to answer the question of what a people ought to do. Presently he gave up his struggle to get at what was troubling him and reverted to the language of the law. But we can catch him trying to shape intuition into an articulate premise if we read in full his sentence about perverting the meaning of liberty, "I think that the word 'liberty,' in the 14th Amendment, is perverted when it is held to prevent the natural outcome of a dominant opinion, unless it can be said that a rational and fair man necessarily would admit that the statute proposed would infringe fundamental principles as they have been understood by the traditions of our people and our law."

And who was more rational and fair-minded than Justice

Holmes? Who better knew fundamental principles as they have been understood by the traditions of our people than Captain Holmes, shot in the chest and in the stomach at Balls Bluff, in the neck at Antietam, in the leg at Chancellorsville, the young Union officer wounded beyond belief as his Brahmin father was making common cause with Moncure Conway and Conway's "various unknown dingy-linened friends of progress?"

Notes

INTRODUCTION

1. James M. McPherson, *The Abolitionist Legacy: From Reconstruction to the NAACP* (Princeton, N.J.: Princeton University Press, 1975), 4–5. See also David B. Davis, "Anti-slavery or Abolition," *Reviews in American History*, I (March, 1973), 95–99.
2. Jane H. Pease and William H. Pease, *They Who Would Be Free: Blacks' Search for Freedom, 1830–1861* (New York: Atheneum, 1974), 3–16.

MISSION TO ENGLAND

1. Moncure Conway Diary, April 21, 1863, in Moncure D. Conway, *Autobiography, Memories and Experiences* (Boston: Houghton Mifflin, 1904), I, 389.
2. Frank P. Stearns, *The Life and Public Services of George Luther Stearns* (Philadelphia: J. B. Lippincott, 1907), 274. Stearns refers to a series of dinner parties attended by his father, George Luther Stearns, Wendell Phillips, Emerson, and Conway. Inasmuch as Stearns was nursing a longstanding grudge against Conway, this was lavish praise indeed.

3. *Atlantic Monthly*, X (November, 1862), 644–46.

4. Conway, *Autobiography*, I, 388.

5. Conway was scheduled to stay abroad until October, 1863. Ralph Waldo Emerson to William Emerson, March 11, 1863, in Ralph Rusk (ed.), *The Letters of Ralph Waldo Emerson* (New York: Columbia University Press, 1939), V, 319.

6. Aileen S. Kraditor, *Means and Ends in American Abolition: Garrison and His Critics on Strategy and Tactics, 1834–50* (New York: Vintage, 1970), 18–19.

7. *Ibid.*, 212.

8. Wendell Phillips, *Speeches, Lectures, and Letters* (Boston: Lee and Shepard, 1884), 396–414. James M. McPherson, *The Struggle for Equality: Abolitionists and the Negro in the Civil War and Reconstruction* (Princeton, N.J.: Princeton University Press, 1964), 29–51.

9. Phillips, *Speeches*, 414. Emphasis added.

10. *Ibid.*, 243–44: Robert D. Marcus, "Wendell Phillips and American Institutions," *Journal of American History*, LVI (June, 1969), 41–58.

11. The importance that Phillips and Conway's other backers attached to his mission is suggested in a speech Phillips made at the time Conway was recruited to go to England: "The South stands with both hands, holding loaded revolvers, and, lest she should lose any time [reloading the revolvers], John Bull is behind with additional pistols to hand the moment she needs them." Phillips, *Speeches*, 553.

12. The account of Conway in England is based on *Autobiography*, I, 390–432. All quotations are from this source.

13. The reaction may be followed in the *New York Tribune*, June 30, July 1, July 2, 1863. Almost fifty years after the event the episode was still so nettlesome that the old warriors were still trying to dissociate themselves from it. Stearns, *The Life and Public Service of George Luther Stearns*, 263–64.

14. Here it is important to distinguish between *opportunity* and *test*. The opportunity to strike an anti-institutional stance (perhaps a pose) exits when the institutions themselves are not endangered. At such time the luxury of destructive rhetoric is possible. Conversely the test comes when institutions are in perceived danger, when the rhetoric itself might be fulfilled. The disunionists were confronted twice with the test: at the time of Lincoln's response to the Fort Sumter attack and when they learned of Conway's challenge.

15. David Herreshoff, *American Disciples of Marx: From the Age of Jackson to the Progressive Era* (Detroit: Wayne State University Press, 1967), 30, 48–52.

VIRGINIA

1. This is Conway's estimate of his father's estate. The 1860 census lists the value of Walker P. Conway's real property at $6,000, his personal property at $20,000. Free Population Schedule, Stafford County, Va., Census, 1860, p. 819.

2. Margaret Conway to Conway, November 6 [1855?], in Conway Collection, Columbia University. Hereinafter, unless otherwise specified all Conway letters are from the Columbia University Collection.

3. *Ibid.*, October 10, 1855.

4. *Ibid.*, March 24, October, 1855.

5. *Ibid.*, July 10, 1857.

6. Conway, *Autobiography*, I, 6.

7. Walker Peyton Conway to Conway, September 18, 1854. It is worth noting that the Conway slaves were augmented over the years, thus affirming Walter Peyton Conway's allegiance to the slave system. In 1840 he owned nine slaves; in 1850, twenty-three; in 1860, twenty-eight. Of the 461 slaveholders in Stafford County in 1860, only 16 owned more slaves than he.

Some puzzlements lie embedded in these stark census data. The sex-age distributions—

indicators of presumptive fertility—of the Conway slaves for this twenty-year period raise questions about the slaves' increase. For example, in 1840 Conway owned three male slaves, two of whom were over twenty years old. In 1850 he owned eleven males, five of whom were over twenty years old and Charles Humstead, who would have been over twenty years old in 1850, had been sold because of his incendiary prank. Where have the three "new" adult males come from? The presumption is that Conway was actively acquiring slave property, in the face of his wife's express misgivings.

One also wonders what else might lie in these census data. In the 1840 census Walker Conway's household listing is put toward the middle of the Stafford County returns. In 1860, although twenty-eight people in Stafford County are credited with owning property of a greater value than he, his name leads the list. Is it random chance, or does the census taker have a keen sense for the grades and subleties in the Falmouth-Stafford County pecking order, and in 1860 puts Conway first among the county's leading property holders? Population Schedule, Stafford County, Virginia Census 1840; Free Population Schedules, Stafford County, Virginia Census, 1850 and 1860; Slave Schedules, Stafford County, Virginia Census, 1850 and 1860.

These data also illustrate the temptations that beset a polemicist. Compare them with the portrait Conway drew of his home and Stafford County when he was on the English mission during the Civil War. In *Testimonies Concerning Slavery* Conway is the expert witness; he proposes to tell the English only what he knows firsthand "from a region where Slavery exists in its mildest form." Falmouth and Stafford County are inhabited by two classes, "the very rich," of which there are "five or six" persons, and the "very poor." Walker Conway is one of the rich, and he is given ownership of "fifty or sixty" slaves; although he is describing the Falmouth of his childhood, a time when his father owned ten slaves. Moncure Conway, *Testimonies Concerning Slavery* (London: Chapman and Hall, 1864), 1–3.

8. Margaret Conway to Conway, July 5, 1856, September 30, 1862.

9. *Ibid.*, November 6 [1855?]. It is this letter that provides the justification for locating Margaret Conway's hostility to slavery before the mid-1850s, when her extant letters show it.

10. Conway, *Autobiography*, I, 6.

11. The single instance in which Conway produces his mother as a witness against slavery is *after* he became an abolitionist.

12. Walker Peyton Conway to Conway September 18, 1854.

13. George M. Frederickson, *The Inner Civil War: Northern Intellectuals and the Crisis of the Union* (New York: Harper and Row, 1968), 126.

14. The book finally begins to charm out of its sheer implausibility. For example, Thoreau stops a lynch mob in its tracks by calling out, "Doubtless . . . you all remember that fine passage in the Bhagavadgita where Krishna says to Arjuna, Thou and I have met many times.' [After that abjuration] The mob was breathless. . . . The ringleaders vainly tried to rally their forces."

15. Conway's biographer summarily judges *Pine and Palm* in a brief paragraph. "It was a passable little tale set in the years of the Civil War [actually, it concludes before the war breaks out]. Although his practice of drawing heavily and obviously on his own experiences for scenes and characters lent a certain realism to his work, Conway did not have the artist's ability to heighten and deepen experience until it bore the stamp of truth. He was inclined to confound actuality with reality. If *Pine and Palm* proved anything, it was that Conway was not a novelist." Mary Elizabeth Burtis, *Moncure Conway, 1832–1907* (New Brunswick: Rutgers University Press, 1952), 201. For an alternative interpretation, one that makes the novel an exercise in ideology, see Frederickson, *Inner Civil War*, 126–27.

16. Margaret Conway to Conway, undated [October, 1855?], and October 10, 1855, in which she says, "Your father has assigned me the encourager, if not the originator, of your [rebelliousness]."

17. Mary E. Burtis, "Moncure Conway: Earthward Pilgrim," in *John and Mary's College: The Boyd Lee Spahr Lectures in Americana, 1951–1956* (Westwood, N.J.: Fleming H. Revel, 1956), 249.

18. Toward the end of his life Conway repaid his debt to Elizabeth Daniel. She was the granddaughter of Edmund Randolph, who was the first attorney general of the United States and later secretary of state whose career had been wrecked by charges of peculation and treason. Conway wrote a biography that was intended to clear Elizabeth Daniel's grandfather from any taint of these ancient impeachments. A work of "love and justice," the *Randolph* was a long delayed acknowledgment of this woman who had "honored" him "with her attention, intelligence and culture," and had given him his first encouragement to write, to get things down on paper as precisely as he could—to *work* at thinking. Moncure Conway, *Omitted Chapters of History Disclosed in the Life and Papers of Edmund Randolph* (New York: Putnam's, 1888), vi.

19. The phrase is Herman Hesse's by which he means the epiphanylike experience of a youth, when, in the most unexpected circumstances, a boy suddenly glimpses his own future. It is revealed to him what he wants to do, and what he will do. He knows what his vocation is.

THE MORAL CHOICE

1. Charles C. Sellers, *Dickinson College: A History* (Middletown, Conn.: Wesleyan University Press, 1973), 195–229.

2. Conway Journal, January 9, 1848, in Conway Collection.

3. For some elliptical evidence suggesting the contrary, see Conway to Ellen Dana, November 18, 1857, Conway to Ellen Conway, January 22, 1862, in Conway Collection.

4. [Moncure Conway] "Flirtation: Being an Essay by a New Contributor," *Southern Literary Messenger*, XV (June, 1849), 345–49.

5. For the short stories, see Conway Journal, December–January, 1847–48. Conway mentions the novel, unfortunately destroyed, in a letter to his sister, Mildred Conway Sawyer, April 16, 1897, cited in Burtis, *Conway*, 15.

6. Conway Journal, January 7–March 21, 1848.

7. "Notes About Carlisle," *ca.* 1848–49, quoted in *Autobiography*, I, 56. Italics added.

8. I have been unable to find the story in the *Herald* for 1846, and have relied on Conway's precis, *Autobiography*, I, 63.

9. Walker Peyton Conway to Conway, September 18, 1845.

10. For the revelation and the skylark vision, see Conway, *Autobiography* I, 78–79. My analysis of this episode centers on the continuation of the adolescent revival of the Oedipal conflict. According to Bruno Bettelheim, the renewal of the conflict "depends very much on the structure of family and society" insofar as they augment and support a parent's insistent demand for obedience. In the case of the Conways these structures could certainly support the father's implacable desire for his son, irrespective of the role played by the mother. By way of qualifying the interpretation I have placed on *Pine and Palm*, I want to suggest that Monc's conflict with his father was perhaps as much of a struggle to *free* his mother's body, as a fight *for* it. Bruno Bettelheim, "The Problem of Generations" in Erik H. Erikson (ed.), *The Challenge of Youth* (New York: Doubleday, 1965), 82–83.

11. Moncure Conway, *Free Schools in Virginia: A Plea of Education, Virtue and Thrift vs. Ignorance, Vice, and Poverty* Fredericksburg: n.p., 1850). For fifty-three printed pages he argued the need for a statewide public school system. Conventional in its mode—basic principles first established: "Education is the injunction of Nature"; "This law of nature is a Duty"; then on to specifics: *e.g.* a refutation of the morally damaging effects "from the promiscuous association of boys and girls" in school—*Free Schools* is a showcase for Monc's talents and abilities, as well as his catholic reading habits. He writes a graceful lucid polemic,

touching all bases from abstract humane duty, native historical pride to self-interest. He rings in as some of his sources and authorities, Horace in the original, Schiller in translation, Henning's *Statutes*, the *Edinburgh Review*, the *Westminster Review*, Redgrave's *Report on Crime*, and Horace Mann's *Reports*, a paper on "the gold formation of Virginia" published by the Assembly of the American Scientific Convention, and even manages to work in such esoterica as Henry IV's sumptuary law against wearing jewelry, and the incidence of witches and vampires in Servia [sic] and Wallachia.

12. For Janney's activities, see Patricia Hicklin, "Gentle Agitator: Samuel M. Janney and the Antislavery Movement in Virginia, 1842–1851," *Journal of Southern History*, XXXVII (May, 1971), 159–90.

13. [Moncure Conway], "A Webster Case in Europe," *Southern Literary Messenger*, XVII (January, 1851), 50–54. The story takes an epistolary form. A European is corresponding with his American friend. The letter is submitted to *S.L.M.* by the American, "M.C., Warrenton, Va., October 1850."

14. This recalls a similar function of the orphan device in *Pine and Palm*.

15. Moncure Conway, "Diversity of [the] Origins of Races—Slavery," December, 1850, in Conway Collection.

16. William Stanton, *The Leopard's Spots: Scientific Attitudes Toward Race in America, 1815–59* (Chicago: University of Chicago Press, 1960), 110–12.

17. *Ibid.*, passim; Frank W. Ryan, "The Southern Quarterly Review, 1842–1857: A Study in Thought and in the Old South" (Ph.D. dissertation, University of North Carolina, 1956), 284–85, 353–57. See also George M. Frederickson, *The Black Image in The White Mind: The Debate on Afro-American Character and Destiny, 1817–1914* (New York: Harper and Row, 1971), 71–96.

18. Ryan, "Southern Quarterly Review," 284, 300.

19. Walker Peyton Conway to Conway, September 18, 1854, in Conway Collection.

20. *Autobiography*, I, 94.

21. The exception seems to have been a sermon Monc preached against dancing. "Hearing that some Methodist young ladies had danced at a ball, I preached so severely against such pleasures that the family resented it and joined another church."

22. Moncure D. Conway, *Emerson at Home and Abroad* (Boston: J. R. Osgood, 1882), 5.

23. Dickson D. Bruce, Jr., *And They All Sang Hallelujah: Plain-Folk Camp-Meeting Religion, 1800–1845* (Knoxville: University of Tennessee Press, 1974), 61–95.

24. The Conway-Emerson letters are in the Conway Collection.

25. He also exonerates himself from the accusation that he left the Methodists because he "aspired to something grander than life" with them. The Methodists did not give him up without retaliation. See the reference to the Methodist newspaper *Zion's Herald* in which parting shots are aimed at him, in *Autobiography*, I, 130.

26. Emphasis added. This passage is elided when portions of the letter are quoted in Burtis, *Conway*, 27–28.

27. It is well to remember that the "mark of Cain" was not, as is often thought, a brand for being a murderer. It was God's guarantee of safety for the murderer.

28. Conway to Emerson, March 3, 1854.

29. I am suggesting that Monc made only a partial identification with Cain. The nature of his "sin" is different from Cain's. Thus: "I heard the Voice of God saying [to me for my sin] as It did to Cain for his sin—'I will set a mark on thee.'"

These matters are, of course, partially speculative and the interpretation I have offered is arguable. But any alternative interpretation must answer this question: Why, when he wrote about his "rack and thumbscrew" time, did Conway suppress the "Voice of God" letter, which describes and illustrates his torment?

The "Cain" (*i.e.* the murderous son) interpretation also adds another dimension to Monc's struggle to free himself from "the God of the creeds." It is this God Who licenses the "parricide" that Monc will undertake through his ministry and Who guarantees Monc's safety after the assault. God therefore becomes deeply implicated in Monc's "murderous" actions; indeed He compels Monc to persist in them and bring out in the open that which previously was disguised and maybe even unconscious. No wonder Monc cries out that his ideas of "Good & Evil" are confused; and what better way to mitigate the horror of confronting what he really wants to do than by holding the God of the creeds responsible for his actions?

30. Emphasis added.

31. Erik H. Erikson, *Childhood and Society* (New York: Norton, 1963), 257. The phrases are taken from Erikson's theoretical formulation which offers an explanation for the origins of moralistic surveillance, prohibition, and a "self-righteousness... most intolerantly turned against others," all of which traits Monc abundantly displayed. The formulation is richly suggestive relative to Monc, though I have not attempted in any rigorous way to apply Erikson's "blueprint of the life-stages" to him.

32. *Christian Advocate and Journal*, August 12, 1852 to February 10, 1853, with installments bearing such titles as "history," "Machinery," "Appliances," "Bane and Antidote."

33. Reading about "Jesuitism" in *Autobiography* one would never suspect that it is sheer ferocity. "Jesuitism" is presented as another step in the development of the gentle, sweet-tempered young man of rational goodwill whose only concern, as he frees himself from the dogmas, is the heartbreak he inflicts upon his parents.

34. Moncure Conway, "Children and Their Literature," *Southern Literary Messenger*, XVIII (November, 1852), 681–85. *Autobiography* does not mention "Children."

35. Emphasis added.

36. In *Autobiography* Conway presents his "new ideas on Slavery" as an accomplished fact. His "abolitionism" appears full-blown without any hint or warning of its development or coming.

NORTH

1. For example, the *Atlantic Monthly's* claims about his *Rejected Stone* and *Golden Hour*.

2. Oliver Wendell Holmes to John L. Motley, February 3, 1862, in John T. Morse, *The Life and Letters of Oliver Wendell Holmes* (Boston: Houghton Mifflin, 1896), II, 162–63; A. N. Wright *et al* to Conway, August 18, 1856, in Conway Collection. The judge was Benjamin Curtis, who commended Conway's sermons to Holmes. In the *Autobiography*, Conway says of the summer and fall of 1856's "Letters from eminent men in all parts of the country brought me daily applause," I, 246.

3. Holmes to Motley, February 3, 1862, in Morse, *Life and Letters of Oliver Wendell Holmes*.

4. But for other frictions on the Commonwealth see Conway Journal, February 6, 1863.

5. Conway Journal, May 3, 1853.

6. Of particular help in sorting through these relationships is Lewis Perry, *Radical Abolitionism: Anarchy and the Government of God in Antislavery Thought* (Ithaca, N.Y.: Cornell University Press, 1973), esp. 55–91.

7. Walker Conway to Conway, September 18, 1854, Margaret Conway to Conway, March 24, October, 1855, July 5, 1856, in Conway Collection.

8. Margaret Conway to Conway, November 6, [1856]. An elided version of this letter is in the *Autobiography*, I, 249–50; the "pining" sentence is from Margaret Conway to Conway, July 5, 1856, in Conway Collection.

9. Margaret Conway to Conway, June 2, 1857, in Conway Collection.

10. *Ibid.*, February 17, July 10, 1857. With the letter of the latter date—written a year before the marriage—the correspondence between mother and son seems to have ended. There is one subsequent letter (September 30, 1862) in which she says that she reads the

Commonwealth with "avidity"; it is the "connecting link" between them. And there is a final letter (May 4, 1883) in which Conway says to her, "My heart goes out to you with a love beyond my power to write." Thus the bulk of the Margaret Daniel Conway correspondence comes at the time between what she called Conway's "transition" to radical abolition and his announcement of his intention to marry.

These are remarkable letters in which three distinct persons are revealed: mother, lover, and one of God's true suffering saints. If I have emphasized her as lover, it is because I believe that it was in that role that her son developed his relationship with her. But she is a striking person in her own right, as I have tried to suggest earlier in this essay. Gentle, of massive integrity, wise (for example, she sees clearly her son's driving ambitions, and fears them for his sake), and of great quiet courage, when Virginia seceded she seems to have exiled herself from Falmouth. She lived in Maryland with her daughter Mildred, whom she called an old fogey for opposing the Emancipation Proclamation.

11. Ralph Waldo Emerson to Ellen Emerson, July 17, 1863 in Rusk, *Emerson Letters*, V, 333.

THE WAX DOLL AND THE COVENANTERS' DAUGHTER

1. Jane Grey Swisshelm to George W. Julian, February 3, 1877, in George W. Julian Collection, Library of Congress. Apart from the bracketed insertions I have made no editorial corrections of the letter.

2. Julian to Swisshelm, February 14, 1877, in Julian Collection.

3. All quotations in this chapter are from Jane Swisshelm's autobiography, *Half a Century*, unless otherwise annotated.

4. W. Melancthon Glasgow, *History of the Reformed Presbyterian Church in America: With Sketches of All Her Ministry, Congregations, Missions, Institutions, Etc., and Embellished with Over Fifty Portraits and Engravings* (Baltimore: Hill and Harvey, 1888), 75–81, 368–77, and *passim*; Leonard J. Trinterud, *The Forming of an American Tradition: A Re-Examination of Colonial Presbyterianism* (Philadelphia: Westminster Press, 1949), 47–48, 137–65, and *passim*.

5. Jane's Biblical reference, which is garbled, is to the Song of Songs, 6:13. *Shunamite* is properly *Shulamite*, a "maiden"; but a "company of two armies" is correct. The verse opens to a long passage in which the writer evokes the maiden in lush, erotic imagery. The story of the Shulamite is about "sensuous, youthful, passionate love; love that is 'hungry as the Sea.'" Jane therefore intimates what I have suggested, an erotic woman in conflict with an austere daughter of Calvin.

6. Richard C. Wade, *The Urban Frontier: Pioneer Life in Early Pittsburgh, Cincinnati, Lexington, Louisville, and St. Louis* (Chicago: University of Chicago Press, 1964), 39–49, and especially, 166–69.

7. Glasgow, *Reformed Presbyterian Church*, 440–42.

8. *Ibid.*, 79. For a summary of the religious aspects of generic abolition of which the New Light Covenanters might provide a case study, see Cushing Strout, *The New Heaven and New Earth: Political Religion in America* (New York: Harper and Row, 1974), 158–72.

9. Glasgow, *Reformed Presbyterian Church*, 87–101.

10. *Swisshelm* v. *Swisshelm*, 56 Penna. 475ff. (1868).

11. Wade, *Urban Frontier*, 327–30.

12. *Dollar Newspaper*, December 6, 20, 1843, with the identifying initials J.[ennie] D.[eans].

13. *Saturday Museum* [the predecessor to the *Gazette*], June 5, 1844; *Dollar Newspaper*, June 12, 1844.

14. The "Black Gag," properly a General Conference resolution, forbade Negro Methodists from testifying against white Methodists in a church trial in any state that prohibited Negro testimony against whites in civil courts.

15. Another way the connection between abolition and woman's rights might be explored is suggested by Ann Dummett, "Racism and Sexism: A False Analogy," *New Blackfriars,* LXI (November, 1975), 484–92.

THE *Visiter*

1. James Philip Hyatt, "Jeremiah," in *The Interpreter's Bible; The Holy Scriptures in The King James and Revised Standard Versions with General Articles and Introduction, Exegesis, Exposition for each book of The Bible* (New York and Nashville: Abington Press, 1954), V, 782.

2. Contradictory evidence comes from *The History of Pittsburgh and Environs* (New York: American Historical Society, 1922), II, 452–57. Without reference, the editors say that the *Visiter* was financed by Charles Avery, a Pittsburgh manufacturer and abolitionist. There is no mention of Avery or any other subsidizers in *Half a Century* or in the *Visiter* itself. Swisshelm always claimed that she was indebted to no person or organizations for financial support. If Avery did subvent the *Visiter,* he was one of the most silent partners there ever was in American journalism.

3. Probably there was another reason for Swisshelm's selling the *Visiter.* The birth of her only child, a daughter whom she called Zoe, coincided with the sale of the paper. While Jane makes no mention of the child's birth in her account of disposing of the paper, one cannot help but believe that it was important, perhaps crucial, to her decision. At last, after sixteen years of marriage, she had borne "a living child." She had to that extent fulfilled her conception of herself as a woman. And she meant to play the role of mother as fully and as unencumbered as possible.

4. No copy of the offending issue survives. Jane apparently destroyed all copies she could lay her hands on. The edition is even missing from her personal collection bound in the Minnesota Historical Collection.

5. Eleanor Flexner, *Century of Struggle: The Woman's Rights Movement in the United States* (New York: Atheneum, 1968), 84.

6. Amelia Bloomer to Jane G. Swisshelm, August 28, 1880; Frances E. Willard to Jane G. Swisshelm, November 26, 1880, in Mitchell Papers, Minnesota Historical Society.

7. Elizabeth Cady Staton et al., *The History of Woman Suffrage* (Rochester, N.Y.: Charles Mann), I, 387.

8. The following account is drawn from Leland D. Baldwin, *Pittsburgh: The Story of a City* (Pittsburgh: University of Pittsburgh Press, 1937), 221–28; and *The History of Pittsburgh and Environs* (New York: American Historical Society, 1922), II, 452–57. For a careful analysis of the relationship between Pittsburgh social conditions and politics, see Michael Holt, *Forging a Majority: The Formation of the Republican Party in Pittsburgh, 1848–1860* (New Haven: Yale University Press, 1969).

9. Baldwin, *Pittsburgh,* 222.

10. For perceptive observations on the abolitionists' doomsday scenario with its interchangeable secular devils and saints, see David B. Davis, *The Slave Power Conspiracy and the Paranoid Style* (Baton Rouge: Louisiana State University Press, 1969), esp. 62–86. See also David B. Davis, "Some Themes of Counter-Subversion: An Analysis of Anti-Masonic, Anti-Catholic, and Anti-Mormon Literature," *Mississippi Valley Historical Review,* XLVII (1960), 205–24.

ST. CLOUD

1. William B. Mitchell, *History of Stearns County Minnesota* (Chicago: H. C. Cooper, 1915), II, 1404–1406.

2. Daniel S. B. Johnston, "A Red River Townsite Speculation in 1857," *Minnesota Historical Society Collections*, XV (1909–14), 411–34; Mitchell, *History of Stearns County*, II, 1404–1406. Mitchell is especially useful because he was Swisshelm's nephew. As a teenager he helped her publish the *Visiter*, and in 1863 she either sold or gave the newspaper to him.

3. Mitchell, *Stearns County*, II, 1404–1406. Brott's railroads were less "imaginary" than visionary. At this time the federal government was making millions of acres of public land available to the territory as railroad grants. Unlike the usual practice of giving a state or a territory a specific amount of public land which in turn was disposed by the legislature, the law designated "in general way the routes of the roads to be built." One of these routes was to serve the northern frontier, angling toward the Canadian border, and Brott hoped to bring it through St. Cloud, linking the "embryo metropolises" he was laying out. When the business was done St. Cloud was on the route opening railroad communications between St. Paul and Canada. To that extent Brott's *Advertiser* had served its purpose, and Sylvanus Lowry had done his job. William W. Folwell, *History of Minnesota* (St. Paul: Minnesota Historical Society, 1921), II, 37–39. See also his "The Five Million Loan," *Minnesota Historical Collections*, XV (1909–15), 189–214.

4. Information about the Lowrys is drawn from Folwell, *History of Minnesota*, II, 28; W. H. C. Folsom, *Fifty Years in the Northwest* (N.p.: Pioneer Press, 1888), 25; William B. Mitchell, "St. Cloud in the Territorial Period," *Minnesota Historical Society Collections*, XII, 639; Minnesota Special Census, Stearns County, 1857.

5. Mitchell, "St. Cloud in the Territorial Period," 639. See also his *Stearns County*, 326–37.

6. Folwell, *History of Minnesota*, II, 37–39.

7. There was still another Swisshelm relative in the migration. James McKelvy was James Swisshelm's nephew. He was a young lawyer who began his practice in St. Cloud in 1857. Whether he migrated with the Mitchell-Swisshelm group or followed them is not clear. Mitchell, *History of Stearns County*, I, 530–31.

8. Quoted in Folwell, *History of Minnesota*, I, 403–404.

9. Rebecca M. Cathcart, "A Sheaf of Remembrances," *Minnesota Historical Society Collections*, XV, 530.

10. *Half a Century*, of course, makes no suggestion that there was a connection between Swisshelm's decision to return to the public life and her conviction that she had irretrievably lost James. She leads the reader to believe that the break was permanent when she left Pittsburgh. But to accept her version is to neglect the only piece of evidence describing her intentions at the time. When she arrived at St. Paul and was interviewed by a writer for a local newspaper, she was reported as saying that she intended to "make her residence in this territory for one year." St. Paul *Daily Pioneer and Democrat*, June 23, 1857, quoted in George S. Hage, *Newspapers on the Minnesota Frontier, 1849–1860* (St. Paul: Minnesota Historical Society, 1967), 83. See also, Daniel S. B. Johnston, "Minnesota Journalism from 1858 to 1865," *Minnesota Historical Society Collections*, XII, 188.

11. Johnston, "A Red River Townsite Speculation in 1857," p. 434.

12. Information about Miller is drawn from Mitchell, *Stearns County*, I, 324; Folwell, *History of Minnesota*, II, 335; St. Cloud *Visiter*; St. Cloud *Democrat*.

13. Sylvanus Lowry to Jane Grey Swisshelm, 1862 [?], quoted in *Half a Century*, 233. Emphasis added.

14. Mitchell, *Stearns County*, I, 171.

15. Mitchell, *Stearns County*, II, 1404–1406. Sources give varying accounts of how Swisshelm came to own the *Visiter*. I have followed Mitchell's version because I have found him the most reliable on other counts. The best alternative account has Brott retaining ownership of the physical plant and giving her editorial control and full financial responsibility for the

paper. Regardless of the variations, all sources agree on the fundamental point: she was free to publish whatever she wanted.

16. Agur is the unidentifiable author of Proverbs 30. Swisshelm's allusion possibly provides come clues to her mind in December, 1857. Probably her reference relates to the eighth verse in which Agur wants "neither poverty or riches"; that is, she is neither rich nor poor. She has some money that might be used as working capital for a newspaper, but not much. Of more interest is the mood of the short chapter. There are sufficient passages in it to suggest that Agur is much on her mind, because the writer speaks so clearly to her as she comes to realize that she has lost James forever. The exegete finds the thrust of the chapter in the direction of the "insatiable" (the "barren womb"), the "incomprehensible" ("the way of a man with a maid"), and the "unsupportable" ("an unloved woman"). He also finds much of the chapter "difficult," "unquestionable," and "conjectural." Therefore to attempt to find anything like a conclusive reason for the reference to Agur is a parlous undertaking. Nevertheless one must wonder why, as she was making the most mundane calculations about type fonts, subscription lists, and such, the obscure Agur and the message about a relationship between a man and a woman, flashed through her mind.

17. John H. Randall, "The Beginning of Railroad Building in Minnesota," *Minnesota Historical Society Collections*, XV, 216.

18. Johnston, "A Red River Townsite Speculation in 1857," 433–34.

19. Folwell, *History of Minnesota*, II, 34.

20. Johnston, "A Red River Townsite Speculation in 1857," 421; Mitchell, *Stearns County*, I, 185.

21. Folwell, *History of Minnesota*, II, 33.

22. This and the preceding paragraph are based upon Cathcart, "Sheaf of Remembrances," 515–52.

23. Mitchell, *Stearns County*, II, 1077–78, quoting a "contemporary."

24. The following account is based upon Mitchell, *Stearns County*, II, 1434–46; and the two volumes, *passim*, for information relating to individual settlers.

25. In *Half a Century* Swisshelm glosses the threat: "If you ever again attempt to publish a paper in St. Cloud, you yourself will be as summarily dealt with as your office has been." The gloss is necessary in order to keep the threat within the context she chose to present the fight; as a contest between slavery and freedom, and freedom of the press versus oppression of speech—in short, vital issues of principle. With these at stake she could scarcely permit the *Visiter* to be described as a "nuisance" or let the brothel imagery suggest that she was engaged in a bitter personal quarrel that had nothing to do with "principle."

26. Russel B. Nye, *Fettered Freedom: Civil Liberties and the Slavery Controversy 1830–1860* (East Lansing: Michigan State College Press, 1949), 99; 94–138.

27. Mitchell, *Stearns County*, II, 1405.

28. Brott, "Autobiography," in Mitchell, *Stearns County*, II, 1409.

29. J. G. S. to Elizabeth Mitchell, 1859, in William B. Mitchell Papers, Minnesota Historical Society.

30. S. J. Fisher, "Reminiscences of Jane Grey Swisshelm," *Western Pennsylvania Historical Magazine*, IV (1921), 165–74.

31. Pittsburg *Chronicle Telegraph*, July 22, 1884.

BIOGRAPHY, AUTOBIOGRAPHY AND THE SEARCH FOR THE LOST PAST

1. Frederick Douglass, *The Life and Times of Frederick Douglass* (Boston: DeWolfe and Fiske, 1892), 582.

2. Douglass to Reverend J. W. Beckett, undated, in Frederick Douglass Papers, Frederick Douglass Memorial Home, Anacostia, D.C. (Library of Congress Microfilm Copy).

3. Benjamin Quarles, *Frederick Douglass* (Washington: Associated Publishers, 1948); Philip S. Foner, *Frederick Douglass: A Biography* (New York: Citadel Press, 1964); Booker T. Washington, *Frederick Douglass* (Philadelphia: George W. Jacobs, 1906); Frederic M. Holland, *Frederick Douglass: The Colored Orator* (New York: Funk and Wagnalls, 1891); Charles W. Chesnutt, *Frederick Douglass* (Boston: Small, Maynard, 1899); James M. Gregory, *Frederick Douglass, the Orator: Containing an Account of His Life; His Eminent Public Services; His Brilliant Career as Orator; Selections from His Speeches and Writing* (Springfield, Mass.: Willey, 1893).

4. For review of the history of the autobiographies see Frederick Douglass, *The Narrative of the Life of Frederick Douglass an American Slave* (ed). Benjamin Quarles (Cambridge: Harvard University Press, 1960), xiii–xvi.

5. Roy Pascal, *Design and Truth in Autobiography* (Cambridge: Harvard University Press, 1960), esp. 61–83, 179–85.

6. *Ibid.*

7. Quarles, *Douglass*, 6 and *passim*.

8. David Brion Davis, *The Problem of Slavery in the Age of Revolution 1770–1823* (Ithaca: Cornell University Press, 1975), 44–49.

9. Quarles, *Douglass*, 335.

10. Douglass, *Life and Times*, 641–42.

11. Quarles, *Douglass*, 335–36. See, for example, the correspondence between W. W. Guthrie and Douglass in Douglass Papers, especially the letter of September 4, 1885.

12. Frederick Douglass to Charles Douglass, *seriatim*, in Douglass Papers.

13. Foner's source for the combined motive of escape (implied) and commitment to abolition (explicit) is Douglass' speech at Baltimore in 1870 celebrating the ratification of the Fifteenth Amendment. It was a speech in which "his thoughts rambled":

Forty years ago I sat on Kennard's wharf, at the foot of Philpot Street, and saw men and women chained and put on the ship to go to New Orleans. I then resolved that whatever power I had should be devoted to the freeing of my race. For thirty years, in the midst of all opposition I have endeavored to fulfill my pledge. I am here today to pledge myself that whatever remains to me of life shall go in the same direction. Foner, *Douglass*, 273; and, for this section of the essay, *passim*.

For a paraphrased version in which Foner establishes the motive for escape and leadership, see *ibid.*, 19. Douglass himself did not offer the combined motive in his *Narrative*, the autobiographical fragment he wrote shortly after he publicly embraced abolition. As he recounted his Baltimore experience the only reference he made to abolition was to tell of his curiosity about the words *abolition* and *abolitionist*: "Here I was perplexed." After he learned the meaning of the words, he "always drew near when [they were] spoken, expecting to hear something of importance to myself and fellowslaves." *Narrative*, 68–69.

14. Richard D. Altick, *Lives and Letters: A History of Literary Biography in England and America* (New York: Knopf, 1965), 332–34; Margaret Oliphant, "The Ethics of Biography," in James L. Clifford (ed.), *Biography as an Art* (New York: Oxford University Press, 1962), 97–102; John A. Garraty, *The Nature of Biography* (New York: Knopf, 1957), 97–104.

15. Douglass, *Life and Times*, 581–82. The summary appears in both editions, 1881 and 1892.

16. *Ibid.*

17. Pascal, *Design and Truth in Autobiography*.

18. Douglass, *Life and Times*, 22.

19. All the Douglass biographers follow Douglass in this strategy, Benjamin Quarles most closely. The first chapter of his biography is precisely intended to show that the processes of self-identification had been completed when Douglass escaped slavery.

20. In one sense Douglass' first two autobiographies perform the function of diaries. They are immediate accounts of his life as he understood it at the time he wrote. They provide the materials for the subsequent rewritings in which the earlier materials are taken and reshaped according to a lengthening perspective of experience.

21. Notwithstanding an autobiographer's power to juxtapose, reverse, blend, or in count-less ways distort the historical past to serve his own end his control is limited by his purpose: the creation of the self-portrait. Even with his great power an autobiographer can never be a solipsist. He cannot paint his picture as he *would* have it but as he is *permitted* to have it. The external world—society—intrudes upon him. In a sense an autobiographer is a mediator between a person who wanted to be himself and society. Almost as a third person, he tells the story of what was possible for him, not what was desired.

The point is illustrated by Douglass' accounts of the reason he was sent from Tuckahoe to Baltimore. Between the *Narrative* and the *Life and Times* there is a striking shift in his understanding of his power to control, that is, the power to "be himself." In the *Narrative* he is willing to risk being "deemed superstitious, and even egotistical" as he claims "a special interposition of divine Providence in my favor." Saved from the stupifying life at Tuckahoe, he is confident that he is God's special child. "Ministering angels" attend him. Investing himself with God's favor, and by committing himself to a belief in providential intervention in history he moves forward in life radiating an unconquerable power. Society holds no strictures for him; he can indeed "be himself." *Narrative*, 55–56.

But in the *Life and Times*, Providence and synergism have been dismissed. He may have been saved from living his life at Tuckahoe, but it was because of "mere circumstance" determined by events external to him over which he had no control and which cannot be interpreted as evidence of a special dispensation. Society has closed in around him. The providential child has become the man who is trapped by the unaccountable accidents of secular society and history. Not only events but an identity are forced on him. *Life and Times*, 90, 716. Also see, Erik Erikson, "On the Nature of Psycho-Historical Evidence: In Search of Gandhi," *Daedalus* (Summer, 1968), 695–730, especially 701–703.

NANTUCKET: CONFIRMATION, BETRAYAL, AND REBIRTH

1. This passage attempts to evoke Douglass' conception of slavery's system of time and its relationship with being. Possibly these observations are not applicable in certain other in-stances, as suggested by Eugene D. Genovese, *Roll, Jordan, Roll: The World the Slaves Made* (New York, Panthenon, 1974), 293, as he writes, "Douglass may have exaggerated the determination of the slaveholders as a class to suppress [such] information." But Douglass did not exaggerate for himself the importance of knowing his age and such things and of having access to records that would carry him beyond memory and invention.

This passage is also at variance with the claims made for the slaves' persistent "institu-tional arrangements," particularly those providing "a coherent social and cultural repertoire [a 'past'] to draw upon." The reader is again reminded that I am describing only Douglass' situation and his understanding of it. It is precisely his lack of a persistent, coherent reper-toire that informs both his life and his life stories. Indeed—using repertoire in its true meaning—Douglass' autobiographies may be read as the list of parts an actor is prepared to play upon demand. See Herbert G. Gutman, *The Black Family in Slavery and Freedom, 1750–1925* (New York: Pantheon, 1976), 303.

2. Douglass Diary, March 17, 1894. Aaron Anthony was Douglass' first owner and mas-ter. "Captain" Thomas Auld and his brother Hugh Auld were related by marriage to Aaron Anthony, and were successively Douglass' masters.

Douglass' memory flaws, which raise all sorts of questions concerning the historical relia-bility of the autobiographies, are demonstrated by comparing this diary notation with his

1845 recollection that Aaron Anthony died about four years (*ca.* 1828–29) after he had been sent to Baltimore to serve in Hugh Auld's household (*ca.* 1824–25). That is, there is a five- or six-year discrepancy in the dates of his movements, a discrepancy that is as revealing as it is important because Douglass used the occasion of the settlement of Anthony's estate not only as a reference point for his own movements, but also as the background for one of his most evocative attacks on the slave system. *Narrative*, 73. The same recollection and the same time sequence appear expanded and embellished in *Bondage and Freedom* and in the *Life and Times*.

According to the three versions, when Aaron Anthony died his estate was "immediately" evaluated for settlement and division, which meant that Douglass was sent back to the eastern shore as part of the "valuation of the property." All the slaves "were ranked with horses, sheep, and swine." There was the traditional tumult and anxiety: who would go to the evil new master, who would go the kind mistress, who would be sold South? And so forth. "At this moment I saw more clearly than ever the brutalizing effects of slavery upon both slave and slaveholder." Douglass calculated himself to be "between ten and eleven years old" when Aaron Anthony's estate was divided.

Accepting his traditional—and self-given—birthdate of 1817 as accurate, the settlement of the estate would have occurred *ca.* 1827–28. Or accepting his statement that he was sent to Baltimore when he was "seven or eight" in relation with his birthdate of 1817, the estate settlement would have been *ca.* 1828–29. But to relate Doctor Sears's date of Captain Anthony's death with the "immediate" settlement skews Douglass' chronology.

There are several alternative possibilities: (1) The settlement was "immediate" and Douglass was ten or eleven years of age. This would revise the traditional birthdate to *ca.* 1812–13. (2) The settlement was not "immediate," but the evaluation and division occurred some years after Anthony's death. This might save both the traditional birthdate and Douglass' estimate of his age at the time of the settlement, but it does so at the cost of throwing out his claim that settlement followed hard after Anthony's death. (3) Doctor Sears's information is wrong. But this is the most difficult of all the possibilities to accept. After all, with whatever passed for the family archives Doctor Sears might have had access to the death date of his great-grandfather. (4) The death and settlement did occur as Douglass claims, but he was not returned to Anthony's home as he says. It is possible that he created a personal myth in order to describe a social reality. The only certainty is that Douglass' account and Doctor Sears's information cannot be reconciled.

Furthermore, there is an inconsistency between little Thomas Auld's birthdate of 1824 and Douglass' accounts of the boy. In the autobiographies Douglass leaves the clear impression that when he was sent to Baltimore as Tommy's playmate, Tommy was his contemporary. Surely there is no indication in the autobiographies that Tommy was an infant or a small child. And to compound the difficulty raised by Tommy Auld's age, Doctor Sears's "facts" have Aaron Anthony dying in November, 1823, and the boy being born in January, 1824, and Douglass supposedly was in Baltimore serving Tommy when he was called back for the settlement "immediately" after Anthony's death.

The point at issue is not Douglass' literal accuracy. The question of the historical accuracy of Douglass' work has been examined about as far as the ephemeral sources allow by Benjamin Quarles in his introduction to the *Narrative*, pp. xxi–xxiv. The point is simple: Even after he had created a past for himself in the autobiographies, Douglass never gave up the quest for a past that did not depend solely upon his memory—or upon his creative powers.

3. Douglass, *Narrative*, 23; Douglass, *Life and Times*, 26, 537.
4. Thomas E. Sears to Douglass, February 18, 1885, in Douglass Papers.
5. *Ibid.*, April 15, 1886.
6. *Ibid.*, April 24, 1886.
7. Frederick Douglass to J. M. Rusk, undated, in Douglass Papers. Douglass asks for a

place in the "Agricultural Bureau" for Nellie Jenkins. He identified her as a member of "the family to which I belonged as a slave," then goes on to say, "Not only her necessity but my former relation to her family will increase my sense of obligation," if his request is honored. For all the strictures Douglass laid against his masters and their families, there is an ambivalence in his attitude and actions toward them, and they toward him. Of all Douglass' biographers only Booker T. Washington observes an obvious point: the Aulds' basic kindness to Douglass. Surely after the first, and abortive, escape attempt, Thomas Auld's response was not characteristic of the vindictive master. His "punishment" was to retrieve Douglass from his field-hand life to Baltimore, which put him closer to freedom. It is not difficult to find in Auld's actions an invitation to escape; indeed Douglass is virtually set up to make a successful escape. At any event Douglass was brought back to Baltimore to learn a trade in order to prepare him for emancipation, which is consistent with what is probably the fact of the matter of the Auld-Douglass relationship: Frederick Douglass was half-brother to Lucretia Auld, Thomas Auld's wife. As the relationship between Douglass and the Aulds runs its course, it begins to take on the outline of the Joseph story, with Douglass playing Joseph in Pharaoh's court for the Auld descendants. Late in his life Douglass connected his life and Joseph's. Diary, February 14, 1887.

8. Douglass, *Life and Times*, 89.

9. *Ibid.*, 90.

10. See correspondence in Douglass Papers, summer, 1891.

11. This letter is not in the Douglass Papers, but the fact that he wrote it is established in Douglass to "Captain" Auld, September 15, 1891, in Douglass Papers.

12. *Ibid.*

13. Douglass, *Life and Times*, 537.

14. Diary, March 17, 1894. The remarkable feature of this final establishment of the date he went to Baltimore is that Douglass had either forgot the chronology he had consistently maintained through his several autobiographies, one that fixes Anthony's death approximately four years after he arrived in Baltimore, or else he threw the old chronology out the window. In any case, and in all versions—both autobiographical and diary—he remained consistent on one thing, the year that he came to Baltimore. Apparently he was determined to have 1825 as that year, regardless of the route by which he came to it. Everything else in one way or another yields to fixing that date. The question then is rather obvious: why was he so solicitous about the year he went to Baltimore? Why is it so important, and why must it be maintained? Could it be that it was in effect his birthdate; only when he came to Baltimore was he "born" and began to "live"? But this speculation still leaves unanswered the question, why must the year be 1825? Only one thing may be unquestionably inferred: the year he went to Baltimore is the one great reference point in Douglass' life as a slave.

15. Douglass, *Life and Times*, 22–24; Douglass, *Bondage and Freedom*, Introduction.

16. For a later statement on motivation, see Benjamin Quarles, "Abolition's Different Drummer: Frederick Douglass," in Martin Duberman (ed.) *The Antislavery Vanguard* (Princeton: Princeton University Press, 1965), 126.

17. Douglass, *Narrative*, 153.

18. *Ibid.*, 151.

19. *Ibid.*, 153.

20. Douglass, *Bondage and Freedom*, 360; Douglass *Life and Times*, 268. Emphasis added.

21. Douglass, *Narrative*, 26.

22. Wendell Phillips to Elizabeth Pease, February 24, 1845, quoted in Foner, *Douglass*, 386.

23. Edmund Quincy to Caroline Weston, October 21, 1841; Evelina A. Smith to Caroline Weston, December 12, 1841, both in Weston Papers, Boston Public Library.

24. Leon F. Litwack, "The Emancipation of the Negro Abolitionist," in Duberman (ed.), *Antislavery Vanguard*, 137–55; Leon F. Litwack, *North of Slavery: The Negro in the Free States, 1790–1860* (Chicago: University of Chicago Press, 1961), 214–46.

25. Douglass, *Life and Times*, 269.

26. Isabel Jennings to Maria W. Chapman, August 2, 1847, in Weston Papers, Boston Public Library.

27. See for example, R. D. Webb to Maria W. Chapman, undated [1846?]: Douglass "is intensely suspicious"; and Douglass' crackling acerbating letter on "betrayal" to Maria W. Chapman, March 24, 1846, in Chapman Papers, Boston Public Library.

28. Foner, *Douglass*, 94. Benjamin Quarles also implies a moratorium or hiatus in Douglass' life. In a subsequent essay on Douglass as a reformer, Quarles writes about the "mature" Douglass, suggesting that before *ca.* 1852, that is, until the break with the Garrisonians, Douglass was "immature" or incomplete "as a Negro." But Quarles, like Foner, does not attempt to explain why Douglass became "mature." Quarles, "Abolition's Different Drummer," in Martin Duberman (ed.), *The Antislavery Vanguard*, 130.

THE HIGHLAND CHIEF, THE AFRICAN QUEEN, AND THE GARDEN OF EDEN

1. On his father, compare *Narrative*, 24–25, *Bondage and Freedom*, 51–52, and *Life and Times*, 27–28. On his mother, compare *Narrative*, 24–25, *Bondage and Freedom*, 52–60, and *Life and Times*, 27, 36–39.

2. James C. Prichard, *The Natural History of Man: Comprising Inquiries into the Modifying Influence of Physical and Moral Agencies on the Different Tribes of the Human Family* (London: H. Bailliere, 1848), 157 and *passim*.

3. *Bondage and Freedom*, 40–42; *Narrative*, 26.

4. George Shepperson, "Frederick Douglass and Scotland," *Journal of Negro History*, XXXVIII (July, 1953), 307. Why Douglass' mother gave him the "pretentious and long" name is uncertain. It may be that Harriet Bailey was following the slaves' "necronymic naming practices" or the "common practice" of naming male children after uncles described by Herbert Gutman, but I know of no evidence supporting either possibility. Indeed, in the case of Douglass the current findings on slave families, naming practices, kinship networks and obligations arising between the kin do not seem very applicable. Most applicable is Douglass' development of a "fictive" kinship with his mother, but that, of course, proceeds from situations and needs altogether different from the context Gutman employs. On the matter of slave kinships and obligations Douglass is more useful for describing conditions that may have prevailed for other slaves than for himself. He rather carefully distances himself from *them*; he is an observer, not a participant. Herbert G. Gutman, *The Black Family in Slavery and Freedom, 1750–1925*, 192–200, and for an example of "distancing," see p. 218.

5. Douglass to "Dear Friend" [Isabel Jennings], September, 1846, in Douglass Papers; Douglass to William Lloyd Garrison, January 27, 1846, in Foner, *Life and Writings*, I, 133; Shepperson, "Douglass and Scotland," 307–21.

6. Compare the "Dear Isa" letters—Douglass to Isabel Jennings—with those he wrote to the Garrisonians, *ca.* 1845–46, in Douglass Papers. Isabel Jennings, an English antislavery worker and Douglass' hostess, admirer, and confidante, was able to elicit a warmth and a confidence that is manifestly lacking in the Garrisonians' correspondence.

7. Douglass to "William" [A. White], July 30, 1845, in Douglass Papers.

8. Anna W. Weston to [?], March 6, 1843, in Weston Papers.

9. William Lloyd Garrison to Helen E. Garrison, n.d., *ca.* October–November, 1847; *ibid.*, May 14, 1853, in Garrison Papers.

10. Mrs. C. B. Clarkson to Maria W. Chapman, August 2, 1846, in Chapman Papers.

11. I have found no instance of Douglass "losing his voice" before the break with Garrison. William Lloyd Garrison to Helen F. Garrison, August 20, 1847; *ibid.*, September 10, 1847; Garrison to *Liberator*, August 25, 1847, in Walter M. Merrill (ed.), *Letters of William Lloyd Garrison: No Union with Slaveholders, 1841-1849* (Cambridge: Harvard University Press, 1973), 516, 526-27, 519.

12. William Lloyd Garrison to Samuel J. May, March 21, 1856, in Garrison Papers, Boston Public Library. Apparently the Garrisonians were earlier troubled by Douglass' relationships with white women. Isabel Jennings, Douglass' English mediator, assured the Garrisonians that while Douglass was in England he "evinced the highest regard for his wife and child—had Mrs. Douglass been a well educated woman and in all respects a companion [for?] him, he would not have avoided more entirely any of these confidential conversations which some persons like to have with young ladies when the latter are willing. . . . This may seem ridiculous to tell you and yet when one learns he has strong feelings, it raises the respect one feels for him." Isabel Jennings to Maria Weston Chapman, October 2, 1847, in Chapman Papers.

13. "What Am I to You," undated [1883?], in Douglass Papers. There are two drafts of the poem, the second considerably longer and more revealing than the first. In the second draft Douglass emphasizes the "truthfulness" of what he is saying. One also observes that Douglass makes Helen Pitts's "whiteness" godly.

14. Douglass to James Redpath, July 29, 1871, in Joseph A. Borome (ed.), "Some Additional Light on Frederick Douglass," *Journal of Negro History*, XXXVIII (April, 1953), 217.

SELF-CREATION AND SOCIAL IMAGINATION

1. Claude Levi-Strauss, *The Savage Mind* (Chicago: University of Chicago Press, 1966), 261.

2. Wendell Phillips Garrison to Swisshelm, August 15, 1880, in Mitchell Papers, Minnesota Historical Society. Particularly, Garrison inquires about the provenance of the slogan about the Constitution being a covenant with death and an agreement with hell. He thought his father had coined the phrase and was surprised to learn that the Covenanters were using it *ca.* 1810.

3. Swisshelm to Mary Mitchell, March 7, 1865, in Mitchell Papers, Minnesota Historical Society; Prospectus for the *Reconstructionist*, n.d. [October, 1865?]. Copies of the paper are rare. A Prospectus is in the Western Reserve Historical Society; a few editions are in the Minnesota Historical Society.

4. There were two qualifications. Provision for desegregated public schools and the desegregated cemeteries were dropped from the civil rights bill. To that extent the act itself was a flawed "crowning work," and the reconciliation of abolition's moral vision for American blacks and the law of the land was incomplete. But nonetheless—and this is the point to be stressed—the limits of abolition's social imagination are clearly revealed. The bill with its open school and open cemetery provisions was the agreed capstone of the abolition edifice. David Donald, *Charles Sumner and the Rights of Man* (New York: Knopf, 1970), 531; James McPherson, "Abolitionists and the Civil Rights Act of 1875," *Journal of American History*, LII (December, 1965), 493-510; Charles Fairman, *Reconstruction and Reunion, 1864-1888*, Pt. 1, Vol. VI of *The Oliver Wendell Holmes Devise: History of the Supreme Court of the United States* (8 vols.; New York: Macmillan, 1971-).

5. For example, William Gillette, *The Right to Vote: Politics and the Passage of the Fifteenth Amendment* (Baltimore: Johns Hopkins Press, 1965). For a somewhat different view, LaWanda and John H. Cox, "Negro Suffrage and Republican Politics: The Problem of Motivation in Reconstruction Historiography," *Journal of Southern History*, XXXIII (August, 1967), 303-30.

6. Here some notice must be taken of the interventionist public policies proposed by abolitionists that seem inconsistent with the proposition of the marketplace, which is jealous of the property right. The most significant of these proposals was "a comprehensive program of agrarian reform, including the confiscation and redistribution of land" in the former Confederacy. But if one follows the line of argument established by George Julian, one of the staunchest abolitionists, then a logic emerges that is consistent with the proposition of the marketplace. Julian aimed at destroying a specific kind of property, only "land monopoly," which was the correlative of labor monopoly, one of which forms was bond slavery. Both "monopolies" must be destroyed because both clog the mechanism of the marketplace and destroy "Real liberty."

Insofar as the "friends" of the blacks were concerned, the proposal of confiscation and land reform was another signal of their "insistently maintained [faith] that, *given a fair chance the Negro would show as much capacity as the white man to make his own unaided way.*" Emphasis added. The intricacies and "ambiguities" of this matter are skillfully explored in LaWanda Cox, "The Promise of Land for the Freedman," *Mississippi Valley Historical Review*, XLV (December, 1958), 413–40.

My outline of the Reconstruction racial settlement might seem to imply a predetermined consistency between political action and ideology that I do not intend. Many recent books on Reconstruction have shown conclusively that the Reconstruction settlement depended upon a concatenation of events and situations that scarcely could have been anticipated in 1865, or 1861, or in the 1850s when the "reconstruction" of the South and the nation began to enter the northern political vocabulary. Nor do I mean to imply a unanimity for abolitionists in the Reconstruction congresses or among their abolitionist constituents, especially on specific economic policies. But as these divisions were over "means, rather than . . . ends," the results of "Equality Before the Law" were fairly free from dispute. David Montgomery, *Beyond Equality: Labor and the Radical Republicans 1862–1872* (New York: Knopf, 1967), 85, 240, 421.

The point I wish to make was set forth long ago by Georges Clemenceau, who was then a young journalist and an admiring friend of the abolitionists, especially Wendell Phillips. Reporting for the Paris *Times*, of the lurching, patched-together settlement, he wrote: "Most of the radicals of today embarked on the abolitionist sea without any clear ideas of where the course would lead [and] they arrived at their present position only after being forced from one reform to another."

But the "sea" (abolition's social imagination) was finite. The sailors could not sail beyond its limits. Thus as Reconstruction ran its course a pleasing congruence of political action and abolition ideology, a fairly close matching of public policy and ideas, was achieved. Georges Clemenceau, *American Reconstruction, 1865–1870*, ed. Fernand Baldensperger (New York: Dial, 1928), 277–78. See also, Joseph A. Kulash, "Abolitionists in an Acquisitive Age: Economic Liberalism in the American Antislavery Movement" (M.A. thesis, University of North Carolina, 1972).

7. "'Wake Samson'—the Last Article Written by Mrs. Jane G. Swisshelm Before Her Death—from *Chicago Tribune*" [undated, spring, 1885?], Scrapbook, in Mitchell Papers, Minnesota Historical Society.

8. Garrison to Samuel J. May, September 28, 1860, in Garrison Papers, Boston Public Library.

9. I am not suggesting that Douglass worked directly from Grund and Tocqueville, but rather that he was drawing from a folklore and culture they describe. As for Tocqueville's prophecy about "a chance of salvation," it goes awry after foretelling white political separation. He speculated that secession would be peaceful. Then racial war would break out in the South, ending with the whites, like the Moors in Spain, being driven out. Alexis de Tocqueville, *Democracy in America* (New York: Harper and Row, 1966,), 328–29.

10. August Meier, "Frederick Douglass' Vision for America: A Case Study in

Nineteenth-Century Negro Protest," in Harold M. Hyman and Leonard W. Levy (eds.), *Freedom and Reform: Essays in Honor of Henry Steele Commager* (New York: Harper and Row, 1967), 127–48; esp. 138–41.

11. The reader is reminded that I am concerned here with a creative writer's imaginative operations. That is, because of his need to imaginatively adjust the "boundary" of abolition Conway achieved a unique perspective on it. He is obviously dissociated from the contemporary anti-imperialist argument which descended from mugwumpery and which never laid the axe to the roots of a national morality as did Conway. For people such as Carl Schurz, Thomas Wentworth Higginson, or the second generation Garrisons—all of whom were movers and shakers in the Anti-Imperialist League and who carried the abolitionist tradition literally in their bodies—the abolitionist-imperialist connection would have been inconceivable, or the most wretched perversity. For a discussion of their ideas see Robert L. Beisner, *Twelve Against Empire: The Anti-Imperialists, 1898–1900* (New York: McGraw-Hill, 1968), particularly 215–39; and James M. McPherson, *The Abolitionist Legacy: From Reconstruction to the NAACP*, (Princeton: Princeton University Press, 1975), 322–30.

12. The *Autobiography* summarized Conway's ideas. They are set out more fully in "Liberty: A Historical Study"; "Liberty: A Contemporary Study"; "Liberty: Our Lingering Chains," *Open Court*, November 30, December 14, 28, 1893, pp. 3887–88, 3905–3906, 3919–21.

HENRY WRIGHT

1. Joseph W. Krutch, *Henry David Thoreau* (New York: Dell, 1965), 155. The journal entry, June 17, 1853, is from Bradford Torrey (ed.), *The Writings of Henry David Thoreau* (Boston: Houghton Mifflin, 1906), XI, 263–65.

2. Henry C. Wright, *The Empire of the Mother Over the Character and Destiny of the Race* (Boston: B. Marsh, 1863), 1.

3. Perry, *Radical Abolitionism: Anarchy and the Government of God in Antislavery Thought* (Ithaca: Cornell University Press), 18.

4. Henry C. Wright, *Human Life: Illustrated in My Individual Experience as a Child, a Youth, and a Man* (Boston, 1849), 156. All quotations in this biographical section are taken from this source.

5. Wright to Maria W. Chapman, May 2, 1839, in Perry, *Radical Abolitionism*, 90.

6. Peter Michelson, *The Aesthetics of Pornography* (New York: Herder and Herder, 1971), particularly "Pornography as Moral Rhetoric" and "Pornography and Moral Anarchy," 88–107 and 160–79.

7. For a documentation of the abolitionist sexual propaganda and an exploration of many of its implications, see Ronald G. Walters, "The Erotic South: Civilization and Sexuality in American Abolition," *American Quarterly*, XXV (May, 1973), 177–201.

8. Mrs. A. M. French, *Slavery in South Carolina and the Ex-Slaves: Or the Port Royal Mission* (New York: Winchell M. French, 1862), especially 190 and the chapters "Free Labor" and "Heart Service," the latter particularly, 82–92.

9. Henry C. Wright, *Marriage and Parentage: Or the Reproductive Element in Man as a Means to His Elevation and Happiness* (Boston: B. Marsh, 1855), 104. All of the following quotations are from this source and *The Empire of the Mother*.

10. Charles E. Rosenberg, "Sexuality, Class and Role in Nineteenth-Century America," *American Quarterly*, XXV (May, 1973), 131–53; Carroll Smith-Rosenberg and Charles Rosenberg, "The Female Animal: Medical and Biological Views of Woman and Her Role in Nineteenth-Century America," *Journal of American History*, LX (September, 1973), 332–56.

11. Rosenberg, "Sexuality, Class and Role in 19th-Century America," 131–53; Herbert

G. Gutman, "Work, Culture, and Society in Industrializing America, 1815–1919," *American Historical Review*, LXXVIII (June, 1973), 531–87.

12. On the matter of a woman's power to "control" her body, Wright's contemporary, Dr. Charles Knowlton was considerably more pertinent. He developed the douche syringe. Knowlton's social ideas justifying the syringe are generally consistent with Wright's, but he seems innocent of the severe self-disciplined repressiveness for women that is so important for Wright, which perhaps helps explain why Knowlton's *Fruits of Philosophy* was suppressed and Knowlton himself was on two occasions fined and jailed. Charles Knowlton, *The Fruits of Philosophy or The Private Companion of Adult People* (Mt. Vernon, N.Y.: Peter Pauper Press, 1937); Charles Knowlton, *Two Remarkable Lectures Delivered in Boston by Dr. C. Knowlton on the Day of His Leaving the Jail at East Cambridge, March 31, 1833, Where He Had Been Imprisoned for Publishing a Book* (Boston: A. Kneeland, 1833); Norman E. Himes, *Medical History of Contraception* (Baltimore: Williams and Wilkins, 1936), 226–29; and more generally, 260–85.

13. It is useful to note the many similarities between Wright's ideas and those of Catharine Beecher, the most celebrated of the Beecher offspring until she was displaced from the top rung of fame in the 1850s by Harriet and Henry Ward. The similarities are all the more striking because of Wright's reputation of being an "extreme case," while Catharine, though she bore it a "cosmic grudge," "actually endorsed as much as she rejected of . . . tradition." She "desir[ed] to break old molds of thought and formulate new ones." But her "significance lies not in [her] originality, but in [her] capacity to present old ideas in new form." Indeed, her mature work may be read as the philosophical complement to Wright's descriptive sexual sociology, both of which are essentially conserving. Like Wright, she "locat[ed] the nation's moral center in the home," over which the women presided. It was up to the men to "weather the storms of democratic liberty" raging outside. Not incidentally, her proposal for this sexual division of labor was made in her *Essay on Slavery and Abolitionism with Reference to the Duty of American Females.* It was through this domestic arrangement that "the fathers, the husbands, and the sons" would be morally armed to battle slavery. Katheryn K. Sklar, *Catharine Beecher: A Study in American Domesticity* (New Haven: Yale University, 1973), 135–36, 244–57, and *passim.*

14. Karl Polanyi, *The Great Transformation: The Political and Economic Origins of Our Time* (Boston: Beacon, 1957), 84–85 and *passim.*

SALMON CHASE

1. A fuller itemization of this "remarkable catalogue" is in Kraditor, *Means and Ends in American Abolition,* 150–52.

2. Quentin Anderson, *The Imperial Self: An Essay in American Literary and Cultural History* (New York, 1971), 230–31; Frederick Somkin, *Unquiet Eagle: Memory and Desire in the Idea of American Freedom,* (Ithaca: Cornell University Press, 1967), 6–7 and *passim.*

3. Lawrence J. Friedman, *Inventors of the Promised Land* (New York: Knopf, 1975), 44–67.

4. Joshua Giddings to Chase, "Confidential," December 7, 1860, in Salmon P. Chase Papers, Historical Society of Pennsylvania; Willie Lee Rose, *Rehearsal for Reconstruction: The Port Royal Experiment* (New York: Vintage, n.d.), 17.

5. Chase to Charles Sumner, January 21 and March 15, 1850, in Chase-Sumner Correspondence, Houghton Library, Harvard University.

6. Chase to Charles Cleveland, October 22, 1841, in Salmon P. Chase Papers, Library of Congress. Emphasis added. The words in brackets are surmised from partially illegible words in the manuscript letter.

7. Eric Foner, *Free Soil, Free Labor, Free Men: The Ideology of the Republican Party*

Before the Civil War (New York: Oxford, 1970), 11–39 and *passim;* Richard H. Sewell, *Ballots for Freedom: Antislavery Politics in the United States 1837–1860* (New York: Oxford, 1976), 121–157, 204–206.

8. James G. Birney to Chase, February 2, 1841, in Chase Papers, Library of Congress.

9. Chase to E. L. Pierce, September 20, 1854, in E. L. Pierce Papers, Houghton Library, Harvard University.

10. Chase to Sidney Howard Gay, April 28, 1847; Chase to Gay, "Strictly Private," January 3, 1855, in S. H. Gay Collection, Butler Library, Columbia University.

11. Chase to Mrs. Randall Hunt, November 30, 1860, in Robert B. Warden, *An Account of the Private Life and Public Services of Salmon Portland Chase* (Cincinnati: Wilstach, Baldwin, 1874), 366–67. Emphasis in original.

12. Chase to Winfield Scott, December 29, 1860, *ibid.*, 368.

13. Giddings to Chase, November 23, 1846, in Chase Papers, Historical Society of Pennsylvania; Chase to Gay, April 28, 1847, in Gay Collection.

14. Warden, *Chase,* 329, 529.

15. Chase to Pierce, September 13, 1858, in Pierce Papers.

16. Jerome Frank, *Law and the Modern Mind* (Gloucester: Peter Smith, 1970), particularly Chap. 2, "A Partial Explanation," 14–23. See also Frank's careful qualifications in the "Preface to [the] Sixth Printing," xxiv–xxv. Similar qualifications are attached to this paragraph.

17. Chase Diary, January 13, 1829; Chase to Charles Cleveland, October 22, 1841, in Chase Papers, Library of Congress. Chase to Charles Sumner, March 15, 1850, in Chase-Sumner Correspondence.

18. This paragraph and the following six paragraphs are based on Chase to ?, June 8, 1828, in Chase Papers, Library of Congress; General S. Bernard to Chase, July 17, 1829, in Chase Papers, Historical Society of Pennsylvania; Diary, *passim;* "Trowbridge Letters," in Jacob W. Schuckers, *The Life and Public Services of Salmon Portland Chase, United States Senator and Governor of Ohio; Secretary of the Treasury, and Chief Justice of the United States* (New York: D. Appleton, 1874), 29; Chase to Charles Cleveland, February, 1828, in *ibid.,* 28; Chase to Thomas Sparhawk, September 30, 1829, in Arthur M. Schlesinger, "Salmon P. Chase: Undergraduate and Pedagogue," *Ohio Archaeological and Historical Publications,* XXVIII (1919), 154–55; Warden, *Chase,* 242; Chase, Commonplace Book (1828?) in Chase Papers, Library of Congress; Alice Chase to Chase, November 10, 1831, in Chase Papers, Library of Congress. David Mark to Chase, May 6, 1826, in Chase Papers, Historical Society of Pennsylvania.

19. James S. Young, *The Washington Community, 1800–1828* (New York: Harcourt, Brace and World, n.d.), 213–18.

20. Alexander Ralyton Chase to Chase, November 4, 1825; Chase to Thomas Sparhawk, April 20, 1829, in Chase Papers, Library of Congress.

21. Chase Diary, April 16, 1829; Chase to Charles Cleveland, March 18, 1830, in Chase Papers, Library of Congress.

22. Schuckers, *Chase,* 28–30.

23. Joseph C. Robert, "William Wirt, Virginian," *Virginia Magazine of History and Biography,* LXX (1972), 396, 419; Wirt to Judge Carr, January 6, 1833; Wirt to N. W. Miller, December 20, 1833, in John P. Kennedy, *Memoirs of William Wirt: Attorney General of the United States* (Philadelphia: Blanchard and Lea, 1851), II, 249–51.

24. Friedman, *Inventors of the Promised Land,* 52, 56.

25. William Wirt, *A Discourse on the Lives and Character of Thomas Jefferson and John Adams, Who Both Died on the Fourth of July, 1826. . . .* (Washington: Gales and Seaton, 1826) *passim;* Robert, "William Wirt," 398.

26. "Autobiographical Memoir," in Kennedy, *Memoirs of William Wirt,* I, 38.

27. Chase to Charles Cleveland, May 28, 1829, in Chase Papers, Library of Congress.

28. For the "movement" of the cities and the "annihalted" mountains, see Chase Diary, December 27, 1829, in Library of Congress. The other quotations are from the diary throughout 1829.

29. Chase Diary, January 12, 1829, in Library of Congress. Emphasis added.

30. Chase to Thomas Sparhawk, January 15, 1830, in Schlesinger, "Salmon P. Chase," 157.

31. Major L. Wilson, *Space, Time and Freedom: The Quest for Nationality and the Irrepressible Conflict, 1815–1861* (Westport, Conn.: Greenwood Press, 1974), 189–91; 195–97.

32. Chase to Charles Cleveland, May 28, 1829, in Chase Papers, Library of Congress.

33. Daniel H. Calhoun, *Professional Lives in America: Structure and Aspiration, 1750–1850* (Cambridge: Harvard University Press, 1965), 85–87; Kennedy, *Memoirs of William Wirt*, II, 355–56.

34. Chase to Charles Cleveland, March 18, 1830; Chase to Joseph Denison, November, 1831, in Chase Papers, Library of Congress.

35. Chase to Denison, November, 1831, *ibid.; Cincinnati Gazette*, February, 1838, quoted in Warden, *Chase*, 258.

36. Chase to Charles Cleveland, October 22, 1841, in Chase Papers, Library of Congress.

37. Chase Diary, August 20, 1840, in Library of Congress.

38. *Ibid.;* Warden, *Chase*, 794.

39. Chase to Joseph Denison, November 10, 1827, in Chase Papers, Library of Congress.

40. Fairman, *Reconstruction and Reunion, 1864–88*, 1394; Stanley I. Kutler, "Reconstruction and the Supreme Court: The Numbers Game Reconsidered," *Journal of Southern History*, XXXII (February, 1966), 57.

THOMAS COOLEY

1. Subsequent to the writing of this chapter, Phillip S. Paludan, *A Covenant with Death: The Constitution, Law, and Equality in the Civil War Era* (Urbana: University of Illinois Press, 1975) has been published. Cooley is one of the legists Paludan discusses. By way of his book I was led to Alan Jones's work on Cooley. My chapter on Cooley stands virtually as it was written before I learned of Jones's writings. I am gratified that in some instances the lines I develop here seem to parallel those already laid out more extensively by him, particularly in "Thomas M. Cooley and 'Laissez-Faire Constitutionalism': A Reconsideration," *Journal of American History*, LIII (March, 1967), 751–71.

2. For a portion of such an inquiry see James M. McPherson, *The Abolitionist Legacy: From Reconstruction to the NAACP* (Princeton: Princeton University Press, 1975).

3. Clyde E. Jacobs, *Law Writers and the Courts: The Influence of Thomas M. Cooley, Christopher G. Tiedeman, and John F. Dillon on American Constitutional Law* (Berkeley: University of California Press, 1954), 24.

4. Benjamin R. Twiss, *Lawyers and the Constitution: How Laissez-Faire Came to the Supreme Court* (Princeton: Princeton University Press, 1942), 11, 28.

5. Thomas M. Cooley, *A Treatise on the Constitutional Limitations Which Rest Upon the Legislative Power of the State of the American Union* (Boston: Little, Brown, 1871), iv.

6. Sidney Fine, *Laissez-Faire and the General Welfare State: A Study of Conflict in American Thought, 1865–1901* (Ann Arbor, University of Michigan Press, 1956), 142.

7. Twiss, *Lawyers and the Constitution*, 18, 24, 34–35, and *passim*; John P. Roche, "Entrepreneurial Liberty and the Fourteenth Amendment," *Labor History* (Winter, 1963), 3–31; and for Cooley's typically assigned role in the post-Appomattox development of constitutional law, Fine, *Laissez-Faire and the General Welfare State*, 139–44.

8. Twiss, *Lawyers and the Constitution*, 10–12.

9. *Ibid.*, 39.

10. Harry B. Hutchins, "Thomas McIntyre Cooley," in William D. Lewis (ed.), *Great American Lawyers* (Philadelphia: John C. Winston, 1909), VII, 431–91; Jerome C. Knowlton, "Thomas McIntyre Cooley," *Michigan Law Review* (March, 1907), V, 309; Gilbert John Clark, *Life Sketches of Eminent Lawyers* (Kansas City: Vernon Law Book Co., 1895), I, 204–205.

11. Whitney R. Cross, *The Burned-Over District: The Social and Intellectual History of Enthusiastic Religion in Western New York, 1800–1850* (New York: Harper and Row, 1965), ix. All the following quotations about the district are drawn from this source.

12. Cooley, "Revolutions," *Western Literary Messenger*, XVI (March, 1851), 8; "A Plate from Glory Illustrated," *ibid.* (August, 1851), 1; "Room and Bread for All," *ibid.* (September, 1851), 33.

13. Cooley, "Address on Laying the Corner Stone of the New Court House . . . at Adrian, June 28, 1884," in Arthur R. Kooker, "The Antislavery Movement in Michigan, 1796–1840: A Study in Humanitarianism on the American Frontier" (Ph.D. dissertation, University of Michigan, 1930), 253.

14. For an exposition of Cooley's formal ideas see Jones, "Thomas M. Cooley and 'Laissez-Faire Constitutionalism': A Reconsideration," 751–71. Jones's discussion is supplemented by Paludan, *A Covenant with Death*, 252–54.

15. For this sketch I have relied chiefly on William E. Nelson, "The Impact of the Anti-slavery Movement upon Styles of Judicial Reasoning in Nineteenth Century America," *Harvard Law Review*, LXXXVII (January, 1975), 513–66. I have also drawn on Charles W. McCurdy, "Justice Field and the Jurisprudence of Government-Business Relations: Some Parameters of Laissez-Faire Constitutionalism, 1863–1897," *Journal of American History*, LXI (March, 1975), 970–1005; Jacobus ten Broek, *The Antislavery Origins of the Fourteenth Amendment* (Berkeley: University of California Press, 1951), and Howard Jay Graham, "The Early Antislavery Background of the Fourteenth Amendment," *Wisconsin Law Review* (May, 1950), 479–507; and *ibid.* (July, 1950), 610–66. All uncited quoted material is drawn from these sources. Robert M. Cover, *Justice Accused: Antislavery and the Judicial Process* (New Haven: Yale University Press, 1975), and Paludan, *A Covenant with Death* have extended the discussion of the racial aspects of abolitionist constitutionalism. Where I have quoted from either I acknowledge my reference by specific citation.

16. Cover, *Justice Accused*, 7, 119 ff and 172.

17. Insofar as it established citizens' rights, according to Cooley, the Fourteenth Amendment was redundant; it simply disposed of "some arguments which disputed" the claims he established here for blacks. *Constitutional Limitations*, 2nd ed., 294–97. But also see Paludan, *Covenant with Death*, 261.

18. Cooley, *Constitutional Limitations*, 1st ed. 34–37.

19. The people *ex. rel. Detroit and Howell Railroad Company* v. *Township Board of Salem*, 20 Mich. 487 (1870).

20. *People* v. *Board of Education of Detroit*, 18 Mich. 400 (1869).

21. This is apparently a reference to *People* v. *Dean* 14 Mich. 406 (1866), a quaint case involving the physical criteria useful for establishing a voter's race, which led the judges to expatiate on such matters as "nose pullers" and "nose measurers."

22. Cooley seems never to have defined these words in *Constitutional Limitations*. A reader is left to infer their definition, the chief inference coming from all those principles and rights expressed in the declaration of rights for the protection of individuals and minorities.

Developing the themes of equality and liberty, and establishing their connection with private property, Cooley often sounds like Josiah Warren, who is usually identified as the founder of philosophical anarchism in the United States. For example, compare *Salem* with "Government and Its True Function," in Josiah Warren, *True Civilization and Immediate Necessity and the Last Ground of Hope for Mankind.* . . . (Boston; n.p., 1863), esp. 10, 22, 32–33.

SELECTED BIBLIOGRAPHY

BOOKS

Altick, Richard D. *Lives and Letters: A History of Literary Biography in England and America.* New York: Knopf, 1965.

Anderson, Quentin. *The Imperial Self: An Essay in American Literary and Cultural History.* New York: Knopf, 1971.

Baldwin, Leland. *Pittsburgh: The Story of a City.* Pittsburgh: University of Pittsburgh Press, 1937.

Beisner, Robert L. *Twelve Against Empire: The Anti-Imperialists, 1898–1900.* New York: McGraw Hill, 1968.

Berthoff, Rowland T. *An Unsettled People: Social Order and Disorder in American History.* New York: Harper and Row, 1971.

Bruce, Dickson, D. *And They All Sang Hallelujah: Plain-Folk Camp-Meeting Religion, 1800–1845.* Knoxville: University of Tennessee Press, 1974.

Burtis, Mary E. *Moncure Conway 1832–1907.* New Brunswick: Rutgers University Press, 1953.

373

_____. *John and Mary's College: The Boyd Lee Spahr Lectures in Americana, 1951–1956*. Westwood, N.J.: Fleming N. Revel, 1956.

Calhoun, David H. *Professional Lives in America: Structure and Aspiration, 1750–1850*. Cambridge: Harvard University Press, 1965.

Chesnutt, Charles W. *Frederick Douglass*. Boston: Small, Maynard, 1899.

Clark, Gilbert J. *Life Sketches of Eminent Lawyers*. Kansas City: Vernon Law Book Company, 1895.

Clemenceau, Georges. *American Reconstruction, 1865–1870*. Edited by Fernand Baldensperger. New York: Dial, 1928.

Clifford, James L., ed. *Biography as an Art*, New York: Oxford University Press, 1962.

Conway, Moncure D. *Autobiography, Memories and Experiences*. Boston: Houghton Mifflin, 1904.

_____. *Emerson at Home and Abroad*. Boston: Osgood and Company, 1882.

_____. *Omitted Chapters of History Disclosed in the Life and Papers of Edmund Randolph, Governor of Virginia; First Attorney-General; United States Secretary of State*. New York: Putnam's, 1888.

_____. *Pine and Palm*. New York: Henry Holt, 1887.

_____. *Testimonies Concerning Slavery*. London: Chapman and Hall, 1864.

_____. *The Golden Hour*. Boston: Ticknor and Fields, 1862.

_____. *The Rejected Stone: or Insurrection vs. Resurrection in America*. Boston: Walker, Wise, 1861.

Cooley, Thomas M. *A Treatise on the Constitutional Limitations which Rest upon the Legislative Power of the States of the American Union*. Boston: Little, Brown, 1871.

Cross, Whitney R. *The Burned-Over District: The Social and Intellectual History of Enthusiastic Religion in Western New York, 1800–1850*. New York: Harper and Row, 1965.

Daniel, Frederick S. *The Richmond Examiner During the War; or, the Writings of John M. Daniel, with a Memoir of His Life, by His Brother*. New York: Arno, 1970.

Davis, David B. *The Slave Power Conspiracy and the Paranoid Style*. Baton Rouge: Louisiana State University Press, 1969.

Donald, David H. *Charles Sumner and the Rights of Man*. New York: Knopf, 1970.

Douglass, Frederick. *My Bondage and My Freedom*. New York: Miller, Orton and Mulligan, 1855.

_____. *Life and Times of Frederick Douglass, Written by Himself. His Early Life as a Slave, his escape from Bondage, and His Complete History to the Present Time, Including His Connection with the Antislavery Movement*. Hartford, Conn.: Park, 1881.

_____. *Life and Times of Frederick Douglass. . . .* Boston: De Wolfe, Fiske, 1892.

_____. *The Narrative of the Life of Frederick Douglass: An American Slave*. Cambridge: Harvard University Press, 1960.

Duberman, Martin, ed. *The Antislavery Vanguard: New Essays on the Abolitionists.* Princeton: Princeton University Press, 1965.

Easton, Loyd D. *Hegel's First American Followers. The Ohio Hegelians: John B. Stallo, Peter Kaufman, Moncure Conway, and August Willich, with Key Writings.* Miami: Ohio University Press, 1966.

Erikson, Erik H. *Childhood and Society.* New York: Norton, 1963.

————, ed. *The Challenge of Youth.* New York: Doubleday, 1965.

Fairman, Charles M. *Reconstruction and Reunion, 1864–1888. The Oliver Wendell Holmes Devise: History of the Supreme Court of the United States.* New York: Macmillan, 1971.

Fine, Sidney. *Laissez-Faire and the General Welfare State: A Study of Conflict in American Thought, 1865–1901.* Ann Arbor: University of Michigan Press, 1956.

Flexner, Eleanor. *Century of Struggle: The Woman's Rights Movement in the United States.* New York: Atheneum, 1968.

Folsom, W. H. C. *Fifty Years in the Northwest.* N.p.: Pioneer Press, 1888.

Folwell, William W. *History of Minnesota.* St. Paul: Minnesota Historical Society, 1921.

Foner, Eric. *Free Soil, Free Labor, Free Men: The Ideology of the Republican Party Before the Civil War.* New York: Oxford University Press, 1970.

Foner, Philip S. *Frederick Douglass: A Biography.* New York: Citadel Press, 1964.

————. *The Life and Writings of Frederick Douglass.* New York: International, 1955.

Frank, Jerome. *Law and the Modern Mind.* Gloucester: Peter Smith, 1970.

Frederickson, George M. *The Inner Civil War: Northern Intellectuals and the Crisis of the Union.* New York: Harper and Row, 1968.

————. *The Black Image in the White Mind: The Debate on Afro-American Character and Destiny, 1817–1914.* New York: Harper and Row, 1971.

French, Mrs. A[usta] M. *Slavery in South Carolina and The Ex-Slaves: or the Port Royal Mission.* New York: Winchell M. French, 1862.

Friedman, Lawrence. *Inventors of the Promised Land.* New York: Knopf, 1975.

Gara, Larry. *The Liberty Line: The Legend of the Underground Railroad.* Lexington: University of Kentucky Press, 1961.

Garraty, John A. *The Nature of Biography.* New York: Knopf, 1957.

Genovese, Eugene D. *Roll, Jordan, Roll: The World the Slaves Made.* New York: Pantheon, 1974.

Gillette, William. *The Right to Vote: Politics and the Passage of the Fifteenth Amendment.* Baltimore: Johns Hopkins Press, 1965.

Glasgow, W. Melancthon. *History of the Reformed Presbyterian Church in America: With Sketches of All Her Ministry, Congregations, Missions, Institutions, Etc., and Embellished with over Fifty Portraits and Engravings.* Baltimore: Hill and Harvey, 1888.

Gregory, James M. *Frederick Douglass, the Orator: Containing an Account of*

His Life, His Eminent Public Services, His Brilliant Career as Orator; Selections from His Speeches and Writings. Springfield, Mass.: Wiley, 1893.

Gutman, Herbert G. *The Black Family in Slavery and Freedom, 1750–1925.* New York: Pantheon, 1976.

Hage, George S. *Newspapers on the Minnesota Frontier, 1849–1860.* St. Paul: Minnesota Historical Society, 1967.

Hahn, Emily. *Once Upon a Pedestal.* New York: New American Library, 1975.

Herreshoff, David. *American Disciples of Marx: From the Age of Jackson to the Progressive Era.* Detroit: Wayne State University Press, 1967.

Himes, Norman E. *Medical History of Contraception.* Baltimore: Williams and Wilkins, 1936.

Holland, Frederic M. *Frederick Douglass: The Colored Orator.* New York: Funk and Wagnalls, 1891.

Holt, Michael. *Forging a Majority: The Formation of the Republican Party in Pittsburgh, 1848–1860.* New Haven: Yale University Press, 1969.

Hyman, Harold M. and Leonard W. Levy, eds. *Freedom and Reform: Essays in Honor of Henry Steele Commager.* New York: Harper and Row, 1967.

_____. *Interpreter's Bible: The Holy Scripture in the King James and Revised Standard Versions with General Articles and Introduction, Exegesis, Exposition for Each Book of the Bible.* New York and Nashville: Abington, 1954.

Jacobs, Clyde E. *Law Writers and the Courts: The Influence of Thomas M. Cooley, Christopher G. Tiedman, and John F. Dillon on American Constitutional Law.* Berkeley: University of California Press, 1954.

Kennedy, John P. *Memoirs of William Wirt: Attorney General of the United States.* Philadelphia: Blanchard and Lea, 1851.

Knowlton, Charles. *The Fruits of Philosophy or the Private Companion of Adult People.* Mt. Vernon, N.Y.: Peter Pauper Press, 1937.

Kraditor, Aileen S. *Means and Ends in American Abolition: Garrison and His Critics on Strategy and Tactics, 1834–1850.* New York: Vintage, 1970.

Krutch, Joseph W. *Henry David Thoreau.* New York: Dell, 1965.

Larsen, Arthur J. *Crusader and Feminist: Letters of Jane Grey Swisshelm, 1856–1865.* St. Paul: Minnesota Historical Society, 1934.

Lewis, William D., ed. *Great American Lawyers.* Philadelphia: John C. Winston, 1909.

Levi-Strauss, Claude. *The Savage Mind.* Chicago: University of Chicago Press, 1966.

Litwack, Leon F. *North of Slavery: The Negro in the Free States, 1790–1860.* Chicago: University of Chicago Press, 1961.

McPherson, James M. *The Abolition Legacy: From Reconstruction to the NAACP.* Princeton: Princeton University Press, 1975.

_____. *The Struggle for Equality: Abolitionists and the Negro in the Civil War.* Princeton: Princeton University Press, 1964.

Merrill, Walter M., ed. *Letters of William Lloyd Garrison: No Union With Slaveholders, 1841–1849.* Cambridge: Harvard University Press, 1973.

Michelson, Peter. *The Aesthetics of Pornography.* New York: Herder and Herder, 1971.

Mitchell, William B. *History of Stearns County Minnesota.* Chicago: H. C. Cooper, 1915.

Montgomery, David. *Beyond Equality: Labor and the Radical Republicans 1862–1872.* New York: Knopf, 1967.

Morse, John T. *The Life and Letters of Oliver Wendell Holmes.* Boston: Houghton Mifflin, 1896.

Nye, Russell B. *Fettered Freedom: Civil Liberties and the Slavery Controversy, 1830–1860.* East Lansing: Michigan State College Press, 1949.

Pascal, Roy. *Design and Truth in Autobiography.* Cambridge: Harvard University Press, 1960.

Paludan, Phillip S. *A Covenant with Death: The Constitution, Law and Equality in the Civil War Era.* Urbana: University of Illinois Press, 1975.

Pease, Jane N. and William N. *They Who Would Be Free: Blacks' Search for Freedom, 1830–1861.* New York: Atheneum, 1974.

Perry, Lewis. *Radical Abolitionism: Anarchy and the Government of God in Antislavery Thought.* Ithaca: Cornell University Press, 1973.

Phillips, Wendell. *Speeches, Lectures, and Letters.* Boston: Lee and Shepard, 1884.

Polanyi, Karl. *The Great Transformation: The Political and Economic Origins of Our Time.* Boston: Beacon, 1957.

Prichard, James C. *The Natural History of Man: Comprising Inquiries into the Modifying Influence of Physical and Moral Agencies on the Different Tribes of the Human Family.* London: N. Bailliere, 1848.

Quarles, Benjamin. *Frederick Douglass.* Washington: Associated Publishers, 1948.

Riegel, Robert E. *American Feminists.* Lawrence: University of Kansas Press, 1963.

Rose, Willie Lee. *Rehearsal for Reconstruction: The Port Royal Experiment.* New York: Vintage, n.d.

Rusk, Ralph, ed. *The Letters of Ralph Waldo Emerson.* New York: Columbia University Press, 1939.

Schuckers, Jacob W. *The Life and Public Services of Salmon Portland Chase, United States Senator and Governor of Ohio: Secretary of the Treasury, and Chief Justice of the United States.* New York: D. Appleton, 1874.

Sellers, Charles C. *Dickinson College: A History.* Middleton, Conn.: Wesleyan University Press, 1973.

Sewell, Richard H. *Ballots for Freedom: Antislavery Politics in the United States 1837–1860.* New York: Oxford University Press, 1976.

Sklar, Kathryn K. *Catharine Beecher: A Study in American Domesticity.* New Haven: Yale University Press, 1973.

Somkin, Frederick,. *Unquiet Eagle: Memory and Desire in the Idea of American Freedom.* Ithaca: Cornell University Press, 1967.

Stanton, Elizabeth C. et al. *The History of Woman Suffrage.* Rochester: Charles Mann, 1881.

Stanton, William. *The Leopard's Spots: Scientific Attitudes Toward Race in America, 1815–1859.* Chicago: University of Chicago Press, 1960.

Stearns, Frank P. *The Life and Public Service of George Luther Stearns.* Philadelphia: Lippincott, 1907.

Strout, Cushing. *The New Heaven and New Earth: Political Religion in America.* New York: Harper and Row, 1974.

Swisshelm, Jane Grey. *Half a Century.* Chicago: n.p., 1880.

ten Broek, Jacobus. *The Antislavery Origins of the Fourteenth Amendment.* Berkeley: University of California Press, 1951.

Thorp, Margaret F. *Female Persuasion: Six Strong-Minded Women.* New Haven: Yale University Press, 1949.

Torrey, Bradford, ed. *The Writings of Henry David Thoreau.* Boston: Houghton Mifflin, 1906.

Trinterud, Leonard J. *The Forming of an American Tradition: A Re-Examination of Colonial Presbyterianism.* Philadelphia: Westminster Press, 1949.

Twiss, Benjamin R. *Lawyers and the Constitution: How Laissez-Faire Came to the Supreme Court.* Princeton: Princeton University Press, 1942.

Wade, Richard C. *The Urban Frontier: Pioneer Life in Early Pittsburgh, Cincinnati, Lexington, Louisville, and St. Louis.* Chicago: University of Chicago Press, 1964.

Warden, Robert B. *An Account of the Private Life and Public Services of Salmon Portland Chase.* Cincinnati: Wilstach, Baldwin, 1874.

Warren, Josiah. *True Civilization and Immediate Necessity and the Last Ground of Hope for Mankind.* Boston: n.p., 1863.

Washington, Booker T. *Frederick Douglass.* Philadelphia: George W. Jacobs. 1906.

Wilson, Major L. *Space, Time and Freedom: The Quest for Nationality and the Irrepressible Conflict, 1815–1861.* Westport, Conn.: Greenwood Press, 1974.

Wright, Henry C. *Human Life: Illustrated in My Individual Experience as a Child, a Youth, and a Man.* Boston: n.p., 1849.

———. *Marriage and Parentage: Or, the Reproductive Element in Man as a Means to His Elevation and Happiness.* Boston: B. Marsh, 1855.

———. *The Empire of the Mother over the Character and Destiny of the Race.* Boston: B. Marsh, 1863.

Young, James S. *The Washington Community, 1800–1828.* New York: Harcourt, Brace and World, n.d.

ARTICLES AND PAMPHLETS

Berthoff, Rowland. "The American Social Order: A Conservative Hypothesis." *American Historical Review,* LXV (April, 1960), 495–514.

Borome, Joseph A., ed. "Some Additional Light on Frederick Douglass." *Journal of Negro History,* XXXVIII (April, 1953), 214–24.

Cathcart, Rebecca M. "A Sheaf of Remembrances." *Minnesota Historical Society Collections*, XV (1915), 515–52.

[Conway, Moncure D.] "A Webster Case in Europe." *Southern Literary Messenger*, XVII (January, 1851), 50–54.

———. "Children and Their Literature." *Southern Literary Messenger*, XVIII (November, 1852), 681–85.

———. "Flirtation: Being an Essay by a New Contributor." *Southern Literary Messenger*, XV (June, 1849), 345–49.

———. *Free Schools in Virginia: A Plea of Education, Virtue and Thrift vs. Ignorance, Vice, and Poverty.* N.p.: Fredericksburg [1850].

———. "Jesuitism." *Christian Advocate and Journal*, August 12, 1852–February 10, 1853.

———. "Liberty: A Historical Study." *Open Court*. November 30, 1893.

———. "Liberty: A Contemporary Study." *Open Court*. December 14, 1893.

———. "Liberty: Our Lingering Chains." *Open Court*. December 28, 1893.

Cox, LaWanda. "The Promise of Land for the Freedmen." *Mississippi Valley Historical Review*, XLV (December, 1958), 413–40.

Cox, LaWanda and John H. "Negro Suffrage and Republican Politics: The Problem of Motivation in Reconstruction Historiography." *Journal of Southern History*, XXXIII (August, 1967), 303–30.

Davis, David B. "Antislavery or Abolition." *Reviews in American History*, I (March, 1973), 95–99.

———. "Some Themes of Countersubversion: An Analysis of Anti-Masonic, Anti-Catholic, and Anti-Mormon Literature." *Mississippi Valley Historical Review*, XLVII (September, 1960), 205–24.

Dummett, Ann. "Racism and Sexism: A False Analogy." *New Blackfriars*, LXI (November, 1975), 484–92.

Erikson, Erik H. "On the Nature of Psycho-Historical Evidence: In Search of Gandhi." *Daedalus* (Summer, 1968), 695–730.

Fisher, S. J. "Reminiscences of Jane Grey Swisshelm." *Western Pennsylvania Historical Magazine*, IV (July, 1921), 165–74.

Folwell, William W. "The Five Million Loan." *Minnesota Historical Collections*, XV (1909–15), 189–214.

Graham, Howard Jay. "The Early Antislavery Background of the Fourteenth Amendment. *Wisconsin Law Review* (May, 1950), 479–507.

Gutman, Herbert G. "Work, Culture and Society in Industrializing America, 1815–1919." *American Historical Review*, LXXVIII (June, 1973), 531–88.

Hicklin, Patricia. "Gentle Agitator: Samuel M. Janney and the Antislavery Movement in Virginia, 1842–1851." *Journal of Southern History*, XXXVII (May, 1971) 159–90.

Johnston, Daniel S. B. "A Red River Townsite Speculation in 1857." *Minnesota Historical Society Collections*, XV (1909–1914), 411–31.

———. "Minnesota Journalism From 1858 to 1865." *Minnesota Historical Society Collections*, X (1900–1904), 247–351.

————. "Minnesota Journalism From 1858 to 1865." *Minnesota Historical Society Collections*, XII (1905–1908), 183–262.

Jones, Alan. "Thomas M. Cooley and 'Laissez-Faire Constitutionalism': A Reconsideration." *Journal of American History*, LII (March, 1967), 751–71.

Klement, Frank. "Jane Grey Swisshelm." *Abraham Lincoln Quarterly*, VI (December, 1950), 227–38.

Knowlton, Charles. *Two Remarkable Lectures Delivered in Boston by Dr. C. Knowlton on the Day of His Leaving the Jail at East Cambridge, March 31, 1833, Where He Had Been Imprisoned for Publishing a Book.* Boston: A. Kneeland, 1833.

Knowlton, Jerome C. "Thomas McIntyre Cooley." *Michigan Law Review*, V (March, 1907), 309–25.

Kutler, Stanley I. "Reconstruction and the Supreme Court: The Numbers Game Reconsidered." *Journal of Southern History*, XXXII (February, 1966), 42–58.

McCurdy, Charles W. "Justice Field and the Jurisprudence of Government-Business Relations: Some Parameters of Laissez-Faire Constitutionalism, 1863–1897." *Journal of American History*, LXI (March, 1975), 970–1005.

McPherson, James M. "Abolitionists and the Civil Rights Act of 1875." *Journal of American History*, LII (December, 1965), 493–510.

Marcus, Robert D. "Wendell Phillips and American Institutions." *Journal of American History*, LVI (June, 1969), 41–58.

Nelson, William E. "The Impact of the Antislavery Movement upon Styles of Judicial Reasoning in Nineteenth Century America." *Harvard Law Review* LXXXVII (January, 1975), 513–66.

Perry, Lewis. "Psychohistory and the Abolitionists: Reflections on Martin Duberman and the Neoabilitionism of the 1960s." *Reviews in American History*, II (September, 1974), 309–22.

Randall, John H. "The Beginning of Railroad Building in Minnesota." *Minnesota Historical Society Collections*, XV (1909–1914), 215–20.

Robert, Joseph C. "William Wirt, Virginian." *Virginia Magazine of History and Biography*, LXX (1972), 387–441.

Roche, John P. "Entrepreneurial Liberty and the Fourteenth Amendment." *Labor History*, IX (Winter, 1963), 3–31.

Rosenberg, Charles E. "Sexuality, Class and Role in Nineteenth Century America." *American Quarterly*, XXV (May, 1973), 131–53.

Schlesinger, A. M. "Salmon P. Chase: Undergraduate and Pedagogue." *Ohio Archaeological and Historical Publications*, XXVIII (1919), 119–61.

Shepperson, George. "Frederick Douglass and Scotland." *Journal of Negro History*, XXXVIII (July, 1953), 307–21.

Shippee, Lester B. "Jane Grey Swisshelm: Agitator." *Mississippi Valley Historical Review*, VII (December, 1920), 206–227.

Smith-Rosenberg, Carroll and Charles E. Rosenberg. "The Female Animal: Medical and Biological Views of Woman and Her Role in Nineteenth-Century America." *Journal of American History*, LX (September, 1973), 332–56.

Stearn, Bertha-Monica. "Reform Periodicals and Female Reformers, 1830–1860."

American Historical Review, XXXVII (July, 1932), 678–99.

Walters, Ronald G. "The Erotic South: Civilization and Sexuality in American Abolition." *American Quarterly*, XXV (May, 1973), 177–201.

Wirt, William. *A Discourse on the Lives and Character of Thomas Jefferson and John Adams, Who Both Died on the Fourth of July, 1826.* Washington: Gales and Seaton, 1826.

MANUSCRIPTS (LISTED BY REPOSITORY)

Boston Public Library, Boston, Massachusetts.
  Chapman, Maria W. Papers.
  Garrison, William Lloyd. Papers.
  May, Samuel. Papers.
  Weston, Anne W. Papers.
Columbia University, New York.
  Conway, Moncure D. Collection.
  Gay, Sidney H. Collection.
Harvard University, Cambridge.
  Chase-Sumner. Correspondence.
  Giddings-Sumner. Correspondence.
  Higginson, Thomas W. Collection.
  Pierce, E. L. Papers.
Historical Society of Pennsylvania, Philadelphia.
  Chase, Salmon P. Papers.
Library of Congress, Washington, D.C.
  Chase, Salmon P. Papers.
  Douglass, Frederick. Papers (microfilm).
  Giddings-Julian Collection.
Minnesota Historial Society, St. Paul.
  Mitchell, William B. Papers.
New-York Historical Society, New York.
  Chase, Salmon P. Papers.
  Smith, Gerritt. Papers.
  Spooner, Lysander. Papers.
New York Public Library, New York.
  Bryant-Godwin Collection.
  Child-Shaw Correspondence.
  Tilton, Theodore. Papers.
Ohio State Archives and Historical Society, Columbus.
  Giddings, Joshua R. Papers.

THESES AND DISSERTATIONS

Kooker, Arthur R. "The Antislavery Movement in Michigan, 1796–1840: A Study in American Humanitarianism on the American Frontier." Ph.D. dissertation, University of Michigan, 1930.

Kulash, Joseph A. "Abolitionists in an Acquisitive Age: Economic Liberalism in the American Antislavery Movement." M.A. thesis, University of North Carolina, 1972.

Ryan, Frank W. *"The Southern Quarterly Review, 1842–1857: A Study in Thought and in the Old South."* Ph.D. dissertation, University of North Carolina, 1956.

NEWSPAPERS AND MAGAZINES

New York *Tribune*, June–July, 1863.
Philadelphia *Dollar Newspaper*, June 12, 1844.
Philadelphia *Saturday Museum*, June 5, 1844.
Pittsburgh *Chronicle Telegraph*, July 22, 1884.
Pittsburgh *Saturday Visiter*, December 20, 1847–August 28, 1852.
San Francisco *Mirror of the Times*, December 12, 1857.
St. Cloud (Minn.) *Democrat*, August 5, 1858–June 11, 1863.
St. Cloud (Minn.) *Visiter*, December 10, 1857–July 29, 1858.
Washington (D.C.) *Reconstructionist*, March 10, 20, 1866.
Western Literary Messenger, March, August, September, 1851.
Weekly Anglo-African, 1859–60.

CENSUS

Minnesota Special Census. Stearns County. 1857.
Virginia Census. Stafford County. Population Schedule. 1840.
Virginia Census. Stafford County. Free Population Schedule. 1850, 1860.
Virginia Census. Stafford County. Slave Schedule. 1850, 1860.

COURT REPORTS

Pennsylvania Supreme Court Reports. 1868.
Michigan Supreme Court Reports. 1866, 1869, 1870.
United States Supreme Court Reports. 1869, 1873.

Index

Abolition: agenda of, 306; and American nationality, 18; and anti-Catholicism, 161–66; and anti-institutionalism, 7; and the Constitution, 150–51; and constitutionalism, 340–42; definition of, xx; and disunion, 8; indicts slavery, 112; radical abolition's contentions, 17; on sexuality, 288–90; social imagination of, 266–67, 276–77, 302–303, 305–306, 330; social mechanics of, 269–70; and social morality, 269–70; and Union, 306–308; values of, 6–7, 170
Abolitionists as creative writers, 266
Adams, Charles F.: criticizes Conway, 17; mentioned, 6
Adams, Henry, 39
Adams, Mrs. John Q., 65

Advertiser (St. Cloud), 175, 180, 184, 194
Agassiz, Louis, 59, 81
Allen, William, 44
American Antislavery Society, 8
American Commonwealth, 331
American nationality, 19
Anderson, Quentin, 307
Andover Seminary, 280–84
Anthony, Aaron, 231, 235, 254. *See also* Douglass, Frederick
Anthony, Susan B., 156, 159
Anti-Catholicism, 69, 72, 161–66, 195, 203, *See also* Abolition; Swisshelm, Jane
Anti-institutionalism: in historiography of abolition, 7; putative equalities of, 20
Anti-Slavery Standard, 269
Auld, "Captain," 234

Auld, Hugh, 231, 233, 235, 241
Auld, Sophia, 231, 233
Auld, Thomas (Captain), 231
Auld, Thomas, 231, 233
Autobiography, defined, xvi
Avery, Charles, 358
"A Webster Case in Europe," 56–58
Awful Disclosures of the Hotel Dieu Nunnery of Montreal, 162

Bailey, Gamaliel, 63
Bailey, Harriet, 244, 250–55. *See also* Douglass, Frederick
Baird, Spencer, 44
Baltimore Conference, 43. *See also* Conway, Walker P.
Barker, Joe, 161
Barstow, George, 181
Belief Not Fancy, 100
Biography, method of, xvi
Black, John, 99, 102–103
Black Bourgeoisie, 218
Bloomer, Amelia, 159
Bright, John, 4
Brooke, Roger, 63, 65
Brown, John, 8, 35, 148
Browning, Robert, 4, 14, 38
Brott, George F., 175, 183, 187
Burned Over District, 337–39
Burroughs, John, 38
Bruce, Blanche K., 210
Bryce, James, 331

Cannon, Mary, 98, 111, 118, 120, 127
Cannon, Thomas, 92, 97
Cannon, William, 98, 100
Carlyle, Thomas, 4, 14, 38
Carnegie, Andrew, 216
Catholics: in Stearns County, 194–95. *See also* Anti-Catholicism
Chapman, Maria W., 91, 258
Chase, Ithamar, 314
Chase, Philander, 315, 318
Chase, Salmon P.: and analysis of slavery, 309; career of, 308–11; as Chief Justice, 329; chooses profession, 317–18; on disunion, 311; early career of, 326–27; early life of, 314–15; education of, 315; and election of 1828, pp. 322–24; on free labor, 328–29; relationship with Wirt, 318–20; as schoolmaster, 315–17;

on Unionism, 311–13; mentioned, 150, 339, 341. *See also* Wirt, William
Child, Lydia M., 91
"Children and Their Literature," 73–74
Christian Advocate and Journal, 71
Civil Rights Act (1875), 270, 275
Cleveland, Grover, 215
Cobden, Richard, 38
Colfax, Schuyler, 204
Commercial Journal, 128
Commonwealth, 4, 79, 269
Conference of Western Unitarian Churches, 84
Constitutionalism: and slavery, 150–51; 340–41; 102, 128, 168, 313. *See also* Chase, Salmon; Cooley, Thomas
Constitutional Limitations: as abolitionist statement, 342–44; as moral tract, 348; mentioned 331, 332, 338–48 *passim*
Conway, Catherine, 24
Conway, Ellen Dana, 5, 17, 84–85
Conway, Eustace, 75
Conway, Margaret Daniel: slave dowry of, 24–25; marriage of, 27; and slavery, 30–31; in *Pine and Palm,* 35–37; on son's marriage, 84; mentioned, 55, 71, 75
Conway, Mildred, 24
Conway, Moncure D.: and *Autobiography,* xvi, 71, 73, 80, 83, 86; and autobiographical fiction, 47, 56–58, 59–60; 71–73, 73–74; abolition achievement of, 4–5; birth and early life, 22–27; relationship with father, 72, 74; relationship with mother, 33, 36–38; religious conversion of, 45–46, 47–48, 61–62; at Dickinson College, 44, 50, 69–71; and Methodism, 39, 42, 45, 52, 62, 63–65, 66–67, 70; at Harvard Divinity School, 74, 78, 79–81; writes for *Liberator,* 81; Unitarian ministry, 69, edits *Dial,* 84; edits *Commonwealth,* 79; marriage, 84; mission to England, 14–18; illnesses of, 18, 48, 53, 61, 73; later career of, 85; social ideas of, 273–76; mentioned, 350
Conway, Peter, 24
Conway, Peyton, 24, 43
Conway, Richard, 24
Conway, Walker Peyton: origins of, 21–22; character of, 26, 33; and religion, 22–23, 27, 29, 30, 32, 43, 48, 49; mar-

riage of, 27; and slavery, 25, 29–30, 60; property of, 23, 352–53; relationship with son, 51, 74–76, 81–82; mentioned, 55
Cooley, Thomas M. Sr., 337
Cooley, Thomas M: childhood and family of, 335–37; poetry of, 338; and politics, 339; career of, 333–37; on laissez-faire, 333. *See also* Burned Over District; *Constitutional Limitations*
Coventanters, 92–94, 96, 102–103
Coverature, 121
Crooks, George R., 44
Croswell, Charles, 334
Curtis, George W., 4

Dana, Charles, 84
Daniel, Elizabeth, 40
Daniel, John M., 40
Daniel, Peter, 40
Daniel, Travers, 40
Darwin, Charles, 38
Dial, 84
Dickinson College, 39, 43, 44
Disunion, 8, 9–11, 12, 123, 311. *See also* Abolition
"Diversity of [the] Origins of Races—Slavery," 38, 60, 61, 72
Dollar Newspaper, 122, 123
Donnelly, Ignatius, 204
Douglass, Frederick: autobiographies of, xix, xvii, 212, 226–27, 228, 236, 243; age and birthdate of, 209, 362–63; source of name, 255–56, 365; and concern for past, 211, 230–31, 248; accounts of father, 249–50; accounts of mother, 250–55; and lost patrimony, 256; breaks with Garrisonians, 258–59; marriages of, 237, 261; social ideas of, 271–73. *See also* Bailey, Harriet; Foner, Philip; Quarles, Benjamin

Elkins, Stanley, 7
Emerson, Ralph Waldo: and relationship with Conway, 65–68; mentioned, 4, 38, 74
Emory, Catharine (Kate), 46–47, 50, 70–71
Emory, John, 46
Emory, Robert, 46
Erskine, Ralph, 100

Falmouth, Virginia, 21
Farquhar, William H., 65
Fawcett, Henry, 14
Fitzhugh, George, 60
Folwell, William, 183, 189
Foner, Philip: as Douglass biographer, 218–22, 211, 213, 237, 238, 246; mentioned, xviii
Frazier, Franklin, 218
Fredericksburg Classical and Mathematical Academy, 39
Fredericksburg Southern Rights Association, 51, 60
Free Labor, 165, 289–90, 310
"Free Schools in Virginia," 54, 72
French, Austa, 289

Garibaldi, Giuseppe, 38
Garrison, William L.: and Conway, 18, 79; and Douglass, 8, 81, 210, 237, 256, 272; mentioned, xiv, xx, 4
Garrisonians: and Douglass, 246, 258–59; 213, 239, 306–308
Godey's Lady's Book, 91
Greeley, Horace, 8, 90, 191
Griffiths, Julia, 259
Grow, Galusha, 204
Grund, Francis, 272

Half A Century: as fantasy, 174; as abolition tract, 112–16; xvii, 97, 108, 112, 159, 122
Hamilton, Elizabeth S., 63
Herald of Freedom, 8
Humstead, Charles, 25
Humstead, Maria, 25
Humstead, Peter, 24
Hunt, Leigh, 38
Huxley, Thomas, 38
Hayes, Rutherford B., 221
History of Woman Suffrage, 159
Holmes, Oliver W., 78
Holmes, Oliver W. Jr., 348–50

Independent, 264

James, William, xv, 283
Janney, Samuel, 55
Jennings, Isabel, 245
"Jesuitism", 72–73
Johnson, Oliver, 210

Jones, Charles Colcock, 62
Julian, George W., 89, 91, 204

Kapital, Das, 332, 337, 347
Kraditor, Aileen, 7

Labor, 165
Lady of the Lake, The, 256
Law. *See* Constitutionalism
Legal profession, 326–27, 340
Levi-Strauss, Claude, xiv, xix, 265
Lewis, John, 27
Liberty party, 126
Liberator, 8, 79, 237
Lippencott, Sarah C. (Grace Greenwood), 63
Lochner v. *New York,* 348–49
Longfellow, Henry W., 80, 81
Lowell, James R., 39, 80
Lowes, John L., xvi
Lowry, David, 176
Lowry, Sylvanus, 172–73, 176–77, 178, 180, 185, 190, 194–95
Lukács, Georg, xix

M'Clintock, John, 44
McCurdy, Charles, 342
McPherson, James, xx, 9, 303
Marriage and Parentage, 291–93
Martineau, James, 14
Mason, James M., 17
Mathilda case, 341
Miller, Stephen, 181, 188–89
Minnesota: territory, 174–75; politics, 186
Minor, John B., 55
Mitchell, Elizabeth C., 127, 177, 208
Mitchell, Henry Z., 127, 177, 178, 181
Mitchell, William B., 183
Moncure, Richard: in *Pine and Palm,* 35; mentioned, 40
Moral Marketplace, 166–70, 277
Mott, Lucretia, 156
Murray, Anna, 237. *See also* Douglass, Frederick

Namier, Lewis, xiv
Nantucket Convention, 236, 237, 242–45, 254–55. *See also* Douglass, Frederick
National Intelligencer, 63
Natural History of Man, 252–53
Neale's Saturday Gazette, 122, 123

Neglected Stone, The, 84
Nelson, William, 342
Non-Resistance, 288. *See also* Wright, Henry

O'Conner, Michael, 161, 162
Ohio Hegelians, 84
"Outaliski's Revenge," 49, 57

Panic of 1857, p. 196
Parker, Theodore, 80
Pease, Jane and William, xx
People v. *The Board of Education of Detroit,* 346
People v. *The Township Board of Salem,* 344
Perfectionism, 288. *See also* Wright, Henry
Phillips, Wendell, 8–9, 19, 80, 245, 257; mentioned, 6, 79. *See also* Disunion
Phillips, William, 51
Pine and Palm, 25, 34–38, 353
Pitts, Helen, 259, 261
Political Abolition, 12, 310. *See also* Chase, Salmon
Political Recollections, 91
Pornography, 289
Purvis, Robert, 210

Quarles, Benjamin: as Douglass biographer, 211, 214–16, 222, 237; mentioned, xviii
Quincy, Edmund, 245

Ramsey, Alexander, 204
Reconstructionist, 269
Republican party, 181, 183, 186, 203
Rice, Henry M., 176
Riddle, James, 128
Rogers, Nathaniel P., 7
Ruskin, John, 38

Sadler, George, 44
St. Cloud: early history of, 193–96; and proprietors, 188
St. Cloud Democrat, 200, 202
Sanborn, Frank, 4
Scarlet Letter, The, 133
Scott, Winfield, 311
Sears, Annie, 232
Sears, Thomas, 211, 229, 231

Secret Six, 4
Seneca Falls Convention, 153
Shepley, James, 177, 187, 197
Sketches of the Life and Character of Patrick Henry, 320
Slaughterhouse cases, 329, 330
Slavery in South Carolina and the Ex-Slaves, 289
Smith, Gerrit, 4, 246
Smith, James McCune, 246, 259
Smith, William, 60
Solemn League and Covenant, 92. *See also* Covenanters
Southern Literary Messenger, 51
Sparks, Mrs. Jared, 5, 80
Spencer, Herbert, 38, 275, 348
Spirit of Liberty, 126
Spooner, Lysander, 150
Stanfield, James H., 14
Stanton, Edwin, 108, 154
Stanton, Elizabeth Cady, 156, 159
Stearns, Charles, 175
Stearns, George L., 4
Stearns County, 191
Stephen, Leslie, 4, 14
Stone, Lucy, 91
Stowe, Harriet Beecher, 91
Stringfellow, Thornton, 60
Sumner, Charles, 63, 270, 274, 309
Sumner, William G., 170
Swisshelm, Elizabeth, 109, 110, 116, 121, 124, 172, 178, 180
Swisshelm, Henry, 181
Swisshelm, James, 106, 108, 179, 189. See also *Swisshelm v. Swisshelm*
Swisshelm, Jane G.: autobiography of, xvii, xviii; early life of, 92–93; and Covenanter church, 100, 102; marriage of, 107, 110, 111; sexuality of, 102, 132–35, 160; as domesticated woman, 122; in Louisville, 112–22, 169; as "Jennie Deans," 122; early journalism of, 126, 128; reform theory of, 148–49; abolition theory of, 166; on slavery, 149–53; on race, 151–53; conspiracy theses of, 160–61, 165; and anti-Catholicism, 161–66; and woman's rights, 127–28, 129–35, 153–60; and constitutionalism, 168; in Minnesota, 172 ff; health of, 125, 147; later career and social ideas of, 267–71

Swisshelm v. Swisshelm, 108–109
Swisshelm, "Zoe," 109, 172, 179, 180, 205

Taylor, Peter A., 14
Texas v. White, 329
The Golden Hour, 84
Theodore Parker Society, 4
Thoreau, Henry, D., 7, 80, 278–79
Time, slave culture's, 229–30
Tocqueville, Alexis de, 150, 272, 331
Tracts for Today, 84

Unionism, 306–308, 311. *See also* Disunion

Virginia Constitutional Convention, 55
Visiter (Pittsburg): founding of, 136; naming, 139–44; external Unionism, 306–308, 311. *See also* Disunion

Virginia Constitutional Convention, 55
Visiter (Pittsburg): founding of, 136; naming, 139–44; external history of, 144; internal history of, 144–47; and anti-Catholicism, 163
Visiter (St. Cloud): founding of, 173, 185; wrecked, 198; reestablished, 199–202

Warren, Josiah, 78
Washington, Booker T., 213
Wellford, Beverly, 60
"What Am I to You," 259–60
Wilson, John, 193, 195
Wirt, William, 318, 319–21. *See also* Salmon Chase
Woman's Rights, 127–28, 132, 160, 299–300. *See also* Swisshelm, Jane; Wright, Henry
Wright, Elizar, 4
Wright, Henry C.: early years, 279–80; at Andover Seminary, 280–84; ministerial career of, 284–85; marriage of, 284; perfectionism and nonresistance of, 286–87; and Garrisonians, 288; social criticism of, 296–97; human sexuality, 290–94; writings of, 291; and woman's rights, 299–300, social imagination, 302–303; mentioned, 307, 339

Zion's Herald, 80